Gators Offshore and Upriver

The U.S. Navy's Amphibious Ships and Underwater Demolition Teams, and Royal Australian Navy Clearance Divers in Vietnam

During the Vietnam War, 142 "gators" (amphibious ships) served in the combat zone. As deeper-draft ships landed Marines on assault beaches by boat or helicopter, World War II-era tank landing ships operated on shallow, winding rivers. Scores of minimal-draft vessels were required to support inland combat action beyond the reach of the cruisers and destroyers serving on the gunline offshore. Therefore, dozens of "mothballed" landing ships were returned to service. These "Ts" served as mobile support bases for river patrol boats and assault helicopters, and ran the rivers to deliver vital cargos to Allied troops, and other units of the "Brown Water Navy." Each day brought the possibility of ambush by the enemy concealed in dense jungle along the banks. Most insidious were swimmer-sappers who used the chocolate-colored waters to hide their movements while placing explosives on vessels lying at anchor or alongside a pier. One such attack against the *Westchester County* killed or injured many sailors and embarked soldiers. This activity spurred Royal Australian Navy clearance divers being called into service. Their inspections of thousands of ship hulls, rudders, and anchor chains, and heroic removal and rendering harmless of deadly ordnance they found, saved many ships and lives. For those interested in learning about Sailors who fought "in country," this companion to *On the Gunline* is the book you're looking for. One hundred and ninety photographs, maps, and diagrams; appendices; and an index to full-names, places, and subjects add value to this work.

Gators Offshore and Upriver

The U.S. Navy's Amphibious Ships and Underwater Demolition Teams, and Royal Australian Navy Clearance Divers in Vietnam

Cdr. David D. Bruhn, USN (Retired)

HERITAGE BOOKS
2019

HERITAGE BOOKS
AN IMPRINT OF HERITAGE BOOKS, INC.

Books, CDs, and more—Worldwide

For our listing of thousands of titles see our website
at
www.HeritageBooks.com

Published 2019 by
HERITAGE BOOKS, INC.
Publishing Division
5810 Ruatan Street
Berwyn Heights, Md. 20740

Copyright © 2019 Cdr. David D. Bruhn, USN (Retired)

All rights reserved. No part of this book may be reproduced or transmitted in any form or by any means, electronic or mechanical, including photocopying, recording or by any information storage and retrieval system without written permission from the author, except for the inclusion of brief quotations in a review.

International Standard Book Number
Paperbound: 978-0-7884-5906-1

To the officers and men who served aboard amphibious ships in Vietnam, the Marines carried to assault landings by Amphibious Ready Groups, frogmen of Underwater Demolition Teams 11 and 12, and the intrepid Royal Australian Navy Clearance Diving Team Three members.

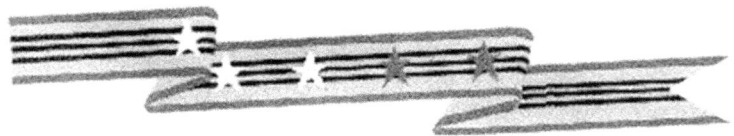

CAMPAIGNS
1. Vietnam Advisory Campaign (15 March 1962-7 March 1965)
2. Vietnam Defense Campaign (8 March-24 December 1965)
3. Vietnamese Counteroffensive (25 December 1965-30 June 1966)
4. Vietnamese Counteroffensive (1 July 1966-31 May 1967) Phase II
5. Vietnamese Counteroffensive (1 June 1967-29 January 1968) Phase III
6. Tet Counteroffensive (30 January-1 April 1968)
7. Vietnamese Counteroffensive (2 April-30 June 1968) Phase IV
8. Vietnamese Counteroffensive (1 July-1 November 1968) Phase V
9. Vietnamese Counteroffensive (2 November 1968-22 February 1969) Phase VI
10. Tet 69/Counteroffensive (23 February-8 June 1969)
11. Vietnam Summer-Fall 1969 (9 June-31 October 1969)
12. Vietnam Winter-Spring 1970 (1 November 1969-30 April 1970)
13. Sanctuary Counteroffensive (1 May-30 June 1970)
14. Vietnamese Counteroffensive (1 July 1970-30 June 1971) Phase VII
15. Consolidation I (1 Jul 1971-30 Nov 1971)
16. Consolidation II (1 Dec 1971-29 Mar 1972)
17. Vietnam Ceasefire Campaign (30 Mar 1972-28 Jan 1973)

Contents

Foreword by Dr. Edward J. Marolda		xiii
Foreword by Captain John D. White II, USN (Retired)		xv
Foreword by Commodore Hector Donohue, AM RAN (Retired)		xvii
Acknowledgements		xxi
Preface		xxvii
1.	Viet Cong Sappers Nearly Sink USS *Westchester County*	1
2.	Amphibious Ships in Vietnam	13
3.	Prelude to the Vietnam War	37
4.	Land the Marines	45
5.	Initial Operations and Raids	49
6.	Special Landing Force/UDT in 1966	65
7.	Operation DECKHOUSE V	95
8.	Establishment of the Mobile Riverine Force	103
9.	Work Horses of the Amphibious Force	129
10.	Inception of the River Patrol Force	153
11.	ARG Alfa's Landings in 1967	171
12.	1968 Tet Offensive	191
13.	Operation SEALORDS	199
14.	Swimmer-Sapper Attack on the MV *Heredia*	209
15.	Final ARG/SLF Operations	219
16.	Vietnamization Begins	225
17.	Cambodian Incursion	231
18.	Swimmer-Sapper Attack on USS *Meeker County*	241
19.	Final U.S. Involvement in Vietnam – 1971 to 1973	247
20.	Operation FREQUENT WIND	253
21.	The *Mayaguez* Incident	265
Postscript		275
Appendices		
A.	Amphibious Ship Unit Awards Summary	287
B.	Royal Australian Navy CDT 3 Unit Awards	297
C.	Navy Unit Citation for Mobile Support Base LSTs	303
D.	Presidential Unit Citations Awarded LSTs	305
E.	BM1 James E. Williams Medal of Honor Citation	313
F.	Commander, Naval Forces Vietnam Letter to CDT 3	315
G.	VNN Ships that Escaped to the Philippines	317
Bibliography/Notes		319
Index		347

About the Author — 369

Photos and Illustrations

Acknowledgements-1: Richard DeRosset	xxi
Acknowledgements-2: Capt. John D. White, USN	xxii
Acknowledgements-3: Donald (Scotty) Allan	xxiii
Acknowledgements-4: Michael A. Harris	xxiii
Acknowledgements-5: Ens. Arnold E. Resnicoff, USNR	xxiv
Acknowledgements-6: Robert Kermen	xxv
Acknowledgements-7: Ron Swart	xxvi
Preface-1: Alan Halldorson aboard the USS *Caddo Parish*	xxviii
Preface-2: USS *Washtenaw County* with her bow doors open	xxxi
Preface-3: 3rd Marine Division Amtraks shuttling supplies	xxxi
Preface-4: Unidentified member of a Battalion Landing Team	xxxii
Preface-5: UH-34 helicopter taking off from the USS *Princeton*	xxxiii
Preface-6: Hospital ship USS *Repose* off South Vietnam	xxxiv
Preface-7: UDT 12 members at Danang, South Vietnam	xxxv
Preface-8: USS *Tunny* off Mare Island Navy Shipyard	xxxvi
Preface-9: Repair ship USS *Jason* at anchor off Vung Tau	xxxix
Preface-10: Four RAN CDT 3 (4th Contingent) members	xlii
Preface-11: LST beaching ramp at Vung Tau, South Vietnam	xliii
Preface-12: USS *Garrett County* on the Co Chien River	xliv
Preface-13: Painting of a mining attack on USS *Westchester County*	xlvi
1-1: USS *Westchester County* under way	1
1-2: USS *Westchester County* with riverine craft alongside	2
1-3: Self-propelled barracks ship USS *Benewah*	3
1-4: Viet Cong swimmer-sappers planning a mission	4
1-5: Damage wrought by enemy mines to USS *Westchester County*	6
1-6: Pontoon and guard shack wrecked by exploding mines	7
2-1: Barracks ship USS *Colleton* with troop carriers alongside	14
2-2: High speed transport USS *Cook* under way	16
2-3: Landing craft repair ship USS *Krishna* at anchor	17
2-4: Inshore fire support ship USS *Carronade* under way	22
2-5: Inshore fire support ship USS *St. Francis River* under way	23
2-6: Amphibious force command ship USS *Eldorado* under way	24
2-7: Flag plot aboard the amphibious command ship USS *Estes*	25
2-8: Amphibious assault ship USS *Boxer* operating helicopters	26
2-9: USS *Inchon* anchored in Haiphong Harbor, North Vietnam	27
2-10: USS *Iwo Jima*, *Thomaston*, and *Vancouver* proceeding together	28
2-11: Landing vehicles move past the transport dock USS *Ogden*	29
2-12: Dock landing ship USS *Oak Hill* off Oahu, Hawaii	30

2-13: Dock landing ship USS *Comstock*   31
2-14: LVTs circle dock landing ship USS *Point Defiance*   32
2-15: Amphibious cargo ship USS *Mobile* under way   33
2-16: Amphibious cargo ship USS *Tulare* under way   34
2-17: Amphibious transport USS *Paul Revere* departing San Diego   36
3-1: Poster of Ho Chi Minh, ruler of North Vietnam   37
3-2: Boat landing on the Mekong River, French Indochina   38
3-3: French Adm Thierry D'Angenlieu and Gen. Richard Brunot   40
3-4: Refugees board the tank landing ship USS *LST-516*   42
3-5: General and flag officers await arrival of refugees in Saigon   43
3-6: General Westmoreland and Admirals Moorer and Veth   44
4-1: U.S. Marines wade ashore at Danang, South Vietnam   45
4-2: Rear Adm. Donald W. Wulzen, USN   46
4-3: Amphibious command ship USS *Mount McKinley* under way   47
4-4: Members of the 9th Marine Expeditionary Brigade   48
5-1: Assault craft from USS *Talladega* in Operation STARLITE   51
5-2: Marines preparing to board assault craft   52
5-3: Flight deck of USS *Iwo Jima*   54
5-4: Ships with Marines embarked, proceeding to South Vietnam   55
5-5: First wave of Marine infantry come ashore at Tam Quan   56
5-6: Marines sweep the village of Phu Thu in South Vietnam   58
5-7: Flight deck aboard the USS *Valley Forge*   61
5-8: Infamous rice paddies of South Vietnam   61
6-1: Chu Lai Peninsula, South Vietnam, January 1966   65
6-2: Gen. William Westmoreland with Capt. Paul J. Knapp   66
6-3: Marines of the 4th Regiment, 3rd Marine Division   68
6-4: Marines of E Company, 2nd Battalion, 4th Regiment   68
6-5: Panji-staked gully provides rough going for Marines   70
6-6: Marines aboard the amphibious assault ship USS *Princeton*   71
6-7: Amphibious assault ship USS *Princeton* standing out of port   72
6-8: Two OV-10A Bronco aircraft from VAL-4   75
6-9: Destroyer USS *Walker* off Cape Henry, Virginia   77
6-10: High speed transport USS *Cook* under way   78
6-11: Medium landing ship (rocket) USS *Clarion River* under way   79
6-12: Light cruiser USS *Oklahoma City* in a tight turn to port   80
6-13: UDT 12 members during landings at Danang   81
6-14: USS *Iwo Jima*, USS *Thomaston*, and USS *Vancouver*   83
6-15: Painting by Bruce Fletcher of the Battle of Long Tan   84
6-16: UH-1D gunships of the 135th Assault Helicopter Company   86
6-17: Amphibious transport submarine USS *Perch* off Hawaii   88
6-18: Two LCMs lay to off the dock landing ship USS *Thomaston*   91
6-19: Heavy cruiser USS *St. Paul* under way   93

7-1: Amphibious tractor moves away from USS *Coconino County* 95
7-2: Briefing of Marines aboard the USS *Coconino County* 97
7-3: Transport of troops up the Co Chien River 99
7-4: Painting *Operation Market Time* by Gene Klebe, 1965 100
7-5: USS *Garrett County* on the Co Chien River, Mekong Delta 101
7-6: Monitor *M-91-1* patrols a river of the Mekong Delta 102
8-1: An armored transport carrier offloads U.S. Army personnel 103
8-2: VNN River Assault Group LCM on a South Vietnam river 104
8-3: U.S. Navy admirals aboard USS *Benewah* 105
8-4: A monitor transiting the Mang Thit Canal, Mekong Delta 107
8-5: An assault support patrol boat patrolling a canal 108
8-6: *APL-26* serving as mothership for landing craft and tugs 109
8-7: Assault troop carrier *ATC-112-7* near the village of My Tho 111
8-8: Mobile Riverine Force units exchange fire with the enemy 112
8-9: Game Warden Base at Nha Be 114
8-10: Two Viet Cong in the Rung Sat Special Zone 114
8-11: A U.S. Army helicopter lands on *ATC(H) R-92-2* 120
8-12: Landing craft repair ship USS *Askari* with craft alongside 120
8-13: A monitor fitted with a 105mm howitzer, and bar armor 123
8-14: A B-52 releases bombs over a coastal area 126
9-1: Tank landing ships practicing beaching off San Diego 129
9-2: A truck boards USS *Newport* near Little Creek, Virginia 131
9-3: Homeward bound pennant displaying ten stars 141
10-1: Vietnamese Navy commandament riverine craft 155
10-2: Vietnamese Navy "FOM" river patrol boat 155
10-3: Dock landing ship USS *Tortuga* under way 156
10-4: USS *Carronade* and *White River* off Danang 157
10-5: SS *Eastern Mariner* after being mined in 1965 158
10-6: HMAS *Bungaree* at Sydney, New South Wales, Australia 159
10-7: Minesweeping boat *MSB-49* on the Saigon River 163
10-8: Navy SEALS aboard a converted "Mike" boat 164
10-9: A PACV (patrol air cushion vehicle) in the Plain of Reeds 166
10-10: Boatswain's Mate First James Elliott Williams, U.S. Navy 168
10-11: Dock landing ship USS *Comstock* at Chu Lai 169
10-12: Russian MKB contact mine 170
11-1: Marines moving up a slope in the northern Asha Valley 171
11-2: A Marine walking through a Vietnamese village 174
11-3: Cruiser USS *Providence* firing her guns 178
11-4: Marines sweeping an area in search of enemy forces 179
11-5: A Marine radioman silhouetted against the shoreline 184
11-6: A Marine mortarman carries his weapon on his shoulder 185
11-7: A Navy spotter aboard an Army "bird dog" aircraft 186

Foreword

David Bruhn's *Gators Offshore and Upriver* presents a detailed and lavishly illustrated study of the contribution during the Vietnam War of the U.S. and Australian forces that operated along South Vietnam's 1,200-mile coastline and on the country's myriad rivers and canals. He focuses on the ships of the amphibious fleet that carried Marines of the Special Landing Force to battle on the coast and in the swamps near Saigon; on the LSTs that enabled the Navy's River Patrol Force and the Army-Navy Mobile Riverine Force to fight far from the sea in the Mekong Delta; and the vital contribution of the Royal Australian Navy's Clearance Diving Team 3.

We learn how the sailors of these units braved fire and accomplished their missions during Operation Game Warden, the Tet Offensive, the SEALORDS Campaign, the Cambodian incursion, and the enemy swimmer-sapper campaign to sink allied ships and craft. Indeed, critical to the success of allied arms was the work of the U.S. underwater demolition team and explosive ordnance disposal personnel and the Australian divers who operated to frustrate enemy swimmer-sapper attacks. Also covered are amphibious and anti-mining operations with the Vietnam Navy, the Vietnamization Program, and Frequent Wind, the evacuation of South Vietnam.

We gain an appreciation of the sacrifices made by the men who paid the ultimate price, including the twenty-five crewmen of USS *Westchester County* (LST 1167) killed when underwater explosions tore into their ship on 1 November 1968. Appendices identify awards given to the U.S. amphibious and Australian units and a listing of the ships of the Vietnam Navy that survived the evacuation from South Vietnam in 1975 to reach the Philippines. In short, this volume should be on the shelf of any serious student of the Vietnam War and the contribution of many courageous and dedicated American and Australian sailors.

Edward J. Marolda, Former Director of Naval History (Acting) and Senior Historian of the Navy

Foreword

All History is relevant to someone, and some history is of interest to everyone. This book, however, should be of interest to anyone who served in the Services at the time of the Vietnam War, and to everyone else, because it is a window to events not well-known nor remembered today.

Very diverse elements of all the United States Services made contributions to the effort, and so did other countries, particularly Australia; during which many men and women made incredible achievements, performed duties under the most adverse, dangerous environment of the time, and exhibited loyalty and a sense of duty regardless of personal opinion and a hostile attitude from the general population at home.

Reading this book brought back memories of my in-country tour 1966-1967 when assigned as a Vietnamese Navy advisor in the Market Time operations (the coastal Junk Force element, in my case), and subsequent deployments on the USS *Polk County* (LST-1084) in 1967 and 1968/69, and on the USS *Parsons* (DDG-33) in 1972 and 1973.

David Bruhn has compiled detailed information on the forces in the Vietnam theater, concentrating on the US amphibious Navy involved from the first assignments of US elements in the early 1960s through March 1973 (when all US forces were out of Vietnam), to the dramatic culminating events of the North Vietnamese takeover in 1975. He lists where Navy and Marine units were located, what they did, and why (the objectives and expectations—some of which were not always realized).

This book is an excellent resource to anyone researching involvement in the Vietnam conflict of Amphibious Forces, and those of the US Coast Guard. At that time, the US Navy had about 965 ships, of which over 15% were amphibious force-related; most of which were deployed to Vietnam at various times. Fifty-four of these ships were in Landing Ship Flotilla ONE, alone; 50 of which were LSTs. Today, the US Navy has fewer than 300 ships in commission; about 33 of them are amphibious warfare ships.

Along the way, David gives glimpses of truly remarkable individual heroism and initiative, and expands insight into the lives of the few who received this Nation's highest decoration, the Medal of Honor. Reading the account of Boatswain's Mate 1st Class James Williams, a MOH recipient, is an inspiration.

The Vietnam conflict is largely viewed as a solely US fight, but David makes it clear it was a United Nations effort, listing armed forces from other countries, principally Australia.

The Vietnam era is ancient history to most of our populations today. Barely mentioned in textbooks, it is most often recorded as a tragedy. David brings out the fallacy of this. On the deck level, individuals responded to events with purpose, determination, and heroism.

While reading these accounts, one should keep in mind that this book covers events that happened nearly 50 years ago. It was a time before cell phones, digital photographs, Skype, and GPS (or any reliable electronic navigation).

We take our instant communication for granted today, but at that time, in that place, even 2-way radios were mostly line-of-sight, and did not always work. In life-or-death situations—which were many—when radio communication failed, individual field commanders had to make operational and tactical decisions on-the-spot. With no opportunity to seek guidance from higher authority, and potential great costs associated with any delay in decisive action, relatively junior leaders had to act independently, and did so, again and again, to protect those under their charge. This book recounts many such actions.

John D. White II
Captain, U.S. Navy (Retired)
Arlington, Virginia

Foreword

David Bruhn's *Gators Offshore and Upriver* provides a thorough insight into the extensive series of amphibious landings conducted by the US Marine Corps Special Landing Force during the Vietnam War. He also reviews the role amphibious ships played in the activities undertaken by the coastal surveillance force (TF 115), the river patrol force (TF 116), the mobile riverine force (TF 117) and Operation SEALORDS (TF 194). As such, it complements the description of naval activity in that war in his earlier book *On the Gunline*, which outlined the major role the surface combatants played, supporting the troops ashore.

As the book demonstrates, the Gator Navy provided a valuable contribution to the war effort, the Landing Ship Tanks (LST) being the work horses, comprising 62 of the 142 amphibious ships deployed to the war zone. Before examining the many amphibious operations undertaken, the author provides an extensive description of the various ship classes that make up the Gator Navy. This is a valuable reference section and useful to the reader to gain additional information about particular types or classes of ships.

Direct support to the campaign in South Vietnam was provided by the long-established Amphibious Ready Group and Special Landing Force (ARG/SLF). This powerful, versatile, and mobile formation supported assault operations along the length of the South Vietnamese littoral. The book clearly shows how versatile and important this sea-based support was to the war effort. The amphibious force was often used to extend the allied flank at sea, block enemy movements, land troops behind the enemy, and to reinforce front-line units.

The significant contribution to the brown-water navy illustrates how versatile the Gator Navy proved to be with the LSTs becoming the 'battleships of the Delta War.' They also provided support facilities to the many boats in the river patrol force and the mobile riverine force. One of the most significant features on these afloat bases were the helicopter pads. Helicopters evacuated the wounded and provided patrol boats with reconnaissance and fire support.

The impact of a swimmer-sapper attack in the Mekong Delta in November 1968 on the LST USS *Westchester County* is described in the opening chapter of *Gators Offshore and Upriver*. This attack resulted in 25 personnel being killed and 22 wounded which accounted for the US Navy's greatest single-incident combat loss of life during the entire Vietnam War. This incident also marked an increase in swimmer-sapper activity. In early 1969, I was sent to Vietnam to brief COMNAVFOR-V staff on RAN swimmer saboteur defence concepts and to assist in the development of US Navy doctrine on combating the swimmer-sapper issue. Operational research papers undertaken by the RAN Research Laboratory were also provided, as they underpinned the broad doctrine. Many of the measures proposed were adopted as standing operating procedures.

North Vietnamese sappers were assault or shock troops, which in today's parlance would be designated as Special Forces. Naval sapper targets included commercial and military shipping, bridges and piers, and bases near waterways. Between 1962 and 1969 there were some 88 successful attacks against shipping in Vietnamese waters, resulting in some 210 personnel killed and 325 wounded. Only 20 enemy sappers were killed or captured, emphasising the extremely advantageous payoff to the enemy of this type of attack.

The book also includes the contribution made by the small RAN clearance diving team, CDT 3. It operated within Operation Market Time (Task Force 115) and was fully integrated within the US Navy EOD Mobile Unit Pacific. The team was involved in thwarting two swimmer-sapper attacks on shipping in Vung Tau in May 1969 and June 1970. The first incident resulted in the recovery of two modern Soviet BPM-2 limpet mines in mint condition. It also participated in Operation SEALORDS, which resulted in them receiving a Presidential Unit Citation.

As the US Command became increasingly aware of the versatility and positive 'can do' mind-set of the Australian clearance divers, they were regularly employed as the 'immediate response team' to any EOD/diving/salvage incident which was 'outside the square.' Vietnam proved to be the testing ground for the RAN Clearance Diving Branch and it confirmed that the selection and training process was turning out men made of the 'right stuff.'

David Bruhn has produced an excellent and comprehensive book, clearly showing the contribution of the Gator Navy to the overall war effort in Vietnam. As well as providing a reference on the various classes of amphibious ships, the book gives an interesting description of the many amphibious landings conducted, and the role amphibious ships played in support of the brown-water navy, within the larger backdrop of the war.

Commodore Hector Donohue AM RAN (Rtd)

Acknowledgements

The stunning painting by Richard DeRosset gracing the cover is of a mining attack on the tank landing ship USS *Westchester County* by Viet Cong swimmer-sappers. Rapid actions by a crew devastated by many casualties, saved the ship from sinking. Two holes blown in her hull were sufficiently large for a Boston whaler to pass through her starboard side, and enter flooded compartments to take out deceased and injured personnel. Richard's brilliant work results from immense talent, and much time spent at sea as a "bluejacket" in the Navy, a deckhand aboard fishing vessels and later, master of the small tanker *Pacific Trojan*.

Photo Acknowledgements-1

Artist Richard DeRosset signing prints of his painting of the torpedoing of the heavy cruiser USS *Indianapolis* (CA-35).
Courtesy of Richard DeRosset

I am greatly indebted to Dr. Edward J. Marolda, who was kind enough to pen a foreword, and whose articles and books on the Vietnam War were of great assistance. Of particular value was his seminal book, *By Sea, Air, and Land: An Illustrated History of the U. S. Navy and the War in Southeast Asia*. Dr. Marolda served as the Acting Director of Naval

History and Senior Historian of the Navy. In 2017 the U.S. Naval Historical Foundation honored him with its Commodore Dudley W. Knox Naval History Lifetime Achievement Award. Marolda has written scores of books and articles. An expert on Vietnam, he taught courses at Georgetown University in Washington, D.C. on the Vietnam War and on the Cold War in the Far East.

Captain John D. White II, USN (Retired) offers unique insight and perspective in his foreword, borne of much sea duty experience (both inshore and offshore) in Vietnam, and subsequent command tours during a very distinguished career in the amphibious force. As a mid-grade officer in Vietnam, he commanded the tank landing ship USS *Polk County* (LST-1084) in 1967 and 1968/69, and was executive officer of the guided-missile destroyer USS *Parsons* (DDG-33) in 1972 and 1973. Later, he was assigned as executive officer of the amphibious cargo ship USS *Mobile* (LKA-115), and as commanding officer of Assault Craft Unit One, tank landing ship USS *Tuscaloosa* (LST-1187), and amphibious transport dock USS *Raleigh* (LPD-1). Ashore, he served in the Bureau of Naval Personnel, and on the Navy Staff in Washington, DC.

Photo Acknowledgements-2

Capt. John D. White II, USN, in 1987 while on active duty.
Courtesy of John White

Commodore Hector Donohue, AM RAN (Retired), provides valuable Australian perspective and assessment in his foreword, and graciously contributed much material, a good part drawn from *United and Undaunted: the first 100 years: a history of diving in the Royal Australian Navy 1911-2011*, which he co-authored with Comdr. Edward W. (Jake) Linton, RAN (Retired). Donohue began his career in the RAN in 1955 as a seaman officer and subsequently sub-specialized as a clearance diver and torpedo and anti-submarine officer. His service in the RAN included command of the destroyer escort HMAS *Yarra* and the guided missile frigate HMAS *Darwin*. Ashore, he held a number of senior positions in Defence policy and force development prior to retirement in mid-1991.

I am also very appreciative of assistance provided by Donald (Scotty) Allan, a former RAN clearance diver and current historian for the Royal Australian Navy Clearance Divers Association. Scotty shared with me his own experience, as well as certificates, citations, photos and stories related to the contributions of CDT 3 in Vietnam. Michael A. Harris, Scotty's American counterpart as the historian for the Mobile Riverine Force Association, provided much assistance as well.

I am particularly appreciative of help lent me by Albert Moore for this book and over the past several years. The founder and former long-serving president of the MRFA, Moore served in several units in Vietnam, including duty aboard the USS *Benewah* (APB-35).

Photo Acknowledgements-3

Photo Acknowledgements-4

Left: Scotty engaged in diving in Sydney Harbour in 1972.
Courtesy of Donald (Scotty) Allan
Right: Michael A. Harris at the Rach Soi Vietnamese Naval Base in December 1968, while assigned as a radioman/.50-cal. gunner to the troop carrier *ATC-152-1*.
Courtesy of Michael Harris

Many other individuals also contributed to this book. Naval Historian and Vietnam War expert John Hodges and Lead Reference Archivist Dale Gordon, assisted with research and provided materials held by the Naval History and Heritage Command. Rabbi Arnold E. Resnicoff of Washington, D.C., a former officer aboard the tank landing ship *Hunterdon County*, provided information about, and reviewed the chapter related to, the Cambodian Incursion.

Ens. Arnold E. Resnicoff, USNR, aboard USS *Hunterdon County* (LST-838), 1970. Courtesy of Rabbi Arnold E. Resnicoff.

Capt. Robert Kermen, USNR (Retired), read the manuscript and provided comments based on his diverse duty as an enlisted man in Vietnam. This duty included that of gunner aboard the armored troop carrier *ATC-112-7* (with River Division 112), as a Journalist Third Class aboard the gun cruiser USS *St. Paul* (CA-73), and assignment ashore working for the historian on commander, Naval Forces Vietnam's staff.

Photo Acknowledgements-6

Capt. Robert J. Kermen, USNR (Retired)
Courtesy of Bob Kermen

Commander Ron Swart, USN (Retired) has lent his expertise to other books by the author and did so again. After achieving the rank of Mineman Chief Petty Officer, he was commissioned to Ensign (LDO Surface Ordnance). Subsequently, he served three tours as a Mobile Mine Unit commanding officer; two tours on the Mine Warfare Command staff as chief staff officer to commander, Mobile Mine Assembly Group; and finally as commander, Mobile Mine Assembly Group. He is currently the editor of *DASHPOT*, the newsletter of the Association of Minemen.

Photo Acknowledgements-7

Formal portrait of Commander Ron Swart, LDO, USN, while still on active duty. His command at sea, and command ashore insignia, attest to a remarkable career. Courtesy of Ron Swart

I am also indebted to Frank and David Zebley for providing some perspective on duty in Vietnam with the U.S. Marines. Frank was a Navy Corpsman with Lima Company 3rd Battalion, 4th Marine Regiment from January 1967 until September 1967, before transfer to the 2nd Medical Battalion in Hue. David served in the Marine Corps from October 1973 to August 1976, as an anti-tank assault man. His unit, or members of it, were involved in Operation EAGLE PULL in Cambodia, Operation FREQUENT WIND in the Republic of Vietnam, and the *Mayaguez* Incident in Cambodia.

Finally, a tip of the hat to Lynn Marie Tosello, who has edited several books for me. Her keen eye, piercing intellect, active pen, and appreciation for eloquence and prose, has been supplemented by ever-increasing knowledge of naval and maritime-related subjects. In short, she ensures that "bright work" gets properly shined, lines are taut, and that there are no significant "holidays" in overall coverage.

Preface

The true rule for the Military is to seize such property as is needed for Military uses and reasons, and let the rest alone.

—President Abraham Lincoln in a letter to Joseph J. Reynolds, dated January 20, 1865.

Lying offshore, ready to act, the presence of ships and Marines sometimes means much more than just having air power or ship's fire, when it comes to deterring a crisis. And the ships and Marines may not have to do anything but lie offshore. It is hard to lie offshore with a C-141 or C-130 full of airborne troops.

—Gen. Colin Powell, U. S. Army, chairman, Joint Chiefs of Staff, during Operation DESERT STORM.

Simply stated the mission of the Squadron is the transportation of Marines and their equipment. However, this includes assault landings and the use of helicopters for vertical envelopment. It requires the constant exercise of much skill and endurance by all hands. Elements of the Squadron are constantly on call to serve in amphibious operations whether they are in the United States or in the Western Pacific.

—U.S. Navy Public Affairs statement regarding Amphibious Squadron Three.[1]

The Halldorson brothers, Michael and Alan—both Navy veterans of the Vietnam War—are partially responsible for this book, and its predecessor and companion, *On the Gunline*. Mike, who authored *Navy Daze: Coming of Age in the 1960s Aboard a Navy Destroyer*, once asked me, "When are you going to write a book about destroyers?" The result was a book devoted to the 270 U.S. Navy combatant ships, and four Royal Australian Navy destroyers, that served on the gunline during the Vietnam War. I later met Alan, who served aboard the USS *Caddo Parish* (LST-515) and USS *Iredell County* (LST-839) in the dangerous, confined inland waters of the Republic of Vietnam. After acknowledging our work pertaining to destroyers, he posed the question, "Where are all the books on amphibious ships?"

Alan's two tank landing ships were old, World War II veterans, commissioned in January and December 1944, respectively. The destroyer USS *Hopewell* (DD-681), which Mike served aboard off the Vietnam coast, was even older, commissioned in September 1943. One duty which the brothers shared (Mike off the South Vietnamese coast providing gunfire support for allied ground forces, and Alan running rivers in South Vietnam delivering food, ammunition and other materiel to river ports) was assignment to gun mounts. The chief difference was that warships normally only set General Quarters and manned gun mounts before fire missions. "Gators" in confined inland waters did so whenever the possibility of attack existed; while passing close enough to a river bank to come under enemy automatic weapons, recoilless rifle, rocket-propelled grenade, or small arms fire—and sometimes when beached, berthed, or anchored handling cargo.

Photo Preface-1

Alan Halldorson standing next to the forward 40mm mount aboard the USS *Caddo Parish* (LST-515) on 22 November 1968. The tank landing ship was beached at Dong Tam, South Vietnam, to deliver cargo.
Courtesy of Alan Halldorson

LARGE NUMBERS OF GATORS SERVED IN VIETNAM

Likely few Americans are aware of the numbers of amphibious ships that served in Vietnam during the war in Southeast Asia. There was ample newspaper and television coverage of aircraft carriers in the Tonkin Gulf carrying out Rolling Thunder bombing missions, and of cruisers and destroyers off the coast shelling enemy positions ashore, but not much of the activities of the gators. Of the 142 amphibious ships deployed at various times to the war zone, 62 (44 percent) were LSTs (tank landing ships).

Quantities by Ship Type	Quantities by Ship Type
4 AGC/LCC (amphibious force command ship)	4 IFS (inshore fire support ship)
12 AKA/LKA (amphibious cargo ship)	7 LPD (amphibious transport dock)
15 APA (attack transport)	8 LPH (amphibious assault ship)
3 APB (self-propelled barracks ship)	18 LSD (dock landing ship)
3 APD (high speed transport)	62 LST (tank landing ship)
5 ARL (landing craft repair ship)	

Twenty-three of the one hundred, forty-two gators earned three or more combat action ribbons (CR), as well as other unit awards. Of these ships, all but six—the landing craft repair ships *Askari* and *Sphinx*, high-speed transport *Cook*, inshore fire support ship *Carronade*, rocket ship *White River*, and amphibious assault ship *Tripoli*—were LSTs.

CR	PUC	NUC	MUC	Ship	Ship Class
7		1	2	*Page County* (LST-1076)	LST-542
6	2		4	*Harnett County* (LST-821)	LST-542
5	2		8	*Jennings County* (LST-846)	LST-542
5	2		5	*Askari* (ARL-30)	*Achelous*
5		4	3	*Tom Green County* (LST-1159)	LST-1156
5	1		2	*Sphinx* (ARL-24)	*Achelous*
4	1		5	*Whitfield County* (LST-1169)	LST-1156
4			2	*Luzerne County* (LST-902)	LST-542
4	1	1	1	*Iredell County* (LST-839)	LST-542
4		1	2	*Caddo Parish* (LST-515)	*LST-491*
4		1	1	*Meeker County* (LST-980)	LST-542
4			2	*Coconino County* (LST-603)	LST-542
4			2	*Cook* (APD-130)	*Crosley*
3	2		8	*Hunterdon County* (LST-838)	LST-542
3	1	4	5	*Vernon County* (LST-1161)	LST-1156
3		4	2	*Westchester County* (LST-1167)	LST-1156
3		2	1	*Carronade* (IFS-1)	*Carronade*
3		2	1	*White River* (LSMR/LFR-536)	LSM(R)-501
3		2	1	*Tripoli* (LPH-10)	*Iwo Jima*
3			2	*Hickman County* (LST-825)	LST-542
3			2	*Madera County* (LST-905)	LST-542
3			1	*Floyd County* (LST-762)	LST-542
3			1	*Wexford County* (LST-1168)	LST-1156

LST-491: No name for class
LST-542: *Chelan*-class
LST-1156: *Terrebonne Parish*-class

PUC: Presidential Unit Citation
NUC: Navy Unit Commendation
MUC: Meritorious Unit Commendation

A summary of the unit awards garnered by all 142 amphibious ships may be found in Appendix A. Chapter 2 provides readers an overview of the various types of amphibious ships that served in Vietnam, before progressing into operations—the heart of the book. Former crew members of LSTs desiring greater detail about these "work horses," will find information related to the ships and their parent Landing Ship Squadrons or Flotilla in Chapter 9.

UNHERALDED U.S. NAVY AMPHIBIOUS READINESS GROUP/MARINE CORPS SPECIAL LANDING FORCE

Many books and articles exist, rightly extolling the heroic actions of the crews of "Swift boats" (PCFs) that plied the coves and coastal waters of South Vietnam, and those of river patrol boats (PBRs) and "Seawolf" helicopters (UH-1B gunships) which engaged in combat on and over inland waters. There are few published works, other than by Marine Corps historians, devoted to the U.S. Seventh Fleet's Amphibious Readiness Group/Marine Corps Special Landing Force teams. To help address this inequity, Chapters 4-7, 11, and 15 are devoted to the subject.

When many people think about amphibious operations, they likely picture the Normandy Landings on 6 June 1944. On that date, in the most famous assault from the sea in World War II, and of all time, British, Canadian, and American forces landed at Utah, Omaha, Gold, Sword, and Juno beaches in the largest amphibious operation in history. Some might also recall the large-scale amphibious assault on the walled city of Inchon during the Korean War. That operation, codenamed CHROMITE—involving 75,000 troops and 261 naval vessels, and which led to the recapture of the South Korean capital of Seoul—began on 15 September 1950 and ended on 19 September.

Few people, outside those who were involved, were likely aware of the numerous amphibious operations and raids carried out by the Seventh Fleet's Amphibious Ready Group and Marine Corps Special Landing Force (ARG/SLF) in Vietnam. In support of allied ground combat, this versatile, and mobile formation struck along the length of the South Vietnamese coastline and far inland. The ARG usually consisted of a handful of amphibious ships: typically, a helicopter assault ship (LPH), a dock landing ship (LSD), an attack transport (APA) or a transport dock (LPD), and a tank landing ship (LST). Additional gators augmented this force as necessary.[2]

A Battalion Landing Team, the heart of the Special Landing Force, was a task unit built around a Marine Corps infantry battalion. Such a battalion was composed of four rifle platoons, one weapons platoon, and one headquarters and service company, consisting of an 81mm mortar platoon, a 106mm recoilless rifle platoon, and a flame thrower section. To this core group, several specialized units were attached to provide support. The BLT's artillery support came from a battery of tanks and other types of fire power. Also attached were amphibious tractors, an engineer shore party, reconnaissance party, and motor transport units.³

Photo Preface-2

USS *Washtenaw County* (LST-1166) with her bow doors open to launch amphibious craft in support of Operation DECKHOUSE V. Two Marine Corps amphibious tractors are moving along the beach, with a UH-1 helicopter approaching, at right. Naval History and Heritage Command photograph #NH 103692

Photo Preface-3

3rd Marine Division Amtraks shuttle supplies to forces conducting clearing operations along the Cua Viet River supply route, 1968.
Marine Corps photograph A191224

Photo Preface-4

Unidentified member of a Battalion Landing Team.
USS *Valley Forge* (LPH-8) Western Pacific 1965-1966 cruise book

The Marine SLF included a medium helicopter squadron equipped with twenty-four UH-34s embarked in the amphibious assault ship. The ground combat element, an infantry battalion landing team, reinforced with artillery, armor, engineer, and other support units, were divided among the ships. This practice enabled landings of men and their equipment on shore by helicopter, or by the forty-one tracked landing vehicles (LVTs) carried aboard the ships, or by both methods. The LVTs were commonly called "Amtraks."[4]

Photo Preface-5

Marine UH-34 helicopter taking off from the flight deck of the amphibious assault ship USS *Princeton* (LPH-5) to land Marines in the Vietcong-saturated Rung Sat Zone in South Vietnam, 26 March 1966. The landing was part of Operation JACKSTAY. National Archives photograph #K-31417

NAVAL SUPPORT FOR AMPHIBIOUS OPERATIONS

The Seventh Fleet provided additional assistance for amphibious operations, including air cover by carrier aircraft, naval gunfire support, supply by the Logistic Support Force, and medical support by hospital ships *Repose* (AH-16) and *Sanctuary* (AH-17) positioned close offshore.[5]

Photo Preface-6

Hospital ship USS *Repose* (AH-16) off the South Vietnamese coast, 22 April 1966. Equipped with a heliport astern, medical staff, and advanced medical facilities, she was credited with saving many lives during the Vietnam War.
National Archives photograph #K-31174

Naval personnel also supported the Marine Special Landing Force as medical corpsmen, chaplains, and spotters in 1st Air Naval Gunfire Liaison Company detachments. Underwater Demolition Team, SEAL, and Beachmaster units supported operations on shore.[6]

Photo Preface-7

UDT 12 members on Red Beach, Danang, South Vietnam, prior to the landing of the 2nd Battalion, 3rd Marines, 10 April 1965.
Defense Department Marine Corps photograph A185082

James George Vanos (better known as Jesse "the body" Ventura, a former professional wrestler who would later serve as governor of the state of Minnesota) and Jan Vanos, his older brother, were both members of Underwater Demolition Team 12. Jim Vanos graduated with BUD/S class 58 in December 1970, and joined UDT 12 after additional requisite training.[7]

As needed, transport submarines *Perch* (APSS-313), *Tunny* (APSS-282), and *Grayback* (LPSS-574) carried Navy underwater demolition teams, SEALs, and South Vietnamese Marines to points off prospective landing beaches. The naval special warfare men then quietly exited the boats, swam or rowed rubber rafts through the surf, and carried out vital reconnaissance or other special operations ashore.[8]

Operating from Subic Bay in the Philippines, *Perch* had begun training in 1963 with Marine Special Forces, UDT teams, and special operations units from allies in covert reconnaissance missions. When the Vietnam War began for the submarine in 1965, her deck armament consisted of two 40mm guns and .50-caliber machine guns that could be mounted on the conning tower. In March, she participated in

JUNGLE DRUM III, an exercise in which a 75-man Marine Corps reconnaissance force was landed on the Malay Peninsula. At year's end, in support of Operation MARKET TIME, the interdiction of communist supply and infiltration along the South Vietnamese coast, *Perch* conducted amphibious landings as part of Operation DAGGER THRUST. Information about these and other actions—including one believed to be the last surface combat action involving a U.S. submarine—may be found in Chapters 5 and 6.⁹

Photo Preface-8

Guided missile submarine USS *Tunny* (SSG-282) off the Mare Island Navy Shipyard, 16 April 1953. She was converted to a troop-carrying submarine in 1966 (APSS-282), and reclassified an amphibious transport submarine (LPSS-282) on 1 January 1969. Naval History and Heritage Command photograph #NH 90809

Three high speed transports—*Alex Diachenko* (ADP-123), *Cook* (ADP-130), and *Weiss* (ADP-135)—also delivered and recovered beach reconnaissance teams, albeit not as stealthily as by transport submarine.

IMPORTANT ROYAL AUSTRALIAN NAVY SUPPORT

Australia was the only ally to provide naval support to the United States during the war. The contributions of RAN Helicopter Flight Vietnam are briefly addressed in Chapter 6, along with heroic actions of the 1st Australian (Army) Task Force during the Battle of Long Tan. The other RAN naval unit in country, Clearance Diving Team Three, was charged with protecting merchant and military shipping at the port of Vung Tau. Ships lying at anchor, or pierside were vulnerable to enemy swimmer-sapper attacks. The crews of vessels that called at Vung Tau between mid-February 1967 and mid-August 1970, owe the Aussie divers a debt of gratitude for the thousands of hull, rudder, and anchor chain inspections they performed—searching for and, when found, rendering harmless emplaced explosives.

Chapter 1 describes a mining attack against USS *Westchester County* on the night of 1 November 1968, which resulted in great loss of life and damage to the tank landing ship. Vulnerability to attack extended to areas other than ports; she'd been anchored on the My Tho River with other units of the Mobile Riverine Force. Between January 1962 and June 1969, there were 88 successful swimmer attacks against shipping, which killed more than 210 personnel and wounded 325. In comparison, only 20 enemy sappers were killed or captured for all attacks—whether successful or not—emphasizing the advantageous payoff to the enemy of this type of warfare.[10]

Swimmer-sappers were specialist North Vietnamese divers and Viet Cong who received nine months training in North Vietnam. At completion, they were capable of assembling and positioning land mines, command-detonated mines, and water mines. Enemy saboteurs, equipped with a snorkel, limpet mine, grenades, signal flare, and a nylon line, used currents and floating debris to assist in their approach to a target. Challenges they faced (other than detection) included low water temperatures, strong currents, and difficulty in navigating underwater (swimming to targets) at night. Mines (acoustic, magnetic, or pressure-detonated) were often transported by sampan to the area of the attack, slung beneath the vessel's keel, if there was sufficient boat traffic, for the 'minelayer' to proceed about its business unnoticed.[11]

The U.S. Navy's Inshore Undersea Warfare Group One, Western Pacific Detachment, was responsible for the protection of shipping in the principal anchorages of South Vietnam against underwater attack. Operation STABLE DOOR provided harbor defense at Cam Ranh Bay, Qui Nhon, Danang, Cua Viet, Nha Trang, Vung Tau, and Saigon. Each harbor defense unit:

- Maintained continuous visual and radar surveillance of harbor approaches and anchorage areas; and
- Operated harbor patrol boats to intercept and search local craft, maintain a vigilant watch for enemy swimmers or floating objects which could be mines, and carry Explosive Ordnance Disposal (EOD) divers for inspection of ships' hulls and anchor chains[12]

Harbor patrols involved periodically dropping grenades into the water during random sweeps, and watching for bubbles that might mark a sapper's approach. Occasionally bodies washed up on the beach as evidence of their success, or ships suffered damage to explosives as evidence of their failure. Inspection of ships' hulls and anchor chains by EOD personnel, and removal/neutralization of mines found, lessened such occurrences. However, despite much effort by harbor defenses, enemy swimmers were elusive, and sabotage attempts on ships continued throughout the war. It was not until January 1968 that the first swimmer was captured by a STABLE DOOR unit.[13]

Although the scope of this book does not include harbor defense, short chapters 14 and 18, and portions of Chapters 6 and 13 as well as the postscript, are devoted to the elite group of forty-nine officers and men that comprised the RAN Clearance Diving Team Three (CDT 3).[14]

ROYAL AUSTRALIAN NAVY CDT 3 IN VIETNAM

> *Our primary role at Vung Tau was ship protection. The biggest threat was diver laid mines. We went out every night into the harbour. The tidal streams in VungTau are very swift and we normally conducted our patrol two hours before and two hours after slack water. We were required to check all vessels for mines. We checked anchor chains in case a mine or other device had been attached to them. The tidal stream would then drag the charge back alongside the hull, which would detonate the mine magnetically. Alternately the attack swimmer would place a limpet mine directly against the hull and leave it there with a timing mechanism.*
>
> *We did a lot of things we couldn't put in our reports. As OIC, I was not authorised to go into an ambush, or assault a VC held position or take part in a search and destroy sweep, but all of these things happened during CDT 3's time in Vietnam.*
>
> —Lt. Alexander Donald, RAN, officer in charge of Clearance Diving Team 3 during its sixth rotation to Vietnam, remarking on activities from 12 August 1969 to 31 March 1970.[15]

The RAN approved the formation of Clearance Diving Team Three in late 1966 as one element of a larger naval contribution to the war in Vietnam, and the team arrived in country on 6 February 1967. The Aussies were initially attached to a U.S. Navy EOD unit based in Saigon. They relocated to Vung Tau twelve days later, with living quarters in a disused ammunition bunker, part of an old French-built coastal fort in the harbour entrance control post ("VC Hill") in the Nui Lon area. From their elevated position, the clearance divers had a commanding view of their primary area of responsibility—Vung Tau Harbor seaward to Long Son Island—for the defense of shipping against enemy attack. Their duties included inspecting shipping in the Vung Tau anchorages, or berthed pierside, for improvised explosive devices.[16]

Photo Preface-9

Repair ship USS *Jason* (AR-8) at anchor off Vung Tau in 1968 with a nest of small ships moored to port and the coastal minesweeper USS *Woodpecker* (MSC-209) moored starboard aft while refueling.
Naval History and Heritage Command photograph #NH 107752

Vung Tau lay at the end of a peninsula jutting into the South China Sea, adjacent to Cape St. Jacques at the southernmost tip. Westward of the peninsula were three peaks of about 700 feet. The team took up living quarters on the seaward slope of the center peak ("VC Hill"). Vung Tau had two anchorages where merchant ships waited before proceeding to Saigon, forty-five miles to the northwest, via the Long Tau Channel through the Rung Sat mangrove swamps. Vessels lying in these anchorages were inviting targets for swimmer-sapper attacks.[17]

Inspection of anchor chains, rudders, and propellers was done daily as a routine measure, while hull searches were performed on request, or following a report of a suspected swimmer in an anchorage. A tidal range of ten feet and currents of 4-6 knots in the Vung Tau anchorages hindered ship hull inspections. Fortunately, these conditions also made mining difficult for swimmer-sappers.[18]

TEAM REDESIGNATION/COMPOSITION/ROTATIONS

Clearance Diving Team 3 was designated EODMUPAC Team 21 in October 1967 for U.S. Navy purposes, signifying that it was functioning as part of the USN Explosive Ordnance Disposal Mobile Unit, Pacific. This designation was subsequently changed to EODMUPAC Team 35. CDT 3 contingents, comprised of one officer and five sailors, were considered to offer a two-team capacity. The standard U.S. Navy EOD Team was one officer and three enlisted.[19]

Eight contingents of CDT 3 personnel deployed to Vietnam—serving at Vung Tau from 6 February 1967 to 14 August 1970, and later at Danang, from 15 August 1970 to 19 April 1971. (During its time at Vung Tau, CDT 3 searched 7,441 ships.) The beginning and ending dates in the table reflect when the officers in charge relieved one another of their duties, with one exception. The Sixth Contingent left Australia for Vietnam on 12 August 1969.[20]

Royal Australian Navy Clearance Diving Team Three
(Sequential Deployments to Vietnam)

Beginning	Ending	Officer in Charge
	First Contingent	
6 Feb 1967	25 Aug 1967	Lt. Michael T. E. Shotter, RAN
	Second Contingent	
25 Aug 1967	26 Feb 1968	Lt. Robert J. Burns, GM RAN
	Third Contingent	
26 Feb 1968	28 Aug 1968	Lt. William D. H. Lees, RAN
	Fourth Contingent	
28 Aug 1968	26 Feb 1969	Lt. Clement J. Littleton, RAN
	Fifth Contingent	
26 Feb 1969	12 Aug 1969*	Lt. Allan A. Davis, RAN
	Sixth Contingent	
12 Aug 1969*	31 Mar 1970	Lt. Alexander Donald, RAN
	Seventh Contingent	
31 Mar 1970	29 Oct 1970	Lt. Ross S. Blue, RAN
	Eighth Contingent	
29 Oct 1970	19 Apr 1971	Lt. Edward W. Linton, BEM RAN[21]

CHANGES IN PROCEDURES/DISESTABLISHMENT

In late January 1969, it was decided that most ship inspections were to be made at night as this was the most common time for enemy attacks. These night inspections began on 5 February 1970. Clearance Diving Team Three's responsibility for Operation STABLE DOOR at Vung Tau came to an end on 14 August 1970 when the Australians were relieved by two South Vietnamese Navy teams.[22]

The following day, CDT 3 divers, their monkey mascot ('WRAN EOD Fred') and equipment were airlifted to Danang in two C-130 Hercules aircraft. At Danang, the team was quartered at U.S. Navy

Support Facility, Camp Tien Sha, and became part of the security department of the facility. The divers were responsible for providing harbor patrols, EOD for the harbor area, naval policing, and ensuring physical security of the base.[23]

On 19 April 1971, CDT 3 relinquished its responsibilities to a U.S. Army EOD section and prepared for return to Australia. The arrival of the Eighth Contingent in Sydney on 5 May, marked the end of Clearance Diving Team 3's four years of duty in Vietnam. For its service in the war, CDT 3 was awarded the U.S. Presidential Unit Citation for extraordinary heroism in action against an armed enemy—the highest award for heroism a unit may receive, and equivalent of the Navy Cross for an individual—the U.S. Navy Meritorious Unit Commendation, and the U.S. Navy Unit Commendation, three times.[24]

Upon arrival on Australian soil, CDT 3 was disbanded, with the provision "to be reformed again at the discretion of the Australian Naval Board." The divers took up fleet support duties with Clearance Diving Teams One and Two, until CDT 3 was reactivated for overseas wartime deployments, including in 1991 for the Gulf War, and again in 2003 for the Iraq War.[25]

UNIT AWARDS AND INDIVIDUAL HONOURS

| Distinguished Service Cross | Distinguished Service Medal | British Empire Medal | Mention in Despatches Clasp | U.S. Army Commendation Medal |

Receipt of the unit awards, as well as Australian and United States individual honours made Clearance Diving Team Three the most highly decorated Australian unit during the Vietnam War. Citations for the unit awards may be found in Appendix B. Members of CDT 3 awarded individual honours are identified below, followed by a photograph of recipients of the U.S. Presidential Unit Citation.

Distinguished Service Cross	
Lt. Alexander Donald, RAN	
Distinguished Service Medal	
ABCD John A. Aldenhoven, RAN	LSCD Phillip C. Kember, RAN

British Empire Medal	
CPOCD Albert V. Rashleigh, RAN	
Mention in Despatches	
CPOCD Barrie J. Bailey, RAN	ABCD Jeffrey L. Garrett, RAN
U.S. Army Commendation Medal	
CPOCD John F. C. Dollar, RAN	LSCD Russel L. Steer, RAN
POCD John Kershler, RAN	ABCD Bogdan K. Wojcik, RAN
ABCD Gerald Kingston, RAN	

CPOCD: Chief Petty Officer Clearance Diver (CD)　　LSCD: Leading Seaman CD
POCD: Petty Officer CD　　ABCD: Able Seaman CD

Photo Preface-10

Four of the six Clearance Diving Team Three (4th Contingent) members awarded a PUC for their participation in Operation SEA LORDS. The photograph was taken at the Royal Australian Navy Diving School HMAS Penguin in 2014. L-R: Robert Spicer; Colin Darling; Robert Cox (deceased) is represented by Sally Broom Cox and daughter; Barry Wilson; and Clement Littleton. David Rhook is not pictured.
Courtesy of Don (Scotty) Allan

CDT 3 (Fourth Contingent to serve in Vietnam)

Lt. Clement J. Littleton, RAN	LSCD David N. Rhook, RAN
POCD Robert J. Cox, RAN	ABCD Colin L. Darling, RAN
POCD Barry W. Wilson, RAN	ABCD Robert H. Spicer, RAN

"AUSSIE" POEM

This prayer for Clearance Divers was penned by Chaplain Peter Ball (assisted by POCD Frederick Asher and ABCD Donald Allan), when onboard HMAS *Perth* in late 1970. He came ashore and visited Lt. Jake Linton, OIC of the 8th Contingent and his team at their base in Camp Tien Sha, Danang, for three days and presented the poem to them. Compliments of Commodore Hector Donohue, AM RAN (Rtd.)

> O God in Heaven hear our plea
> For clearance divers 'neath the sea
> While in the ocean's dark embrace
> Keep us thy sons within thy grace
> And hear us lord, o thou who saves
> For us thy servants 'neath the waves

LST SUPPORT OF OTHER COMBAT OPERATIONS

As might be expected, deep-draft "amphibs"—command ships, helicopter carriers, transport docks, dock landing ships, cargo ships, and transports—did not operate in inland waters. When not participating in assault landings, they carried out other Seventh Fleet tasking. Tank landing ships were on the rivers (as well as offshore), joining barracks ships and landing craft repair ships in support of Task Force 116 (the River Patrol Force), Task Force 117 (the Mobile Riverine Force), and later the SEA LORDS Campaign. Less frequently, LSTs supported patrol craft engaged in Operation MARKET TIME (Task Force 115): offshore interdiction efforts to stop the North Vietnamese flow of troops, war material, and supplies by sea into South Vietnam.

Photo Preface-11

Preparation of a new ramp as LSTs approach to offload at Vung Tau.
National Archives photograph #K-36318

Tank landing ships were extremely versatile owing to shallow drafts which allowed them to ply waters denied vessels that drew more water, and because they could beach to offload cargo. This was particularly desirable at underdeveloped ports with limited pier space and/or constricted anchorages. Specific to the support of River Patrol and Mobile Riverine Forces, four specially modified "T's" served as "mother ships" for patrol craft and "Seawolf" assault helicopters.

Photo Preface-12

Garrett County (LST-786) on the Co Chien River, Mekong Delta, South Vietnam. A naval UH-1B helicopter is landing on her deck, and three PBR Boats are alongside, June 1968. National Archive photograph #K-51441

Chapters 8, 10, and 13 are devoted to the Mobile Riverine Force, River Patrol Force, and SEA LORDS Campaign, and the involvement of "amphibs" (primarily LSTs) with these forces. Four of the most highly decorated tank landing ships—*Garrett County* (LST-786), *Harnett County* (LST-821), *Hunterdon County* (LST-838), and *Jennings County* (LST-846)—served as mobile support bases for river patrol boats and helicopters on the rivers of the Mekong Delta. *Garrett County* is not listed in the earlier table because the ships are rank-ordered by number of combat action ribbons earned. However, in addition to her two CRs, she was notably awarded a Presidential Unit Citation, and six Navy Unit Citations. One of these citations may be found in Appendix C.

In May 1970, *Hunterdon County* had the distinction of being the first commissioned U.S. naval vessel to enter Cambodian waters, during an operation termed the "Cambodian Incursion." The entry of U.S. military forces into Cambodia angered many in Congress and set off a wave of anti-war demonstrations—including one at Kent State

University that resulted in the killing of four students by National Guard troops. "Cambodian Incursion" is the title and subject of Chapter 17.

DEPARTURE OF U.S. FORCES FROM VIETNAM

Presidential candidate Richard M. Nixon pledged during his campaign to get America out of the Vietnam War and, following his election and inauguration, he took action to fulfil this promise. His administration's resultant "Vietnamization" program, which preceded the Cambodian Incursion, is the subject of Chapter 16. Chapter 19 covers the final U.S. involvement in Vietnam from 1971 to 1973.

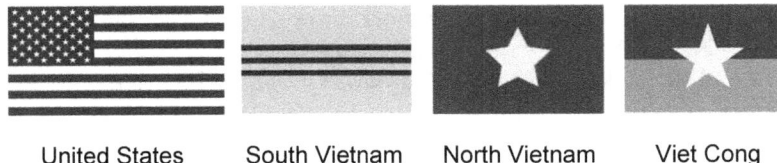

United States   South Vietnam   North Vietnam   Viet Cong

After years of negotiations from 1968 to 1973, the Paris Agreement of January 1973 between the U.S., South Vietnam, North Vietnam, and the National Liberation Front (Viet Cong) provided that prisoners of war would be returned and that the North Vietnam military and U.S. military personnel had to be out of South Vietnam by 29 March 1973, except for U. S. embassy personnel. All U.S. Navy and Marine Corps personnel, with the exception of the officers assigned to the Defense Attaché Office and the Marines of the Embassy Security Detachment, Saigon, left Vietnam on that date for Honolulu, Hawaii.[26]

OPERATIONS FREQUENT WIND AND EAGLE PULL, AND THE UNFORTUNATE *MAYAGUEZ* INCIDENT

> *We're going to have to send you back to rescue the Vietnamese navy. We forgot 'em. And if we don't get them or any part of them, they're all probably going to be killed.*
>
> —Directive to Comdr. Paul H. Jacobs, commanding officer of the destroyer escort USS *Kirk* (DE-1087) from Rear Adm. Donald B. Whitmire, commander of Operation FREQUENT WIND, embarked aboard the command ship *Blue Ridge* (LCC-19).[8]

In late April 1975, with the fall of Saigon to North Vietnamese forces imminent, the U.S. Navy formed Task Force 76 off the coast of South Vietnam. Its mission was to evacuate thousands of Vietnamese who had supported U.S. efforts to stop the Communist takeover of the Republic of Vietnam, and a dwindling number of American civilians still remaining in Vietnam. Chapter 20 describes this operation, code named FREQUENT WIND, following the evacuation by air of Phnom Penh, Cambodia, termed EAGLE PULL. These were the last operations of the Vietnam War involving amphibious ships.

The final chapter of the book deals with recovery of the containership SS *Mayaguez* and her crew, captured by Khmer Rouge forces on 12 May 1975. In a hurried operation ramrodded by President Gerald Ford's National Security Council, because American's reputation was seemingly at stake, forty-three Marines, sailors, and airmen lost their lives saving the forty mariners.

Preface-13

Painting by Richard DeRosset, depicting a Viet Cong swimmer-sapper mining attack on the tank landing ship USS *Westchester County* (LST-1167), on 1 November 1968, in which the U.S. Navy suffered it greatest loss of life in a single incident, as a result of enemy action, during the entire Vietnam War.

1

Viet Cong Sappers Nearly Sink USS *Westchester County*

Sapper action is a special action which requires special effort and special skills to perform.

—Remark by Ho Chi Minh in an address delivered on 19 March 1967 at the Sapper Training School in North Vietnam, located at the headquarters of the 305th Sapper Group.[1]

Photo 1-1

USS *Westchester County* (LST-1167) under way, date and location unknown. U.S. Navy photo from *All Hands* magazine, September 1973

Few Americans have heard of the *Westchester County* (LST-1167), a 384-foot tank landing ship commissioned on 10 March 1954. Fewer still are aware that aboard her, the United States Navy tragically suffered its greatest loss of life in a single incident as the result of enemy action during the entire Vietnam War.

At 0322 on 1 November 1968, the stillness of the Mekong Delta was shattered by two enormous explosions, which blasted gaping holes in the starboard side of the tank landing ship *Westchester County*—opening the interior of the ship to the muddy waters of the My Tho River. As most of her crew, soldiers and other Riverine Force personnel berthed aboard, slept, Viet Cong swimmer-sappers (frogmen) had evaded Base Interdiction & Defense craft (riverine craft) patrolling as a deterrent to just such an attack, and silently approached the anchored ship. The messenger of the watch had just gone below to wake reliefs for those on duty, when a pair of mines detonated simultaneously. Estimated to contain between 150 and 500 pounds of explosives, the mines were attached amidships to the starboard side of the ship's hull.[2]

Photo 1-2

USS *Westchester County* (LST-1167) with riverine craft alongside.
Courtesy of Albert Moore, founder and long-serving president of the Mobile Riverine Force Association

The tank landing ship was functioning as an ammunition and supply ship serving with the joint Army-Navy Mobile Riverine Force (Task Force 117). On this day, she was attached to Mobile Riverine Group Alfa, and also serving as a temporary home and base to 175 soldiers of the 9th Infantry Division's B Company, 3rd Battalion of the 60th Riverine Infantry, and to the crews of Navy River Assault Division 111. At the time of the attack, "Wesco" (as she was referred to by her crew) was anchored midstream on the My Tho River, in the vicinity of My Tho, forty miles upstream from the seaport of Vung Tau. Clustered in a rough semicircle around her were the self-propelled barracks ship *Benewah* (APB-35), the landing craft repair ship *Askari* (ARL-30), two large barracks barges, a small salvage vessel, and scores of armored riverine assault craft sporting coats of green paint.³

Photo 1-3

The self-propelled barracks ship USS *Benewah* (APB-35), flagship of the joint Army-Navy Mobile Riverine Force (Task Force 117), lies at anchor in waters of the Mekong Delta, with armored troop carriers (ATCs) nearby, November 1967. National Archives photograph #USN 1142271

Moored alongside *Westchester County*'s starboard side were three "ammi" (huge aluminum pontoon barges), separated from the ship by a floating 50-foot-long teak log, called a camel, which acted as a fender to protect the side of the ship. Linked together, the three barges functioned as a combination pier, loading dock, and ammunition and gasoline storage depot. Numerous craft (monitors, assault support patrol boats, and armored troop carriers) of River Assault Division 111 were made up to the ammis. Five UH-1B Iroquois ("Seawolf") attack helicopters were staged on Wesco's upper deck. Stored below on her tank deck, were more than 350 tons (about ten truckloads) of high explosives and ammunition.⁴

Typical precautions against enemy attack had been in effect. The 384-foot tank landing ship was darkened, with only anchor lights showing. Forward and aft, 3"/50-caliber rapid-fire guns were loaded, manned by partial crews, and armed lookouts were posted on deck. A watch team was in place on the bridge and, in the bowels of the ship, engine room personnel stood ready to answer engine commands from the bridge, should *Westchester County* need to get under way. In the distance, muffled thumps could be heard as riverine craft patrolled the anchorage area, periodically dropping concussion grenades to ward off enemy frogmen. Below deck, in the crowded berthing compartments, Navy and Army personnel slept peacefully.[5]

NORTH VIETNAMESE SWIMMER-SAPPERS

Photo 1-4

At a camp in the jungle, Viet Cong swimmer-sappers study a map in preparation for a demolition attack on a bridge in Phuoc Tuy Province, November 1971. The original photograph was captured from the Viet Cong.
Australian War Memorial photograph P01003.021

The team of swimmers that had affixed the explosives to the hull of *Westchester County* were "sappers," members of the Bo Doi Dac Cong ("soldiers in special forces"), a highly organized, well-trained and well-equipped organization that carried out special operations. The term "sapper" originated from the French word *saper*, a reference to French soldiers who dug narrow trenches, or "saps," toward an enemy fort to provide a somewhat protected channel for moving men and artillery closer to the fort in preparation for an assault. The term "sapper" currently refers more broadly to combat engineers who carry out a variety of construction and demolition duties. In Vietnam, American troops used the name primarily for North Vietnamese Army (NVA) and

Viet Cong (VC) units that used tactics more akin to those of commandos than to the work of engineers.[6]

Prior to the Tet Offensive in early 1968 (a coordinated series of North Vietnamese and Viet Cong attacks against targets all across South Vietnam), the sappers in the south were controlled by the Viet Cong and operated independently of the North Vietnamese Army. After the Viet Cong suffered massive casualties during Tet, all sapper operations in South Vietnam were supervised by the 429th Sapper Group, which reported directly to the Sapper High Command, a department in the NVA High Command in Hanoi. Training centers in South Vietnam and Cambodia were run by the 429th Sapper Group, while the centers in North Vietnam and Laos were directed from the NVA High Command. The instruction typically lasted three to eighteen months, depending on whether trainees would be soldiers in regular units or raiders operating outside a formal military structure.[7]

On 27 December 1970, five South Vietnamese Popular Forces platoons and helicopter gunships engaged a platoon of the 126th NVA Naval Sapper Regiment in the First Coastal Zone, which they wiped out, with nineteen killed and one, badly wounded, captured. The dead had empty packs and floatation bladders, indicating that they were returning from a mine emplacement mission. The prisoner revealed that his unit had travelled from the vicinity of Vinh Linh City, North Vietnam, to the Cua Viet River where they placed two 50kg pressure mines on the night of 24 December.[8]

The POW was a nineteen-year-old NVA private first class from Thanh Hoa Province in North Vietnam. He revealed that the 126th Regiment consisted of four companies of 50 to 60 men, each made up of four platoons. His training, conducted in Haiphong, had included two months of swimming instruction, two to three months of demolition training, and a similar period of political indoctrination.[9]

Within the Sapper Group were three distinct types of sapper units. Urban sappers were devoted to intelligence gathering, terrorism, assassination, and special operations in large urban areas such as Saigon and Hue. Field sappers conducted operations against U.S. and South Vietnamese troops, trained other Communist troops as sappers, and provided Communist leadership an elite force for lightning raids. Naval swimmer-sappers were responsible for attacking merchant and naval shipping, bridges, and bases near waterways. Merchant ships delivering munitions and other materials to Vietnamese ports in support of the allied war effort were popular targets, as were ships and barges of the Mobile Riverine Force that berthed large numbers of American soldiers, and lesser numbers of Riverine Force personnel.[10]

An attack on a waterborne vessel called for the placement of one or more explosive charges directly onto the hull of the target. The first challenge confronting the swimmers was to arrive at the target covertly. Depending on where the vessel was moored or anchored, the swimmers had to get their explosive charges to the target by swimming from shore or being dropped off by sampan. Once close enough to the target, a two-man swimmer cell normally swam covertly beneath the water's surface using snorkels, each dragging an individual charge or working together to carry a single large charge. The two members normally tied a rope between themselves to facilitate the attack and prevent themselves from becoming separated.[11]

Approaching the vessel, the pair tried to catch the anchor chain between them using their rope. If successful in snaring the chain, this action secured them against any currents that might propel them away from the ship. The swimmers could then maneuver and place the charge or charges against the hull of the target. The explosive(s) were attached, either magnetically or tied to the hull, and the fuses activated. The latter could be either command detonated or time-delayed, but time-delayed seemed to be the preferred method as it required no additional activity by the swimmers, whose goal was to escape undetected and survive the mission.[12]

SUBSTANTIAL DAMAGE TO TANK LANDING SHIP

Photo 1-5

Clear view of the damage wrought by enemy limpet mines to the hull of USS *Westchester County*, following the removal of the pontoons and the riverine craft that were made up along her starboard side.
Courtesy of Albert Moore

A waxing gibbous moon provided some illumination in an otherwise dark night, however, the full scope of damage to the ship could not be ascertained until daybreak. Dawn's early light revealed a pair of gaping,

10-foot holes, and the ship listing 11-degrees to starboard. Above, on Wesco's main deck, two of the choppers were wrecked beyond repair. The inboard ammi along her starboard side was crumpled, with dozens of damaged light anti-tank rockets, Claymore mines, blocks of C-4 plastic explosive, flares, grenades, and other loose ordnance strewn across its twisted deck.[13]

The forward half of the teakwood camel had been obliterated, and the remaining twenty-five feet driven through the ammi's aluminum hull (as shown in the below photograph) with the splintered remainder scattered over the decks of the pontoon and the ship. The pontoon's guard shack was wrecked, and several assault craft moored to the ammi (not shown) were severely damaged and in danger of sinking.[14]

Photo 1-6

Pontoon and guard shack wrecked by two exploding mines attached to *Westchester County*'s hull evidence the force that opened her hull, killing and wounding many sailors and soldiers sleeping in adjacent berthing spaces.
Courtesy of Albert Moore

DESPERATE EFFORTS BY CREW TO SAVE SHIP

The mines had been placed between the pontoons and the ship's hull, resulting in the force of the explosions travelling upward, through hull plating and fuel tanks, and into berthing compartments. In an instant, visibility within the ship was reduced to zero as lighting was knocked out, and the air filled with steam and vaporized diesel fuel.[15]

As river water flowed into *Westchester County*, she began listing to starboard. General Quarters was sounded, and survivors able to do so, groped in the tangled darkness to reach battle stations or aid wounded shipmates. The ship's commanding officer, Lt. Comdr. John W. Branin, was thrown from his bunk by the blast. Believing his ship was under rocket attack, he picked himself up off the deck, and quickly made his way to the bridge. Once there, Branin and his executive officer, Lt. Richard Jensen, faced a grim situation. Early reports indicated severe damage amidships and suggested heavy casualties, especially among the senior petty officers—leaving more junior, or untrained personnel, to rapidly carry out critical functions.[16]

Compounding these challenges, oil-slick decks made movement around the ship extremely hazardous, and communications between repair parties and damage control central (directing repair actions) was almost negligible. Of great concern, two-thirds of the tank deck, which ran nearly the entire length of the ship, was being used for ammunition storage. More than 10,000 rounds of 105mm and 155mm howitzer ammunition were stacked alongside pallets of 20mm cannon ammunition, boxes of C-4 plastic explosive, Claymore mines, white phosphorous ammunition, and cases of flares and pyrotechnics. Loose and damaged ammunition now lay scattered about the deck, blanketed by a mist of fuel oil. With just one spark, *Westchester County* and the other vessels of the Mobile Riverine Force anchored nearby could be obliterated, and the sailors and soldiers aboard them killed by an explosion of unimaginable magnitude.[17]

Branin's immediate problem was saving his ship from sinking. As tons of water continued flowing in through her ruptured hull plating, and she heeled over, ever farther, he thought for an instant that she would roll completely over. Fortunately, the *Westchester County* had a ballasting system which allowed her (like other LSTs) to "ballast down" off an assault beach, rest on the bottom in shallow water, and open her bow doors to discharge her craft. This was done by filling internal tanks provided for that purpose with water. When ready to do so, it was easy to pump out the water, float clear, and stand out to sea.[18]

Importantly, the ship had water in her ballast tanks, and Branin knew that if water could be pumped out of her forward starboard tanks, this action could reverse, or nearly offset, the effects of the water flooding into the ship. Miraculously, there was still electrical power to the pumps and, with the damage control officer providing precise instructions to Petty Officer Second Class Rick Russell, the ship slowly started rolling back to a more even keel.[19]

With many of the senior petty officers aboard killed or incapacitated, junior petty officers, seamen, and firemen stepped up, taking charge at battle stations suddenly undermanned and without leaders. The 22-year-old Russell, finding himself alone in the forward pumping station, had contacted the bridge via sound-powered phones, reported in, and stood by for orders.[20]

CORPSMAN'S HEROIC ACTIONS SAVES LIVES

Amidships on the second deck, in the senior petty officers' berthing compartment, Hospital Corpsman First Class John S. Sullivan had, like many others, been flung from his rack (bed). Knocked unconscious by the blast, he found himself, upon coming to, lying half on the deck and half in a gaping hole, and pulled himself away from the opening. With the General Quarters alarm sounding, Sullivan skirted the hole and began crawling through the wreckage toward the sound of voices.[21]

In this and other adjacent crowded sleeping areas, the blasts had rolled the deck beneath the occupants upward and back, leaving only a cramped crawl space between the deck and overhead, which was now jammed with twisted metal and mangled bodies. Below, in the Army berthing spaces, men, bedding, weapons, ammunition, and personal gear were hurled about, just before the waters of the My Tho began flooding these areas via breeches in the hull.[22]

Sullivan located two injured shipmates, sandwiched between the remains of their bunks and tons of tangled steel, pinned in the wreckage. Both had multiple injuries and Sullivan, injured himself, treated them by touch in the darkness. After providing first aid as best he could, Sullivan pried the men free and, with the help of an impromptu rescue team, evacuated them to a higher deck. Of the eleven men who slept in the First-Class Petty Officers' berthing area, three had been in other parts of the ship on watch. Five of the those present had been killed outright. Sullivan and his two shipmates were the only sailors to emerge alive from the compartment after the explosions.[23]

Sullivan headed for the bridge, with leg bleeding, to find out where else he was needed As soon as it became evident the ship was not under sustained attack, Branin released non-vital men from their topside battle stations to assist with rescue and casualty evacuation. However, until blowers could clear the lower decks of vaporized fuel, the use of cutting torches was out of the question. Chain falls, pry bars, come-alongs (hand-operated winches), and screw jacks were used to gain access to, and free men trapped in the wreckage. Sealed battle lanterns and portable lighting equipment safe to use, provided illumination. On the tank deck, fire party personnel stood by with hoses at the ready, while sailors gingerly collected damaged ammunition, gently setting it aside until it could be disposed of.[24]

While a corpsman from River Assault Division 111 tended to the wounded in sick bay, Sullivan returned to the devastated berthing areas.

Two men discovered still alive in one of the partially flooded lower compartments, were pinned in their racks against the overhead by a huge sheet of steel. Directly below them, sunlight and river water entered the ship. Sullivan made his way into the wreckage, rendered first aid and provided encouragement, until the metal could be pried back far enough to pull the wounded sailors free. A 13.3-foot Boston whaler ("skimmer") then proceeded into the wrecked and flooded compartment through a hole in the ship's hull to take them to safety.[25]

MAKESHIFT REPAIRS

The day after the mining attack—which killed 25 men and wounded 23 others aboard *Westchester County*—the entire Mobile Riverine Force moved from My Tho to Dong Tam. Located on the north bank of the Mekong River, Dong Tam was the home of the Army's 9th Division and its Navy counterpart. A few days after arrival there, Branin beached the Wesco on a river bank near Dong Tam, in order to expose enough of the hull at low tide to fully assess the damage to his ship and to plan temporary repairs.[26]

With the help of a repair division from the landing craft repair ship *Askari*, and a team from Naval Support Activity, Dong Tam, Wesco's crew worked around-the-clock for two weeks, building a cofferdam to keep the river at bay, and cutting away mangled steel in preparation for temporary hull repairs. Finding that necessary structural steel plating and I-beams were unavailable locally through Navy sources, Branin decided to follow a time-honored Navy tradition.[27]

That night, a party sent ashore to find and "liberate" the needed materials found at an Army engineer compound near Dong Tam: a stockpile of portable bridging equipment, including assorted I-beams and plenty of steel plating. Once available at the ship site, within hours the "commandeered" beams and plating were cut to the proper size and welded into place to serve as hull patches.[28]

VOYAGE TO YOKOSUKA

On 14 November, with the help of a large Navy tug, the *Westchester County* came off the bank, and proceeded downriver to the South China Sea and a 2,500-mile voyage home to Yokosuka, Japan, for dry-docking and permanent repairs. Her passage home was not an easy one. Rough seas generated by a typhoon she was unable to avoid, caused cracks and ruptures in the temporary repairs, and she began taking on water. By the time the LST entered Tokyo Bay on 25 November, flooding had overwhelmed pumps capable of dewatering 3,200 gallons per minute. Nevertheless, the intrepid ship and crew made it safely into port.[29]

The following day, *Westchester County* entered dry dock at the U.S. Naval Ship Repair facility in Yokosuka where she remained until 5 February 1969.[30]

RETURN TO COMBAT DUTY

Upon completion of refresher training and upkeep, *Westchester County* got under way on 10 March 1969 for the Vietnam coast. She continued to make regular deployments to Vietnam until she was decommissioned on 30 November 1973. During her service to the nation and the Navy, she earned a host of unit and service awards:

- Combat Action Ribbon (3)
- Navy Unit Commendation Ribbon (3)
- Meritorious Unit Commendation Ribbon (2)
- National Defense Service Medal
- Armed Forces Expeditionary Medal (3)
- Vietnam Service Medal (16)
- Republic of Vietnam Gallantry Cross Unit Citation (27)
- Republic of Vietnam Campaign Medal with 1960s device[31]

AWARDS FOR VALOR

More than thirty-six personal awards and commendations were awarded to the ship's crew for its performance during and immediately after the 1 November attack. Lt. Comdr. John W. Branin received the Bronze Star Medal. Hospital Corpsman First Class John S. Sullivan received the Silver Star Medal and the Purple Heart Medal.[32]

LEST WE FORGET

The Republic of Vietnam suffered two killed in the mining attack; a South Vietnamese sailor, and Le von Ba, a "Tiger Scout" interpreter. Comprising the remaining twenty-three killed were seventeen members of ship's company, one member of River Assault Division 111, and five members of the U.S. Army's 9th Infantry Division. The body of Engineman Third Class Harry J. Kenney was never recovered.

USS *Westchester County* (17)

SA Jackie C. Carter	SK1 Aristotoles D. Ibanez
SK1 Richard C. Cartwright	YN1 Jerry S. Leonard
QM2 Chester D. Dale	RM3 Joseph A. Miller
RD3 Keith W. Duffy	RM1 Rodney W. Peters
SN Timothy C. Dunning	YN3 Cary F. Rundle
PN1 David G. Fell	RM3 Reinhard J. Schnurrer
ETN2 Thomas G. Funke	QM2 Thomas H. Smith
RM3 Gerald E. Hamm	CS1 Anthony R. Torcivia
SN Floyd W. Houghtaling	

River Assault Squadron 11, Division 111 (1)

EN3 Harry J. Kenney

B Company, 3rd Battalion, 60th Infantry, 9th Infantry Division (5)

SP4 Leslie V. Bowman	SP4 Paul D. Jose
SP4 Wilfredo Cintron-Mendez	SGT Dennis K. O'Connor[33]
PFC Ernest F. Cooke[33]	

2

Amphibious Ships in Vietnam

When I received orders to the USS Benewah (APB-35), I had never heard of an APB. My orders specified I should attend C.I. School prior to joining the ship's company. I had never heard of a C.I. School. After the yeoman and I went through some paper work, I found out what an APB was and what C.I. School meant. (Counter Insurgency) Oh Boy!!

—Albert Moore, former crewmember aboard the self-propelled barracks ship USS *Benewah*, during her service in Vietnam.[1]

One hundred thirty-nine amphibious ships, and four self-propelled barracks ships (functioning as troop transports), served in Vietnam. Some plied inland waters in support of riverine operations and combat ashore. These ships, as well as the river patrol boats and assault craft they supported, were collectively known as "the Brown Water Navy," in reference to the muddy river waters on which they operated. Other ships carried out blue water amphibious landings along the coast of Vietnam. Some, mostly tank landing ships, did both. Some readers may wish to skip the summary information contained in the next two dozen pages, press ahead to the heart of the book, and return as necessary, to learn more about particular types or classes of ships.

The commissioning dates in the tables reflect when ships were placed in full commission; some were earlier in reduced commission, for transit from builder's yard to fitting out yard. The quantities of officers and men listed refer to ship's company, and not to embarked troops aboard ships that carried them. Finally, propulsion machinery and armament cited may vary slightly among ships of the same class or over the service life of the ships. Minor differences between ships, and upgrades to weapons systems were not uncommon.

MOBILE RIVERINE FORCE "GREEN FLEET" SHIPS

There are not too many ex-sailors around today who can claim to have served aboard a "Green Ship." The "Green Ship Fleet" in Vietnam consisted of nine World War II tank landing ships (LSTs) converted into self-propelled barracks ships (APBs) and landing craft repair ships

(ARLs), and three high speed transports (APDs). The APDs had been laid down as destroyer escorts, and then converted in the builders' yards to carry Marines and landing craft. Shallow-draft tank landing ships, and other types with deeper drafts, which operated farther offshore, were readily available. As needed, they were taken out of reserve fleets where they'd been "mothballed" (laid up) after World War II or the Korean War, and, following modernization, pressed back into service. Some of the APLs (non-self-propelled barracks ships), which are not covered in this book, were also painted green.[2]

U.S. Seventh Fleet ships assigned to amphibious ready groups in support of Marine landings along the coast sported standard Navy grey coats of paint. Some of these ships entered river ports as necessary to deliver war materials and cargo, or served upriver for periods of time with the Mobile Riverine Force (Task Force 117). One such was the tank landing ship *Westchester County* (LST-1167). As detailed in Chapter One, while functioning as "ammunition ship" in 1968, she was nearly lost to a mine attack carried out by Viet Cong swimmer-sappers.

The following review of amphibious ships begins with those that served entirely, or primarily with the "Green Fleet," followed by tank landing ships. Comprising 62 of the 142 vessels to which this book is devoted, they were the most numerous of any type. Discussion then progresses to overviews of ships of the offshore amphibious forces.

SELF-PROPELLED BARRACKS SHIPS

Photo 2-1

Barracks ship USS *Colleton* (APB-36) with armored troop carriers alongside in the Mekong Delta, South Vietnam.
Naval History and Heritage Command photograph #L45-55.02.01

APBs *Benewah*, *Colleton*, *Mercer*, and *Nueces* were self-propelled barracks ships built on *LST-542* class hulls. *Benewah*, the lead ship in the class, entered the Philadelphia Naval Shipyard in July 1966 for conversion and modernization prior to return to active duty. Although retaining her designation of APB-35, she was converted to a brigade command ship and served as the flagship for commander, River Assault Flotilla One. She was recommissioned on 28 January 1967. *Colleton* was completed in September 1945 but, due to the end of World War II, was placed in "reserve" until 1967.[3]

Benewah-class Self-propelled Barracks Ship – 4 ships
328 feet, 4,000 tons, 12 knots, 12 officers, 129 enlisted
Two General Motors diesel engines; two 3"/50 gun mounts,
two quad 40mm mounts, twenty .50- and .30-cal machine guns

Ship	Comm.	Ship	Comm.
Benewah (APB-35)	9 Mar 46	*Mercer* (APB-39)	19 Sep 45
Colleton (APB-36)	28 Jan 67	*Nueces* (APB-40)	30 Nov 45

Benewah's original armament was two 20mm mounts. In 1967, these guns were replaced by two 3"/50 gun mounts, two quad-barreled 40mm mounts, and twenty strategically placed .50- and .30-caliber machine guns. She carried twenty-five fiberglass assault boats, utilized by Army troops who made her their base of operations. A large helicopter landing platform built over her superstructure was also used for deploying troops and receiving casualties.[4]

Ordered to Vietnam on 22 February 1967, *Benewah* stopped at Pearl Harbor for a short upkeep while en route to the combat zone. While in Hawaii, her crew painted the ship an Army olive green. The sailors generally agreed that their mission was unique, and looked forward to serving on a ship that looked a little different. Different she was, as witnessed on 22 April, when greeted by the flashing light of a Navy warship, which signaled ... "Welcome to Vietnam, whatever you are!"[5]

HIGH SPEED TRANSPORTS

The three high speed transports that served in Vietnam had been laid down in their builder's yards as *Rudderow*-class destroyer escorts and converted to auxiliary personnel destroyers (APDs) during construction. During World War II, scores of destroyers and destroyer escorts were transformed into high speed transports in support of Marine Corps amphibious operations. Some boilers were removed from destroyers to make room for troop and cargo space. The smaller destroyer escorts, having but a single boiler room, had no boilers to spare. The destroyers and destroyer escorts lost all of their torpedo tubes and some guns during conversion.[6]

Photo 2-2

High speed transport USS *Cook* (APD-130) under way, circa 1962.
Naval History and Heritage Command photograph #L45-64.01.01

The high-speed transports were much faster than cargo ships. They retained some firepower, but sacrificed their primary anti-submarine weapons (torpedoes) to free up deck space to carry troops and landing craft. Fast and agile, with shallow drafts, APDs proved ideal for operating along hostile coasts and small islands, landing Marines ashore, and providing limited naval gunfire during operations and recovery of troops. However, trading off warfare capabilities in order to employ the destroyers/destroyer escorts as troop transports came with a cost. The lightly armed APDs proved vulnerable in combat and many were lost or damaged in World War II as a result of enemy action.[7]

Crosley-class High Speed Transport – 3 ships
306 feet, 2,130 tons (full load), 23.6 knots, 12 officers, 192 enlisted
Two Babcox and Wilcox "D" Express type boilers, two General Electric turbines; one 5"/38 gun mount, three twin 40mm mounts, six single 20mm mounts, two depth charge racks

Ship	Comm.	Ship	Comm.
Alex Diachenko (APD-123)	8 Dec 44	*Weiss* (APD-135)	7 Jul 45
Cook (APD-130)	25 Apr 45		

LANDING CRAFT REPAIR SHIPS

Photo 2-3

The landing craft repair ship USS *Krishna* (ARL-38), anchored off the island of Phu Quoc while serving as the only joint Navy-Coast Guard operations-communications center since World War II. *Krishna*'s mission was to function as mother ship for U.S. Navy and Coast Guard patrol boats working to prevent infiltration of supplies and ammunition to the Viet Cong, February 1966.
National Archives photograph #USN 1116903

Five World War II vintage *Achelous*-class landing craft repair ships—*Askari, Indra, Krishna, Satyr,* and *Sphinx*—served in Vietnam. The five were laid down as tank landing ships, and then converted. Modification from LST to ARL mainly involved transforming the large interior tank deck into a number of shops and storerooms, and adding two large cargo booms forward and a large 60-ton A-frame boom amidships. *Krishna* was the only U.S. Navy ship to bear that name, and only one of two (along with *Indra*) to be named after a Hindu deity.[8]

Achelous-class Landing Craft Repair Ship – 5 ships
327 feet, 3,960 tons (full load), 10 knots, 21 officers, 232 enlisted
Two General Motors 12-567A Detroit twelve-cylinder diesel engines;
two 18-quad 40mm mounts, six .50-caliber machine guns

Ship	Comm.	Ship	Comm.
Askari (ARL-30)	23 Jul 45	*Satyr* (ARL-23)	28 Apr 45
Indra (ARL-37)	2 Oct 45	*Sphinx* (ARL-24)	10 May 45
Krishna (ARL-38)	3 Dec 45		

Askari, the most highly decorated of the five ARLs, garnered five Combat Action Ribbons, two Presidential Unit Citations, and five Navy Unit Commendations during the Vietnam War. (Since only one ribbon for each is authorized, a bronze star is affixed for each additional award. A silver star denotes five awards.) Commissioned on 23 July 1945, her subsequent duty (prior to being decommissioned on 21 March 1956 at Astoria, Oregon, and laid up in the Pacific Reserve Fleet) was quite interesting. It included earning four battle stars during the Korean War, followed by participation in nuclear weapons tests in the Marshall Islands, and transportation of refugees from North to South Vietnam as part of Operation PASSAGE TO FREEDOM.[9]

Passage to Freedom duties carried out by her and other ships are taken up in the next chapter. Although *Askari*'s support of nuclear tests are outside the scope of this book, they highlight the diversity of duties levied on the ARLs. *Sphinx* ended her naval service as an intelligence gathering ship. While deployed for a lengthy period in the late 1980s in Pacific waters off Nicaragua in Central American, her duties included eavesdropping on communications of the Sandinista government and looking for arms traffic in the Gulf of Fonseca.[10]

Askari spent four months in 1948 at Enewetak Atoll (also spelled Eniwetok) in the Marshall Islands, providing maintenance services to landing craft operating in support of Operation SANDSTONE nuclear bomb tests. Three tests (designated X-Ray, Yoke, and Zebra) took place between 15 April and 15 May. The thirty-four Navy ships that participated in the tests comprised Task Group 7.3, organized into eight functional areas. Most of the ships remained at Enewetak during the tests, except for the destroyers, which routinely were on surveillance patrols of the area.[11]

Four of the amphibious ships present for the tests later took part in the Vietnam War. *Mount McKinley* (AGC-7), the flagship, was anchored off Parry Island for all three shots. The attack transport *Pickaway* (APA-222) was part of the main naval task unit, and the remaining two ships, dock landing ship *Comstock* (LSD-19) and the *Askari* (ARL-30), were part of the boat pool unit. *Comstock* was the mother ship, and *Askari* the repair ship, for the amphibious craft and small boats which provided water transportation for personnel aboard the ships involved in scientific operations.[12]

Map 2-1

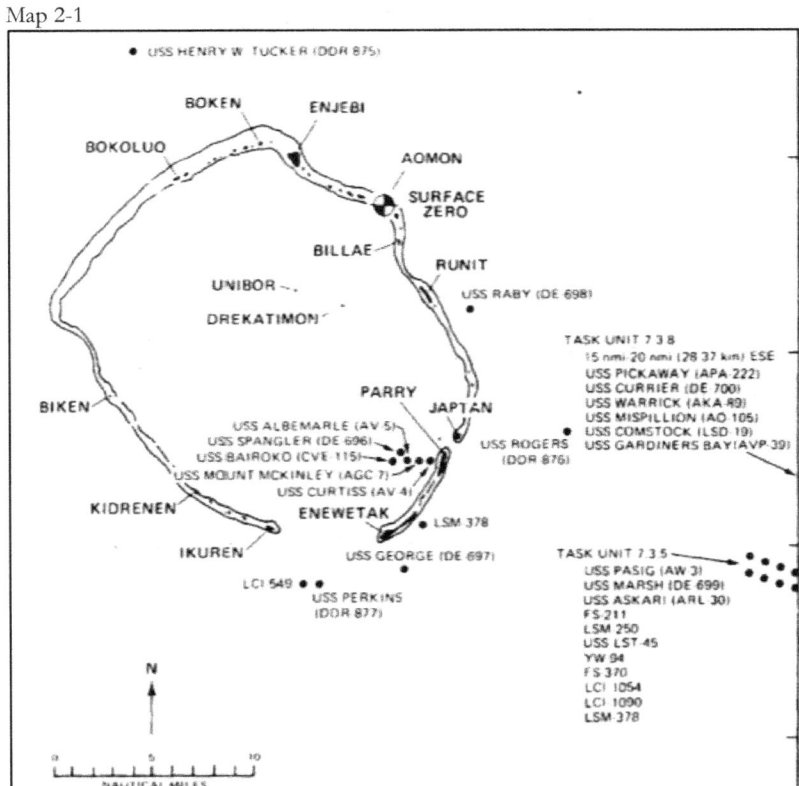

Enewetak Atoll in the Marshall Islands
Source: "Operation Sandstone 1948"
(http://nuclearweaponarchive.org/Usa/Tests/Sandston.html: accessed 25 December 2018).

TANK LANDING SHIPS

The bulk of the tank landing ships that served in Vietnam, 44 of 63, were of World War II vintage. The crews of such ships in World War II referred to them as "Large, Slow Targets"—an acknowledgement of their LST designations, and appraisal of their vulnerability to attack by enemy forces. Stretching 328 feet in length, with shallow drafts enabling them to easily beach to land assault troops and heavy equipment ashore, the LSTs could make a mere 11.6 knots. Bear in mind, this benchmark was obtained during post-construction trials when the ships were new—not after years of service, with tired engines and, dirty hulls while deployed.

WORLD WAR II VINTAGE TANK LANDING SHIPS

LST-1 Class (no name for class) – 1 ship
328 feet, 4,080 tons (full load), 11.6 knots, 11 officers, 104 enlisted
Two General Motors 12-567A, 900hp diesel engines; two twin 40mm mounts, four single 40mm mounts, twelve single 20mm mounts

Ship	Comm.
Blanco County (LST-344)	14 Jan 43

LST-491 Class (no name for class) – 4 ships
328 feet, 4,080 tons (full load), 11.6 knots, 13 officers, 104 enlisted
Two General Motors 12-567A, 900hp diesel engines; two twin 40mm mounts, four single 40mm mounts, twelve single 20mm mounts

Ship	Comm.	Ship	Comm.
Bulloch County (LST-509)	20 Jan 44	*Caroline County* (LST-525)	14 Feb 44
Caddo Parish (LST-515)	28 Jan 44	*Chase County* (LST-532)	20 Jan 44

LST-542 Class (*Chelan County*-class) – 37 ships
328 feet, 4,080 tons (full load), 11.6 knots, 13 officers, 104 enlisted
Two General Motors 12-567A, 900hp diesel engines; two twin 40mm mounts, four single 40mm mounts, twelve single 20mm mounts

Ship	Comm.	Ship	Comm.
Chesterfield County (LST-551)	14 Apr 44	*Mahnomen County* (LST-912)	21 May 44
Clarke County (LST-601)	25 Mar 44	*Meeker County* (LST-980)	26 Feb 44
Coconino County (LST-603)	5 Apr 44	*Monmouth County* (LST-1032)	1 Aug 44
Floyd County (LST-762)	5 Sep 44	*Nye County* (LST-1067)	24 Mar 45
Garrett County (LST-786)	28 Aug 44	*Outagamie County* (LST-1073)	17 Apr 45
Hampshire County (LST-819)	14 Nov 44	*Page County* (LST-1076)	1 May 45
Harnett County (LST-821)	22 Nov 44	*Park County* (LST-1077)	8 May 45
Henry County (LST-824)	30 Nov 44	*Pitkin County* (LST-1082)	7 Feb 45
Hickman County (LST-825)	8 Dec 44	*Polk County* (LST-1084)	7 Feb 45
Holmes County (LST-836)	25 Nov 44	*Pulaski County* (LST-1088)	27 Mar 45
Hunterdon County (LST-838)	4 Dec 44	*San Joaquin County* (LST-1122)	14 Feb 45
Iredell County (LST-839)	6 Dec 44	*Sedgwick County* (LST-1123)	19 Feb 45

Jennings County (LST-846)	9 Jan 45	*Snohomish County* (LST-1126)	28 Feb 45
Jerome County (LST-848)	20 Jan 45	*St. Clair County* (LST-1096)	2 Feb 45
Kemper County (LST-854)	14 Dec 44	*Stone County* (LST-1141)	9 May 45
Litchfield County (LST-901)	11 Jan 45	*Summit County* (LST-1146)	30 May 45
New London County (LST-1066)	20 Mar 45	*Sumner County* (LST-1148)	9 Jun 45
Luzerne County (LST-902)	15 Jan 45	*Sutter County* (LST-1150)	20 Jun 45
Madera County (LST-905)	29 Jan 45		

POST WORLD WAR II TANK LANDING SHIPS

LSTs of two post-WWII classes served in Vietnam. Both classes were larger, faster, and with increased manning in comparison to the WWII vintage ships. Moreover, as shown below, each of these classes was more capable than its predecessor.

LST-1156 Class (*Terrebonne Parish*-class) – 10 ships
384 feet, 5,800 tons (full load), 14 knots, 16 officers, 189 enlisted
Four General Motors 16-278A diesel engines; three
twin 3"/50 gun mounts, five single 20mm mounts

Ship	Comm.	Ship	Comm.
Terrell County (LST-1157)	14 Mar 53	*Washtenaw County* (LST-1166)	29 Oct 53
Tioga County (LST-1158)	1 Jul 55	*Westchester County* (LST-1167)	10 Mar 54
Tom Green County (LST-1159)	12 Sep 53	*Wexford County* (LST-1168)	15 Jun 54
Vernon County (LST-1161)	18 May 53	*Whitfield County* (LST-1169)	14 Sep 54
Washoe County (LST-1165)	30 Nov 53	*Windham County* (LST-1170)	15 Dec 54

LST-1179 Class (*Newport*-class) – 10 ships
522 feet, 8,550 tons (full load), 27 knots, 14 officers, 241 enlisted
Six 16-cylinder Electro Motive Engines (EMD 645 E-5) diesel engines;
two twin 3"/50 gun mounts; upgraded: two 25mm chain guns, six
.50-caliber machine guns, one 20mm Phalanx (CIWS)

Ship	Comm.	Ship	Comm.
Cayuga (LST-1186)	8 Aug 70	*Racine* (LST-1191)	9 Jul 71
Frederick (LST-1184)	11 Apr 70	*San Bernardino* (LST-1189)	27 Mar 71
Fresno (LST-1182)	22 Nov 69	*Schenectady* (LST-1185)	13 Jun 70
Manitowoc (LST-1180)	24 Jan 70	*Sumter* (LST-1181)	20 Jun 70
Peoria (LST-1183)	21 Feb 70	*Tuscaloosa* (LST-1187)	24 Oct 70

INSHORE FIRE SUPPORT SHIPS

Photo 2-4

Inshore fire support ship USS *Carronade* (IFS-1) south of Danang, South Vietnam, ready to provide fire support to U.S. Marines, 11 November 1967.
National Archives photograph #USN 1127944

The *Carronade*—a one-of-a-kind ship designed and developed to fire rockets at close inshore targets—and three old converted LSMRs (Medium Landing Ship, Rocket), which comprised the other units of Inshore Fire Support Division 93, were the "betwixt and between" vessels of the amphibious force. Owing to their combined unique rocket firing capabilities, the division provided important warfare support to inshore Mobile Riverine Force operations, and Marine Corps landings along the coast.

Carronade-class Inshore Fire Support Ship – 1 ship
245 feet, 1,500 tons, 15 knots, 10 officers, 132 enlisted
Diesel propulsion; one single 5"/38 gun mount,
eight rocket launchers, two 40mm mounts

Ship	Comm.
Carronade (IFS/LFR-1)	25 May 55

Photo 2-5

Inshore fire support ship USS *St. Francis River* (LFR-525) en route to U.S. Naval Support Facility, Cam Ranh Bay, South Vietnam, to load ammunition, July 1969.
National Archives photograph #USN 1140633

***LSM(R)-401* Class Landing Ship Medium (Rocket) – 1 ship**
203 feet, 1,084 tons (full load), 12.6 knots, 5 officers, 133 enlisted
Two General Motors 16-287A diesel engines; one single 5"/38 gun mount, two twin 40mm mounts, four twin 20mm mounts, eight twin tube 5-inch rocket launchers, two .50-cal machine guns on the fo'c'sle, two .30-cal machine guns on the bridge wings

Ship	Comm.
Clarion River (LFR-409)	16 May 45

***LSM(R)-501* Class Landing Ship Medium (Rocket) – 2 ships**
Two General Motors 16-287A diesel engines; one single 5"/38 gun mount, two twin 40mm mounts, four twin 20mm mounts, ten twin tube 5-inch rocket launchers, four 4.2-inch mortars

Ship	Comm.	Ship	Comm.
St. Francis River (LFR-525)	14 Aug 45	*White River* (LFR-536)	28 Nov 45

The Navy changed the designation of the *Clarion River*, *St. Francis River*, and *White River* on 1 January 1969 from LSM(R) to LFR (inshore fire support ship).

AMPHIBIOUS READY GROUP (ARG/SLF) SHIPS

Up to this point, discussion of amphibious ships has been limited to those that primarily supported Mobile Riverine Force operations. The remaining sixty-four ships were larger and of deeper draft. When operating together, they were designated an Amphibious Ready Group, aboard which was embarked a Marine Corps Special Landing Force, or other troops.

- Amphibious Force Command Ship (AGC/LCC) – four
- Amphibious Assault Ship, Helicopter (LPH) – eight
- Amphibious Transport Dock (LPD) – seven
- Amphibious Cargo Ship (AKA/LKA) – twelve
- Attack Transport (APA)- fifteen
- Dock Landing Ship (LSD) – eighteen

AMPHIBIOUS FORCE COMMAND SHIPS

Photo 2-6

Amphibious force command ship USS *Eldorado* (LCC-11).
National Archives photograph #K-92078

Amphibious command ships were designed to provide command and control capabilities for amphibious invasions. The AGC designation (which predated LCC) was based on "miscellaneous unclassified vessels" AG, and sub-class C, with three possible meanings, command, control, or communications. It became associated with amphibious force flagships, since all AGCs were these type vessels. Three of the AGC/LCC command ships in Vietnam were of WWII vintage; the remaining one, *Blue Ridge* (LCC-19) was newly constructed.

Photo 2-7

Flag plot aboard the amphibious command ship USS *Estes* (AGC-12). The sailor, whose arm is shown in the foreground, is writing backwards with a grease pencil on a Plexiglas status board to provide information to users in the command center. National Archives photograph #USN 1113998-B

Blue Ridge-class Command Ship – 1 ship
634 feet, 18,874 tons, 23 knots, 52 officers, 790 enlisted
Two boilers, one steam turbine, single propeller, 22,000hp;
two 25mm Bushmaster guns, four .50-cal. machine guns,
two 20mm Phalanx (CIWS)

Ship	Comm.
Blue Ridge (LCC-19)	14 Nov 70

Mount McKinley-class Amphibious Force Command Ship – 3 ships
459 feet, 12,580 tons (full load), 16.4 knots, 54 officers, 568 enlisted
Two Babcock & Wilcox boilers, one General Electric geared turbine,
single propeller, 6,000shp; two single 5"/38 gun mounts, four
twin 40mm mounts, ten twin 20mm gun mounts

Ship	Comm.	Ship	Comm.
Eldorado (AGC/LCC-11)	26 Aug 44	*Mount McKinley* (AGC-7)	1 May 44
Estes (AGC-12)	9 Oct 44		

AMPHIBIOUS ASSAULT SHIP, HELICOPTER

Photo 2-8

Amphibious assault ship USS *Boxer* (LPH-4), circa mid-1960s, with six UH-34 Sea Horse helicopters flying in formation in the foreground, and a *Forrest Sherman*-class destroyer in the background.
Naval History and Heritage Command photograph #NH 107671

Three of the eight amphibious assault ships that served in Vietnam were former *Essex*-class aircraft carriers. Although the ships were extensively modified internally as part of their conversion to Landing Platform Helicopter (LPH), they retained the classic appearance of World War II *Essex* carriers.

Boxer-class Amphibious Assault Ship, Helicopter – 3 ships
888 feet, 36,457 tons (full load), 33 knots, 1,200 ship's complement
Eight 565psi boilers, four turbines, four propellers, 75,000shp

Ship	Comm.	Ship	Comm.
Boxer (LPH-4)	15 Apr 45	*Valley Forge* (LPH-8)	3 Nov 46
Princeton (LPH-5)	18 Nov 45		

The modern *Iwo Jima*-class amphibious assault ships were built to transport more than 1,700 Marine assault troops into inland combat areas by helicopter. This technique of vertical envelopment offered flexibility and surprise. This was particularly true when employed with traditional landing craft operations. Combat-ready Marines flown in behind enemy defenses could isolate strategic strong points, disrupt enemy communications, and converge with beach-landed Marines to achieve their combined objectives.[13]

Photo 2-9

USS *Inchon* (LPH-12) anchored in Haiphong Harbor, North Vietnam, on 20 June 1973, during Operation END SWEEP. A CH-46D helicopter is flying off her port, and five other CH-46s, seven H-53s, and one UH-1 are visible on her flight deck. Naval History and Heritage Command photograph #NH 107678

Iwo Jima-class Amphibious Assault Ship, Helicopter – 5 ships
592 feet, 18,474 tons (full load), 22 knots, 667 ship's complement
Two 600 psi boilers, one turbine, one propeller, 22,000shp; four 3"/50 gun mounts, (modifications) two 3"/50s removed and replaced with eight-cell Sea Sparrow BPDMS launchers, two Phalanx CIWS added

Ship	Comm.	Ship	Comm.
Inchon (LPH-12)	20 Jun 70	*Okinawa* (LPH-3)	14 Apr 62
Iwo Jima (LPH-2)	26 Aug 61	*Tripoli* (LPH-10)	6 Aug 66
New Orleans (LPH-11)	16 Nov 68		

AMPHIBIOUS TRANSPORT DOCK

The *Raleigh/Austin*-class transport docks were a combination dock landing ship (LSD) and assault transport (APA). They were designed to carry Marines, or cargo, or some combination of these, employing their two CH-46 helicopters and landing craft. *Austin*-class LPDs were based on the design of the earlier *Raleigh*-class.[14]

Raleigh-class Amphibious Transport Dock – 1 ship
522 feet, 14,113 tons (full load), 20 knots, 436 ship's complement
Two boilers, two geared turbines, two propellers, 24,000shp;
(as built) four twin 3"/50 gun mounts, (early 1970s)
three twin 3"/50 mounts, one CIWS

Ship	Comm.
Vancouver (LPD-2)	11 May 63

Photo 2-10

The three ships of a 20-knot amphibious ready group—*Iwo Jima* (LPH-2), *Thomaston* (LSD-28), and *Vancouver* (LPD-2)—proceeding together during Operation DECKHOUSE V, 4 January 1967.
National Archives photograph #USN 1119682

Photo 2-11

LVTP landing vehicles loaded with Marines move past the amphibious transport dock USS *Ogden* (LPD-5) during Operation BEACON HILL I, 20 March 1967. National Archives photograph #USN 1121212

Austin-class **Amphibious Transport Dock – 6 ships**
522 feet, 16,914 tons (full load), 21 knots, 24 officers, 396 enlisted
Two Babcock & Wilcox boilers, two steam turbines, two shafts,
24,000shp; two 25mm guns, two CIWS, eight .50-cal. machine guns

Ship	Comm.	Ship	Comm.
Cleveland (LPD-7)	21 Apr 67	*Duluth* (LPD-6)	18 Dec 65
Denver (LPD-9)	26 Oct 68	*Juneau* (LPD-10)	12 Jul 69
Dubuque (LPD-8)	1 Sep 67	*Ogden* (LPD-5)	16 Jun 65

DOCK LANDING SHIPS

Dock landing ships have a well dock to transport and launch landing craft and amphibious vehicles. Eighteen of these type ships, from four different classes, served in Vietnam. Twelve were World War II vintage, and the remaining five of post-Korean War construction. The newest, *Anchorage*, was commissioned in March 1969.

Photo 2-12

Dock landing ship USS *Oak Hill* (LSD-7) off Oahu, Hawaii, 8 September 1967. National Archives photograph #USN 1126011

Ashland-class Dock Landing Ship – 5 ships
457 feet, 7,930 (seagoing), 17knots, 17 officers, 237 enlisted
Two Babcock and Wilcox 250psi boilers, two Skinner 5-cylinder reciprocating steam engines; one single 5"/38 gun mount in open tub, two quad 40mm mounts, two twin 40mm mounts, sixteen single 20mm mounts

Ship	Comm.	Ship	Comm.
Belle Grove (LSD-2)	9 Aug 43	*Gunston Hall* (LSD-5)	10 Nov 43
Carter Hall (LSD-3)	18 Sep 43	*Oak Hill* (LSD-7)	5 Jan 44
Epping Forest (LSD-4)	11 Oct 43		

Casa Grande-class Dock Landing Ship – 7 ships
457 feet, 7,930 tons (seagoing), 17 knots, 17 officers, 237 enlisted
Two Babcock and Wilcox 250psi boilers, two Newport News
Shipbuilding steam turbines, twin propellers, 7,000shp; original
armament: one single 5"/38 dual purpose gun mount, two quad 40mm
AA gun mounts, two twin 40mm AA gun mounts,
sixteen single 20mm AA gun mounts

Ship	Comm.	Ship	Comm.
Cabildo (LSD-16)	15 Mar 45	*Fort Marion* (LSD-22)	29 Jan 46
Catamount (LSD-17)	15 Mar 45	*Tortuga* (LSD-26)	8 Jun 45
Colonial (LSD-18)	15 May 45	*Whetstone* (LSD-27)	12 Feb 46
Comstock (LSD-19)	2 Jul 45		

Photo 2-13

Dock landing ship USS *Comstock* (LSD-19) prepares to off load troops into landing craft at Chu Lai, South Vietnam, 24 June 1965.
National Archives photograph #USN 1111760

Thomaston-class Dock Landing Ship – 5 ships
510 feet, 11,525 tons (full load), 20 knots, 18 officers, 330 enlisted
Two 600psi boilers, two turbines, two propellers, 24,000shp;
four twin 3"/50 gun mounts, four twin 40mm mounts,
six twin 20mm mounts

Ship	Comm.	Ship	Comm.
Alamo (LSD-33)	24 Aug 56	*Point Defiance* (LSD-31)	31 Mar 55
Hermitage (LSD-34)	14 Dec 56	*Thomaston* (LSD-28)	17 Sep 54
Monticello (LSD-35)	29 Mar 57		

Photo 2-14

LVTs circle USS *Point Defiance* (LSD-31) prior to approach to Vung Mu Beach, during Operation DAGGER THRUST, December 1965.
National Archives photograph #USN 1113997-A

Anchorage-class Dock Landing Ship – 1 ship
553 feet, 14,095 tons (full load), 20+ knots, 24 officers, 300 enlisted
Two 600psi boilers, two De Laval turbines, two propellers, 24,000shp;
four twin 3"/50 gun mounts, two CIWS mounts,
two 25mm Bushmaster chain guns

Ship	Comm.
Anchorage (LSD-36)	15 Mar 69

AMPHIBIOUS CARGO SHIPS (YOU CALL, WE HAUL)

Amphibious cargo ships were designed specifically to carry troops, heavy equipment, and supplies in support of amphibious assaults, and to provide naval gunfire support during those assaults. In World War II and afterward, these type ships were designated Attack Cargo Ships (AKA). In 1969, the remaining AKAs were renamed Amphibious Cargo Ships with the designation LKA, one shared with new *Charleston*-class amphibious cargo ships.

Photo 2-15

USS *Mobile* (LKA-115) under way in the Pacific on 24 January 1971.
Naval History and Heritage Command photograph #NH 107726

Charleston-class Amphibious Cargo Ship – 4 ships
575 feet, 18,589 tons (full load), 20 knots, 34 officers, 375 enlisted
Two boilers, one geared turbine, one propeller, 22,000shp; four
twin 3"/50 gun mounts, updated with two 20mm CIWS

Ship	Comm.	Ship	Comm.
Charleston (LKA-113)	14 Dec 68	*Mobile* (LKA-115)	29 Sep 69
Durham (LKA-114)	24 May 69	*St. Louis* (LKA-116)	22 Nov 69

Andromeda-class Attack Cargo Ship – 3 ships
459 feet, 14,200 tons (limiting), 16.5 knots, 24 officers, 223 enlisted
Two Foster and Wheeler 450psi boilers, one General Electric steam
turbine, single propeller, 6,000shp; one single 5"/38 gun mount,
four twin 40mm mounts, eighteen single 20mm mounts

Ship	Comm.	Ship	Comm.
Mathews (AKA-96)	5 Mar 45	*Winston* (AKA-94/LKA-94)	19 Jan 45
Merrick (AKA-97)	31 Mar 45		

Tolland-class Amphibious Cargo Ship – 4 ships
459 feet, 14,160 tons (limiting), 16.5 knots, 35 officers, 387 enlisted
Two Combustion Engineering 450psi boilers, one General Electric
turbine, one propeller, 6,000shp; one single 5"/38 gun mount,
four twin 40mm mounts, sixteen single 20mm mounts

Ship	Comm.	Ship	Comm.
Seminole (AKA-104)	8 Mar 45	*Union* (AKA-106)	4 Dec 44
Skagit (AKA-105)	2 May 45	*Washburn* (AKA-108)	17 May 45

Tulare-class Amphibious Cargo Ship – 1 ship
564 feet, 16,000 tons (full load), 20 knots, 435 ship's complement
Geared turbine, single propeller;
six twin 3"/50 gun mounts, six .50-cal. machine guns

Ship	Comm.
Tulare (AKA-112)	12 Jan 56

Photo 2-16

USS *Tulare* (LKA-112) under way in the Pacific on 30 January 1969.
Naval History and Heritage Command photograph #NH 107732

ATTACK TRANSPORTS

Attack Transports were designed to carry assault troops and support equipment to the site of amphibious operations. APAs could transport a full battalion of troops and disembark them with their own landing craft. APAs then stood off the beachhead ready to evacuate troops and casualties. All APAs still in Navy inventory on 1 January 1969 were redesignated LPAs (Amphibious transports).

Arthur Middleton-class Attack Transport – 1 ship
489 feet, 18,000 tons (full load), 18.4 knots, 37 officers, 475 enlisted
Two Foster and Wheeler 465psi boilers, one General Electric turbine,
one propeller, 8,500shp; four single 3"/50 gun mounts, two twin 40mm
mounts, eight single 20mm mounts, four .50-cal. machine guns

Ship	Comm.
George Clymer (APA-27)	15 Jun 42

Crescent City-class Attack Transport – 1 ship
491 feet, 14,247 tons (full load), 16 knots, 48 officers, 510 enlisted
Two Babcock & Wilcox 450 boilers, one General Electric turbine,
single propeller, 7,800shp; one single 5"/38 gun mount,
three single 3"/50 mounts, two twin 40mm mounts,
four twin 20mm mounts

Ship	Comm.
Calvert (APA-32)	1 Oct 42

Bayfield-class Attack Transport – 3 ships
492 feet, 16,100 tons (full load), 18.4 knots, 51 officers, 524 enlisted
Two Combustion Engineering 465psi boilers, one General Electric
geared turbine, single propeller, 8,500shp; two single 5"/38 gun
mounts, two quad 1.1" mounts (replaced by two single 40mm mounts),
two twin 40mm mounts, eighteen single 20mm mounts

Ship	Comm.	Ship	Comm.
Bayfield (APA-33)	20 Nov 43	*Henrico* (APA-45)	26 Nov 43
Cavalier (APA-37)	15 Jan 44		

Haskell-class Attack Transport – 9 ships
455 feet, 14,837 tons (full load), 17.7 knots, 56 officers, 480 enlisted
Two Babcock and Wilcox header-type 465psi boilers, one
Westinghouse turbine, one propeller, 8,500shp;
one single 5"/38 gun mount, four twin 40mm mounts,
one quad 40mm mount, ten single 20mm mounts

Ship	Comm.	Ship	Comm.
Bexar (APA-237)	9 Oct 45	*Okanogan* (APA-220)	3 Dec 44
Lenawee (APA-195)	11 Oct 44	*Pickaway* (APA-222)	12 Dec 44
Magoffin (APA-199)	25 Oct 44	*Renville* (APA-227)	15 Nov 44
Montrose (APA-212)	2 Nov 44	*Talladega* (APA-208)	31 Oct 44
Navarro (APA-215)	15 Nov 44		

Paul Revere-class Amphibious Transport – 1 ship
563 feet, 16,828 tons (full load), 20 knots, 414 ship's complement
One geared turbine, single propeller, 19,250shp; four 3"/50 guns

Ship	Comm.
Paul Revere (APA-248)	3 Sep 58

Photo 2-17

USS *Paul Revere* (APA-248) outbound to sea from San Diego, date unknown.
U.S. Navy photograph courtesy of NavSource and Mike Smolinski

3

Prelude to the Vietnam War

You can kill ten of my men for every one I kill of yours, but even at those odds, you will lose and I will win.

—Remark by Ho Chi Minh to the French in the late 1940s.

Photo 3-1

In Hanoi, a large parade poster shows Ho Chi Minh, ruler of North Vietnam, shaking hands with party chairman Mao Tse-Tung of Communist China, symbolizing Peking backing of the North Vietnamese Campaign against South Vietnam.
U.S. Information Agency photograph #65-1277

FRENCH INVOLVEMENT IN INDOCHINA

Prior to American involvement in Southeast Asia, the French had long occupied Vietnam and adjacent Cambodia and Laos. It began in September 1858, with a Franco-Spanish expedition to the city of Tourane (Danang). After the subsequent French conquest of Saigon and three southern provinces, the Vietnamese government was forced to cede the southern portion of the country to France in 1862. The resulting French colony was named Cochinchina and, in 1887, France added the balance of Vietnam as well as Cambodia to its empire to create the Indochina Union. "French Indochina," as it was commonly known, was later expanded by the accession of Laos in 1893, followed by that of Kouang-Tcheou-Wan, a small enclave on the south coast of China ceded to France as a leased territory, in 1900.[1]

Photo 3-2

Boat landing on the Mekong River, French Indochina, circa 1931.
Naval History and Heritage Command photograph #NH 80423

Japan occupied French Indochina in September 1940, but left the French colonial government intact before taking over administration of the area as a protectorate, near the end of World War II. After recognizing in 1945 that defeat was inevitable, Japan allowed the countries that made up the Indochina Union to proclaim their independence from France. This freedom was short-lived in the case of Laos and Cambodia, which readily accepted the return of the French overlords later that year. Vietnam proved much different, as Ho Chi Minh, the leader of the Indochina Communist Party, was unyielding in his desire to rid the country of foreign dominance. Shortly after the surrender of Japan in August 1945, Ho announced the establishment of a provisional government in Hanoi with Bao Dai as supreme counselor and, a few days later, declared Vietnam's independence.[2]

Ho Chi Minh was born in central Vietnam in 1890 and left the country in 1911 as an adult. During a lengthy absence, he joined the French Communist Party in 1920, and then travelled from Paris to Moscow to become, four years later, a full-fledged Communist agent, and eventually to Hong Kong to form the Indochina Communist Party in 1940. The following year, Ho returned covertly to Vietnam and, from inside China on the Vietnamese border, established the Vietnam Revolutionary League ("Vinh Minh"). Under Gen. Vo Nguyen Giap, the Vinh Minh began a guerrilla campaign against the Japanese that continued until the end of World War II. Following Japan's surrender, British forces landed in Saigon on 13 September 1945, and thereafter returned authority to the French. That November, Ho Chi Minh dissolved the Indochina Communist Party and replaced it with the Association for Marxist Studies in an effort to broaden his base of support.[3]

A few months earlier, the heads of the Soviet Union, the United Kingdom, and the United States had met at Potsdam, Germany, to determine how to administer a defeated Germany following its surrender on 8 May 1945. Goals of the conference included establishing post-war order, resolving peace treaty issues, and countering the effects of war. Following discussion about the Japanese occupation of French Indochina, on 26 July 1945, Harry S. Truman, Winston Churchill, and Chiang Kai-shek issued the Potsdam Declaration calling for the surrender of Japan. In a related decision, the allied leaders determined that the British would disarm the Japanese forces in southern Vietnam, and the Chinese nationalists would perform this function north of the sixteenth parallel.[4]

Following Japan's surrender on 2 September 1945 and the allied disarmament of its troops, China agreed in February 1946 to withdraw its forces from North Vietnam, and the French and Viet Minh reached an accord in March that recognized Vietnam as a "free state" within the French Union. However, any resulting goodwill between the two parties disappeared three months later when Adm. Thierry d'Argenlieu, the French high commissioner for Cochinchina, violated the agreement by proclaiming a separate government for Cochinchina. Hostilities between the two factions resulted and, after negotiations broke down,

French warships bombarded Haiphong Harbor and French troops occupied Hanoi, forcing Ho Chi Minh to withdraw his forces from the city and create a rural base from which to operate.⁵

Photo 3-3

French Rear Admiral Thierry D'Angenlieu (in white) walking with (at his left, in blue) French General Richard Brunot, location and date unknown.
Naval History and Heritage Command photograph #NH 121080

The French Indochina War, fought from 19 December 1946 to 1 August 1954, between the French Union's French Far East Expeditionary Corps (led by France and supported by Bao Dai's Vietnamese National Army) and the Viet Minh (led by Ho Chi Minh and Gen. Vo Nguyen Giap) had begun. Most fighting took place in Tonkin, the northern part of Vietnam, although the conflict engulfed parts of the entire country and extended into the neighboring French Indochina protectorates of Laos and Cambodia.⁶

After seven long years, with Laos and Cambodia demanding their independence and a majority of the French National Assembly expressing a desire for a negotiated end to the war, the French government finally granted the protectorates their freedom. In 1941, the French enthroned Prince Norodom Sihanouk, at the age of eighteen, as the ruler of Cambodia, believing him easily controlled. This assumption would prove false. In 1953, after having increasingly demanded full independence of the kingdom from the French colonists and their departure from Cambodia, Sihanouk embarked on a world tour to publicize his campaign. Fearing retribution for this action, he afterwards went into voluntary exile in Battambang Province, joined by

30,000 Cambodian troops and police. The French government granted Cambodia its independence on 9 November 1953. It made the same concession to Laos the preceding month.[7]

FRENCH DEFEAT AT DIEN BIEN PHU

> [Dien Bien Phu] was the first time that a non-European colonial independence movement had evolved through all the stages from guerrilla bands to a conventionally organized and equipped army able to defeat a modern Western occupier in pitched battle.
>
> —Martin Windrow, military historian quoted in the Boston Globe, 4 January 2005.

The final blow to France's tenuous hold on what remained of the Indochina Union was delivered by Viet Minh communist revolutionaries in a stunning defeat of the French Far East Expeditionary Corps at the Battle of Dien Bien Phu. The battle took place from 13 March to 7 May 1954 in northwestern Vietnam near the Chinese and Laotian borders. The Vo Nguyen Giap-led Viet Minh occupied the highlands surrounding the battlefield, besieged the French with heavy artillery fire and, after a lengthy siege, overran their garrison and killed or captured most of the forces. Of the French soldiers captured, few survived the ensuing grim death march to Viet Minh prison camps located 300 miles to the east.[8]

The Battle of Dien Bien Phu was the defining conflict of the French Indochina War, and the crushing French defeat influenced negotiations over the future of Indochina. Agreements reached at the Geneva Convention, in July 1954, called for the cessation of hostilities in Vietnam, Cambodia, and Laos, and temporarily divided Vietnam at the seventeenth parallel, pending elections in 1956 to choose a national government that would administer a reunified county. Until then, the Viet Minh would remain in charge of North Vietnam, while the State of Vietnam (which succeeded the Provisional Central Government of Vietnam that existed from 1948-1949) controlled the South, and French forces gradually withdrew from Vietnam as the situation stabilized. Bao Dai, the former emperor of Vietnam (8 January 1926-25 August 1945), was the State of Vietnam's chief of state, and Ngo Dinh Diem its prime minister. Neither the United States nor the State of Vietnam signed the Geneva Accords. The United States indicated that it would not disturb the agreements, but would view renewed aggression with concern. Ngo

Dinh Diem rejected the idea of a nationwide election, believing that a free open-ballet vote was impossible in the communist North.⁹

Photo 3-4

Refugees board the tank landing ship USS *LST-516* for their journey from Haiphong to Saigon, October 1954, as part of Operation PASSAGE TO FREEDOM. National Archives photograph #80-G-652364

The accords also stipulated a period of grace ending on 18 May 1955, in which people could move freely between the two Vietnams before the border at the seventeenth parallel was sealed. During this period, an estimated 310,000 Vietnamese civilians, soldiers, and non-Vietnamese members of the French Army fled to the south by sea as part of the U.S. Navy Operation PASSAGE TO FREEDOM. In total, the cargo vessels and tank carriers that participated in the evacuation as part of Task Force Ninety would make 109 southbound voyages carrying their charges to freedom. The first vessel to embark refugees was the *Menard* (AFA-201) in the fall of 1954. Other task force units included the *Bayfield* (APA-33) and *Montague* (AKA-98), and the USNS *General A. W. Brewster* (T-AP-155). The French Navy and Air Force transported another 500,000 refugees.[10]

U.S. NAVY'S GROWING ROLE IN VIETNAM

Photo 3-5

Rear Adm. Aaron P. Storres, USN; an unidentified civilian; Lt. Gen. John W. O'Daniel, USA, chief of MAAG (Military Assistance Advisory Group) Vietnam; Rear Adm. Lorenzo S. Sabin Jr., USN; and U.S. Ambassador to Vietnam Donald R. Heath await arrival in Saigon of the 100,000th refugee, September 1954.
National Archives photograph #80-G-647030

The U.S. Navy's initial advisory effort in Vietnam began in October 1950 with the establishment of a Navy Section, within the U.S. Military Assistance and Advisory Group (MAAG), staffed by eight officers and enlisted men. The primary mission of the Navy Section was to provide aid that would help strengthen the coastal and river security of Vietnam. This effort gradually expanded as the section supervised the transfer of craft and equipment to the Vietnamese Navy; furnished military advisors to training centers, the Saigon shipyard, and the coastal and river patrol units; and provided assistance to the Vietnamese Marine Corps.[11]

The U.S. Military Assistance Command Vietnam (MACV) was established on 8 February 1962, following a significant increase in the number of American military personnel in Vietnam. Located at the Tan Son Nhut Air Base outside Saigon, the unified command was responsible for American military activities in Vietnam, while the MAAG continued to administer the military aid program. The functions of the MAAG were absorbed by the MACV in May 1964, and the former Navy Section of the MAAG became the Naval Advisory Group under the U.S. Military Assistance Command. On 10 May 1965, Rear Adm. Norvell G. Ward, USN, assumed the duties of chief, Naval Advisory Group, and on 1 April 1966, the new and concurrent title and responsibilities of commander, Naval Forces Vietnam.[12]

Photo 3-6

Adm. Thomas H. Moorer (chief of Naval Operations designate), at left, is greeted by Gen. William C. Westmoreland, USA, commander, U.S. Military Assistance Command Vietnam (MACV), and Rear Adm. Kenneth L. Veth, commander, U.S. Naval Forces Vietnam (NavForV), on his arrival in Saigon on 27 June 1967.
Naval History and Heritage Command photograph #NH 104909

4

Land the Marines

It seems clear that our national policy towards SVN [South Vietnam] is shifting from one in which we attempted to maintain an 'advisory' image in SVN to one of active and overt U.S. participation.

—Observation by Adm. Thomas H. Moorer, commander, Pacific Fleet, to chief of Naval Operations, Adm. David L. McDonald. Moorer also conveyed to McDonald that his fleet was "on the scene with the capacity and…are ready to go."[1]

Photo 4-1

U.S. Marines wade ashore from a mechanized landing craft (LCM) at Danang, South Vietnam, March 1965.
National Archives photograph #USN 1142247

On 26 February 1965, President Lyndon B. Johnson authorized the deployment to Danang of two Marine battalion landing teams, a medium helicopter squadron, and headquarters elements of the 9th Marine Expeditionary Brigade. The Marines were to protect the airbase at the coastal city (the primary entry point for Americans flying into Vietnam) against Viet Cong and regular North Vietnamese attack, thus freeing South Vietnamese troops for other combat duties.[2]

This directive was carried out on 8 March. At dawn on that day, Rear Adm. Donald W. Wulzen gave the traditional order, "land the landing force." *Mount McKinley* (AGC-7), the flagship of the Seventh Fleet Amphibious Strike Force; *Vancouver* (LPD-2); *Henrico* (APA-45); and *Union* (AKA-106) then began disembarking Marines into landing craft. Upon emerging from the surf at Red Beach Two, north of Danang, the 3rd Battalion, 9th Marines, became the first battalion-size American ground combat unit deployed ashore in Vietnam.[3]

Photo 4-2

Rear Adm. Donald W. Wulzen, USN.
USS *Eldorado* (AGC-11) Western Pacific 1965-1966 cruise book

Photo 4-3

Amphibious command ship USS *Mount McKinley* (AGC-7) under way. Naval History and Heritage Command photograph #NH 107683

Rear Admiral Wulzen, commander, Amphibious Force, U.S. Seventh Fleet, was embarked aboard the *Mount McKinley*. Charged with the rapid movement of combat troops to trouble spots throughout the Western Pacific, he and his seagoing staff of 35 officers and 80 men were based at Subic Bay. In this capacity, Wulzen was the direct representative of commander, Amphibious Forces, U.S. Pacific Fleet, whose headquarters were in Coronado, California.[4]

First ashore was Battalion Landing Team 3/9 under the command of Lt. Col. Charles E. McPartlin Jr., which made the beach at 0815. Although a clear demonstration that the Marines had arrived, the landing was an administrative landing in friendly territory, rather than an assault landing on an enemy-held beach. Clad in full battle gear and carrying M-14 rifles, the Marines were met by sightseers and four American soldiers with a sign declaring, "Welcome, Gallant Marines." Less than two hours later, Battalion Landing Team 1/3 began arriving via helicopters at the Danang air base.[5]

Even before all 3,500 members of the 9th Marine Expeditionary Brigade arrived at Danang, American leaders were considering the use of Marines followed by Army units in active operations against the Viet Cong. The solely defense mission was shelved on 1 April 1965 when President Johnson authorized the Marines at Danang to move out and engage Viet Cong and North Vietnamese forces in combat.[6]

EASY LANDING, BUT GRUELING COMBAT AHEAD

Photo 4-4

Members of the 9th Marine Expeditionary Brigade landing at Danang, March 1965. Marine Corps photograph A183183

It took the 9th Marine Expeditionary Brigade almost the entire day on 8 March (D-Day), to get all its men and materiel ashore. Watching the proceedings was Nguyen Tien, who at age 24 had been a Viet Cong guerrilla for five years. He was on the beach that morning to observe the landings. Upon viewing the Marines "carrying too much gear and sweating like pigs," he wondered, "are they going to be able to fight in the heat?" But he also recognized that the entry of American combat troops into the war meant trouble.

> When I saw the Americans arrive, I knew the war was about to get harder — it was going to be more ferocious, and it was going to last a lot longer. A lot more people were going to die, and if we weren't very determined, we weren't going to win.[7]

5

Initial Operations and Raids

Within a week of the Marines landing at Danang, representatives from the U.S. Military Assistance Command Vietnam (MACV) and the U.S. Pacific Fleet reached an agreement on 14 March 1965, for the conduct of Operation MARKET TIME. In support of this naval coastal surveillance campaign, the agreement contained provisions for carrying out amphibious raids using South Vietnamese Marines, U.S. Marine battalions, or combined forces. General William C. Westmoreland and Admiral Roy L. Johnson ratified the results of the Saigon conference, and forwarded it to Admiral U. S. G. Sharp, commander in chief, Pacific, on 14 May for approval. On 9 June, Westmoreland informed Sharp that U.S. amphibious operations would be welcome and inquired about the status of the 14 March agreement. CincPac replied that it was still under review, but that U.S. raids could commence.[1]

In preparation, Lt. Col. Charles H. Bodley's battalion landing team (BLT 3/7) and Lt. Col. Norman G. Ewers' helicopter squadron (HMM-163), embarked in the ships of Task Group 76.5 (the Seventh Fleet designation for the Amphibious Ready Group) on 24 June. Ewers was the senior of the two officers, and became the commander of the Special Landing Force (SLF) as well as retaining command of his squadron. The task group—*Iwo Jima* (LPH-2), *Point Defiance* (LSD-31), and *Talladega* (APA-208)—under Capt. David A. Scott, USN, sailed from Buckner Bay, Okinawa, on 26 June, bound for South Vietnam.[2]

The first mission of the SLF was protection of the U.S. Army's large logistic facilities at Qui Nhon. Because of increased enemy activity in II Corps, and fear of a Communist offensive there, Westmoreland had requested the deployment of a Marine battalion to Qui Nhon until Army infantry forces arrived. On 1 July, Bodley's BLT 3/7 landed at Qui Nhon. The battalion remained ashore for six days until relieved by Lt. Leon N. Utter's BLT 2/7. Reembarked, the SLF remained offshore with HMM-163 flying from the *Iwo Jima* to provide helicopter support. HMM-163 was relieved on 20 July, by a ten-plane detachment from

HMM-161, and the ARG/SLF then reverted to its role as the Pacific Fleet's ready reserve and proceeded to Subic Bay.[3]

The first major battle and regimental-size clash between U.S. and enemy forces during the Vietnam War came the following month. Between 18-24 August 1965, units from the 3rd Marine Division, III Marine Amphibious Force, fought the Viet Cong 1st Regiment south of the newly established Marine base at Chu Lai.[4]

OPERATION STARLITE

> *Our colonel pulled the entire 4th Marine Regiment together and said we were going on an operation at 0500. I'll never forget his words. He said, 'we are going to be fighting an enemy that's had 20 plus years of fighting experience. They are called the Viet Cong, but you are Marines. You are better trained. You can deal with this. I expect all of you to come home.'*
>
> *As soon as we landed all we saw were explosions and heard weapons firing. I saw the VCs coming out of holes. I saw more of them coming. I thought, 'our guys were getting slaughtered.' I started shooting them. I saw helicopters taken down by mortars. It was a nightmare.... We were being shot from every angle. We kept advancing. The enemy was everywhere. When we arrived at the village close by, the Marines figured out that the VC had tunnels that connected the village to the surrounding areas.*
>
> —Benjamin Palermo, who served with G Company, 2nd Battalion, 4th Marine Regiment during Operation Starlite in August 1965.[5]

On 15 August, Maj. Gen. Lam Quang Thi, the South Vietnamese Army commander in I Corps, informed Lt. Gen. Lewis Walt, the senior Marine in Vietnam, that he had an enemy defector who had been drafted into the Viet Cong the previous spring. The 17-year-old disclosed that the 1st Viet Cong Regiment had moved onto the Van Tuong Peninsula just south of the new Marine base at Chu Lai. Because the Marines had previously received conflicting agent reports and other intelligence that placed the unit in multiple locations, they weren't sure how credible this new information was.[6]

Then they received a lucky break. A National Security Agency Signals Intelligence analyst in Saigon identified that transmissions from a radio known to be used by the headquarters of the 1st Viet Cong Regiment were originating from the Van Tuong Peninsula. Recognizing an opportunity to destroy an important enemy unit, and eliminate the threat it presented, Walt decided to act before the enemy attacked the

Marine base at Chu Lai or melted away into the western hills. The resultant operation, STARLITE, involved a simultaneous amphibious assault and vertical envelopment. The plan called for landing Marines on a beach on one side of the enemy and inserting Marines by helicopter on the other, in order to trap the Viet Cong force between them.[7]

The tank landing ship *Vernon County* (LST-1161), which happened to be landing and loading supplies at Chu Lai, was tasked to support the operation. After embarking elements of the 3rd Battalion, 3rd Marines (BLT 3/3 under Lt. Col. Joseph E. Muir) she sailed south along the coast to An Thuong and put the troops ashore.[8]

Photo 5-1

Assault craft from USS *Talladega* (APA-208) carrying Marines to a landing site for Operation STARLITE.
USS *Talladega* 1965-1966 cruise book

What started out as a search-and-destroy operation soon escalated into a battalion-sized offensive. The 1st Viet Cong Regiment was a professional organization of battle-hardened fighters, commanded by Col. Le Huu Tru, who had led a battalion at the iconic battle at Dien Bien Phu against the French in 1954. The Marines thwarted enemy movement toward Chu Lai, some nine miles to the north, with the main battle taking place in the Van Truong village complex. It was the first big battle for the Marines, which decimated the 60th VC Battalion and severely crippled the 40th Battalion.[9]

Photo 5-2

Marines embarked in the attack transport USS *Talladega* preparing to board assault craft. USS *Talladega* (APA-208) 1965-1966 cruise book

The Marines discovered at Van Truong communication equipment, documents, munitions, rice, and propaganda indicating that the hamlet had served as a VC command post.[10]

COMPLETING REQUIRMENTS LEVIED ON THE SLF

Following STARLITE, Brig. Gen. Melvin D. Henderson (Task Force 79 commander, and the senior Marine officer in the Seventh Fleet) expressed concerns to Lt. Gen. Victor H. Krulak about the earlier involuntary diversion of the SLF from training and refitting, to salvage operations:

> It appears that both the battalion commander and the SLF commander were concerned about the degradation of physical fitness of Marine personnel caused by confinement aboard ship.... The SLF commander although concerned, felt that higher authority was directing these movements with full appreciation of effect on integrity and readiness of SLF and refrained from objecting or coming upon the air to set forth his concern.[11]

This complaint stemmed from a decision by the Navy on 22 July, to divert the ships of the ARG to assist in a salvage mission off Pratas Reef (200 miles southeast of Hong Kong), where the destroyer *Frank Knox* (DD-742) had run aground. *Talladega* (APA-208) and *Iwo Jima* (LPH-2) remained at the salvage site until 31 July, while *Point Defiance* (LSD-31) unloaded some of its equipment at Subic Bay to free up more deck space. Returning to the salvage operation, she remained on scene until 19 August, when all three ships were ordered to Vietnam so that the SLF could participate in STARLITE.[12]

The SLF commander contended that splitting the amphibious ready group to optimize support for the salvage operation had resulted in leaving behind some equipment unloaded by the *Port Defiance* at Subic. This action, in turn, caused the incremental arrival of Battalion Landing Team 3/7 in the battle area.[13]

Before any action was taken regarding the complaint, Henderson was succeeded by Maj. Gen. Lewis J. Fields (commanding general of the 1st Marine Division) as commanding general, Fleet Marine Force, Seventh Fleet. Fields had his own doubts about command relationships within the Seventh Fleet. He believed that the organization of the SLF "was still a reflection of our peacetime activities in the Western Pacific," and "to think that whoever was senior of the two commanders, helicopter squadron or infantry battalion, would command the SLF as well as his own unit was ridiculous...." Fields wanted an expanded headquarters to command both the helicopter squadron and infantry battalion, "leaving their commanders to carry out the duties for which they had been intended and assigned."[14]

Vice Adm. Paul B. Blackburn Jr. did not concur with the proposed organizational changes, and indicated that he would "make all decisions concerning the organization of the Seventh Fleet." He did advocate for the creation of an additional SLF in the Seventh Fleet, which would justify an amphibious brigade headquarters. However, his proposal was similarly denied by commander in chief, Pacific Fleet. Admiral Johnson informed Blackburn that with the continuing commitment of forces to Vietnam, there were neither enough Marine troops nor helicopters in the Western Pacific to form a second Special Landing Force.[15]

Meanwhile, following STARLITE and a short refurbishing visit to Subic Bay, BLT 3/7 disembarked at Chu Lai and was attached to III Marine Amphibious Force in early September. The ARG proceeded to Okinawa and embarked Lt. Col. Robert T. Hanifin's BLT 2/11, the new SLF battalion. HMM-163 remained the SLF helicopter squadron, and Ewers kept his dual-role as commander of both the SLF and the squadron. The ARG/SLF returned to Vietnam on 10 September 1965, and served as the covering force for the landing of the U.S. Army's 1st Cavalry Division (Airmobile) at Qui Nhon.[16]

SERIES OF DAGGER THRUST AMPHIBIOUS RAIDS

Photo 5-3

Flight deck of the USS *Iwo Jima* (LPH-2) with Marines boarding helicopters for a landing on the Vung Mu Peninsula, South Vietnam, during Operation DAGGER THRUST. National Archives photograph #USN 1114000-D

While off Qui Nhon, the SLF made preparations to conduct a series of amphibious raids, in support of the MARKET TIME anti-infiltration operations. The raids were to be quick thrusts by the SLF into suspected enemy concentration points, followed by immediate retraction of the landing force. Since no permanent beachhead was to be established, the Navy amphibious commander would retain control of the Marine forces ashore in accordance with established amphibious doctrine. Rear Adm. Donald W. Wulzen (CTF 76) was designated the amphibious task force commander for the DAGGER THRUST mission.[17]

The operation was to consist of three raids in rapid succession on widely dispersed coastal areas to seek out Viet Cong along the beach and in nearby villages. After carrying out the first raid on the Vung Mu Peninsula (twenty miles south of Qui Nhon), the SLF was to strike next, fifty miles to the south in the Ben Goi area (twenty-seven miles north of Nha Trang). The third target was Tam Quan, thirty miles south of Quang Ngai City.[18]

On 22 September, the amphibious command ship *Estes* (AGC-12), and high-speed transport *Diachenko* (APD-123) rendezvoused with the ships of the ARG off Qui Nhon. Embarked aboard *Estes* were Rear Admiral Wulzen and Col. Edwin G. Winstead, the commander of the landing force. The task force then proceeded to Chu Lai where the SLF carried out a rehearsal for DAGGER THRUST. After backloading the assault forces, the task force—joined by the destroyers *Leonard F. Mason* (DD-852) and *Ernest G. Small* (DDR-838)—moved south to Vung Mu.[19]

Photo 5-4

Ships of commander Task Force 76 proceed through the twilight to South Vietnam, with Marines embarked, to conduct Operation DAGGER THRUST. Naval Heritage and History Command photograph #USN 1111528

The results of the DAGGER THRUST raids were disappointing. For Dagger Thrust I, the SLF landed over the beach and by helicopter on the morning of 25 September. After searching the peninsula and finding no sign of the enemy battalion believed to be there, the Marines re-embarked and proceeded to Ben Goi Bay. In preparation for Dagger Thrust II, three Marine reconnaissance teams from a detachment aboard the *Iwo Jima* transferred to the high speed transport *Diachenko*. Accompanied by South Vietnamese UDT personnel, they went ashore in small boats on the evening of 27 September. None reported finding the enemy, and Wulzen cancelled the landing.[20]

The battalion came ashore at Tam Quan on 1 October for Dagger Thrust III, and encountered some resistance from local guerrillas. The following day, Hanifin received orders "to break contact and withdraw."

Admiral Sharp had directed that the SLF (the Pacific Command's contingency force) be re-embarked and sail for Indonesian waters, ending the first DAGGER THRUST series.[21]

Photo 5-5

First wave of Marine infantry come ashore at Tam Quan during Dagger Thrust III. Marine Corps photograph 1114002

In the evening of 30 September, a group of Indonesian Army conspirators had gathered in Jakarta with the aim of kidnapping and killing seven army generals. By dawn on 1 October, six of the generals were dead; the seventh had escaped. Later that morning, the so-called September 30th Movement announced that it had seized power to forestall a coup against the president by a group of generals. The Indonesian Communist Party (PKI) maintained that the coup attempt was an internal affair of the army. Army leadership insisted that it was part of a PKI plot to seize power and subsequently embarked on a mission to purge the country of the perceived communist threat.[22]

CHANGES IN THE SPECIAL LANDING FORCE

In October 1965, following the Indonesian alert, there was a change in the composition of the ARG/SLF. *Valley Forge* (LPH-8), *Montrose* (APA-212), and *Monticello* (LSD-35) replaced *Iwo Jima*, *Talladega*, and *Point Defiance*. In related personnel changes: Capt. Thomas R. Weschler relieved Capt. David A. Scott as the ARG commander; Lt. Col. Mervin

B. Porter's HMM-261 replaced HMM-163 as the SLF helicopter squadron, and Porter relieved Ewers as the SLF commander.[23]

The exchange of the ships and helicopter squadron assigned to the ARG/SLF was routine and had been planned for some time, but Generals Krulak and Fields took this occasion to institute their long-desired restructuring of the SLF command and staff. On 17 October, Krulak notified Headquarters Marine Corps that "due to accelerated tempo...increased complexity of command and control, and for continuity," Fields was assigning a Marine colonel, "with an initial staff of three officers and five men," to the SLF. Col. John R. Burnett assumed command from Lieutenant Colonel Porter on 18 October and, with the SLF reconstituted and restructured, plans were initiated for a second series of DAGGER THRUST raids.[24]

THE SAIGON CONFERENCE

Following the first Dagger Thrust raids, General Westmoreland had proposed convening a joint MACV-CincPacFlt conference in Saigon to discuss the raids and to plan future ones. Westmoreland was dissatisfied with the limited authority he enjoyed over the SLF, and wanted an arrangement in which it would be unnecessary for him to go to the Seventh Fleet when he desired to employ the Special Landing Force.[25]

One item of contention between the MACV and CincPacFlt staffs was the criteria for establishing an amphibious objective area (AOA) during an amphibious landing or raid in Vietnam. According to existing doctrine, the amphibious task force commander controlled all air, land, and sea forces in the AOA during an amphibious operation. In Vietnam, this practice impinged upon Westmoreland's authority and South Vietnam's sovereignty, regarding the control of air traffic within the AOA and coordination with friendly ground forces operating inland within the perimeter of the AOA.[26]

During the 26-28 October conference, Captain Weschler, the ARG commander and senior officer present, served as chairman. The representatives from the various MACV component commands, as well as the amphibious commands under the jurisdiction of CincPacFlt, agreed on three specific targets for the next series of DAGGER THRUST raids to take place from 25 November through 7 December. They also agreed that the requirement for specific raid notification could be reduced from 60 to 24 hours. Finally, they resolved the sensitive issue of command and control of air and ground units in the area of operations. The agreed-upon solution was to simply reduce the size of the geographical AOAs to a 10-mile arc inland and a 25-mile arc seaward unless a specific target situation dictated an increase.[27]

The smaller AOA permitted the Navy amphibious task force commander to control naval gunfire and other supporting arms including aviation, while still accommodating civilian air traffic. The commander was to reserve a 10-nautical-mile-wide air corridor at an altitude of 7,000 to 10,000 feet for use by civilian aircraft. This action was possible without any violation of amphibious doctrine, because there was no chance of enemy air opposition and minimal other threats, due to the limited range of Viet Cong anti-aircraft weapons.[28]

SECOND SERIES OF DAGGER THRUST RAIDS

Photo 5-6

Marines of Echo Company, Second Battalion, First Marines sweep the village of Phu Thu on 5 December 1965 during DAGGER THRUST V.
Marine Corps photograph 1114218

Following approval of the recommendations of the Saigon conference by Johnson and Westmoreland, the Seventh Fleet amphibious forces began preparing for the next DAGGER THRUSTs. On 26 November 1965, the ARG/SLF sailed for Lang Ke Ga—a Viet Cong controlled and suspected infiltration point on the coast, ninety miles east of Saigon. Rear Admiral Wulzen aboard the command ship *Eldorado* (AGC-11) joined the amphibious task force for Dagger Thrust IV, with Captain

Weschler the amphibious task force commander, and Colonel Burnett commanding the landing force.[29]

On 30 November, the SLF came ashore at Lang Ke Ga, seventeen miles southwest of Phan Thiet. With the exception of scattered tank traps in the beach area and isolated incidents of small arms-fire, the Marines encountered no opposition. The battalion re-embarked the following day, ending the operation with no casualties on either side.[30]

Dagger Thrust V, the final raid, was launched on 5 December near the Phu Thu village complex, forty miles north of Qui Nhon. This time, the battalion surprised a small Viet Cong force, killing twenty-six enemy and detaining thirty-eight suspects. The Marines sustained casualties of three dead and ten wounded during the operation.[31]

SUBMARINE/UDT SUPPORT OF DAGGER THRUST

Frogmen of Underwater Demolition Team 12 supported Dagger Thrust raids and other amphibious operations in 1965, by conducting prelanding beach reconnaissance. The divers were first carried to survey sites by high speed transports, but by late year, the amphibious transport submarine *Perch* (LPSS-313) had begun to support clandestine coastal reconnaissance missions. Unlike a surface ship, she could deliver and extract UDT personnel with minimal risk of detection by the enemy, as illustrated by a description of standard procedures employed.

In support of a Dagger Thrust amphibious operation, UDT 12 Detachment Charlie was embarked aboard *Perch*. Following arrival off the Vietnamese coast, frogmen assisted by crewmembers, inflated their rubber boats on the afterdeck of the submarine as it lay on the surface. Lines from the boats were fastened to the periscope; the divers boarded the boats; and *Perch* descended to just below the surface. She then slowly towed the boats toward the target beach, until the UDT released them, and paddled quietly and carefully ashore to complete their mission.[32]

While they made the shore and carried out their tasking, *Perch* stood by to assist in vectoring the craft and providing any necessary support. After obtaining the required hydrographic data, and conveying it by radio back to Navy assets, the frogmen remained ashore to provide security for the Marine assault at dawn.[33]

Underwater Demolition Team 12 Detachment Bravo participated in every major amphibious operation in 1965, including PIRANHA in August, STARLITE in September, DAGGER THRUST in October, and BLUE MARLIN in November.[34]

OPERATION HARVEST MOON

HARVEST MOON was a joint U.S. Marine and South Vietnamese Army operation in December 1965, intended to trap Vietcong forces in the Phuoc Ha Valley. Located about halfway between Danang and Chu Lai, the valley was nearly ten miles wide at its mouth, and stretched inland twice that distance, flanked by low foothills and beyond them, towering 1,000-foot mountains.[35]

It and the surrounding area had been a Viet Cong stronghold for many years, with only a few scattered Vietnamese government outposts in the larger towns. One of the outposts was Que Son, the site of an Army of the Republic of Vietnam (ARVN) district headquarters. The Vietnamese outpost had been a thorn in the side of the Viet Cong for some time and in early December, ARVN and the Marines confirmed reports that enemy forces were massing in the valley for an attack on the town. These forces included the reconstituted Viet Cong 1st Regiment, three separate VC battalions, two local force VC companies, and other smaller units.[36]

Fighting the Viet Cong would be a battalion of Marines from the Danang enclave, a battalion from Chu Lai, and the SLF battalion aboard the ARG in the South China Sea. Joining the Marines would be four ARVN battalions. For the thousands of Marines and Vietnamese troops, Harvest Moon would bring bloody combat lasting more than a week in the rice paddies and jungled hills of South Vietnam. The bright autumn moon that inspired the name of the operation was hidden by heavy monsoon clouds that kept the nights in total blackness.[37]

Making matters worse, Harvest Moon would be a "boondocker" battle. (This reference refers to slogging through muddy terrain in combat footwear.) Helicopters played a major role, but heavy clouds and rain often prevented their use, and the only way to move was by foot. Marines sloshed through waist-deep rice paddies, and fought their way through tangled jungle and up muddy hills, burdened by ammo, communications gear, and rations carried in rucks on their backs.[38]

The Harvest Moon offensive opened on 8 December 1965. The 11th Rangers and 1st Battalion, Fifth ARVN Regiment advanced about six miles into the valley before making contact with the Viet Cong. Enveloped by a numerically superior force, the battalion withdrew to higher ground. The rangers suffered moderate casualties, but held until reinforcements arrived the next day.[39]

The 2nd Battalion, Seventh Marines, arrived from Chu Lai on 9 December, and were staged for movement by helicopters to a position deep in the valley. The 3rd Battalion, Third Marines, was still en route, traveling in convoy from Danang to an area in the valley's mouth.

Offshore in the South China Sea, Golf and Foxtrot Companies of the 2nd Battalion, First Marines, were completing final preparations for helicopter lift ashore from the *Valley Forge*, one of the ships of the ARG/SLF. Foxtrot would go in first, followed by Golf Company.[40]

Photo 5-7

Flight deck aboard the USS *Valley Forge* as Marines are heli-lifted by UH-34D helicopters of Medium Helicopter Squadron 261.
USS *Valley Forge* (LPH-8) Western Pacific 1965-1966 cruise book

Photo 5-8

The infamous rice paddies of South Vietnam.
USS *Valley Forge* (LPH-8) Western Pacific 1965-1966 cruise book

Files (groups) of Marines arranged in heli-teams, were staged on the hangar deck while, above them, helicopters from HMM-261 warmed up on the flight deck. On command, the Marines raced up the ladderway to the waiting choppers. As loudspeakers blared the command, "land the landing force," the loaded birds of the helicopter squadron lifted off to head up the valley. The landing zone for Foxtrot was a low hill at the edge of a huge rice-paddy complex covering the valley floor, but the zone proved "too hot" to land the entire company there. Viet Cong dug in around the hill, riddled the helicopters with automatic fire, as the remainder of the company was put down in the paddies and the Marines who landed first joined them.[41]

The Marines of Golf Company were landed on a low hill behind the paddies in which Foxtrot was under fire. Their orders were to move up and reinforce Foxtrot. As the company moved down a draw toward the paddies, Marine jets overhead directed rocket and cannon-fire into Viet Cong positions. As Golf Company entered the paddies to join Foxtrot, they began taking sniper fire and, moving closer to Foxtrot, heavy automatic weapons fire from the front and right flank followed. The Marines continued to move forward until the volume of enemy fire became so intense, the order was passed to keep down until additional air strikes could knock out the remaining VC machine gun positions.[42]

For more than thirty minutes, A-4 Skyhawks and F-4 Phantoms pounded the low hills and tree lines from which the enemy was firing. Finally, the two companies were able to stand up and walk out of the paddies without a round being fired at them. The other two companies of the 2nd Battalion, First Marines, still offshore, were landed the following day and joined Foxtrot and Golf.[43]

On 12 December, B-52 bombers of the U.S. Strategic Air Command carried out the first of four strikes in the valley, dropping 750- and 1,000-pound bombs on Viet Cong area targets. After the initial strike between ridges on the southern edge of the valley, the 3rd Battalion, Third Marines, was heli-lifted to the strike area. It met heavy VC resistance at the mouth of the valley, but quickly routed the enemy. Over the next three days, Marines swept through the valley, capturing tons of enemy equipment. One cave contained bolts of khaki cloth and another nearby, sewing machines to convert fabric into field uniforms. Other caves held stores of ammunition and weapons.[44]

A second B-52 strike was carried out on 14 December and two the next day. Enemy resistance was sporadic through 15 December. Many guerrillas took advantage of the heavy weather and slipped out of the valley under cover of darkness, but others stayed to fight. An enemy squad ambushed the lead elements of Golf Company, as it preceded the

2nd Battalion, First Marines, down a narrow draw. The Viet Cong were all killed, while the Marines suffered only light casualties. The next day, the 2nd Battalion swept northeast as an ARVN reconnaissance company and Echo Company, 2nd Battalion, Ninth Marines, set up blocking positions. The sweep resulted in at least sixty Viet Cong killed and many others wounded.[45]

On 17 December, 3rd Battalion, Third Marines (and attached units), began moving east, and phased out of the operation the following day. The 2nd Battalion, First Marines, followed 3/3 out, and were returned by helicopter to ships in the ARG offshore. The 2nd Battalion, Seventh Marines, also began to pull back out of the valley, continuing to search out VC fortifications and destroy them during this movement. On 18 December, the 2/7 fought the last big battle of Operation HARVEST MOON just outside the village of Ky Phu.[46]

As Golf Company led the battalion in long column out of Ky Phu, two companies of Viet Cong (stretching some 1,000 yards along a tree line, paralleling the Marines' route of march) were waiting to spring an ambush. Golf Company took heavy automatic fire as it neared the center of a rice-paddy complex, and immediately laid down return fire to enable Foxtrot's two forward platoons to pass through them and break the front of the ambush. At the same time, VC in the village opened fire on Hotel Company (bringing up the rear) with automatic weapons and recoilless rifles.[47]

Foxtrot's forward platoons raced back, fighting off Viet Cong trying to split the column, to reinforced Hotel Company. The fighting in the village was brutal. The enemy was firing from well-concealed bunkers, which had to be destroyed with flame throwers and demolitions. At times the combatants were no more than ten yards apart in a fight to the death. When the lengthy battle was over, 105 VC bodies lay before the Marines, and it was estimated that those of another 150 killed or wounded, had been hidden or dragged away. Found with the casualties were many individual and crew-served weapons (which require more than one individual to function).[48]

SPECIAL LANDING FORCE AT YEAR'S END

> *The potential problem with the SLF had nothing to do with its performance or its excellence or its utilization. The difficulty was principally a political one between Navy and Army doctrine.... Specifically, with regard to the SLF the Army wanted operational control. I always felt that once they had been given it, they never would have released it, and the SLF would simply become another Army unit*

> *ashore. We would never be able to get it back aboard ship for use in some other area which might be more important.*
>
> —Adm. John J. Hyland, former commander, U.S. Seventh Fleet.[49]

Lt. Col. Robert T. Hanifin's 2nd Battalion, 1st Marines, suffered twelve dead and fifty-two wounded during HARVEST MOON. Following the operation, the SLF underwent further changes in composition and designation. Vice Adm. John J. Hyland succeeded Blackburn in December as commander, Seventh Fleet. The SLF was redesignated Task Group 79.5, with responsibility for reporting administratively to Maj. Gen. Lewis J. Fields in his capacity as commanding general, Task Force 79 (Seventh Fleet Marine Forces). Within the Special Landing Force, BLT 2/3, commanded by Lt. Col. William K. Horn, became the new SLF battalion on New Year's Eve.[50]

The SLF had proved its value in 1965 as a mobile floating reserve, and its air and ground units played important roles in STARLITE and HARVEST MOON. The DAGGER THRUST raids failed to achieve their overall objective: the quick exploitation of intelligence and resultant contact with large enemy formations. The Navy believed the dismal results were a product of excessive Army requirements and restrictions. Admiral Roy L. Johnson later observed:

> The excessive time involved in planning and coordinating with the MACV levels resulted in completely stale intelligence. Furthermore, by the time MACV had completed his all-important coordination and alerting of ARVN forces and Province Chiefs, we had also completely spooked the VC and they had flown the coop.[51]

6

Special Landing Force/UDT in 1966

Photo 6-1

Chu Lai Peninsula, South Vietnam, January 1966.
Naval History and Heritage Command photograph #NH 74192

As 1966 dawned, the Special Landing Force (SLF) was the only strategic reserve for all of the Far East. This situation resulted from the commitment, by the end of 1965, of most Okinawa-based Marine Forces to Vietnam. Although under the operational control of the Seventh Fleet, the SLF was readily available to General Westmoreland for specific operations in Vietnam.[1]

Marine Col. John R. Burnett was the SLF commander with his headquarters aboard the helicopter amphibious assault ship *Valley Forge* (LPH-8). On 5 January, HMM-362 replaced HMM-261, and Burnett relocated to the attack transport *Paul Revere* (APA-248). The other ships of the amphibious task force were *Montrose* (APA-212) and the dock landing ship *Monticello* (LSD-35). Nearly all of the remainder of January was devoted to planning for Operation DOUBLE EAGLE.[2]

Photo 6-2

Gen. William Westmoreland walking with Capt. Paul J. Knapp, USS *Princeton*'s (LPH-5) commanding officer, in late 1964.
Naval History and Heritage Command photograph #NH 93799

OPERATION DOUBLE EAGLE

> ... the weather was bad. We made a dawn landing which meant that we approached the landing area with no lights. It was tough putting the boats in the water because of the seas and the fact that we could not use lights on deck except for small red lights.... A cruiser and a destroyer [were] firing on the beach before the landings. The initial landings were made by LVT's from the LST and the LSD. The Skagit boats were used to send in supplies as needed. The weather was bad most of the time which made it difficult to off load from the cargo holds.... Most of the Viet Cong escaped. At the end of Double Eagle, another operation was started called Double Eagle II. Marines from Chu Lai and from the [USS] Valley Forge [LPH-8] again tried to attack the Viet Cong and again they were unsuccessful.

>—Thomas Herbert, former officer aboard the attack cargo ship
> USS *Skagit* (AKA-105), describing the initial amphibious
> landings of DOUBLE EAGLE on 28 January 1966.[3]

Double Eagle, which began on 28 January and would conclude on 1 March 1966, was the largest amphibious operation in the war to date. General Westmoreland had earlier, on 7 December, ordered III Marine Amphibious Force and Field Force, Vietnam, to initiate a coordinated offensive during late January against the enemy build up in the region of the I and II Corps border. The main objective of the operation was to engage the North Vietnamese Army's 18th and 95th Regiments and the Viet Cong 2nd Regiment in Quang Ngai Province.[4]

UDT 11 DETACHMENT CHARLIE

In preparation for the operation, frogmen from UDT 11 Detachment Charlie conducted surveys from 3-21 January of coastal areas near Phan Thiet, Cam Ranh, Nha Trang, and Qui Nhon. Immediately prior to DOUBLE EAGLE, submarine *Perch* and these frogmen were called upon to conduct a clandestine beach reconnaissance of the chosen site. Utilizing a slightly different method, the submarine settled on the bottom out about 1,000 yards offshore. Support divers with scuba gear "locked out" of *Perch* using the forward escape trunk, and prepared lines and equipment. UDT members then exited the sub in a similar fashion, breathing from equipment rigged underwater by the divers.[5]

Rubber boats were sent to the surface and inflated, and the frogmen ascended and boarded the craft. They then broke out weaponry, radios, and equipment protected from water intrusion during the lock-out process. As the frogmen proceeded shoreward, the lead boat deployed an acoustic pinger, identifying to the sub its position and course. By directing the craft to come right, come left, or maintain course, *Perch* was able to vector it to the exact landing site, where the recon began. At completion, the frogmen paddled out to sea, attached a line between the boats, and then signaled the submarine. Remaining submerged, *Perch* used her periscope to snag the line, and took the boats in tow. Once sufficiently seaward to escape detection from shore, she surfaced and recovered the UDT and their equipment.[6]

THE AMPHIBIOUS LANDINGS

Capt. William J. Maddocks, USN (commander Amphibious Squadron Five) commanded the amphibious task force assigned to DOUBLE EAGLE, and Colonel Burnett, USMC, the landing force. In accordance with doctrine, Maddocks was to transfer operational control of the ground forces to the III MAF ground commander for the operation, Marine Brig. Gen. Jonas M. Platt, once all the troops were ashore. Although D-Day, 28 January, brought low overcast, light rain, and heavy seas, the first boat waves landed Marines near Thach Tru (in southern Quang Ngai Province) as scheduled.[7]

Photo 6-3

Marines of the 4th Regiment, 3rd Marine Division come ashore on D-Day. Defense Department photograph Marine Corps A186773

Photo 6-4

Marines of E Company, 2nd Battalion, 4th Regiment, scale rocks along the shore on D-Day, after crossing a very narrow landing beach.
Defense Department photograph Marine Corps A186776

Mid-morning, the surf began to build rapidly, delaying debarkation of other elements of the landing force, and deteriorating weather hampered the operation for the rest of the day. General Platt arrived at Red Beach from Chu Lai by mid-afternoon, but was unable to assume operational control of the DOUBLE EAGLE forces because insufficient communication equipment was ashore. As a result, the command of forces ashore remained with the amphibious task force commander, and the commander of the landing force.[8]

DOUBLE EAGLE TASK GROUP COMPOSITION

The flagship (attack transport *Paul Revere*) had led two other APAs, an attack cargo ship (AKA), three LSTs (tank landing ships), two LSD (dock landing ships), a helicopter carrier (*Valley Forge*), a cruiser (*Oklahoma City*), a destroyer (*Barry*), two auxiliaries, and the hospital ship *Repose* to the assault area. As the first wave landed, the destroyer *Barry* and cruiser *Oklahoma City* provided naval gunfire coverage, while eight A-4 Skyhawks and eight F-4B Phantoms were on station overhead. The aircraft were from Marine Air Groups MAG-12 and MAG-11, based at Chu Lai and Danang, respectively.[9]

The ships of Task Group 76.6 are identified in the table, which includes those that took part in DOUBLE EAGLE, the subsequent DOUBLE EAGLE II, or both.

Task Group 76.6

Ship	Commanding Officer
Princeton (LPH-5)	Capt. Thomas James Gallagher Jr., USN
Valley Forge (LPH-8)	Capt. Richard Oscar Madson, USN
Montrose (APA-212)	Capt. Robert Juarez, USN
Navarro (APA-215)	Capt. John Jefferson Love Jr., USN
Paul Revere (APA-248)	Capt. William Robert McDowell Jr., USN
Weiss (APD-135)	Lt. Comdr. Robert Theodore Carterette, USN
Skagit (AKA-105)	Capt. Joe E. Chambliss, USN
Catamount (LSD-17)	Comdr. Arthur Shaw, USN
Fort Marion (LSD-22)	Comdr. Jack E. Waterman, USN
Monticello (LSD-35)	Capt. George William Folta Jr., USN
	Capt. Vincent F. Kelley, USN
Tioga County (LST-1158)	Lt. Comdr. Roger Edgar Ekman, USN
Tom Green County (LST-1159)	Comdr. Burl Abraham Troutman Jr., USN
Westchester County (LST-1167)	Comdr. Norman Thomas Hansen, USN
Windham County (LST-1170)	Lt. Comdr. George Thomas Dyer Jr., USN
Oklahoma City (CLG 5)	Capt. Kendall Washburn Simmons, USN
Topeka (CLG-8)	Capt. Thomas Chapin Buell, USN
Barry (DD-933)	Comdr. Otto Darby Tiderman, USN
O'Brien (DD-725)	Comdr. Charles Stahl Christensen Jr., USN

Orleck (DD-886)	Comdr. Edward Herman Heuer, USN
Elkhorn (AOG-7)	Lt. Comdr. Gordon Lewis Thorpe, USN
Repose (AH-16)	Capt. Eugene Hugh Maher, USN
Safeguard (ARS-25)	Lt. Comdr. Louis Aloysius Downey, USN

RESULTS UNIMPRESSIVE

Photo 6-5

Panji-staked gully provides rough going for Marines of "F" Company, 2nd Battalion, 4th Regiment during Operation DOUBLE EAGLE.
Defense Department photograph Marine Corps A186718

DOUBLE EAGLE II was launched after intelligence sources indicated that large numbers of enemy troops were concentrating twenty-five miles north of Chu Lai, and to the west of Tam Ky, in Quang Tin Province. Essentially the same forces as those which participated in the first DOUBLE EAGLE were utilized. Once again, contact was lighter than expected; 125 Viet Cong killed and 15 captured, with Marine casualties 4 killed and 121 wounded. The operation was terminated on

1 March. The Viet Cong had, once again, avoided significant contact with the SLF, other Marines from the III Marine Amphibious Force (based ashore at Danang), and South Vietnamese units during a sweep near Quang Ngai City and Tam Ky in I Corps.[10]

CHANGES IN COMMAND AND COMPOSITION

Through the end of February 1966, the Special Landing Force was under the administrative control of the 1st Marine Division in Okinawa. With the pending deployment of its division headquarters to Vietnam, a new parent organization had to be found for Marine forces remaining on Okinawa and afloat with the Seventh Fleet. On 1 March, General Krulak activated the 9th Marine Amphibious Brigade, under the command of Col. Herman Hansen Jr.—a World War II flying ace and recipient of the Navy Cross and two Silver Stars. The MAB assumed operational control of most Marine units on Okinawa and also, administrative control of the Special Landing Force.[11]

In a separate action, Battalion Landing Team 1/5 (Lt. Col. Harold L. Coffman) became the new SLF battalion. The 1/5 had traveled from Camp Pendleton, California, with Amphibious Squadron Three ships. After a short exercise off the island of Mindoro in the Philippines, the SLF was ready for the next amphibious landing in South Vietnam.[12]

OPERATION JACKSTAY

Photo 6-6

Marines aboard USS *Princeton* (LPH-5) prepare to board helicopters that will take them to the Rung Sat Special Zone.
Department of Defense photograph Marine Corps A413986

Operation JACKSTAY began shortly after daybreak on 26 March 1966. Spearheaded by the *Princeton* (LPH-5), the attack was launched in LCM-8 landing craft from the *Alamo* (LSD-33) and *Pickaway* (APA-222), and from the *Princeton* in helicopters. *Princeton* was an amphibious assault helicopter carrier and, as such, functioned as a high-speed transport and launching platform for a battalion of Marines and their combat gear. In an assault area, the Marines were embarked in helicopters and landed ashore. They might be used in commando-type operations or, more commonly, in support of conventional amphibious forces. On this day, 1,200 Marines poured ashore and began searching the Rung Sat Special Zone, surrounding the river approaches to Saigon.[13]

Photo 6-7

Amphibious assault ship USS *Princeton* standing out of port.
USS *Princeton* (LPH-5) Far East 1966 cruise book

The dangerous Rung Sat Special Zone, which lay astride the major waterways connecting Saigon (South Vietnam's major port) with the sea, was largely inundated at high tide. During February and early March, the danger posed by the almost undisputed Viet Cong control of this area had been underscored by three attacks made on merchant shipping en route to Saigon. The most recent of these had come on 2 March, when the tanker SS *Paloma* was attacked and set afire only four miles upriver from the site where an ambush had taken place three days earlier against another merchant vessel.[14]

Map 6-1

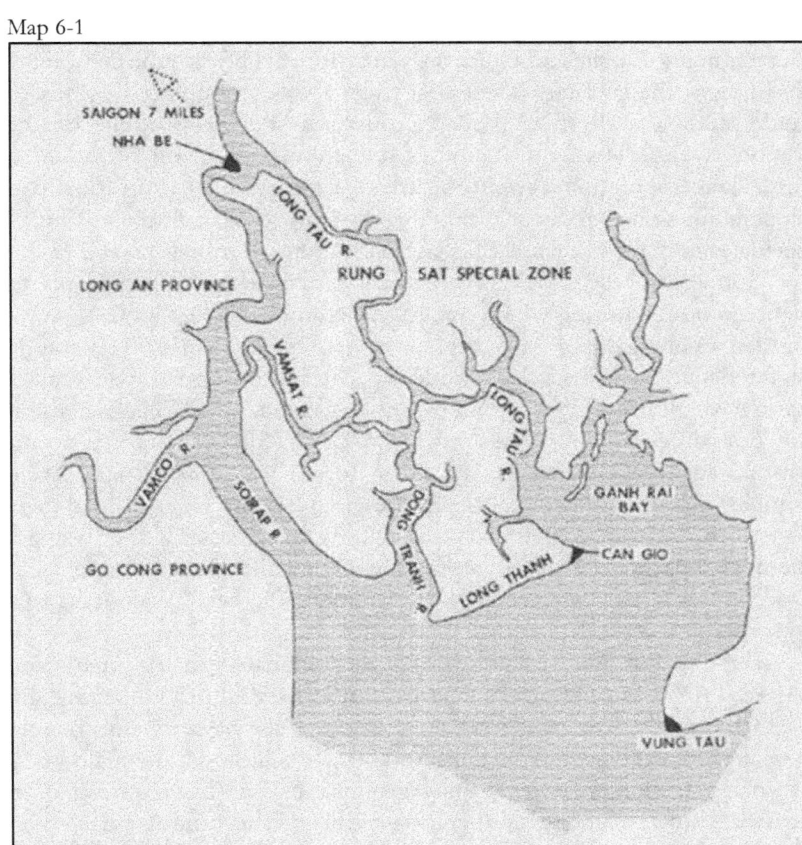

Rung Sat Special Zone
Naval History and Heritage Command Vietnam War Highlights, May 1966

In the aftermath of this attack, General Westmoreland asked that the SLF be committed for about ten days to penetrate the Rung Sat and disrupt Viet Cong activities. The naval force consisted of *Princeton*,

Alamo and *Pickaway*, the attack cargo ship *Merrick* (AKA-97), and the tank landing ships *Henry County* (LST-824) and *Washoe County* (LST-1165). In supporting roles, the high-speed transport *Weiss* (APD-135), with UDT 11 personnel embarked, was assigned for special operations; the destroyer *Robinson* (DDG-12) for naval gunfire support; and rounding out the group, the salvage ship *Reclaimer* (ARS-42). Planes from the carrier *Hancock* (CVA-19) provided air support. *Washoe County* was to serve as an advance base, providing gunfire support arms, ammunition, rations, and water to assault boat groups.[15]

Members of UDT 11 and SEAL Team One were involved in JACKSTAY between 26 March and 7 April. UDT frogmen from Detachments Charlie and Delta slipped ashore at 0300 on the dark, rainy morning of the landing. Their first tasking was to emplace beacons to guide landing craft through dangerous and shallow portions of the Saigon River, following the landings at its mouth. They then conducted surveillance operations; swept the area for mines; and set up four-man blocking positions about 500-800 meters apart to prevent the escape of fleeing enemy forces, while SEALs and Marines combed the area.[16]

Some of these blocking positions remained in place for up to eighteen hours, during which one position ambushed a Viet Cong junk and became engaged in a firefight with its six occupants. The enemy suffered five killed and one wounded. Later, the frogmen were called upon to demolish a captured Viet Cong rest camp. JACKSTAY marked the first time in which elements from UDT, SEALs, Marine Recon Teams, and regular Marine and naval forces joined for a large-scale combat operation. Vietnamese Marines, and LDNN frogmen and their American advisors dispatched to the Rung Sat Special Zone to assist them, also participated in the operation. The contributions of the Lien Doc Nguoi Nhia ("soldiers who fight under the sea") included three river reconnaissance missions.[17]

Despite the large numbers of forces allocated to the operation, JACKSTAY was only partially successful in its goal of eliminating the Viet Cong in the Rung Sat, because the enemy always seemed to be one step ahead and chose not to make a stand. But, although the main body of enemy troops withdrew, small groups of Viet Cong remained to provide some resistance. Operating much of the time waist-deep in water, and with few suitable helicopter landing sites, the Marines would have been literally stuck in the mud, but for the availability of boats and landing craft to transport them between areas.[18]

By completion of the twelve-day operation, sixty-three Viet Cong were reported killed against U.S. casualties of five KIA, two missing, and twenty-four WIA. JACKSTAY resulted in the destruction of three major base complexes upon which the estimated 1,000 Viet Cong in the area had depended.[19]

Photo 6-8

Two OV-10A Bronco aircraft from Light Attack Squadron Four (VAL-4) fly low over narrow, winding waterways of the Rung Sat in search of enemy activity, June 1969. National Archives photograph #USN 1139918

JACKSTAY involved the first joint United States-Vietnamese amphibious operation when, on 31 March, Vietnamese River Assault Groups provided a protective screen and minesweeping escort for U.S. Marines embarked in landing craft. The boat-convoy worked its way seven miles down the narrow Vam Sat River to make the deepest penetration of the Rung Sat Special Zone. The operation resulted in the destruction of Viet Cong training, hospital, and supply complexes.[20]

Comdr. Derwin T. Lamb (commander, Landing Ship Squadron One) received the Bronze Star with Combat "V" for leading an assault boat convoy through a winding, narrow river hemmed in by thick mangrove swamps that provided cover for Viet Cong snipers. His staff medical officer, Lt. H. J. Lauffenberg, MC, USN, received the Bronze Star with "V" and Purple Heart while serving as the assault boat medical officer during the operation.[21]

OPERATION OSAGE

Following JACKSTAY, Col. Richard A. Brenneman relieved Colonel Burnett as SLF commander on 7 April. Two days later, HMM-364 (Col. Daniel A. Sommerville) replaced HMM-362 aboard the *Princeton*. In late April, the Special Landing Force conducted an amphibious operation, OSAGE, in Thua Thien Providence. The Marine BLT was assigned the mission of destroying a VC battalion and elements of an NVA regiment, reported to be operating in the Phu Loc District coastal region.[22]

Map 6-2

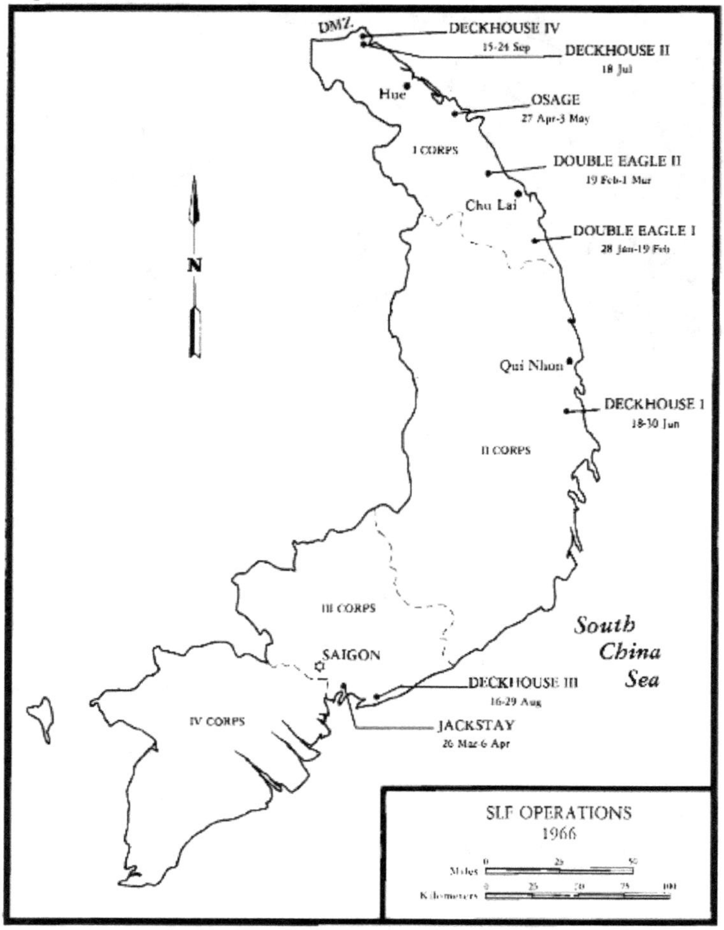

U.S. Seventh Fleet Special Landing Force Operations in 1966
Jack Shulimson's book, *U.S. Marines in Vietnam, An Expanding War 1966*

In support of the 27 April landing, UDT 11 Detachment Delta conducted a recon of the Phu Loc area, twenty miles north of Danang. During the operation, which lasted through 2 May, *Princeton*, *Alamo*, and *Pickaway* were assigned with BLT 1/5 and HMM-364 embarked. Destroyers *John W. Thomason* (DD-760) and *Walker* (DD-517) provided gunfire support. Opposition was light on 27 April against the first wave of nine LVTPs (amphibious assault landing tracked vehicles) and sixteen helicopters. With the exception of delaying and harassing tactics, the enemy again elected not to fight. The Marines killed eight enemy, while suffering eight dead and nine wounded during the operation.[23]

Photo 6-9

Destroyer USS *Walker* (DD-517) off Oahu, Hawaii, on 29 May 1963.
Naval History and Heritage Command photograph #NH 107240

SPECIAL LANDING FORCE'S EXPANDED ROLE

In early May 1966, General Westmoreland suggested to Admiral Sharp that as a result of the changing nature of the war in Vietnam, the original SLF mission was too narrow in scope. Dramatically increased U.S. military forces in Vietnam—and their expanded operations, along with the Navy's MARKET TIME interdiction efforts to stop the flow of troops, war materiel, and supplies by sea into South Vietnam—had been successful in severely restricting the movement of enemy main force units. Accordingly, the requirement for amphibious raids to disrupt the buildup of enemy forces in coastal regions had lessened. Westmoreland recognized that enemy troop concentrations in coastal areas would continue to occur, but he wanted to develop a more responsive procedure to destroy those forces.[24]

An outgrowth of a conference that month was a decision to initiate a broader type of amphibious operation, code named DECKHOUSE. The Deckhouse series was designed to complement Allied land operations against enemy units. The first of these operations, DECKHOUSE I, took place in II Corps, in support of the U.S. 1st Cavalry Division's Operation NATHAN HALE.[25]

DECKHOUSE I

Photo 6-10

High speed transport USS *Cook* (APD-130) under way, circa 1962.
Naval History and Heritage Command photograph #L45-64.01.01

From 16-18 June, UDT 11 conducted clandestine surveys of beaches in the Cau and Cai River areas, operating from the high-speed transport *Cook*. As the first Marines came ashore on 26 June near the River Cau (twenty-five miles south of Qui Nhon), gunfire and rockets from the *Clarion River* (LSMR-409) pounded suspected Viet Cong posts ashore. At the same time, *Princeton* launched helicopters to carry other Marines farther inland to block enemy troops trying to escape the "leathernecks" coming in from the sea. Following their beach reconnaissance, frogmen were aboard Vietnamese Junk Force 21 vessels to stop any Viet Cong trying to escape by water.[26]

Photo 6-11

Medium landing ship (rocket) USS *Clarion River* under way, location and date unknown. Naval History and Heritage Command #NH 86769-KN

After landing, the Marines provided security to one flank of the Army's 1st Cavalry Division, engaged seven miles to the south in NATHAN HALE. Since this operation was not amphibious, the Special Landing Force, once established ashore, came under the operational control of the 1st Cavalry. Deckhouse I terminated on 27 June, and Nathan Hale on the 30th. Although the Marines encountered only scattered resistance, Nathan Hale developed into a nine-battalion operation with over 400 enemy killed. Special Landing Force casualties were three KIA and twenty-one WIA, with sixty-five Viet Cong killed and another seventy-two captured.[27]

Assigned DECKHOUSE I ships/forces are identified in the table:

Amphibious Ready Group (CTG 76.5)	Naval Gunfire Support (CTG 70.8)
Princeton (LPH-5)	*St. Paul* (CA-73)
Alamo (LSD-33)	*John W. Thomason* (DD-760)
Pickaway (APA-222)	*Basilone* (DD-824)
Special Landing Force (CTG 79.5)	*Cook* (APD-130)
BLT 3/5 (1,500 Marines)	*Clarion River* (LSMR-409)
HMM-364 Det VMO-6 (armed helicopters)	*White River* (LSMR-536)

DECKHOUSE II

Shortly after DECKHOUSE I, the SLF rotated helicopter units. On 4 July, HMM-363 (Lt. Col. James D. McGough) relieved HMM-364. The second operation in the DECKHOUSE series took place during the latter part of the month in support of Operation HASTINGS, carried out by the III Marine Amphibious Force.[28]

Following intelligence reports of a large enemy force building up near the coast just south of the DMZ, III MAF had launched HASTINGS on 7 July—a combat reconnaissance operation northwest of Quang Tri City. That same day, Westmoreland requested that the ARG/SLF be stationed off I Corps Tactical Zone coastal waters in an alert status for amphibious support. The units listed below were made available for DECKHOUSE II.[29]

Amphibious Ready Group (CTG 76.5)	Naval Gunfire Support (CTG 70.8)
Princeton (LPH-5)	*Oklahoma City* (CLG-5)
Alamo (LSD-33)	*Lofberg* (DD-759)
Pickaway (APA-222)	*White River* (LSMR-536)
Cook (APD-130)	
Special Landing Force (CTG 79.5)	
BLT 3/5	
HMM-363 Det VMO-6 (armed helicopters)	

Photo 6-12

The light cruiser USS *Oklahoma City* (CLG-5) in a tight turn to port, 16 February 1972. Naval History and Heritage Command photograph #NH 98669

Amphibious ships *Princeton, Alamo, Pickaway*, and *Cook*, with *Lofberg*, and *White River* for gunfire support, departed Danang on 15 July, and proceeded northwest up the Vietnamese coast to the mouth of the Thach Han River. *Cook*, with UDT 11 embarked, conducted a pre-dawn coastal reconnaissance of the landing beach, then screened the approach of the remainder of the task force. Four miles offshore, the cruiser *Oklahoma City* stood by with her 6-inch guns.[30]

Photo 6-13

UDT 12 members on Red Beach during landings at Danang, 13 April 1965. Defense Department photograph Marine Corps A183973

All ships were in position by 0500 on 16 July and the landing was conducted on schedule at 0630. In nearly perfect weather and sea conditions, the first elements of the 2,000-man Special Landing Force began coming ashore by craft and helicopters just north of the Thach Han River (eight miles northeast of Dong Ha). After making Blue Beach, Companies K and I seized An Trung and Diem Ha Trung and, simultaneously, L Company set down about a mile and a half inland. No resistance was encountered. As soon as commander, Landing Force moved ashore, and established his command post about one-half mile inland, the amphibious phase was terminated and the SLF came under the operational control of III MAF.[31]

Battalion Landing Team 3/5 and HMM-363 operated ashore until 30 July, when they re-embarked in the Amphibious Ready Group. No significant contact was made with the enemy. There were no Marine Corps casualties; Viet Cong/North Vietnamese Army lost three KIA.[32]

DECKHOUSE III

> *The ARG/SLF Navy Marine team once again demonstrated its versatility and "Can Do" spirit during the execution of Operation Deckhouse III... The rapid reconstitution of the ARG/SLF, and execution of a second amphibious assault within 33 hours, reflected professional competence and efficient enthusiasm of the highest caliber. To the officers and men who participated in the planning and execution of this operation, I extend a sincere "WELL DONE."*

—Adm. Roy L. Johnson, USN, commander in chief, Pacific Fleet.[33]

On 4 August 1966, BLT 1/26 (First Battalion of the 26th Marines, Lt. Col. Anthony A. Monti), newly arrived from the United States, became the SLF Battalion. After brief training in the Philippines, the Special Landing Force conducted DECKHOUSE III on the Vung Tau Peninsula, sixty miles southwest of Saigon. UDT 11 was involved from 15 to 21 August. Frogmen operating from USS *Cook* conducted two clandestine recons, marking approaches and later leading forces ashore. On the morning of the 16th, the Amphibious Ready Group landed its Marines across difficult beaches in Binh Tuy Province. The landing was in support of the 173rd Airborne Brigade, then engaged in Operation TOLEDO, a search-and-destroy mission to deprive the enemy of valuable caches of arms and supplies.[34]

The Deckhouse III naval force consisted of the amphibious ships *Iwo Jima*, *Vancouver*, and *Thomaston*, as well as the heavy cruiser *St. Paul*, destroyer *John W. Thomason*, and medium landing ship (rocket) *White River* for naval gunfire support.[35]

Deckhouse III Naval Forces

Ship	Commanding Officer
Iwo Jima (LPH-2)	Capt. Nils William Boe, USN
Vancouver (LPD-2)	Capt. Carl Mann Cruse, USN
Thomaston (LSD-28)	Capt. Franklin Taylor Stephens Jr., USN
St. Paul (CA-73)	Capt. Edward Matthew Higgins Jr., USN
John W. Thomason (DD-760)	Comdr. Jack Andrew Christensen, USN
White River (LSMR-536)	Lt. William Clifford Carlson, USN

Photo 6-14

Amphibious Ready Group, comprised of the assault helicopter carrier USS *Iwo Jima* (LPH-2), USS *Thomaston* (LSD-28), and USS *Vancouver* (LPD-2), 4 January 1967. National Archives photograph #USN 1119682

The ultimate results of the operation, which ended on 22 August, were disappointing: only two enemy killed at the cost of four Marines dead and twenty-one wounded. Intelligence indicated that the area had been under control of the Viet Cong for at least one year. The headquarters for the Viet Cong 5th Division was located in the May Tao Secret Zone—a heavily forested area at the intersection of Long Khanh, Phuoc Tuy, and Binh Tuy Provinces, which served as a Viet Cong sanctuary. Also based there were two main force regiments, the 274th and 275th, each with three battalions. However, the Viet Cong either escaped the area, or were successful in avoiding the amphibious forces.[36]

BATTLE OF LONG TAN

During the conduct of DECKHOUSE III, heavy contact was made by the 1st Australian Task Force with the Viet Cong 275th Main Force Regiment and D445 Local Force Battalion. Operating from a newly established base at Nui Dat in Phuoc Tuy Province, the Task Force consisted of two (and after 1967, three) infantry battalions, a troop and later a squadron of Armoured Personnel Carriers from the 1 APC Sqn., and a detachment of the Special Air Service Regiment (SASR).[37]

Photo 6-15

Painting by Bruce Fletcher of a reconstruction of the Battle of Long Tan, Vietnam, 18 August 1966, between Delta Company and Viet Cong forces; several events that happened at intervals during the battle are depicted occurring simultaneously. Image courtesy of Wikimedia Commons

In response to a Viet Cong attack on the base during the night of 17 August 1966, Delta Company of the 6th Battalion, Royal Australian Regiment encountered a large enemy force in a rubber plantation, not far from the small village of Long Tan, on 18 August. Attacked on three flanks by a regimental-sized VC force, 108 Australian and New Zealand soldiers, under Maj. Harry Smith, fought for their lives in torrential rain against an estimated 2,500 enemy. Eighteen Australians lost their lives and twenty-four were wounded during the prolonged combat. After the battle, the bodies of 245 enemy soldiers were found, as well as evidence of the remains of many others having been carried away.

Supported by artillery fire from a base only three miles away, Delta Company held its ground for three hours, while exacting massive casualties on a tenacious and determined enemy. (Fire support was provided by three batteries of 1 Field Regiment sited at Nui Dat, complemented by a battery of medium artillery from the U.S. Army 2/35th Artillery Battalion. Some 3,500 rounds were fired during the battle by the allied forces.) Additional 6th Battalion forces arriving in armoured vehicles on the battlefield at dusk, inflicted further casualties and forced the enemy to withdraw.[39]

Lyndon B. Johnson awarded Delta Company a Presidential Unit Citation and the Australian Government conferred the Australian Unit Citation for Gallantry to D Company in 2009. A number of members also received individual decorations, medals and awards:

Distinguished Service Order (DSO)
Brigadier David Jackson
Lieutenant Colonel Colin Townsend

Member of the Order of the British Empire (MBE)
Captain Maurice 'Morrie' Stanley (NZ)

Military Cross (MC)
Major Harry Smith

Distinguished Conduct Medal (DCM)
Warrant Officer 2 Jack Kirby
Corporal J. Carter

Military Medal (MM)
Sergeant Bob Buick
Private Ron Eglington

Mentioned in Despatches (MID)
Lieutenant Adrian Roberts
Second Lieutenant Geoff Kendall
Second Lieutenant Dave Sabben
Warrant Officer 2 Jack Roughley[40]
Corporal Phil Dobson
Corporal W. R. Moore
Private Bill Akell

Australians commemorate Vietnam Veterans Day on 18 August every year. The day was originally known as Long Tan Day, chosen to honor the men of Delta Company.[41]

I hope that readers will permit a slight detour before resuming Deckhouse III material, in order to pay tribute to an equally heroic Royal Australian Navy unit, which supported ground forces in Vietnam.

RAN HELICOPTER FLIGHT VIETNAM

The Royal Australian Navy played a significant role in Vietnam, with some 13,500 personnel serving there during the war. The ex-aircraft carrier HMAS *Sydney* is well remembered as the 'Vung Tau Ferry,' completing twenty-five trips to Vietnam as a troop and transport carrier. Destroyers HMAS *Hobart, Perth, Brisbane,* and *Vendetta* distinguished themselves on the gunline off the coast. Clearance Divers kept ships and harbors free from mines, and cleared estuaries and rivers of underwater obstacles and explosives. The escort vessels of the RAN and supply ships quietly and efficiently carried out their duties, as the logistic support teams, medical and humanitarian services did also. A lesser known aspect of RAN service in Vietnam was the Royal Australian Navy Helicopter Flight Vietnam (RANHFV).[42]

86   Chapter 6

Official crest of Royal Australian Navy Helicopter Flight Vietnam, and an unofficial patch designed and worn by members of the U.S. Army 135th Assault Helicopter Company, of which RAN Navy Helicopter Flight Vietnam was a part.

The soldiers of D Company could have used some assistance that day from RAN Helicopter Flight Vietnam, which was yet to arrive in country. Royal Australian Navy Helicopter Flight Vietnam was specially formed on 14 July 1967 for service in support of allied forces during the Vietnam War. The first contingent arrived in Vietnam on 16 October 1967, and was quickly integrated with the U.S. Army 135th Assault Helicopter Company (AHC) flying the ubiquitous Iroquois helicopters in both the utility and gun-ship configurations.[43]

Photo 6-16

UH-1D gunships of the 135th Assault Helicopter Company.
Courtesy of Hector Donahue

The 135th AHC, based at Vung Tau, became fully operational and flew its first mission on 3 November 1967. By the end of November, the company had flown 3,182 hours in support of the U.S. Army 9th Infantry Division and the 1st Australian Task Force based at Nui Dat. The usual daily commitment was one UH-1H command and control helicopter, four UH-1C gunships, and ten slicks (unarmed choppers).[44]

Some 200 personnel in four annual contingents were deployed from September 1967 to June 1971 and, flying in support of the South Vietnamese, unquestionably saw the most intense combat of any RAN personnel in the war. The integration of Royal Australian Navy personnel with the 135th Assault Helicopter Company came to an end in mid-1971 as a result of the United States policy of disengagement, and associated training of the South Vietnamese to assume responsibility for their own defence.[45]

Forty-six years after it was disbanded, the RAN Helicopter Flight Vietnam war awarded the Unit Citation for Gallantry. As its name implies, this award is presented to selected Australian Defence Force units for acts of extraordinary gallantry in action.[46]

DECKHOUSE III, PHASE II

Following its attack on the Australians on 18 August, the 275th VC Regiment was believed to have withdrawn east and northeast. The new mission of the ARG/SLF was to conduct a waterborne and heliborne amphibious assault, twelve miles south of the original assault beach, in order to carry out search-and-destroy operations, and establish blocking positions on the east bank of the Rai River. Intelligence indicated that a good percentage of the 5th VC Division was comprised of North Vietnamese Army (NVA) personnel. The NVA 721st Anti-aircraft Company had been infiltrating from the Cambodia border area for the past few months and integrating with 5th Division units.[47]

The combined assault began at 0800 on 22 August and ended in late afternoon on the 29th upon completion of the withdrawal. The operation was launched with seaborne forces landing on Green beach, and a helicopter-lifted assault force in Landing Zone Dove. The assault area was characterized by jungle, swamps, and brush covered plains. Interestingly, the most compelling combat occurred before the assault, between the submarine *Perch* and Viet Cong ashore.[48]

PERCH'S WAR

On 20 August, *Perch* was called upon to conduct clandestine beach surveys, using her fourteen-man detachment from UDT 11 to identify a suitable landing site for the amphibious assault two days later. In preparation for the assault, three rubber IBS (small inflatable boats) filled with frogmen slipped ashore that night and carried out their tasking. The only excitement was some artillery fire from a nearby South Korean army unit, unaware of the landing party's presence. The following night, the 21st, another UDT group was launched. This time, the Viet Cong were lying in wait. From their ambush position they could not accurately pinpoint the frogmen's position in the darkness, and their recoilless rifle fire was ineffective. The team completed the survey. But, in the confusion, the scout swimmers became separated from the other UDT members.[49]

Photo 6-17

Amphibious transport submarine USS *Perch* (LPSS-313) off Hawaii, November 1966. U.S. Navy photograph by PH2 C. A. Komperda

A search party was sent from *Perch*. A short time later, the original group, including the scout swimmers, were recovered by the submarine, which then lay on the surface about 2,000 yards offshore. The search party, however, failed to return. Lt. Ron Seiple, commanding the UDT detachment, and two of his men, launched another boat to find the missing party. Halfway to shore, Seiple ignited a flare to signal to the search party his position. The light it generated spurred shouts from the party, and small arms-fire from Viet Cong on shore.[50]

As Seiple and his men paddled toward the voices, Lt. Comdr. Tom Dykers Jr., *Perch*'s commanding officer, brought the submarine in as close as water depth allowed. Seiple and his boat crew retrieved their fellow UDT, and they returned aboard the submarine as *Perch*'s deck gunners took the enemy under fire with .50-caliber machine guns mounted on the conning tower. The submarine then withdrew seaward. This action was only a primer for what would follow.[51]

During the first two recons, an 85-man South Vietnamese Army (AVRN) force had been inland of the beach to provide protection for the frogmen. As Viet Cong were now moving into the area, they could not return to a friendly base (find sanctuary) before dark, and requested to be berthed aboard *Perch* for the night. This was not possible, owing to space limitations inside the submarine. As an alternative, Dykers ferried the soldiers to the site to be surveyed the following day. Upon arrival, he anchored *Perch* 500 yards offshore in order to provide protection for the AVRN with his deck gun, following their movement ashore.[52]

As darkness fell, Viet Cong were seen moving into positions around the AVRN beach force. It's unclear to the author whether *Perch* was off Brown Beach or adjacent Green Beach, where the assault landings were ultimately made. In any case, both offered much concealment to enemy forces. The 1,100-meter shoreline of Brown Beach was slightly concave. Rocks extended out into the surf from a rocky point at which its right flank terminated. Its left flank ended at a less-defined sandy point. Partly drying shoals, extending as far seaward as fifteen miles, made for a challenging approach to the beach. Sparse brush-covered dunes, immediately rearward of the beach, extended inland about 600 meters. Behind the dunes was dense vegetation.[53]

Green Beach, which lay to the right of the rocky point of Brown Beach, had the same general characteristics. The seaward approaches were unrestricted. However, the beach was backed by massive dunes which dropped off sharply to dense vegetation.[54]

Perch's crew were at battle stations and, upon sighting enemy movement on shore, Dykers ordered the 40mm deck gun crew to fire on the Viet Cong, assembling on the right and left flanks of the ARVN position. An initial and a secondary explosion were observed, believed to have resulted from a hit on an ammunition cache. At first light, Dykers sent in seven motorized-rubber boats to bring the ARVN troops aboard. With them, were nine government sympathizers who, had they remained ashore, would likely have been killed. These civilians were transferred to a Swift boat on patrol in the area.[55]

Once this had been accomplished, *Perch* approached the beach on the surface, where the VC had dug in, in anticipation of the submarine's return. Dykers called for air strikes, then closed to within 1,100 yards of the beach and ordered his .50-caliber and 40mm gunners to open on the enemy emplacements. With each pass, strikes by A-1E Skyraider bombers forced the VC from their foxholes, who then became targets for *Perch*'s guns. Following sufficient attrition of the enemy, Lieutenant Seiple led two waves of motorized rubber boats, filled with UDT and ARVN soldiers, on a mini-amphibious assault of the beach.[56]

After securing the area, and capturing two prisoners, the UDT completed the beach survey as planned. This is believed to be the last surface combat action involving a U.S. submarine. Seiple was awarded the Bronze Star for his actions, and Dykers the Navy Commendation Medal with Combat V device. The crew of the *Perch* termed their fire fights with the Viet Cong, "*Perch*'s War."[57]

DECKHOUSE IV

> *The BLT was opposed by NVA regular troops that fought using conventional tactics. There was little attempt on the part of the enemy to evade our forces. They had prepared positions and waited for the BLT forces to come within range. Fire support was outstanding once all units were ashore and prepared to fire.*
>
> *Naval gunfire support played an important role in the operation, accounting for a significant number of enemy dead and wounded.... The USS ST PAUL (CA-73) provided excellent support, [fire from] her 8" guns being called in as close as 200 yards to friendly lines during the one enemy assault. The enthusiasm and spirit, coupled with good shooting, of the Naval ships, was a significant factor in success of the operation.*
>
> —Observations made by Lt. Col. Anthony A. Monti, USMC, commanding officer, Battalion Landing Team 1/26, in a combat-after-action report for Operation DECKHOUSE IV/PRAIRIE.[58]

The Marines of Battalion Landing Team 1/26 went into action once again on 15 September 1966, this time for DECKHOUSE IV. The mission of the ARG/SLF team for this operation was essentially the same as previous ones in the Deckhouse series:

> Conduct waterborne amphibious assault over Beach BLUE and helicopterborne assault into selected landing zones to conduct

search and destroy operations and screen northern approaches to AOA [area of operations] in support of Operation PRAIRIE.[59]

In preparation for the assault landing on 15 September, two UDT 12 platoons operating from *Perch*, and one from the high-speed transport *Diachenko* performed two separate clandestine recons in the vicinity of the mouth of the Cua Viet River. (DECKHOUSE IV would prove to be *Perch*'s last combat mission. Replaced by the *Tunny*, *Perch* would operate out of Pearl Harbor in Hawaiian waters until 1967 when she became a Naval Reserve Training submarine based in San Diego. After nearly twenty-seven years of service, she was decommissioned and struck from the Naval Register on 1 December 1971.)[60]

Photo 6-18

Two LCM landing craft lay to off the dock landing ship USS *Thomaston* (LSD-28) waiting to begin Operation DECKHOUSE IV on 15 September 1966.
Defense Department photograph Marine Corps K-33207-NPC

The location selected for the landing was a 1 ½-mile-long straight beach, designated "Blue," composed of soft sand, which was firm when wet. The area of operations was within the Central Vietnam lowlands. The lowlands originated in the foothills of the Annam Mountains and terminated at the coast in a wide belt of massive dunes and low sandy shores, except where broken by river mouths and lagoons. The Hieu Giang and Thach Ham rivers, flowing down from the mountains, were the major tributaries which formed the Cua Viet River. Seventy-three-foot "Mike boats" (LCM-8s) could navigate the Cua Viet from its mouth to where it joined the Thach Hau; from there to Quang Tri, only 36-foot landing craft could proceed.[61]

D-Day for DECKHOUSE IV was 15 September. The operation ended at noon on 18 September, when BLT 1/26 came under the operational control of the 4th Marines to participate in Operation PRAIRIE. The landings constituted a seaward arm of the other, much larger operation being carried out by American and South Vietnamese forces ashore; to destroy North Vietnamese Army fortifications, bunkers, and supply caches; and stem intensified infiltration across the DMZ. The amphibious group remained off the coast, until withdrawal of the Special Landing Force in mid-afternoon on 25 September.[62]

Amphibious Ready Group (Task Group 76.5)
BLT 1/26, HMM-363

Ship	Commanding Officer
Iwo Jima (LPH-2)	Capt. Nils William Boe, USN
Vancouver (LPD-2)	Capt. Carl Mann Cruse, USN
Thomaston (LSD-28)	Capt. Franklin Taylor Stephens Jr., USN
St. Paul (CA-73)	Capt. Harry Frederick Fischer Jr., USN
Oklahoma City (CLG-5)	Capt. Kendall Washburn Simmons, USN
Hull (DD-945)	Comdr. Robert Eugene Weeks, USN
Diachenko (APD-123)	Lt. Comdr. Donald Moderl Metzler, USN
St. Francis River (LSMR-525)	Lt. Frederick N. Mangol, USN

During the ten days the Marines were ashore, the dock landing ship *Thomaston* served as primary control ship and boat haven while staging boat convoys carrying supplies nine miles up the Cua Vet River to Dong Ha. Called upon to refuel helicopters from the *Iwo Jima*, the transport dock *Vancouver* assumed the task of primary helicopter refueling ship, which required all-day flight operations during the assault. Aircraft from Marine Medium Helicopter Squadron 363 (HMM-363) launched from *Iwo Jima* lifted Marines into strike zones ashore, and carried out resupply and medevac missions. Later missions included the extraction of forces, picking up U.S. WIA and KIA and returning them to the ship, and transporting five Viet Cong prisoners to Lai An.[63]

COMBAT ASHORE

During operations ashore, the Marines of BLT 1/26 made substantial contact with elements of the 324th B Division, exacting a heavy toll in Viet Cong casualties. Enemy activity was characterized by the use of heavy mortar and automatic weapons fire, in addition to 57mm anti-tank weapons. In one area, an extensive trench, bunker, and tunnel system was encountered. Such positions were used by the enemy to delay and harass friendly units. However, heavy supporting fire forced the enemy to flee north from these positions into the DMZ.[64]

The landing on 15 September, two miles south of the Demilitarized Zone was unopposed, but later that day, division recon encountered an estimated company-size unit. Contact was broken after four hours when supporting fire forced the enemy, wearing black and khaki uniforms, to withdraw. In late afternoon the following day (D+1), Company Bravo received small arms-fire from an estimated 30-40 enemy. Contact was broken after fifty minutes due, once again, to supporting fire. At approximately the same time, Company Delta took small arms-fire from 12 to 20 enemy. Artillery fire was called, and contact was broken. Company D and helicopters then received fire from a village, causing one helicopter to land. Air strikes were called and the fire ceased.[65]

Photo 6-19

Heavy cruiser USS *St. Paul* (CA-73) under way, date and location unknown. Naval History and Heritage Command photograph #L45-248.07.01

Fire support was provided for the battalion landing team by a 105mm howitzer battery, a 107mm howitzer battery, the USS *St. Paul* and USS *Hull*, and by close air support from the 1st Marine Air Wing. In early morning on D+2 (17 September), A Company was attacked by a company-size unit. The enemy, wearing helmets and grass camouflage uniforms, were forced to retreat under supporting arms fire. Contact initiated by the enemy lessened, but probes of friendly positions, harassing small arms-fire, and mortar fire were experienced throughout the operation.[66]

AUTUMN AND YEAR'S END ACTIVITIES

Following DECKHOUSE IV, BLT 3/26 (Lt. Col. Garland T. Beyerle) replaced BLT 1/26, and HMM-362 (Lt. Col. Marshall B. Armstrong) relieved HMM-363. Concern that a major enemy thrust could occur in the DMZ, resulted in a Marine BLT remaining afloat off the northern coast of South Vietnam from October through November 1966. In December, another change occurred in SLF composition when BLT 1/9 (Maj. James L. Day) relieved BLT 3/36. In a separate, but related action, planning was begun for DECKHOUSE V, which was to take place in the Mekong Delta in early 1967.[67]

7

Operation DECKHOUSE V, January 1967

Photo 7-1

An LVTH6A1 amphibious tractor moves shoreward from USS *Coconino County* (LST-603) during Operation DECKHOUSE V. National Archives photograph #USN 1142237

With the exception of DECKHOUSE V (6-15 January), all ARG/SLF operations in 1967 took place in I Corps. As the year broke, there were diverse opinions within the many command levels of the U.S. Armed Forces, regarding the appropriate use of the unique striking force. Within the III Marine Amphibious Force, Marine division and wing commanders wanted control of their battalions and squadrons, which were siphoned off to man the Special Landing Force.[1]

Military Assistance Command Vietnam, and Marine Amphibious Force commanders did not want troops floating off the coast when they could be "in country" and, probably, in contact. On the plus side, the Marines in the SLF did not count against "in country" authorized troop strength and, at minimum, served as a source of reinforcements for land-based forces following commitment of a division's reserve.[2]

As commanders debated what Marine units would provide the SLF with landing forces, and where they would be used, other changes were taking place. In January 1967, the Amphibious Ready Group gained assignment of a tank landing ship (LST), bringing the ARG ship total to five. The other members were an amphibious helicopter assault ship (LPH), a transport dock (LPD), an attack transport (APA), and a dock landing ship (LSD).[3]

In separate, but related actions, the Joint Chiefs of Staff authorized the formation of a second SLF, and directed commitment of the SLFs to extended operations in Vietnam. Neither of these decisions were meant to restrict the areas in which landings took place. Nevertheless, challenges associated with the provision of logistic support would result in SLF operations becoming a purely I Corps function.[4]

Map 7-1

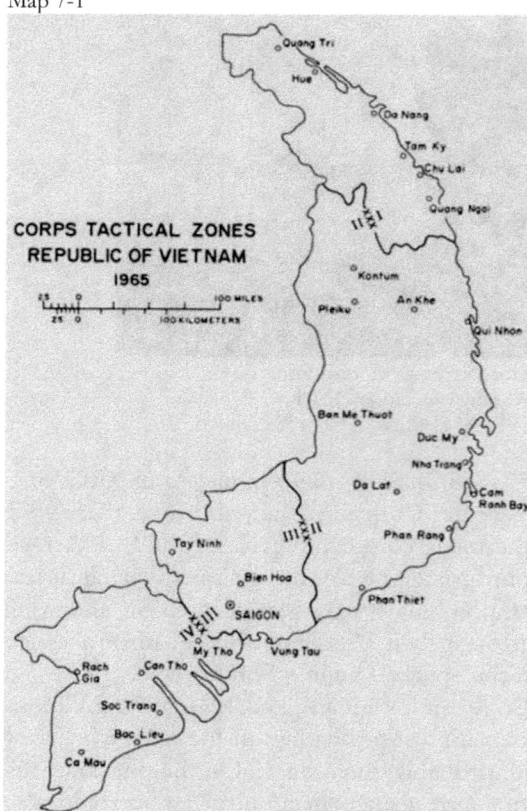

I, II, III, and IV Corps Tactical Zones in South Vietnam

OPERATION DECKHOUSE V

Photo 7-2

Briefing of Marines aboard the tank landing ship USS *Coconino County* (LST-603), in preparation for Operation DECKHOUSE V.
National Archives photograph #K-35611

DECKHOUSE V was both the first SLF operation of 1967, and the first combined U.S./Vietnamese amphibious landing in the Mekong Delta. It was also regrettably—for proponents of the SLF concept— the last landing to take place beyond the boundaries of I Corps. In preparation for D-Day, the ARG (under Capt. John D. Westervelt) proceeded south to the coast of Kien Hoa Province in IV Corps. Comprising Col. Harry D. Wortman's Special Landing Force were BLT 1/9 (Maj. James L. Day) and HMM-362 (Col. Marshall B. Armstrong).[5]

The assault against the Thanh Phong Secret Zone in Kien Hoa Province (a suspected Viet Cong coastal enclave between the Co Chien and Ham Luong rivers) was scheduled for 4 January, but had to be delayed until the morning of the 6th, due to adverse weather. In support of the landing by the 1st Battalion, 9th Marines, *Washtenaw County*, *Coconino County*, and *St. Francis River* conducted the first seaward penetration of the Co Chien River. HMM-362's UH-34 and CH-46 helicopters operating from the *Iwo Jima* lifted the remainder of the Battalion Landing Team and elements of Vietnamese Marine Brigade Force Bravo (primarily the 3rd and 4th battalions).[6]

Amphibious Ready Group and Naval Gunfire Support Ships

Ship	Commanding Officer
Iwo Jima (LPH-2)	Capt. Nils William Boe, USN
	Capt. Francis Xavier Timmes, USN
Vancouver (LPD-2)	Capt. Carl Mann Cruse, USN
Henrico (APA-45)	Capt. Harlan Dale Williams, USN
Thomaston (LSD-28)	Capt. John W. O'Neill, USN
Coconino County (LST-603)	Lt. Timothy Parks Dugan Jr., USN
Washtenaw County (LST-1166)	Lt. Comdr. Alfred John Dillon, USN
Canberra (CAG-2)	Capt. Edwin Miller Rosenberg, USN
St. Francis River (LSMR-525)	
USCGC *Pt. Kennedy* (WPB-82320)	

ADDITIONAL SUPPORT

Operation MARKET TIME units provided exfiltration patrols prior to and during the landings, and helped guide tank landing (LSTs) and rocket ships (LSMRs) into the shallow and unmarked channels of the Co Chien and Ham Luong rivers. PBRs were staged at the Vietnamese Navy Coastal Group 35 base on the Co Chien, and the 34/37 base on the Ham Luong, to provide blocking forces against possible enemy escape by water. Helicopters of HC-1 (Detachment 29) operated from Tra Vinh because the poor weather prevented their flying from the tank landing ship *Jennings County* (LST-846).[7]

UNSPECTACULAR RESULTS AMID DIFFICULTIES

Operation DECKHOUSE V, which lasted until 15 January, produced unspectacular results. The Marines encountered only local force Viet Cong, although prisoners stated that larger VC units had been in the area before the landings. Captain Westervelt was later told that a Philippine radio station had broadcast information that the Marines were headed for the Mekong Delta, when the ARG departed Subic Bay.[8]

In addition to the scarcity of enemy forces encountered, other difficulties marred the execution of the operation. These included poor communications, rough seas, hurried planning, and the necessity for the 4th Battalion, VNMC, to endure a near-record, ship-to-shore landing-craft-movement of twenty-three miles. Captain Westervelt described these difficulties:

> The Navy aspects of the Deckhouse V landings were formidable. Normal operating depths of water for the LPH, LPD and other deep draft ships in the Amphibious Ready Group were about 8 to 10 miles to seaward off the coastal areas of Kien Hoa between the Co Chien and Ham Luong rivers. The 8-inch gun cruiser *Canberra*

had a fire support station some eight miles, as I recall, from the impact areas for her pre-assault bombardment. Water depths adequate for LST and rocket ship passage over the shallow bar into positions for the assault landings [were] obtained only at high tide. Because an early morning landing time was required for the Marine assault forces in the LVT5 vehicles, this meant that, to protect the surprise features of the landings, the LST's and rocket ships had to proceed over the bar late in the preceding evening at high tide to be in position by dawn....

The long distance off-shore required by the principal ARG ships plus the fact that some landing beaches were well upstream from the seaward beaches accounted for the long boat rides (up to 23 miles) required for some of the troops.

The seas were very rough on the original D-Day (4 Jan) and again on 5 Jan, so the actual D-Day on 6 Jan was 2 days late. However, even on the 6th it was not possible to load the [Vietnamese Marines] from the *Henrico* into LCM6's alongside, so *Henrico*, *Thomaston* and *Vancouver* returned to Vung Tau, transferred *Henrico*'s troops to the LPD and LSD so loading could take place in the well decks. The [Vietnamese Marines] actually landed on the 7th.[9]

Photo 7-3

Two LCMs from USS *Vancouver* (LPD-2), an LCU, and a Coast Guard patrol boat transport troops up the Co Chien River, in the Mekong Delta Region as part of Operation DECKHOUSE V, February 1967. A UH-1B helicopter is overhead. National Archives photograph #USN 1120882

Problems were encountered at higher command levels as well. Amphibious doctrine called for the task force commander to control all aircraft in the amphibious operations area. Normally, these aircraft would come from the Navy and Marine Corps. However, the geographical location of Deckhouse V created special circumstances which dictated that all air support come from the Seventh Air Force.

Its commander, Maj. Gen. William W. Momyer, USAF, agreed with Navy control of aircraft in a traditional amphibious assault against a hostile shore. However, with an Air Force air control system already in place in the Mekong Delta, he saw no reason to change it because an amphibious force was temporarily operating in the area. Fortunately, since all future SLF operations were to be in the I Corps area, these complicated command relationships could be avoided.[10]

U.S NAVY TASK FORCES 115, 116, AND 117

Photo 7-4

Painting *Operation Market Time* by Gene Klebe, 1965, depicting the inspection of an indigenous craft in South Vietnamese coastal waters.
Naval History and Heritage Command accession #88-162-K

Up to this point in the book, the coverage of amphibious ships has largely been limited to those assigned to the ARG. Before proceeding further with remaining SLF activities (which will resume in Chapter 11) a review of the Navy's three major task forces in Vietnam is in order. The task forces came into existence sequentially as new requirements were identified, for which the unique capabilities needed did not exist. The first such was a coastal surveillance force.

Task Force 115 (Coastal Surveillance Force) had been established on 30 April 1965 to stem the infiltration of weapons, ammunition, and other war materials into South Vietnam by sea. In support of Operation

MARKET TIME, the U.S. Navy deployed U.S. Navy and U.S. Coast Guard destroyer escorts, ocean minesweepers, cutters, coastal craft, and patrol planes along the country's 1,200-mile coastline.[11]

As war materials flowed into the Mekong Delta from Cambodia, Task Force 116 (River Patrol Force) was stood up on 18 December 1965. To interdict these supplies, 31-foot river patrol boats (PBRs), assisted by armed helicopters, were charged with plying South Vietnam waterways to limit the enemy's use of larger rivers. The code name of this operation was GAME WARDEN.[12]

Photo 7-5

USS *Garrett County* (LST-786) on the Co Chien River, Mekong Delta, in June 1968, while providing support for five PBRs and two UH-1Bs of Operation GAME WARDEN. National Archives photograph #K-51442

By 1966, U.S. troops were committed in large numbers to three of the four corps areas of Vietnam, with only a small number of troops in IV Corps, the Mekong Delta region. This was because: the military situation was not as critical as in the other corps areas; there were no tracts of land where a large military installation could be constructed, without dislocating large numbers of people; and the numerous rivers, streams, and canals which dissected the Delta, severely restricted ground movement. Regarding the latter, military planners were reluctant to commit U.S. troops to the Delta until a solution was found to the mobility problem.[13]

Despite these challenges, the U.S. Army identified fairly early in 1966, a need to insert troops in the Mekong Delta to counter growing communist strength. Joint Army and Navy planning began for the establishment of a Mekong Delta Mobile Afloat Force. On 1 September, River Assault Flotilla One was commissioned at Navy Amphibious Base, Coronado, in California. Commanded by Capt. Wade C. Wells, USN, the flotilla would later expand and receive the concurrent designation Task Force 117 (Mobile Riverine Force). The purpose of the MRF was to locate, surround, and destroy main force Communist combat units in the Delta.[14]

Photo 7-6

U.S. Navy monitor *M-91-1*, a unit of the Mobile Riverine Force (MRF) patrols one of the many rivers that lace the Mekong Delta. Units assigned to the MRF were painted green to make them less noticeable on the jungle-lined Delta rivers.
National Archives photograph #USN 1125095

FORTHCOMING INTRODUCTORY CHAPTERS

The following three chapters introduce the Mobile Riverine Force (Chapter 8), the sixty-two LSTs that served in Vietnam (Chapter 9), and the River Patrol Force (Chapter 10).

8

Establishment of the Mobile Riverine Force

Photo 8-1

An armored transport carrier offloads U.S. Army personnel in the Rung Sat, near Vung Tau during a training exercise. These troops were operating from the USS *Whitfield County* (LST-1169), 13 February 1967.
National Archives photograph #K-36113

On 7 January 1967, the first units of the newly established Riverine Assault Force arrived at Vung Tau aboard the tank landing ship *Whitfield County* (LST-1169). Three days later, commander, River Assault Squadron Nine, his staff, and River Assault Division 91 began training operations off Vung Tau in River Assault Group (RAG) boats on loan from the Vietnamese Navy (VNN). These naval units were joined by elements of the U.S. Army Ninth Infantry Division on 15 January. Shortly after, landing exercises and training began.[1]

Squadron Nine staff were assigned to VNN River Assault Groups in the Rung Sat Special Zone and the Mekong Delta as technical observers. The training they oversaw was intended to acquaint U.S. Army and Navy personnel with the environment in which they would be operating, and familiarize them with local customs and regulations, and rules of engagement.[2]

Photo 8-2

VNN River Assault Group LCM under way on a South Vietnam river, with a full load of troops, circa 1966. This landing craft had been converted for this employment, with living accommodations for a crew of seven forward of the engine compartment, machine gun positions, and a canvas canopy over the cargo space.
Naval History and Heritage Command photograph #NH 43013

MOBILE RIVERINE FORCE (TF 117) COMPOSITION

Photo 8-3

Capt. Wade C. Wells, USN (commander, Mobile Riverine Force), Adm. U. S. G. Sharp, USN (commander in chief, Pacific), and Rear Adm. Kenneth L. Veth, USN (commander, Naval Forces Vietnam), aboard USS *Benewah* (APB-35), November 1967. Naval History and Heritage Command photograph #NH 74283

Commander, Naval Forces Vietnam, activated Task Force 117 under Capt. Wade C. Wells on 28 February 1967. River Assault Squadron Eleven arrived at Vung Tau in March, joining River Assault Squadron Nine. By June, support ship *Kemper County* (LST-854), barracks ships *Benewah* (APB-35) and *Colleton* (APB-36), and other vessels had arrived to round out the Navy's MRF Contingent.[3]

River Assault Flotilla One (Task Force 117)

River Assault Squadron Nine (Task Group 117.1)		River Assault Squadron Eleven (Task Group 117.2)	
River Assault Division 91	River Assault Division 92	River Assault Division 111	River Assault Division 112
13 ATC	13 ATC	13 ATC	13 ATC
3 Monitor	2 Monitor	3 Monitor	2 Monitor
1 CCB	1 CCB	1 CCB	1 CCB
8 ASPB	8 ASPB	8 ASPB	8 ASPB
	1 Refueler		1 Refueler
EOD Team		EOD Team	

River Support Squadron Seven (Task Group 117.3)
Benewah (APB-35), *Colleton* (APB-36), *APL-26*, *Askari* (ARL-30), Support LST (1156-class), *Kalispell* (YTB-784) and *Winnemucca* (YTB-785) Support and salvage craft as assigned

APB:	328-foot self-propelled barracks ship
APL:	Non self-propelled barracks craft
ARL:	327-foot landing craft repair ship (ex-LST)
ASPB:	50-foot assault support patrol boat
ATC:	56-foot armored troop carriers (modified LCM-6 landing craft)
CCB:	61-foot command communications boat
Monitor:	60 or 61-foot heavily-armed craft
YTB:	Large harbor tug

MOBILE RIVERINE FORCE COMMAND STRUCTURE

The architects of the MRF envisioned that it would support an infantry brigade and an artillery battalion using a variety of modified landing craft, support ships, and specially designed assault boats. The strike unit would function essentially as a self-contained amphibious assault force, complete with all support elements except aircraft. Marines would have been the ideal ground component, being specialists in amphibious warfare. However, they were heavily committed in I Corps and unavailable. Thus, a brigade from the 9th Infantry Division would serve as the infantry component of the Mobile Riverine Force.[4]

In addition to transporting infantry and artillery, heavily armed and armored river craft of the naval component of the Mobile Riverine Force would also provide gunfire support for operations ashore. As finally organized, the Mobile Riverine Force consisted of the 2nd Brigade of the 9th Infantry Division and a Navy element under the overall direction of commander, U.S. Military Assistance Command Vietnam. Commanding General, II Field Force Vietnam, exercised operational control of the Army contingent, and commander, Naval Forces Vietnam, the naval component.[5]

SUBSEQUENT EXPANSION AND REORGANIZATION

The MRF was augmented in mid-1968 by the 3rd Brigade, and two additional River Assault Squadrons (Thirteen and Fifteen, established on 14 April 1968 and 11 May 1968, respectively). Upon their joining in early summer, the Mobile Riverine Force was reorganized into Mobile Riverine Group Alfa (Squadrons 9 and 11), and Group Bravo (Squadrons 13 and 15). Each River Assault Squadron was further divided into two river assault divisions.[6]

Each squadron boasted a powerful fleet of five monitors—the "battleships of the Brown Water Navy." The converted landing craft were protected by armor and equipped with .50-caliber, 40mm, and 20mm gun mounts, two 40mm grenade launchers, and an 81mm mortar. Two or three similarly armed and armored 61-foot craft served as command and control boats (CCB). Twenty-six armored troop carriers (modified LCM-6 landing craft) armed with .50-caliber machine guns, rapid fire Mk-19 grenade launchers, and 20mm cannon transported the Riverine Infantry. The craft were also fitted with flame throwers or water cannons to destroy enemy bunkers. Lastly, a modified troop carrier functioned as a refueler for the river force.[7]

Photo 8-4

A Monitor transiting the Mang Thit Canal, Mekong Delta, South Vietnam, June 1968. National Archives photograph #K-52352

In September 1967, each squadron began receiving the first of 8-16 purpose-built assault support patrol boats (ASPBs) for minesweeping and escort duty. All of the riverine craft, with the exception of the ASPBs, were World War II-era mechanized landing craft that had been taken out of mothballs and modified for use in South Vietnam.[8]

Propelled by twin 12-cylinder diesel engines, ASPBs could make about twice the speed of the other riverine craft. The added power and maneuverability of this craft was expected to make it an excellent boat for providing covering fire. However, the riverine operations for which the ASPBs had been specifically designed revealed flaws that affected the survivability of both boat and crew. Munitions easily penetrated the craft, making duty aboard ASPBs and MSRs (ASPBs converted to river minesweepers) among the most dangerous on inland waterways.[9]

Photo 8-5

An Assault Support Patrol Boat patrolling a Mekong Delta canal during Operation CORONADO IX, November 1967. An Army CH-47 helicopter is removing equipment from the temporary artillery fire support base beyond the boat.
National Archives photograph #80-G-K-42552

RIVER SUPPORT SQUADRON SEVEN

The mixture of ships and craft comprising the support squadron of the Mobile Riverine Force included berthing barges, tugs to move non-self-propelled barracks ships (such as the *APL-26*), a landing craft repair ship, and support LSTs. Seventh Fleet tank landing ships rotated in and out of service with the MRF, delivering supplies and serving as ammunition ships.[10]

Photo 8-6

APL-26 serving as mothership for landing craft and tugs, November 1967. National Archives photograph #USN 1142272

DUTY WITH THE MOBILE RIVERINE FORCE

Capt. Robert J. Kermen, USNR (Ret.), who served as an enlisted gunner aboard *ATC-112-7* (a unit of River Assault Division 112) from November 1968 until July 1969, when the armored troop carrier was turned over to the Vietnamese Navy, later described duty aboard her. (His boat was actually the second ATC so designated. Its predecessor was destroyed by a mine in the Cua Viet River on 14 March 1968, with six crewmembers killed and another seriously wounded.)

> We lived on the boat 24 hours a day. Our bunks were metal frames with canvas stretched across them and an air mattress on top. Food consisted of Korean War-era C-rations and LRRPs, which were dehydrated meals much like today's MREs. The food was quite good once you developed a taste for it. We carried 20-30 cases of food at all times as well as several hundred gallons of drinking water. Malaria pills and salt tablets were also a necessary part of our diet. Rarely did we eat aboard the ships we tied up to. In theory, we were supposed to berth, eat, and shower aboard the ships but they were pretty crowded with the Ninth Infantry Division [soldiers] we were supporting. It was just easier to live on the boats.

The uniforms of the Mobile Riverine Force [personnel] were really used only for special events such as inspections and award presentations. Utility greens were the standard issue. Most of the time we were in dungaree or O.D. [olive drab] shorts with jungle boots or tennis shoes. Going into combat, we donned our flak jackets, flak pants, and helmets. Some sailors even wore bandanas to keep sweat from running into their eyes.

Some crews tried to individualize the appearance of their boats by adding everything from state flags to Charles Shultz cartoons. Snoopy sitting on his doghouse was common. Sayings such as "Sat Cong" [Kill Communists] appeared as well. Our officers were pretty tolerant to a point; then the hammer would come down and we would repaint the boat.

Maintenance of our boats was a constant battle in that climate and environment. Rocket hits into the cases of C-rations we carried … were constantly covering the sides of our boats with such delicacies as "beef with spice sauce," "fruit cocktail," and canned ham and eggs (no loss there!).

Cooking aboard the boats was interesting as well. While heat tablets were commonly used, some of us used C-4 explosive, which burns hot and very fast. I shudder today when I think of heating up leftovers at home using that method. C-4 was plentiful. We always had a case or two on hand for use by the Army troops we carried.

Our main mission was to carry troops into combat and insert them for search-and-destroy missions against the Viet Cong in the Mekong Delta…. We loaded troops directly off the ships and usually landed them shortly after sunrise…. The Viet Cong loved to hit us going in because they knew we were carrying troops by our draft…. After a while, these ambush points became predictable and were given names by us—Snoopy's Nose, Rocket Alley, and Blood Alley come to mind. Some of those places were located fairly close to our shore base at Dong Tam.

When we were "off the line," we hauled supplies for the Army, patrolled the Mobile Riverine Base at night, or provided waterborne security for Army artillery barges…. All night long, we would steam back and forth lobbing concussion grenades in the water to discourage swimmers. We had a two-boat patrol and alternated this security every 4 hours. One of the major disadvantages of this duty was that having the boat in long periods of contact with the riverbank allowed rats to come aboard and share our living quarters. They would hide by day and run around at night. Sometimes, they ran across your chest while you were sleeping. This provided another form of recreation. We would remove the bullets from our .38 shells and push the case into a bar of soap thus producing a "soap bullet." Great for short range and they did not ricochet.

Every night, just prior to sunset, the whole MRB, consisting of at least six ships, would shift anchorage and re-anchor after dark. This was done to prevent the VC from targeting the ships easily.

During my tour on the rivers, our boat participated in many and varied assignments. Most of the time was spent in the Delta, but we did go up to the Parrot's Beak on Operation Giant Slingshot as a support boat for the PBRs. We were stationed at Tra Cu and Go Dau Ha. This was the only place we saw blue, clear water.[11]

Photo 8-7

Bob Kermen holding an Ithaca model 37 riot gun, as the *ATC-112-7* operated near the village of My Tho, Mekong Delta, in 1969. While not the first choice for self-defense, the shotgun was the weapon of choice for searching sampans and last-minute detonation of mines floating in patches of water lilies.
Courtesy of Capt. Robert J. Kermen, USNR (Retired).

MRF RELOCATION TO SHORE BASE AT DONG TAM

Photo 8-8

Units of the Mobile Riverine Force exchange fire with enemy positions during Operation CORONADO I.
ComNavForV Monthly Historical Supplement, June 1967

On 1 June 1967, the Mobile Riverine Force left its anchorage at Vung Tau and proceeded to Dong Tam via passage up the My Tho River. Dong Tam was a large Army base carved out of the jungle, about five miles west of My Tho in Dinh Tuong Province. USS *Benewah* (APB-35), the flagship and headquarters of the Mobile Riverine Force, usually lay at anchor off Dong Tam. A detachment of two officers and four enlisted were permanently stationed there to provide administrative support to the river flotilla when its commander was absent.[12]

Riverine Assault Force units spent the first week at Dong Tam, conducting security patrols and troop lifts, and utilized assault landings as part of Operation CORONADO I (7-8 June) to refine doctrine and techniques with elements of the 2nd Brigade. The first operation in the CORONADO series took place in Dinh Tuong Province, eighteen miles west of My Tho. Contact with a reinforced enemy platoon near Ba Rai Creek on 7 June, resulted in four naval personnel being wounded. The extent of the enemy's casualties was unknown.[13]

OPERATIONS IN THE RUNG SAT SPECIAL ZONE

Map 8-1

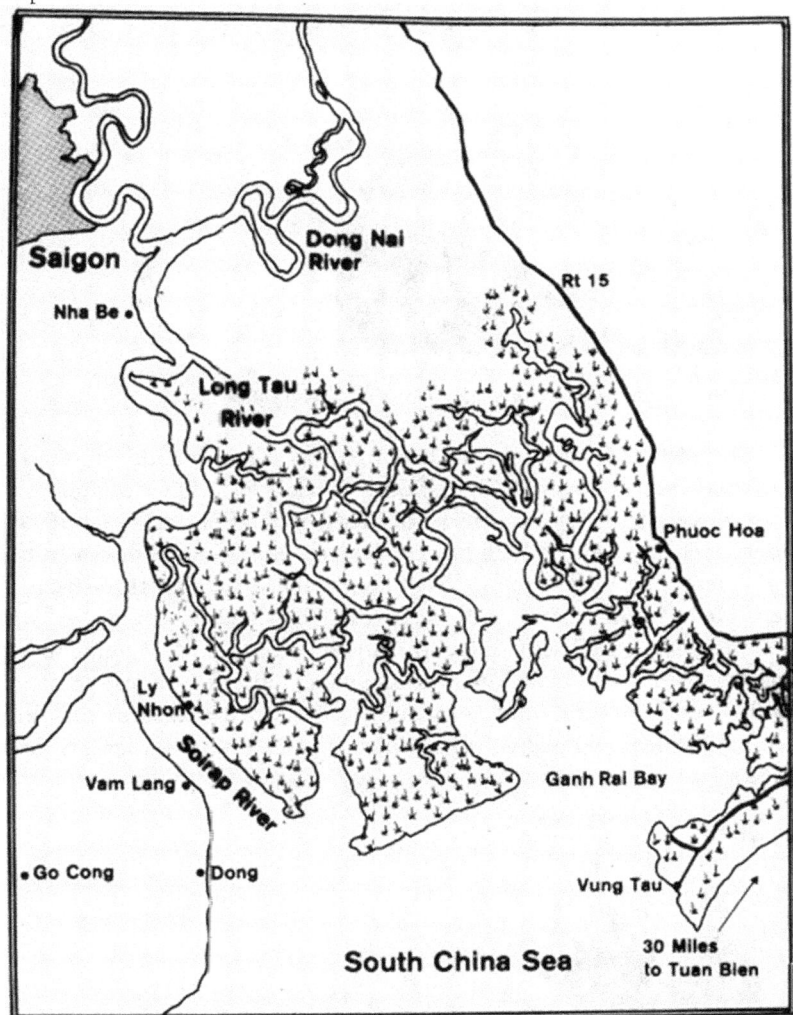

Rung Sat Special Zone. (Soirap is more commonly spelled Soi Rap.)
Naval History and Heritage Command photograph #NH 96343

On 11 June, the bulk of the MRF proceeded to a small base at Nha Be, sited at the junction of the Soi Rap and Long Tau rivers, the main waterways between the port of Saigon and the South China Sea. Located just seven miles south of Saigon, Nha Be would become a major combat and logistics hub during the course of the war. (River Assault Division 112 remained at Dong Tam to conduct local security patrols and troop lift missions throughout the month. No major contact with the enemy occurred during this period.)[14]

Photo 8-9

Game Warden Base at Nha Be, June 1967.
Naval History and Heritage Command photograph #NH 74204

The Mobile Riverine Force anchored off Nha Be and in the week that followed, conducted Operation GREAT BEND, a search-and-destroy sweep in the northern part of the Rung Sat Special Zone (RSSZ) and adjacent area of the Bien Hoa Province. Army troops discovered a large Viet Cong base camp on 16 June, in the Nhon Trach district of Bien Hoa. The camp was near the (believed) location of the headquarters of the Viet Cong commander of the RSSZ. Enemy items seized included a "claymore" (homemade, anti-personnel) mine, a number of grenades, and a quantity of assorted documents and materials—including film from which the below photograph was developed.[15]

Photo 8-10

Two Viet Cong in the Rung Sat Special Zone
Naval History and Heritage Command photograph #NH 64842

OPERATION CONCORDIA I

Diagram 8-2

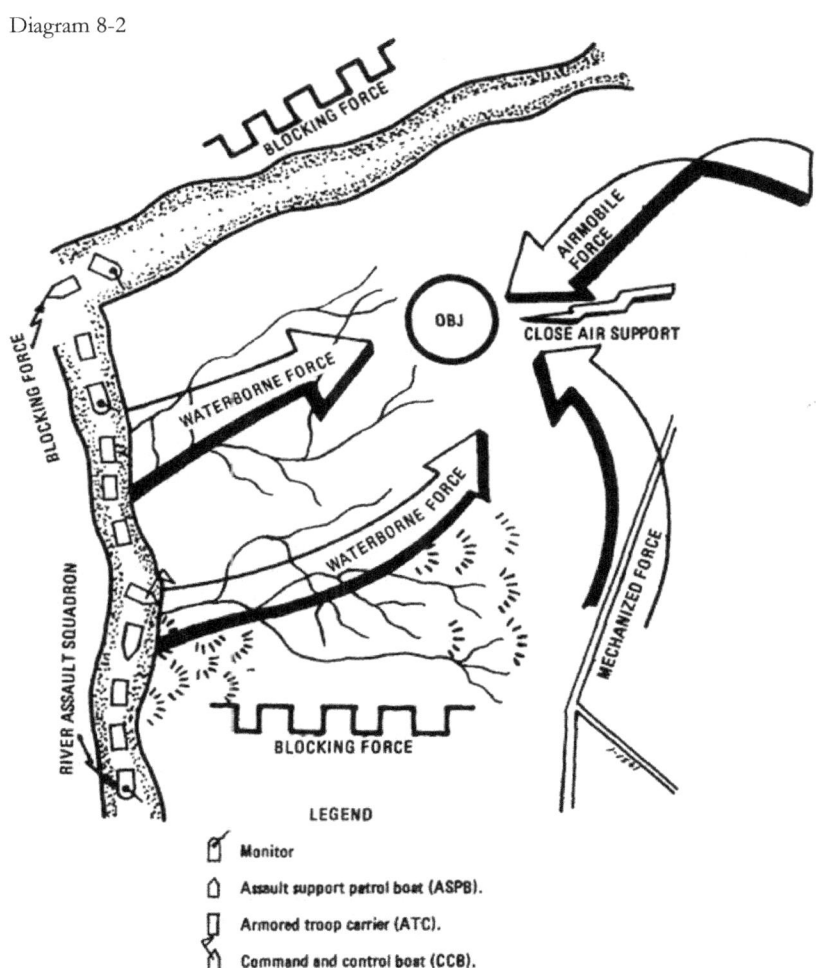

Diagram of coordinated waterborne, airmobile, and mechanized land forces during a generic combat operation involving a River Assault Squadron.
U.S. Army Riverine Warfare Field Manual FM 31-75, January 1971

Upon completion of GREAT BEND on 18 June, the MRF shifted to an anchorage near the confluence of the Vam Co and Soi Rap rivers. Operation CONCORDIA I commenced the following morning, when riverine craft landed three companies of the 4th Battalion, 47th Infantry on the banks of Van Creek. Concurrently, the 2nd Battalion of the Vietnamese Army (ARVN) landed three-and-one-half miles southwest of the 4/47th units; and two companies of the 3rd Battalion, 47th Infantry, one mile south of Can Giouc. The deployed assault forces initially formed a triangle disposition. After the troops were ashore, the Riverine Assault Force took up blocking stations at locations intended to prevent exfiltration—escape of the enemy by water routes.[16]

Intelligence gained mid-morning from a captured Viet Cong village chief revealed that three enemy companies were in place near the base of the triangle, midway between the 4/47th and ARVN positions. In response, C Company of the 4/47th was reembarked and put ashore at the junction of the Nui and Ben Via rivers. Working inland, the company came under heavy fire from entrenched enemy positions, and was pinned down in the open in a stretch of rice paddies. Eight hundred yards away, A Company of the 4/47th (moving in from the northeast to provide assistance) also began taking intense fire.[17]

Riverine Assault Force units engaged enemy emplacements in the tree lines flanking the paddies with 20mm, 40mm, machine-gun, and 81mm mortar fire, reducing the assault on the hard-pressed troops. Combat continued well into the evening, with sustained naval gunfire helping to disrupt the enemy forces. Throughout the engagement, the movements of naval units and troops ashore were coordinated between commander, River Assault Squadron Nine, and the operations officer of the 4/47th, both embarked in RAD 92's command-control boat.[18]

Designated ATCs supplied the troops and naval units with food, water and ammunition; others functioned as medical aid and casualty-clearing stations. During the action, several craft were hit by recoilless rifle and B-40 rocket fire. One boat, *ATC-112-4*, was struck by a rocket below the waterline, forcing it to beach. Following emergency patching, the troop carrier returned to the riverine base under its own power.[19]

The initial phase of CONCORDIA I ended on the evening of 21 June. Two hundred fifty-five Viet Cong were killed during the three days of fighting in which U.S. forces suffered 46 soldiers killed and 15 sailors wounded. Seriously wounded personnel were evacuated to the *Benewah* and *Colleton*, and to the medical facility at Nha Be. The short transit time between the battle area and nearby barracks ships helped to save a number of lives.[20]

During the remainder of June, the MRF remained at the junction of the Vam Co and Soi Rap rivers, carrying out operations in the southeastern districts of Long An Province. No major contact with the enemy developed during this period.[21]

Map 8-3

1 BINH LONG
2 BIEN DUONG
3 BIEN HOA
4 PHUOC TUY
5 TAY NINH
6 HAU NGHIA
7 GIA DINH
8 LONG AN
9 GO CONG
10 KIEN TUONG
11 DINH TUONG
12 KIEN HOA
13 KIEN PHONG
14 SA DEC
15 VINH LONG
16 VINH BINH
17 CHAU DOC
18 AN GIANG
19 PHONG DINH
20 BA XUYEN
21 KIEN GIANG
22 CHUONG THIEN

Provinces of South Vietnam, including Go Cong, Long An, and Dinh Tuong, located to the south and southwest of Saigon
Naval History and Heritage Command photograph #NH96341

CHANGES TO THE MOBILE RIVERINE FORCE

With the arrival on 12 June of two additional monitors, the number of LCM (mechanized landing craft) conversions reached its programmed strength of sixty-eight. In other changes, two large harbor tugs, *Kalispell* (YTB-784) and *Winnemucca* (YTB-785), also joined the force. The tugs were responsible for movement of the two APLs and ammi-pontoons, and performance of any other required towing services. All assault craft on loan from the Vietnamese Navy were returned on 16 June.[22]

OPERATION CONCORDIA II (TASK FORCE 117)

The Mobile Riverine Force operated from anchorage at the junction of the Vam Co and Soi Rap rivers for nearly all of July 1967. Following the conclusion of Operation CONCORDIA II in Long An and Go Cong Provinces, it relocated to Dong Tam (61 miles distant) in response to a reported enemy build-up in Dinh Tuong Province.[23]

On 4 July, units of the MRF embarked elements of the 2nd Brigade, U.S. Ninth Infantry to launch phase III of CONCORDIA II. This operation took place in Go Cong Province, located to the south of Saigon. After landing troops along the west bank of Go Cong Creek, assault craft took up blocking stations in Go Cong and Go Gua creeks to prevent enemy exfiltration from the area. In a series of brief skirmishes, 33 Viet Cong were killed, 78 were captured, and 13 defected. There were no American casualties.[24]

MRF operations in the Can Giouc district of Long An Province commenced on 11 July. Elements of the 3rd and 4th Battalions, U.S. 47th Infantry were landed along the Vang, Mui, and Chim Duoi creeks. West of there, two ARVN battalions went ashore along the Rach Cac River. The waterborne units then took up stations to block escape routes, and provide troop lift and gunfire support. Throughout the day, company-size units were reembarked and relanded elsewhere, in a series of leapfrog movements along Xom Cau Creek.[25]

During one of these movements, the enemy detonated a "claymore" mine as *ATC-112-4* dropped its ramp. Shrapnel wounded seven sailors and four soldiers. Simultaneously, the two monitors in company received recoilless rifle and small arms fire. Return fire followed, and air strikes and artillery fire were delivered into the area.[26]

Following the air strike, A company of the 4/47th made contact with a Viet Cong unit. As the two monitors supported the company, two more monitors were ordered into the area to provide additional fire support. As the assault craft exchanged fire with the enemy, B company of the 4/47th (which had remained afloat to act as a ready-reaction force) was landed along the east bank of Xom Cau Creek. Supported by the two monitors and two ATCs, it swept southward.[27]

Throughout the day, all units exchanged fire with enemy forces armed with B-40 rockets, automatic weapons, and small arms. Several assault craft were hit by enemy fire. That evening, a rocket struck *M-112-1*'s conning station—killing her boat captain, Chief Boatswain's Mate Howard W. Bannister, instantly. Six others aboard the monitor, including the embarked river division commander, were wounded. This action continued for a time, until broken off by the Viet Cong.[28]

The operation ended on 14 July. American casualties were eight killed and forty-five (29 soldiers, 15 sailors, and one Marine) wounded. Viet Cong losses were fifty-nine killed, six captured, three defectors, and numerous weapons seized. The latter included:

- 20 water mines
- 49 individual and 8 crew-served weapons (including three B-40 rocket launchers)
- Several hundred components for grenades[29]

The Mobile Riverine Force continued to operate in Long An Province through late July.[30]

OPERATION CORONADO II

On 25 July, the MRF was ordered to the Dong Tam region. This action followed a series of minings along National Route 4 in Dinh Tuong Province, coupled with mortar attacks against the U.S. base at Dong Tam. CORONADO II commenced on 28 July. The search-and-destroy mission against elements of the Viet Cong 261st and 263rd battalions, and the 514th Provincial Battalion, lasted through 1 August. Enemy losses from it and concurrent CUU LONG 64 by South Vietnamese Army troops included 675 killed. U.S. losses were nine soldiers killed and thirty-three wounded, and another thirty-one sailors wounded.[31]

On a number of occasions, while exchanging fire with enemy units, assault craft were struck with large-caliber rounds. Although damage to the craft was relatively minor, a number of crewmen were wounded. In one such encounter, monitor *91-2* and *ATC 91-10* were hit with B-40 rocket fire. As the craft retired in order to rendezvous with an ATC(H) and transfer wounded personnel, the ATC was again struck by a rocket. Twenty-two Navymen were wounded during that single engagement.[32]

The presence of a helicopter platform atop an ATC provided the Mobile Riverine Force an important capability for handling medical evacuees. The idea to employ a modified armored troop carrier in such a role was conceived by Capt. Wade C. Wells, commander, Task Force 117. Berger M. Shepard of the Naval Research and Development Unit, did the design work. Materials for the platform were obtained in Saigon and delivered to the *Askari*. A frame, fashioned from two-inch piping and three-inch angle iron, was secured by cables and turnbuckles to padeyes in the ATC's welldeck. A section of steel matting fastened to the frame completed fabrication of the landing pad. (The modified craft were Program IV ATCs. Program V ATCs all had flight decks.)[33]

Photo 8-11

A U.S. Army UH-1D helicopter lands on *ATC(H) R-92-2*,
operating as part of the Mobile Riverine Force.
National Archives photograph #USN 1132291

Several craft were struck with recoilless rifle fire or B-40 rockets in July. Generally, the damage was quickly repaired by the *Askari* or the repair facilities at Dong Tam.[34]

Photo 8-12

Landing craft repair ship USS *Askari* (ARL-30), one of the three mobile bases of the Navy's River Assault Flotilla, providing maintenance and support for various craft.
National Archives photograph #USN 1123313

OPERATIONS CORONADO III AND IV

The Mobile Riverine Force relocated to Vung Tau on 4 August 1967 in preparation for Operation GREAT BEND IV (later renamed CORONADO III). Associated search-and-destroy missions in the Can Gio and Quang Xuyen districts of Gia Dinh Province between 7-16 August were aimed at reducing Viet Cong pressure on the main shipping channel to Saigon. Only light contact was made with the enemy as MRF elements destroyed seven bunkers (three by naval gunfire) and seized a quantity of weapons and explosives.[35]

On 18 August, the MRF relocated to the junction of the Vam Co and Soi Rap rivers to prepare for CORONADO IV. Because some of the missions associated with the operation were to occur up to forty miles distant, six ATCs were loaded with supplies and positioned six miles from the area of operations to serve as forward supply points.[36]

When the operation was launched on the 20th, the Riverine Assault Force first conducted reconnaissance-by-fire missions along the banks of the Vam Co River. (This practice involved locating the enemy via return fire.) Ninth Infantry troops (of the 3/47th and 3/60th Battalions) then landed on both banks of the river. Their sweeps failed to produce any major contact with the enemy. Small-unit skirmishes resulted in forty-nine Viet Cong killed and the seizure of a number of weapons. Six U.S. soldiers were wounded during the two-day mission.[37]

From 23 August through month's end, search-and-destroy missions in the Can Giouc district met little resistance. Mobile Riverine Force units killed ten Viet Cong and captured five others. Nearly a hundred enemy bunkers were destroyed and a quantity of munitions ("claymore" mines, blasting caps, detonating cord, and several thousand rounds of small-arms ammunition) seized.[38]

VIET CONG AMBUSH MOBILE RIVERINE FORCE

In September, the Riverine Assault Force suffered its heaviest losses since its activation on 28 February, with six Navymen killed and eighty-four wounded. Most of the casualties were caused by shrapnel from RPG-2 (B-40) and RPG-7 rockets. The introduction of the heavy armor-penetrating RPG-7 rocket with a range of 500 meters posed a much more serious threat to the assault craft of Task Force 117 than did the prevalent RPG-2, with only half the penetration capability and an effective range of just 100 meters.[39]

A majority of these losses occurred on 15 September during a four-hour battle between Riverine Assault Force units and entrenched Viet Cong forces along the Ba Rai Creek in Dinh Tuong Province; which resulted in eighteen craft damaged, three U.S. sailors killed and seventy-seven wounded. History repeated itself in late morning on the twenty-seventh in Ben Tre Creek, forty miles southwest of Saigon. As had occurred during the earlier battle, the Viet Cong ambushed Armored Troop Carriers (ATCs) minesweeping at the head of a small task unit. As the *ATC-91-3* and *ATC-91-10* began taking heavy 57mm recoilless rifle, B-40 rocket, and automatic fire from well-entrenched enemy positions on the east bank, Monitor *M-111-2* moved up and silenced the 57mm fire. Return fire by all the naval units ended the remaining hostile fire. Three sailors were killed and six wounded during the engagement, all crewmembers of ATC minesweepers.[40]

These and previous encounters with the enemy had demonstrated that employing ATCs as minesweepers was less than satisfactory. The slow heavily-armored converted landing craft were slowed even more while conducting chain-drag sweeps, which in turn slowed down the remainder of the assault force, doubling its exposure time in kill zones. The ATCs also had to leave the greater safety offered by the center of the channel and sweep near the bank in order to be effective, which greatly increased the possibility of ambush by Viet Cong. The delivery of the first shipment of (two) Assault Support Patrol Boats (ASPBs) to Vung Tau on 20 September seemed to offer a solution to this problem.[41]

The well-armed craft had been specifically designed for duty in Vietnam and were intended to perform a variety of roles, which included providing escort and protection for ATCs during the troop transport phase of riverine assault; performing minesweeping duties in advance of the river assault squadrons; and acting as a blocking and intercepting force in waters around the area of operation. The fifty-foot ASPBs were fitted with a 20mm cannon, an 81mm mortar, .50-caliber and smaller M-60 machine guns, and two hand cranked Mk-20 grenade launchers.[42]

THREAT POSED BY RIVER MINES

Discussion to this point in the book about the threat posed by mines, had been limited to those emplaced by swimmer-sappers on, or near immobile ships lying at anchor, or berthed alongside a pier. Much larger, and more deadly mines were employed by the Viet Cong against vessels transiting waterways in South Vietnam. Boat crews regularly faced death from mines command-activated by observers hidden in heavy foliage along the banks. The reference to chain drags refers to ATCs (later ASPBs), and other minecraft, streaming astern, lengths of stout chain to which metal spikes were welded every few links. The chain was designed, when dragged across the bottom, to sever electrical wires used by the enemy to remotely detonate the mines.[43]

INTRODUCTION OF BAR ARMOR

To provide Mobile Riverine Force personnel greater protection from RPG attack, bar armor was fitted in assault craft. This "stand-off" was a series of parallel 1-inch concrete reinforcing steel rods surrounding the main deck and topside weapons stations. The bar armor was designed to detonate an RPG (rocket-propelled grenade) or recoilless rifle rounds before they hit the armor plate, diffusing the force of shrapnel.[44]

Photo 8-13

Monitor fitted with a 105mm howitzer, and extensive bar armor, July 1968.
Naval History and Heritage Command photograph #NH 95988

However, this measure provided only a modicum of comfort to boat crews, because the possibility of death or injury still accompanied RPG hits, which affected actions taken by the gunners aboard assault craft. Bob Kermen explained:

> At certain points on the river, we would pass rubber plantations, the property of wealthy French owners living outside the country. They must have had a lot of pull in Washington, because we were told not to return fire, if fired upon from these locations. This was because of the damage our .50-caliber machine guns could cause. Small arms-fire did not greatly concern us, because the bullets bounced off the boat's steel plating. However, all bets were off if

under RPG attack, because they could kill us. In those cases, we engaged with rapid .50-caliber and 20mm high explosive ammo, until the threat was eliminated or we had passed out of range of the enemy.[45]

OPERATIONS CORONADO V, VI, VII, VIII

The Mobile Riverine Force continued applying pressure throughout the Delta and RSSZ in October 1967; killing large numbers of Viet Cong, and destroying numerous structures and bunkers. During sequential CORONADO operations at different locations, combat forces ashore overran a number of enemy base camps, and destroyed or captured large quantities of supplies and ammunition.[46]

Mobile Riverine Force Operations in October 1967

Operation	Dates	Location
Coronado V	12 Sep-5 Oct 67	Kien Hoa and Dinh Tuong Provinces
Coronado VI	11-18 Oct 67	Quang Xuyen district of the RSSZ
Coronado VII	21-23 Oct 67	Can Giouc district of Long An Province
Coronado VIII	27 29 Oct 67	Long Thanh district of Bien Hoa Province

The heaviest combat came in the Cam Son Secret Zone. Operating from Dong Tam, the MRF launched a riverine/airmobile-assault and search-and-destroy mission in the western part of the Ban Long Secret Zone on 5 October. Conducted in coordination with elements of the South Vietnamese Army Seventh Division, the objective was to entrap enemy forces in the Cam Son and Ban Long Secret Zones. Intelligence reports had indicated that the Viet Cong 263rd and 514th main force battalions were located in this area. These forces disrupted lines of communication between the Mekong Delta and Saigon, and also posed a threat to the U.S. Army/Navy units based at Dong Tam.[47]

Mobile Riverine Force contact with the enemy in the Ban Long Secret Zone was light, while the ARVN was heavily engaged in the northwestern part of the Cam Son Secret Zone. On 6 October, the MRF reoriented its forces westward into the Cam Son Secret Zone to encircle an expected Viet Cong movement. That afternoon, troops of the Ninth Infantry gained contact with the 263rd Battalion. The ensuing battle continued until 2200 the following night.[48]

The circle could not be completely closed due to an absence of waterways to the east, where MRF assault craft might otherwise take up blocking positions. However, the enemy was significantly engaged by U.S. and ARVN troops to account for 173 Viet Cong killed, 171 enemy bunkers destroyed, and a large quantity of small-arms ammunition captured. American casualties were six soldiers killed and twenty-five wounded, and one sailor wounded by sniper fire.[49]

The commencement of CORONADO VIII at month's end marked the initial employment of the Royal Thai Army Volunteer Regiment in conjunction with the Mobile Riverine Force. In a separate action, *Westchester County* (LST-1167) relieved *Whitfield County* at Vung Tau on 27 October as the MRF support tank landing ship.[50]

CORONADO IX

The MRF was engaged throughout November in CORONADO IX, which took place north of the My Tho River in the Mekong Delta. The area of operations stretched from the Plain of Reeds area (vicinity of the Cambodian border) east to the Soi Rap River.[51]

In preparation for the operation, the MRF departed Vung Tau on 1 November 1967 for the Dong Tau area, which involved passage via the South China Sea down the coast. Heavy winds and high seas greatly slowed the force, already burdened by a requirement to tow their ammi-pontoons. When the ships reached the relative calm of the Mekong/My Tho rivers, towing speed increased to 10 knots.[52]

During the transit of the Cua Tieu River, an armored troop carrier, *ATC-111-7*, sweeping ahead of the mine task group, surfaced a 170-lb conical-shaped, moored mine, eight miles east of My Tho. This was the first proof that chain-dragging minesweeping operations by TF 117 craft were effective. The water mine was later disarmed by EOD personnel.[53]

CORONADO IX commenced on 2 November on the My Luong Peninsula of Dinh Tuong Province. A week later, operations shifted to the Cam Son and Ban Long Secret Zones of the province. The three-battalion, riverine and airmobile search-and-destroy operation marked the initial deployment of the 5th Battalion of the South Vietnamese Marine Corps (VNMC) as the third maneuver battalion of the Mobile Riverine Force. The South Vietnamese Marines, staging from their base camp on the north side of the My Tho River, near Dong Tam, were supported by River Assault Division 112 throughout the operation.[54]

Later in the month, the MRF relocated to a Mekong River anchorage thirty-two miles west of Dong Tam, to begin operations in western Dinh Tuong and eastern Kien Phong Provinces. The initial phase involved the transit of a riverine assault unit with the VNMC 5th Battalion embarked, thirty-two miles to the area of operations—the MRF's deepest penetration, to date, into the Delta.[55]

During the operation, riverine craft transited waterways laden with obstacles not previously encountered. These included a low bridge spanning the Ruong Stream, six miles northeast of Sa Dec. Removal of the center span allowed continued passage. Concurrently, the Mobile Riverine Force EOD team removed a number of Viet Cong-erected wire barriers from the stream, opening a complex of waterways not used by riverine craft since 1963. This allowed assault craft with embarked Marines to penetrate fifteen miles inland from the Mekong River.[56]

On 20 November, the TF 117 Special Operations Team conducted an intelligence-collection mission on the Con Qui Island complex, four miles east of Sa Dec. Two enemy were killed and two captured. One of the captives, Capt. Nguyen Van Thoi, was a Viet Cong Intelligence Chief in the IV Corps area.[57]

The MRF relocated to Dong Tam the following day, for another phase of operations in the Cam Son Secret Zone. Prior to the Mobile Riverine Force entering the zone on 23 November, a B-52 strike saturated the area. The use of Air Force heavy bombers in this operation indicated the strategic importance assigned to Dinh Tuong by senior military commanders.[58]

Photo 8-14

A B-52 releases bombs over a coastal area, October 1965.
Defense Department photo 94890 USA

BATTLE OF RUONG STREAM

> *To a newcomer in one of these actions, the battle of the boats is incredible. The crossfire between the Viet Cong and our rugged craft at 25 yards is like nothing in naval warfare since the day of the great frigates.*
>
> —Capt. Robert S. Salzer, USN, who had assumed command of Task Force 117 from Capt. Wade C. Wells, on 2 December 1967, describing the Battle of Ruong Stream.[59]

In December 1967, the Mobile Riverine Force concentrated its efforts on locating and destroying major Viet Cong units in a series of riverine operations. On the evening of 3 December, the MRF began relocating assault elements from Dong Tam in preparation for CORONADO XI, to be conducted from 4-6 December in western Dinh Tuong and eastern Kien Phong Provinces. Barge-mounted artillery, accompanied by River Assault Division 92, led the movement. Behind it came RAD 112 (aboard which were the Vietnamese Marine Corps Fifth Infantry Battalion); RAD 111 (carrying the U.S. Army 3/47th Infantry Battalion); and RAD 91 (with the 4/47th Infantry Battalion embarked.)[60]

Battle was joined on 4 December when the Viet Cong ambushed RAD 112 with automatic weapons and rockets shortly after the division entered the Ruong Stream from the Mekong River. After fighting their way, another two miles up the waterway through heavily-bunkered enemy positions to the pre-selected landing zone, the craft were again taken under fire with intense recoilless rifle, automatic weapons, and rocket fire, with the heaviest concentration coming from the west bank. The VNMC battalion landed and immediately launched a counter-attack against the 502nd Viet Cong Battalion and local guerrilla units. Thereafter, River Assault Division 111, which had also taken fire from the initial ambush site as well as from upstream, landed on the western bank just north of the Viet Cong positions. The U.S. Army troops it carried, landed and counterattacked the insurgents, as had the Vietnamese Marines.[61]

Throughout the day-long battle, the riverine craft of RADs 111 and 112 assisted the ground offensive by providing afloat gunfire support and taking up blocking positions to prevent any exfiltration by the Viet Cong from the objective area. During the fighting, division craft sustained forty-three hits (excluding those of automatic weapons and small arms fire) from 57mm recoilless rifles, rockets, and one "claymore" mine, leaving twenty-three boats damaged, but none serious enough to require withdrawal.[62]

This initial phase of CORONADO XI resulted in 266 Viet Cong killed, eight captured and 5,000 rounds of small-arms ammunition and 321 weapons captured. Most of the enemy casualties resulted from fierce fighting by the Vietnamese Marines, who suffered forty killed and 103 wounded. Among personnel of the Riverine Assault Force, two Navymen were killed and 103 wounded.[63]

On 27 December, the Vietnamese Joint General Staff pulled the VNMC 5th Battalion out of the Mobile Riverine Force, and relocated these troops to II Corps. Four days later, *Pitkin County* (LST-1082) relieved *Blanco County* (LST-344) as the MRF resupply LST.[64]

9

Work Horses of the Amphibious Force

Let there be built great ships which can cast upon a beach, in any weather, large numbers of the heaviest tanks.

—Sir Winston Churchill, memo to the War Department, 1940.

Photo 9-1

Tank landing ships practicing beaching off San Diego, California, circa the 1960s. USS *Wexford County* (LST-1168) is in the foreground, with *Jerome County* (LST-848) and *Polk County* (LST-1084) the next two ships off her starboard side.
Naval History and Heritage Command photograph #NH 68713

The bulk of the sixty-two tank landing ships that served in Vietnam were assigned to Landing Ship Squadrons. LandShipRon Two was based at Sasebo, Japan; LandShipRon Three at Guam, Mariana Islands; and LandShipRon Nine at Yokosuka, Japan. Landing Ship Flotilla One in San Diego, later moved forward to Yokosuka. Other LSTs, particularly modern *Newport*-class ships constructed late in the war, were assigned to amphibious squadrons, home ported at San Diego or Long Beach, California, or Little Creek, Virginia.

Four LSTs—*Garrett County*, *Harnett County*, *Hunterdon County*, and *Jennings County*—were taken out of "mothballs," and sent to Vietnam for continuous duty in country. Participating as a unit of Task Force 116 in support of Operation GAME WARDEN, these ships served in the Mekong Delta as mobile support bases for river patrol boats and helicopter gunships.

Before progressing to representative operations, identification of squadrons to which LSTs were assigned, and unit awards earned by individual ships, an introduction of the tank landing ships is in order.

DESIGN AND EVOLUTION OF TANK LANDING SHIPS

The evacuation between 26 May and 4 June 1940 of the British Expeditionary Force, and other Allied troops from the French seaport of Dunkirk, demonstrated to the British Admiralty that the allies needed relatively large, ocean-going ships capable of delivering tanks and other vehicles in amphibious assaults upon the continent of Europe. At their first meeting, during the Argentia Conference in August 1941, President Franklin D. Roosevelt and Prime Minister Winston Churchill confirmed the Admiralty's views. In November 1941, a small delegation from the Admiralty travelled to the United States to share ideas with the Navy's Bureau of Ships with regard to development of the required ships. During this meeting, it was agreed that the Bureau of Ships would design the required vessels.[1]

Within a few days, naval architect John C. Niedermair sketched out an awkward-looking ship, which proved to be the basic design for the 1,051 unnamed LSTs built during World War II. The ship was given a large ballast system that could be filled with sea water to provide necessary stability for ocean passage, and pumped out for beaching operations. The 328-foot LST boasted a 50-foot beam (which distributed the ship's weight over a greater area, and enabled it to ride higher when in landing trim) and a minimum draft of three feet, nine-and-a-half inches. The ship's expansive width permitted a 14-foot wide opening for the bow doors, enabling accommodation of most Allied vehicles. The LST could carry 2,100 tons of tanks and/or vehicles, or other cargo.[2]

Of the 1,051 LSTs, 113 were transferred to Great Britain, and four turned over to the Greek Navy. Another 116 were converted to other ship types, including a number being transformed into landing craft repair ships (ARLs). This involved removing the LST bow ramp and doors, sealing the bow, and adding derricks, booms, and winches to haul landing craft on board. Necessary blacksmith, machine, and electrical workshops were provided on the main deck and tank deck.[3]

The end of World War II left the U.S. Navy with a huge inventory of unneeded tank landing ships. Hundreds were scrapped or sunk. Most of the remaining ones were laid up in reserve fleets, awaiting any future need for them. The successful amphibious assault at Inchon during the Korean War highlighted the utility of LSTs, once again. As a consequence, fifteen new *Terrebonne Parish*-class ships were constructed in the early 1950s. These LSTs were fifty-six feet longer than their predecessors, and faster. Propelled by four, rather than two, diesel engines, they could make 15 knots. Other improvements included the fitting of 3-inch/50 twin mounts (in lieu of 40mm guns) and controllable-pitch propellers that increased the ships' backing power.[4]

On 1 July 1955, U.S. county or parish names (counties in the state of Louisiana are called "parishes") were assigned to all World War II-era LSTs still in commission.

Seven LSTs of the *De Soto County*-class were constructed in the late 1950s. Considered to be the ultimate design employing the traditional "clam shell" bow door configuration, they were capable of 17.5 knots.[5]

COMPLETELY NEW LST SHIP DESIGN

Photo 9-2

A truck boards USS *Newport* (LST-1179) near Little Creek, Virginia, October 1969. National Archives photograph #K-78408

The commissioning of *Newport* (LST-1179) on 7 June 1969, marked the introduction of an entirely new concept in the design of LSTs. She was the first of a new class of twenty, 522-foot, 5,190-ton tank landing ships capable of 20 knots. To obtain that speed, a thirty-ton, 112-foot bow replaced the traditional blunt bow doors of previous LSTs. Supported by two derrick arms, a ramp allowed for the unloading of tanks and other vehicles ashore. Additionally, amphibious vehicles could be launched from her tank deck via a stern gate, and the flight deck could accommodate most Navy helicopters.[6]

SERVICE OF TANK LANDING SHIPS IN VIETNAM

LSTs were the work horses in Vietnam, comprising 62 (44 percent) of the 142 amphibious ships deployed at various times to the war zone.

Number/Ship Type	Number/Ship Type
4 AGC/LCC (amphibious force command ship)	4 IFS (inshore fire support ship)
12 AKA/LKA (amphibious cargo ship)	7 LPD (amphibious transport dock)
15 APA (attack transport)	8 LPH (amphibious assault ship)
3 APB (self-propelled barracks ship)	18 LSD (dock landing ship)
3 APD (high speed transport)	62 LST (tank landing ship)
5 ARL (landing craft repair ship)	

In addition to their being the most plentiful amphibious ship, LSTs were also, arguably, the most versatile of the "gators." Their duties included assignment to:

- Operation MARKET TIME as support ships for "Swift boats" and Coast Guard cutters
- Operation GAME WARDEN as support ships for PBRs and "Seawolf" helicopters
- The Mobile Riverine Force as support ships for various riverine craft, "Seawolf" helicopters, and SEAL detachments, or as ammunition ships
- Amphibious readiness groups carrying Marines to landing sites on the Vietnamese coast

PRESIDENTIAL UNIT CITATIONS AWARDED LSTS

Fourteen LSTs were awarded Presidential Unit Citations during the war for extraordinary heroism in action against an armed enemy. Four of these ships received multiple awards. The PUC is the highest honor a military unit may receive for heroism; the collective degree of valor is the same as that warranting award of the Navy Cross to an individual. These ships are identified below:

- *Garrett County*
- *Hampshire County*
- *Harnett County* (2)
- *Hunterdon County* (2)
- *Iredell County*
- *Jennings County* (2)
- *Jerome County*
- *Sedgwick County*
- *Terrell County*
- *Vernon County*
- *Washoe County*
- *Washtenaw County* (3)
- *Whitfield County*
- *Windham County*

The award citations may be found in Appendix D. USS *Leader* (MSO-490) is included in the following summary, because she replaced *Garrett County* in SEALORDS, and because her PUC was the only such awarded an ocean minesweeper during the war.

U.S. Navy Element of the Mobile Riverine Force (Task Force 117)
29 January - 4 March 1968

Washtenaw County Squadron 9	29 Jan-4 Mar 68	*Jerome County*	29 Jan-18 Feb 68

I Corps River Patrol Group (31 January-29 February 1968)

Garrett County	31 Jan-29 Feb 68	*Hunterdon County*	20-29 Feb 68
Harnett County	31 Jan-29 Feb 68	*Jennings County*	31 Jan-29 Feb 68

Commander Task Group 194.0
(Units Participating in Operation SEALORDS)
18 October - 5 December 1968

Leader (MSO-490)	18 Oct-5 Dec 68	*Jennings County*	18 Oct-5 Dec 68
Washoe County Squadron 9	18 Oct-5 Dec 68	*Hunterdon County*	18 Oct-5 Dec 68

Individual Award for *Harnett County*

Harnett County	12 Dec 68-30 Apr 69

Task Force 115 (Units Participating in Operation SWIFT RAIDER)
6 December 1968 - 31 March 1969

Terrell County Squadron 9	1 Jan-4 Feb 69	*Washtenaw County* Squadron 9	1-31 Mar 69
Washtenaw County Squadron 9	5-23 Feb 69		

U.S. Navy Element of the Mobile Riverine Force (Task Force 117)
25 January - 5 July 1969

Iredell County Squadron 2	25 Jan-15 Feb 69	*Vernon County* Squadron 9	28 Feb-25 May 69
Hampshire County Squadron 3	25 Jan-19 Apr 69	*Whitfield County* Squadron 9	8 May-5 Jul 69
Sedgwick County Squadron 3	23 Apr-6 May 69	*Windham County* Squadron 9	25 Mar-10 May 69

Much tank landing ship work involved delivery of critical materials and supplies to South Vietnamese coastal and river ports in support of all three task forces (115, 116, 117). Enemy threats included rocket-propelled grenade, recoilless rifle, and mortar attack on inland waterways. These, as well as attack by swimmer-sappers, existed while lying at anchor or alongside a pier handling cargo.[7]

One of many tank landing ships that came under enemy attack during the war was *Caddo Parish* (LST-515). An account of this action will be found on page 137, following an introduction of Landing Ship Squadron Two, of which she was a member.[8]

LANDING SHIP SQUADRON TWO, LITTLE CREEK

The U.S. Navy's first and only Reserve Landing Ship Squadron came into existence in May 1963 at Amphibious Base, Little Creek, Virginia. Commanded by Lt. Comdr. Edward J. Brown, it consisted of *Chesterfield County* and *Mahnomen County*. *Chase County* joined in early June, followed on the 19th by *Luzerne County*, *Madera County*, *New London County*, and *Hickman County*. The latter ships arrived after undergoing activation from the Pacific Reserve Fleet in San Diego. By late August, with the arrivals of *Caddo Parish*, *Nye County*, *Pulaski County*, and *Monmouth County*, the squadron was at full strength with eleven ships.[9]

In the summer of 1965, squadron ships joined other naval forces off the Dominican Republic. Civil war had erupted in that country, and President Lyndon B. Johnson dispatched Marines and paratroopers to quell the fighting. The LSTs sent to the Caribbean are identified in the table by the letters AE, denoting their receipt of Armed Forces Expeditionary Medals for the 1965 Dominican Republic Crisis.[10]

That autumn, a requirement was identified in the Western Pacific for additional cargo lift. The war in Vietnam was escalating, very limited port facilities existed in country, and shallow draft landing ships were needed to deliver war materiel. ResLandShipRon Two was the ideal choice for this tasking because its ships were already partially activated and manned. The reserve LSTs were placed in full commission on 21 December 1965. On 25 January, the squadron name was changed to

Landing Ship Squadron Two to reflect its active status. Between 1963-1965, the ships had operated in the Norfolk area with reduced crews of about five officers and thirty enlisted men. In late 1965, crew size was increased to eight officers and ninety men.[11]

That same month, the first contingent of LSTs were making preparations for extended overseas duty with the Pacific Fleet. The first squadron ship left Norfolk on 27 January for the Western Pacific, and the last one on 26 February. By March 1966, most of the ships were in Pearl Harbor, undergoing modified refresher training conducted by commander, Service Force Pacific. The last LST departed Pearl in April, and the squadron soon began operations in the Pacific, working for commander, Military Sea Transportation Service (MSTS), Far East Area. The squadron was based in Sasebo, Japan.[12]

The LSTs were employed transporting bulk materiel to ports in South Vietnam generally inaccessible to other type ships. The cargos brought from Kachsiung and Keelung, Taiwan; Subic Bay, Philippine Islands; and Buckner Bay, Okinawa, were principally cement, but also included vehicles, petroleum, munitions, barbed wire, and general cargo. These bulk items were used to establish bases, and to provide combat equipment for units on the front lines. The deliveries were primarily to Phan Rang, Qui Nhon, Vung Tau, Chu Lai, Nha Trang, and Danang.[13]

Mahnomen County grounded at Chu Lai on 30 December 1966 as a result of typhoon weather. Efforts to refloat her were unsuccessful, and she was decommissioned and struck from the Navy list on 31 January 1967. Other squadron ships then began to be put out of naval service, after a determination was made that the LSTs could be operated more economically by foreign crews. An added benefit would be their officers and men could then serve in more critical billets. A process was begun to decommission the ships at Pusan, Korea, and turn them over to MSTS for civilian manning. Four had been handed over when the Chief of Naval Operations ordered the decommissioning suspended, as a result of an emerging requirement for additional LSTs in Vietnam.[14]

Ship	Decom	Ship	Decom
Mahnomen County	31 Jan 67	*Nye County*	27 Mar 67
New London County	22 Feb 67	*Chase County*	15 Apr 67
Chesterfield County	13 Mar 67	*Pulaski County*	30 Apr 67

The network of streams and rivers in the Mekong Delta, flowing down from Cambodia and Laos, provided an ideal water transportation system for use by ships of relatively shallow draft. The expanded efforts against Viet Cong activities in this area demanded a logistics system, which could be met only by the cargo capacity of LSTs and the LSM (medium landing ship) and LCU (utility landing craft) classes. The remaining LandShipRon Two "Ts" already deployed to Vietnam, were manned and armed with Navy crews, and were capable of carrying large quantities of cargo to the river bases in the Delta. Thus, they were the logical choice to fulfill this requirement.[15]

The squadron's five remaining ships—*Caddo Parish*, *Hickman County*, *Luzerne County*, *Madera County*, and *Monmouth County*—were gradually returned to operational status and commenced logistics support in the Mekong Delta. Their primary movements were between the ports of Saigon, Vung Tau, Dong Tam, and Binh Thuy-Can Tho, utilizing the Mekong and Bassac rivers.[16]

Ship	Recom/ Decom	Disposition
Caddo Parish (LST-515) AE	2 Aug 63/ 26 Nov 69	Transferred to Philippine Navy, 26 Nov 1969, renamed RPS *Bataan* (LT-85)
Chase County (LST-532) AE	Unknown/ 15 Apr 67	Placed in service by the MSTS as USNS *Chase County* (T-LST-532)
Chesterfield County (LST-551) AE	29 Mar 63/ 1 Jun 70	Sold for scrapping in February 1971 to Mitsui and Co., Japan
Clarke County (LST-601)	28 Jul 66/ Jul 70	Transferred to Indonesia, date unknown, renamed KRI *Teluk Saleh* (LST-510)
Hickman County (LST-825) AE	22 Mar 63/ 26 Nov 69	Transferred to Philippine Navy, 26 Nov 1969, renamed RPS *Cagayan* (LT-97)
Iredell County (LST-839)	18 Jun 66/ Jul 70	Transferred to Indonesia, date unknown, renamed KRI *Teluk Bone* (LST-511)
Luzerne County (LST-902) AE	15 Apr 63/ 30 Jun 70	Struck from the Naval Register, 12 Aug 1970; sold to CEMEX, Ensenada, Baja California, as a cement barge
Madera County (LST-905) AE	30 Mar 63/ 26 Nov 69	Transferred to Philippine Navy, 29 Nov 1969, renamed RPS *Ilcos Norte* (LT-98)
Mahnomen County (LST-912)	27 Mar 63/ 31 Jan 67	Ran aground at Chu Lai, South Vietnam on 30 Dec 1966 during a typhoon; demolished by Navy Support Detachment, Chu Lai
Monmouth County (LST-1032) AE	28 May 62/ 12 Aug 70	Sold for scrapping, 11 Sep 1971, to Zidell Exploration Inc., Portland, Oregon
New London County (LST-1066) AE	21 Dec 65/ 27 Feb 67	Placed in service by the MSTS as USNS New *London County* (T-LST-1066)
Nye County (LST-1067) AE	22 May 63/ 27 Mar 67	Transferred to MSTS and placed in service as USNS *Nye County* T-LST-1067
Page County (LST-1076)	28 Nov 60/ 5 Mar 71	Transferred to Greece, date unknown, renamed HS *Kriti* (L-171)
Pulaski County (LST-1088) AE	21 May 63/ Jul 67	Transferred to MSTS and placed in service as USNS *Pulaski County* (T-LST-1088)

RPG ATTACK ON THE *CADDO PARISH*

Caddo Parish (one of only four *LST-491* class ships to serve in Vietnam) had arrived in country in March 1966. Operating out of Vung Tau in a combat support role, she ran munitions and supplies to Chu Lai, Qui Nhon, and Tuy Hoa. In December 1968, the tasks assigned her squadron were increased to include resupply of Riverine Assault Force units in the Mekong Delta. *Luzerne County* had assumed this role in early November, after the mining of *Westchester County* by swimmer-sappers necessitated a replacement by another Mobile Riverine Force LST. Several weeks later, *Caddo Parish* shouldered the permanent assignment of resupply ship on 26 December 1968.[17]

During operations in the Mekong Delta, she called at Nha Be, Dong Tam, Can Tho (Binh Thuy), and other ports accessible to gators of the "Brown Water Navy," and came under fire on several occasions. The most significant attack occurred late-night on 6 March 1969, five kilometers west of Dong Tam, when *Caddo Parish* suffered three rocket-propelled grenade (B-40) hits on her port side. One RPG breeched her hull, spraying a top bunk in a berthing compartment with shrapnel. Three personnel casualties resulted from that and the other detonations. Repairs to the ship were made in Subic Bay, and *Caddo Parish* returned to the Delta to resume her support of the Mobile Riverine Force.[18]

Alan Halldorson, a crewmember aboard *Caddo Parish* and later, her successor in the squadron, *Iredell County*, described his duty aboard the two tank landing ships:

> While I was aboard the *Caddo Parish* and *Iredell County*, we once delivered a company of soldiers and their equipment to Danang, and also stopped at Camranh Bay. We mostly ran the rivers, hauling supplies from Vung Tau, where we were based, to Saigon, Dong Tam, and Can Tho. While supporting the Mobile Riverine Force, we had reefers [refrigerated boxes] on the main deck to transport perishable food.
>
> We normally beached to offload cargo, but might anchor out, if another ship was blocking us, or strong tidal currents prohibited beaching. When beached or at anchor, we shot at anything sighted in the water, because of the threat of sappers and what had happened to the *Westchester County*.
>
> We were beached at Dong Tam when we came under RPG attack. Shrapnel from one of the grenade hits struck a porcelain sink in a crew head, and ceramic shards badly wounded a sailor. Another RPG penetrated a berthing compartment and the explosion blasted a shipmate out of his top rack. The crew cared for the men injured

in the attack. We did not fire back because of an airstrip off the ship's portside, and the possibility that we might hit our own forces.

In addition to the personnel casualties we suffered in the attack, an RPG damaged the motor used to open and close the bow doors. We proceeded to Singapore, and offloaded all of our ammunition in preparation for repairs. However, repairs couldn't be made there because of lack of materials or necessary capabilities, and we were then sent to Subic Bay.

When operating on the rivers, we manned our 40mm guns and .50-caliber machine guns when close enough to a river bank to come under attack. We knew where the dangerous areas were, and usually set port or starboard General Quarters—meaning one-half the crew was at their battle stations with guns manned and ready to fire. If something happened, we would transition to full General Quarters.

In addition to manning weapons, we would also increase our level of readiness by setting material condition Zebra. This refers to closing all doors and hatches, and "dogging" [latching] them shut to increase compartmentation throughout the ship, and by doing so, minimize the spread of fire or flooding, if hit or mined.

I was lucky on one occasion, while running to my battle station, that an engineer was dogging shut a door on the tank deck, leading to the weather deck, which I had to go through to man my gun. I yelled at him to leave it open, but he didn't hear me, completed the job, and departed. I had just begun to open it, but hadn't loosened all the dogs, when it was hit by enemy fire, bending the door. I was struck in the face by some debris, but not seriously hurt. But for his actions, I might well have been a casualty.[19]

UNIT AWARDS EARNED BY SQUADRON TWO SHIPS

Caddo Parish received four Combat Action Ribbons (CR), two Meritorious Unit Commendations (MUC), and one Navy Unit Commendation (NUC) during her Vietnam service. Squadron mate *Iredell County* garnered a Presidential Unit Citation (PUC). *Page County* saw the most combat action and, not unexpectedly, was the most decorated member the squadron. A summary of ship awards may be found in the table. *Chase County*, *Chesterfield County*, *New London County*, and *Pulaski County* did not receive any of those listed.

Former crewmembers, and other interested readers, may find the dates associated with Combat Action Ribbons useful in relating these actions to particular operations.

Ship	Unit Awards
Caddo Parish 7 awards	CR (4): 2-23 Apr 68, 6 Mar 69, 9 Mar 69, 20-21 Mar 69 MUC (2): 1 Sep 68-1 May 69, 2 May-1 Nov 69 NUC (1): 2-21 Nov 70
Chase County	
Chesterfield County	
Clarke County 3 awards	CR (1): 17 Nov-1 Dec 67 MUC (2): 1 Jul 66-31 Mar 68, 18 Nov 69-24 Apr 70
Hickman County 5 awards	CR (3): 2 May 68, 30 May 68, 23 May 69 MUC (2): 1 Sep 68-1 May 69, 2 May-1 Nov 69
Iredell County 7 awards	CR (4): 6-8 Feb 68, 21 Feb 68, 10 Mar 68, 18 Mar 70 PUC (1): 25 Jan-15 Feb 69 MUC (1): 5 Dec 69-24 Apr 70 NUC (1): 11 Nov-31 Dec 68
New London County	
Luzerne County 6 awards	CR (4): 18 Feb 68, 22 Feb 68, 4 Mar 68, 3 Mar 69 MUC (2): 1 Sep 68-1 May 69, 2 May 69-24 Apr 70
Madera County 5 awards	CR (3): 4 Jun 68, 19 Aug 69, 3 Nov 69 MUC (2): 1 Sep 68-1 May 69, 29 May-15 Nov 69
Mahnomen County 1 award	CR (1): 20 Jan 67
Monmouth County 3 awards	MUC (2): 1 Sep 68-1 May 69, 2 May 69-24 Apr 70 NUC (1): 25 Apr-21 Nov 70
Nye County 1 award	CR (1): 9 Jul 66
Page County 10 awards	CR (7): 21 Aug 68, 25 Aug 68, 12-13 Sep 68, 22 Sep 68, 28 Sep 68, 5 Oct 68, 26 Feb 70 MUC (2): 7 Jun-30 Nov 68, 28 Dec 69-24 Apr 70 NUC (1): 25 Apr-31 May 70
Pulaski County	

REMAINING SERVICE OF LANDSHIPRON TWO

Following a Navy decision to replace four of the ships of LandShipRon Two with 542-class LSTs in better material condition, *Page County* and *Stone County* joined the squadron on 28 October 1969, from Landing Ship Squadron One, in San Diego. *Iredell County* and *Clarke County* were reassigned from LandShipRon Three, based at Guam, on 6 November. A short time after these acquisitions, *Caddo Parish*, *Hickman County*, and *Madera County* were decommissioned, on 26 November, without ceremony in the Philippines, and turned over to the Philippine government. The officers and crews of these ships were reassigned to the newly reporting ones.[20]

As *Caddo Parish*'s service to the U.S. Navy came to an end, Alan Halldorson and his shipmates manned the *Iredell County* during her waning time in Vietnam. Electrician's Mate Second John R. Swofford, of the *Iredell County*, later explained how this came about:

I served on the *Iredell County* (LST-839) as an EM2. In November 1969 the USS *Caddo Parrish* (LST-515) was scheduled to be turned over to the Philippine Navy.... A decision was made to swap crews; the *Caddo Parrish* crew would take over the *Iredell County* and the 839 crew was honored to sail the 515 back to the Philippines. However, a couple of the *Iredell County* crew opted to stay on board the 839 and remain in Vietnam. The remainder of us were anxious to get back to Subic Bay. We successfully brought the 515 into Subic, turned the ship over to the Philippine Navy and were placed in transit awaiting new orders.

I remained in Subic pending the arrival of my new ship, the [salvage ship] USS *Current* (ARS-22) out of Pearl Harbor. Once she arrived, I went right back to Vietnam. After arriving...on station, we received a distress call from the *Iredell County* around 0100 hours. She had gone aground in the Delta. The USS *Current* arrived the next day to find the *Iredell County* sitting high and dry on a sand bar. I never thought I would see that ship again.... We eventually pulled the 839 off the sand and she went on her way.[21]

Iredell County relieved *Monmouth County* as Mobile Riverine Force resupply ship on 8 February 1970. Two-and-a-half-months later, these ships, and two of the other three remaining LSTs of the squadron, left Vung Tau for Danang to load Marine Corps cargo for return to the United States. A departure ceremony was held aboard *Clarke County* on 23 April, to bid farewell to Vietnam and the squadron's operational and administrative commanders. At its conclusion, the commodore, Comdr. Robert L. Zipse, USN, ordered homeward bound pennants flown from the ships' masts. The next day, *Iredell County*, *Luzerne County*, *Clarke County*, and *Monmouth County* departed Vung Tau to make the Pacific crossing. *Page County* remained behind to execute remaining tasking, until her scheduled August departure date.[22]

Traditionally, U.S. Navy ships returning from a long overseas deployment display a homeward bound pennant, fabricated by the crew and flown in place of the normal commissioning pennant. Such action is limited to ships that have been outside the United States continuously for 270 or more days. Flown from the time a ship gets under way to proceed to a United States port until sunset on the day of arrival, it consists of white stars on a blue field at the hoist, and is divided red over white at the fly. The pennant has one star to represent the ship's first nine months outside the U.S., plus another star for each additional six months. The length of the pennant is one foot for each member of the crew who has been on duty outside the United States for nine months or more, not to exceed the length of the ship itself.

Photo 9-3

Homeward bound pennant displaying ten stars, signifying continuous deployment for a period of greater than five years overseas.

On 1 May, the four ships sailed from Danang, bound for San Diego, with stops at Guam and Pearl Harbor en route. The final leg of the journey ended on 13 June, at which time it was learned that *Page County*, left behind in Vietnam, would become a part of LandShipRon Three rather than be decommissioned. *Iredell County* and *Clarke County* remained in San Diego, while the *Monmouth County* and *Luzerne County* proceeded up the California coast to join the "mothball fleet" at Vallejo in the San Francisco Bay area.[23]

The staff remained aboard *Iredell County* until 30 June when, at an inactivation ceremony, commander Landing Ship Squadron Two's pennant was hauled down for the last time. *Clarke County* and *Iredell County* were later transferred to Indonesia, while *Luzerne County* and *Monmouth County* were sold to private buyers.[24]

LSTS IN SUPPORT OF OPERATION GAME WARDEN

Four tank landing ships served as mobile support bases for river patrol boats (PBRs) and "Seawolf" helicopter gunships in support of friendly forces ashore and along the rivers of the Mekong Delta. Participating as a unit of Task Force 116 in support of Operation GAME WARDEN, their duty involved continuous operations in country and in contiguous waters, with the exception of overhaul periods.

The number of campaigns in which each of these ships participated, the span of their Vietnam service, and other summary information about them follows.

- *Garrett County* (8)   29 November 1967 - 2 February 1971
- *Harnett County* (11)   12 January 1967 - 21 July 1970
- *Hunterdon County* (10)   5 July 1967 - 31 March 1971
- *Jennings County* (9)   7 November 1966 - 12 August 1970

Ship	Recom/Decom	Disposition
Garrett County (LST-786)	15 Oct 66/ 23 Apr 71	Transferred to South Vietnam, renamed RVNS *Can Tho* (HQ 801)
Harnett County (LST-821)	20 Aug 66/ 12 Oct 70	Transferred to South Vietnam, renamed RVNS *My Tho* (HQ-800)
Hunterdon County (LST-838)	10 Sep 66/ Unknown	Struck and transferred to Malaysia, 1 Aug 71, renamed *Sri Langkawi* (A-1500)
Jennings County (LST-846)	11 Jun 66/ 26 Sep 70	Sold to a mining company for service as an ore barge

Ship	Unit Awards
Garrett County 9 awards	CR (2): 29 Mar 68, 23 Jan 69 PUC (1): 31 Jan-29 Feb 68 NUC (6): 10 Nov 66-30 Jan 68, 1 Mar-30 Sep 68, 1 Oct-2 Dec 68, 3 Mar-6 Aug 69, 10 Sep-31 Dec 69, 6 Sep 70-27 Jan 71
Harnett County 10 awards	CR (6): 13 Jun 67, 29 Dec 67, 23 Dec 68, 29 Jan-1 Feb 69, 15 Mar 69, 24 Mar 69 PUC (2): 31 Jan-29 Feb 68, 12 Dec 68-30 Apr 69 NUC (2): 10 Nov 66-30 Jan 68, 1 Mar-30 Sep 68, 1 Oct-31 Dec 69, 20 Feb-30 Jun 70
Hunterdon County 13 awards	CR (3): 29 Aug 67, 12 Mar 68, 12 Sep 68 PUC (2): 20-29 Feb 68, 18 Oct-5 Dec 68 NUC (8): 10 Nov 66-30 Jan 68, 1 Mar-30 Sep 68, 6 Dec 68-6 Apr 69, 11 May-16 Oct 69, 5 May-30 Jun 70, 19 Jul-1 Aug 70, 2 Aug 70, 1 Jan-19 May 71
Jennings County 15 awards	CR (5): 12 Mar 67, 22 Mar 67, 11 Apr 67, 12 Jun 67, 25 Jun 67 PUC (2): 31 Jan-29 Feb 68, 18 Oct-5 Dec 68 NUC (8): 10 Nov 66-30 Jan 68, 1 Mar-30 Sep 68, 1-17 Oct 68, 6 Dec 68-4 Mar 69, 5 Apr-11 Sep 69, 17 Oct-31 Dec 69, 1 Jul 70-30 Apr 71, 4 Jan-30 Jun 71

A SNAPSHOT OF THE *HUNTERDON COUNTY*'S DUTY

The service of *Hunterdon County*, which took part in the most campaigns of the four ships, included operations in Cambodian waters. On 12 May 1970, she became the first Navy ship to enter Cambodia, when she did so to rearm and refuel helicopters of the U.S. Army and Navy, and the Air Force of the Republic of Vietnam. President Richard Nixon had authorized U.S. combat troops to cross the border from South Vietnam into Cambodia the previous month. This action was aimed at forestalling communist North Vietnamese attacks into South Vietnam from their sanctuaries there, even as the South Vietnamese were being primed to assume more responsibility for the conduct of the war and U.S. forces were being withdrawn.[25]

Hunterdon County remained in Cambodia to provide support to the Vietnamese armed forces and their U.S. Army and Navy advisors longer than any other ship of her type. Her other unique achievements during

Vietnam service included capturing one of the largest Viet Cong caches in the Mekong Delta on 29 March 1969, and setting a record for the farthest transit of the Bassac River by a U.S. commissioned ship in August of that same year. She was subsequently reclassified a patrol craft tender *Hunterdon County* (AGP-838), as also were *Harnett County* (AGP-821) and *Garrett County* (AGP-786).[26]

Hampshire County made three trips into Cambodia in support of the Riverine Force. On one occasion, she ventured to within fifteen miles of Phnom Penh while transferring ammunition to *Hunterdon County*.[27]

LANDING SHIP SQUADRON NINE, YOKOSUKA

Landing Ship Squadron Nine (comprised of eight *Terrebonne Parish*-class LSTs built in the early 1950s) was commissioned at sea on 1 July 1960, and was transferred from San Diego to Yokosuka, Japan, that summer. Six of these ships collectively earned eight Presidential Unit Citations during the Vietnam War—including three by *Washtenaw County* alone.[28]

Over the course of the war, the squadron transported troops, ammunition, and resupply items, including bringing a large portion of the Republic of Korea troops and equipment from Pusan, Korea, to the Republic of Vietnam. Since 1967, ships of the squadron were assigned, on a continuing basis, to the MARKET TIME forces operating in the Mekong Delta. From 1 May 1970, ships also provided continuous support to bases in South Vietnam.[29]

Ship	Com/Decom	Disposition
Terrell County (LST-1157)	14 Mar 53/ 25 Mar 71	Transferred to Greece, renamed HS *Inouse* (L-104)
Tom Green County (LST-1159)	12 Sep 53/ 5 Jan 72	Transferred to Spain, renamed *Conde del Venadito* (L-13)
Vernon County (LST-1161)	18 May 53/ 14 Jun 73	Transferred to Venezuela, 29 June 1973, renamed ARBV *Amazonas* (T-21)
Washoe County (LST-1165)	30 Nov 53/ 25 Nov 70	Placed in service by the Military Sealift Command (MSC) as USNS *Washoe County* (T-LST-1165)
Washtenaw County (LST-1166)	29 Oct 53/ 30 Aug 73	Converted to a Special Minesweeper Ship and redesignated USS *Washtenaw County* (MSS-2), 9 February 1973
Westchester County (LST-1167)	10 Mar 54/ 30 Nov 73	Transferred to Turkey, 27 August 1974, renamed TCG *Serdar* (L-402)
Whitfield County (LST-1169)	14 Sep 54/ 15 Mar 73	Sold to Greece, 1 March 1977, renamed HS *Kos* (L116)
Windham County (LST-1170)	15 Dec 54/ 1 Jun 73	Transferred to Turkey, renamed TCG *Ertugrul* (L-401)

Ship	Unit Awards
Terrell County (LST-1157) 5 awards	PUC (1): 1 Jan-4 Feb 69 MUC (3): 1 Aug 65-31 Mar 68, 18 Jun-4 Aug 67, 1 Apr 68-31 Mar 69 NUC (1): 25 Jun-28 Oct 69
Tom Green County (LST-1159) 12 awards	CR (5): 3 Jul 67, 15 Apr 68, 28 Dec 68, 21 Jan 69, 16 Jun 69 MUC (3): 1 Aug 65-31 Mar 68, 18 Jun-8 Jul 67, 1 Apr 68-31 Mar 69 NUC (4): 1 Apr-25 May 68, 28 Dec 68-24 Jan 69, 3 Nov-16 Dec 70, 4 Apr-10 May 71
Vernon County (LST-1161) 13 awards	CR (3): 21 Nov 66, 9-12 Jun 68, 25 Jan 69 PUC (1): 28 Feb-25 Mar 69 MUC (5): 1 Aug 65-31 Mar 68, 1 Apr-22 May 68, 22 Jun-24 Jul 68, 14 Oct 68-31 Mar 69, 2 Mar-15 Dec 72 NUC (4): 19-25 Jun 67, 23 May-21 Jun 68, 25 Jul-13 Oct 68, 2 Oct-5 Nov 70
Washoe County (LST-1165) 5 awards	CR (1): 2 Apr 66 PUC (1): 18 Oct-5 Dec 68 MUC (2): 1 Aug 65-31 Mar 68, 1 Apr 68-31 Mar 69 NUC (1): 28 Jul-28 Aug 69
Washtenaw County (LST-1166) 11 awards	CR (1): 14 Mar 68 PUC (3): 29 Jan-4 Mar 68, 5-23 Feb 69, 1-31 Mar 69 MUC (4): 1 Aug 65-31 Mar 68, 1 Apr-16 Jun 68, 3-20 Sep 69, 2 Mar-15 Dec 72 NUC (3): 17 Jun-20 Jul 68, 10 Nov-2 Dec 68, 23 Feb-6 Apr 71
Westchester County (LST-1167) 9 awards	CR (3): 9 Sep 66, 11 Dec 67, 31 Oct-1 Nov 68 MUC (2): 1 Aug 65-31 Mar 68, 1 Apr-20 Sep 68 NUC (4): 20 Aug 67-16 Jan 68, 21 Sep-5 Nov 68, 30 Jul-2 Oct 70, 18-30 Jun 71
Whitfield County (LST-1169) 14 awards	CR (4): 24 Jul 68, 10 Jan 69, 30 Apr 69, 18 Jun 69 PUC (1): 8 May-5 Jul 69 MUC (5): 1 Aug 65-31 Mar 68, 1 Apr-17 Jul 68, 25 Sep-30 Nov 68, 25 Jan-31 Mar 69, 2 May-15 Dec 72 NUC (4): 20 Aug-29 Oct 67, 18 Jul-24 Sep 68, 1 Dec 68-24 Jan 69, 9 May-18 Jun 71
Windham County (LST-1170) 6 awards	CR (1): 17 Jan 66 PUC (1): 25 Mar-10 May 69 MUC (4): 1 Aug 65-31 Mar 68, 1 Apr-19 Jun 68, 27 Jul 68-31 Mar 69, 2 Mar-15 Dec 72

Washoe County's duties in 1965 were representative of those of other squadron ships: shuttle runs between Okinawa and Vietnam in support of American forces in country. The loads she carried included Marine Corps, Naval Beach Group, Naval Beach Jumper, and Amphibious Construction Battalion equipment and personnel. Squadron units also supported amphibious landings, and served as Mobile Riverine Force support/resupply ships, and mother ships for patrol vessels engaged in Operation MARKET TIME.[30]

In late summer and early fall of 1966, *Westchester County* was on station off the Ca Mau Peninsula, carrying out other type duties, refueling, replenishing, and serving as a base for boats and crews patrolling the coast of Vietnam to prevent infiltration by sea.[31]

REORGANIZATION OF LANDSHIPRON NINE IN 1967

Landing Ship Squadron Nine was reorganized on 1 November 1967, in concert with the transfer of Landing Ship Flotilla One from San Diego to Yokosuka, Japan. Two of Squadron Nine's existing divisions—LST Division 91 and LST Division 92—were disestablished, and their ships placed directly under commander, Landing Ship Squadron Nine. The four ships of its third division (IFS Division 93)—*Carronade, Clarion River, St. Francis River,* and *White River*—were transferred to commander, Landing Ship Flotilla One, based at Yokosuka, Japan.[32]

Flotilla One also gained four LSTs of Landing Ship Squadron One, permanently deployed in support of Operation GAME WARDEN.

Landing Ship Squadron Nine	
Terrell County (LST-1157)	*Washtenaw County* (LST-1166)
Tom Green County (LST-1159)	*Westchester County* (LST-1167)
Vernon County (LST-1161)	*Whitfield County* (LST-1169)
Washoe County (LST-1165)	*Windham County* (LST-1170)
Landing Ship Flotilla One	
Carronade (IFS-1)	*Garrett County* (LST-786)
Clarion River (LSMR-409)	*Harnett County* (LST-821)
St. Francis River (LSMR-525)	*Hunterdon County* (LST-838)
White River (LSMR-536)	*Jennings County* (LST-846)[33]

SQUADRON COMPOSITION AT YEAR'S END IN 1970

In late autumn in 1970, *Washoe County* and *Terrell County* arrived at Bremerton, Washington, to begin inactivation—reducing Landing Ship Squadron Nine to six ships.[34]

A few days later, Landing Ship Flotilla One was disestablished on 1 December, owing to declining requirements for Seventh Fleet amphibious ships in South Vietnam. Disestablishment of Landing Ship Squadron Three occurred that same day, and *Holmes County, Park County, Pitkin County,* and *Page County* were assigned to Landing Ship Squadron Nine. Squadron Nine was further bolstered by the acquisition of *Garrett County* and *Hunterdon County* from defunct Flotilla One.[35]

At year's end, ten tank landing ships and two patrol craft tenders (converted LSTs) comprised Landing Ship Squadron Nine.

1156-class (*Terrebonne Parish*) Ships	
Tom Green County (LST-1159)	Westchester County (LST-1167)
Vernon County (LST-1161)	Whitfield County (LST-1169)
Washtenaw County (LST-1166)	Windham County (LST-1170)
542-class (World War II vintage) Ships	
Holmes County (LST-836)	Park County (LST-1077)
Page County (LST-1076)	Pitkin County (LST-1082)
AGP (World War II vintage Ships Converted to Patrol Craft Tenders)	
Garrett County (AGP-786)	Hunterdon County (AGP-838)[36]

LANDING SHIP SQUADRON THREE, GUAM

We logistically supported Market Time coastal blockade, Game Warden river patrol, Mobile Riverine Force, and Regional and Popular Force operations in the Mekong Delta; alternating with direct logistical support for Third Marine Amphibious Force holding the northern front along the 17th Parallel....

In Vietnam the Blanco County *delivered vehicles, troops, and supplies (mainly gasoline in drums stacked on pallets 11 feet high on the tank deck and the main deck) to forward combat units; escorted contractors' vessels; and, during three months assigned to Operation Market Time, sustained and directed the operations of a task group of six fast patrol gunboats in blockade operations of enemy controlled sectors.... Patrol boat elements were deployed inshore daily to suppress all activity in the free fire zone at the mouth of the Bo De River in the southern tip of the Mekong Delta.*

When the patrol craft were occupied, Blanco County *occasionally gave chase to stop and inspect the family occupied coastal lighters which entered our area of operations. Overtaking them typically took several hours since our speed advantage on them was only about one knot. When one was in tow alongside, I would step outside the Combat Information Center and assume triggerman position on the M1919A4 machine gun there, watching the occupants assembled on the lighter's stern to see that nothing happened to the boarding party and to make sure that nobody got shot.*

Service on the Blanco County *witnessed a wealth of varied experience and Vietnam is a beautiful country. We saw many red blue and gold enemy flags along the rivers and attracted hostile fire once approaching Vinh Long in the Delta and once at Cua Viet on the DMZ. The ship was heavily armed and we had enough crew to man up to three quarters of our main armament at general quarters battle stations. In the rivers we also kept a man on the bow with an M-1 rifle and the only targets we ever shot at were floating debris that crossed the ship's path.*

—Lawrence P. Blumette, Supply Department head aboard the *Blanco County* (LST-344) from March 1968 to October 1969.[37]

Landing Ship Squadron Three was commissioned on 1 October 1954, with Comdr. Cornelius P. Callahan in command. A decade later, Lt. Comdr. Peter H. Orvis relieved Comdr. Thomas E. Reynolds, the squadron's eighth commander, on 2 September 1965. The seven ships of the squadron—*Tioga County, Stone County, Snohomish County, Polk County, Page County, Kemper County*, and *Floyd County*—subsequently deployed to Vietnam, participating in Operation DOUBLE EAGLE.[38]

As the buildup in Vietnam continued, it became obvious that more tank landing ships were required to support the war effort. Consequently, six LSTs in the Atlantic Reserve Fleet and eleven in the Pacific Reserve Fleet were taken out of "mothballs." They were overhauled and refitted in shipyards in Camden, New Jersey; Baltimore, Maryland; Long Beach, San Diego, and San Francisco, California; and Portland, Oregon, for duty in Vietnam.[39]

Jennings County, Hunterdon County, Harnett County, and *Garrett County* were overhauled in San Francisco. These ships, previously discussed, were modified to serve specifically as support ships for river patrol boats and helicopters. Of the remaining thirteen ships from the Reserve Fleet, *Litchfield County, Park County*, and *Sutter County* were the first three ships to deploy to the Western Pacific in July 1966. *Iredell County* and *Hampshire County* departed San Diego in September 1966 with full loads of materiel to support the Vietnam effort.[40]

On 4 October 1966, Orvis and his staff, embarked in *Pitkin County*, stood out of San Diego in company with *Caroline County*, and *Blanco County*, bound for Guam, Mariana Islands, the new home port of the squadron. *Sedgwick County, Coconino County*, and *Clarke County* arrived in the Western Pacific by the end of 1966. The majority of the ships were initially employed to transport men and materiel between Danang and Chu Lai. Other tasking included moving supplies from Japan, Okinawa, and Taiwan to Vietnam; participating in Operation DECKHOUSE V; and providing support for "Swift boats" in Operation MARKET TIME.[41]

The remaining ships of LandShipRon Three, *Meeker County* and *Bulloch County*, were en route to WestPac in January 1967. That year would find units of the squadron navigating rivers of the Mekong Delta area to beach supplies and equipment at Cua Viet. The primary mission of the squadron was direct amphibious and logistics support of U.S. and Allied operations in South Vietnam.[42]

Although the 542-class LSTs were a quarter-century old, and laboriously slow in comparison to modern ships, they were ideally suited for the role they played in Vietnam. They did not need pierside facilities to offload war supplies. Practically any beach and reasonable surf conditions would suffice, and the LSTs' shallow draft allowed them to ply waterways impassible to other logistics vessels. Nonetheless, a need for their services gradually lessened.[43]

For much of 1969, four ships of the squadron were assigned to Naval Support Activity, Danang; another two to Task Force 117 (Mobile Riverine Force)/Naval Support Activity, Saigon; and a seventh ship to Task Force 115 (Market Time). Three LSTs were kept in the South China Sea, as contingency ships in the event additional materiel movement was required from Danang to Cua Viet and Tan My.[44]

Danang's requirements were lowered to two ships in January 1969. Separately, the Task Force 117 commitment terminated. A draw down of Landing Ship Squadron Three followed. *Blanco County* and *Caroline County* departed Southeast Asia in late March, bound for San Diego. On 1 July, *Coconino County* was turned over to the Vietnamese Navy. These events marked the beginning stages of inactivation of the squadron. In October 1969, *Litchfield County* and *Sedgwick County* were placed out of commission, in reserve.[45]

Snohomish County was decommissioned at Guam in July 1970. *Hampshire County* and *Meeker County* began inactivation in September 1970. Other squadron ships returned to San Diego, and Landing Ship Squadron Three was disestablished on 1 December 1970.[46]

Ship	Recom/ Decom	Disposition
Blanco County (LST-344)	9 Jun 66/ 3 Oct 69	Sold for scrapping, 1 Jul 75, to W. L. Weeks
Bulloch County (LST-509)	20 Oct 50/ 8 Apr 70	Transferred to South Vietnam, renamed RVNS *Qui Nhon* (HQ-504)
Caroline County (LST-525)	9 Jun 66/ early 70	Sold for scrapping by the Defense Reutilization and Marketing Service (DRMS), 1 Aug 75
Clarke County (LST-601)	28 Jul 66/ Jul 70	Transferred to Indonesia, date unknown, renamed KRI *Teluk Saleh* (LST-510)
Coconino County (LST-603)	8 Jun 66/ 4 Apr 69	Transferred to South Vietnam, 4 Apr 69, renamed RVNS *Vung Tau* (HQ-503)
Floyd County (LST-762)	3 Nov 50/ 3 Sep 69	Sold, 4 Dec 75, to Max Rouse & Sons, Beverly Hills, CA
Hampshire County (LST-819)	6 Jul 66/ 19 Dec 70	Sold to Max Rouse & Sons, Beverly Hills, CA
Iredell County (LST-839)	18 Jun 66/ Jul 70	Transferred to Indonesia, renamed KRI *Teluk Bone* (LST-511)
Kemper County (LST-854)	20 Nov 50/ 28 May 69	Transferred to the government of Barbados in July 1975, renamed *Northpoint*
Litchfield County (LST-901)	5 Mar 66/ 7 Dec 69	Sold for scrapping by the DRMS, 1 Jan 77
Meeker County (LST-980)	23 Sep 66/ Dec 70	Sold to Max Rouse & Sons, Beverly Hills, CA

Page County (LST-1076)	28 Nov 60/ 5 Mar 71	Transferred to Greece, date unknown, renamed HS *Kriti* (L-171)
Park County (LST-1077)	9 Apr 66/ unknown	Sold to Mexico, 1 July 1978, renamed ARM *Rio Panuco* (LST-401)
Pitkin County (LST-1082)	9 Jul 66/ 1 Sep 71	Sold to Max Rouse & Sons, Beverly Hills, CA
Polk County (LST-1084)	3 Nov 50/ 30 Oct 69	Sold, 1 December 1975, for scrapping by the DRMS
Sedgwick County (LST-1123)	4 Jun 66/ 6 Dec 69	Sold, 1 August 1976, to Malaysia, renamed KD *Rajah Jaro* (A-1502)
Snohomish County (LST-1126)	28 Feb 45/ 1 Jul 70	Sold for scrapping in January 1971 to Chin Ho Fa Steel and Iron Co. Ltd., Taiwan
Stone County (LST-1141)	3 Nov 50/ May 1970	Transferred to Thailand, 12 March 1970, renamed HTMS *Lanta* (LST-4)
Sutter County (LST-1150)	16 Apr 66/ 12 Mar 71	Sold, 1 November 1975, by the Defense Reutilization and Marketing Service
Tioga County (LST-1158)	20 Jun 53/ 23 Dec 70	*Terrebonne Parish*-class ship commissioned on 20 June 1953; reactivated in 1972 for service with the Military Sealift Command as USNS *Tioga County* (T-LST-1158)

Page County earned seven Combat Action Ribbons and the most unit awards overall. *Hampshire County*, *Iredell County*, and *Sedgwick County* were awarded Presidential Unit Citations. *Snohomish County* was the longest serving, with continuous service since World War II. *Iredell County* and *Page County* were also units of Squadron Two during the war.

Ship	Unit Awards
Blanco County 2 awards	CR (1): 1-2 Jan 1967 NUC (1): 1 Jul 66-31 Mar 68
Bulloch County 1 award	MUC (1): 1 Jul 66-31 Mar 68
Caroline County 3 awards	CR (1) 24 Feb 68 MUC (1): 1 Jul 66-31 Mar 68 NUC (1): 11 Oct-13 Nov 68
Clarke County 3 awards	CR (1): 17 Nov-1 Dec 67 MUC (2): 1 Jul 66-31 Mar 68, 18 Nov 69-24 Apr 70
Coconino County 6 awards	CR (4): 29 Jul 67, 10 Jan 68, 3 Sep 68, 17 Feb 69 MUC (2): 1 Jul 66-31 Mar 68, 10 Nov-8 Dec 68
Floyd County 4 awards	CR (3): 2 Jun 68, 26 Aug 68, 2 Sep 68 MUC (1): 1 Apr-11 Oct 68
Hampshire County 4 awards	CR (2): 7-15 Jan 67, 23 May 70 PUC (1): 25 Jan-19 Apr 69 NUC (1): 22 Apr-27 June 70
Iredell County 7 awards	CR (4) 6-8 Feb 68, 21 Feb 68, 10 Mar 68, 18 Mar 70 PUC (1): 25 Jan-15 Feb 69 MUC (1): 5 Dec 69-24 Apr 70 NUC (1): 11 Nov-31 Dec 68

Kemper County 2 awards	CR (1): 3 Mar 66 NUC (1): 19-25 Jun 67
Litchfield County 3 awards	CR (1): 24 Feb 68 MUC (1): 1 Jul 66-31 Mar 68 NUC (1): 11 Jul-11 Aug 68
Meeker County 6 awards	CR (4): 2 Mar 68, 23 May 68, 14 Oct 68, 28 Jun 70 MUC (1): 1 Jul 66-31 Mar 68 NUC (1): 27 Jun-21 Nov 70
Page County 10 awards	CR (7): 21 Aug 68, 25 Aug 68, 12-13 Sep 68, 22 Sep 68, 28 Sep 68, 5 Oct 68, 26 Feb 70 MUC (2): 7 Jun-30 Nov 68, 28 Dec 69-24 Apr 68 NUC (1): 25 Apr-31 May 70
Park County 7 awards	CR (1): 1 Nov 68 MUC (1): 1 Jul 66-31 Mar 68 NUC (5): 2 Aug-4 Sep 68, 22 Sep-12 Nov 68, 24 Dec 70-26 Jan 71, 28 Feb-2 Apr 71, 10 May-30 Jun 71
Pitkin County 4 awards	MUC (1): 1 Jul 66-31 Mar 68 NUC (3): 2-24 Jun 68, 11 Oct-19 Nov 68, 5 May-24 Dec 70
Polk County	
Sedgwick County 5 awards	CR (2): 5 Mar 68, 11 Mar 68 PUC (1): 23 Apr-6 May 69 MUC (2): 1 Jul 66-16 Feb 68, 5-31 Mar 68
Snohomish County 1 award	CR (1): 17 Nov 68
Stone County 1 award	CR (1): 5 Mar 68
Sutter County 2 awards	MUC (1): 1 Jul 66-31 Mar 68 NUC (1): 16 Nov-17 Dec 68
Tioga County 1 award	CR (1): 16 Feb 66

LANDING SHIP SQUADRON ONE, SAN DIEGO

On 14 January 1966, *Henry County* (LST-824), with commander, Landing Ship Squadron One (Comdr. Derwin T. Lamb, USN) embarked, departed San Diego with *St. Clair County* (LST-1096) and *Snohomish County* (LST-1126) bound for Okinawa. Also embarked were elements of headquarters and support company, Third Amtrac Battalion, First Marine Division. The task unit arrived at Naha on 17 February, after a stop in Pearl Harbor. After offloading was completed, elements of the First Engineering Battalion, First Marines embarked. The task unit sailed on the morning of 19 February for Chu Lai, Vietnam.[47]

While deployed, *Henry County* and *Washoe County* participated in Operation JACKSTAY during which Commander Lamb earned the Bronze Star with Combat "V", and Lt. H. J. Lauffenberg, MC, USNR (staff medical officer), the Bronze Star with "V" and the Purple Heart. (A description of their actions may be found in Chapter 6.) Upon the arrival of Lamb and his staff back in San Diego, they resumed Squadron

Work Horses of the Amphibious Force   151

One inspection, training, and assistance to newly commissioned, returning, and deployed units of Landing Ship Squadrons One and Three.[48]

Four to six ships from Landing Ship Squadron One were assigned to commander, Landing Ship Squadron Three during their deployments to Vietnam in 1968 and 1969. Requirements for the services of these ships lessened in 1969 and terminated in June. *Iredell County* and *Stone County* were later assigned to Landing Ship Squadron Two.[49]

Ship	Recom/ Decom	Disposition
Henry County (LST-824)	5 Sep 59/ unknown	Transferred to Malaysia, 1 Oct 76, renamed KD *Sri Banggi* (A-1501)
Holmes County (LST-836)	3 Nov 50/ 1 Jul 71	Transferred to Singapore and renamed RSN *Endurance* (L-201)
Iredell County (LST-839)	18 Jun 66/ July 1970	Transferred to Indonesia, renamed KRI *Teluk Bone* (LST-511)
Jerome County (LST-848)	7 Dec 59/ 1 Apr 70	Transferred to South Vietnam in Apr 70, renamed RVNS *Nha Trang* (HQ-505)
Outagamie County (LST-1073)	3 Nov 50/ 21 May 71	Transferred to Brazil, renamed *Garcia D'Avilla* (G 28)
St. Clair County (LST-1096)	3 Oct 50/ 26 Sep 69	Sold for scrapping, 1 Dec 75, by Defense Reutilization and Marketing Service
San Joaquin County (LST-1122)	3 Nov 50/ 26 Sep 69	Sold for scrapping, 1 Sep 74, by Defense Reutilization and Marketing Service
Stone County (LST-1141)	3 Nov 50/ May 1970	Transferred to Thailand, 12 Mar 70, renamed HTMS *Lanta* (LST-4)
Summit County (LST-1146)	30 May 45/ 31 Oct 69	Continuously in-service following WWII; sold to Ecuador, 14 Feb 77, renamed *Hualcopo* (T-55)
Sumner County (LST-1148)	3 Oct 50/ 9 Oct 69	Sold, 1 Aug 75, to Frank Ganter, Newport, Rhode Island, used as a barge
Wexford County (LST-1168)	15 Jun 54/ 1 Nov 76	*Terrebonne Parish*-class ship commissioned on 15 Jun 54; Sold to Spain, 29 Oct 71, renamed *Martin Alvarez* (L-12)

Ship	Unit Awards
Henry County 2 awards	CR (2): 29-30 Jan 68, 6 Feb 68
Holmes County 4 awards	CR (1): 30 Oct 68 NUC (3): 19 Jun-17 Aug 67, 26 Jan-3 Mar 71, 2 Apr-10 May 71
Iredell County 7 awards	CR (4) 6-8 Feb 68, 21 Feb 68, 10 Mar 68, 18 Mar 70 PUC (1): 25 Jan-15 Feb 69 MUC (1): 5 Dec 69-24 Apr 70 NUC (1): 11 Nov-31 Dec 68
Jerome County 3 awards	CR (1): 18 Mar 68 PUC (1): 29 Jan-18 Feb 68 MUC (1): 29 Nov 67-1 Jun 68

Outagamie County		
San Joaquin County 1 award	MU (1): 1 Apr-30 Jun 69	
St. Clair County	CR (2): 23-24 Jul 68, 30 Jul 68	
3 awards	NUC (1): 3 Sep-12 Oct 68	
Stone County 1 award	CR (1): 5 Mar 68	
Summit County		
Sumner County	CR (1): 25 Jun 68	
2 awards	NUC (1): 2 Jun-30 Nov 68	
Wexford County	CR (3): 17 Sep 65, 20 Oct 65, 8 Nov 70	
4 awards	MUC (1): 15 Nov 67-22 May 68	

NEWPORT-CLASS TANK LANDING SHIPS

The Pacific Fleet's newest LSTs were home ported in Long Beach or San Diego after commissioning. Two of the ten *Newport*-class ships that served in Vietnam—*Cayuga* and *Schenectady*—earned Combat Action Ribbons on 24 May 1972, and 27 June 1972, respectively. None received PUC, MUCs, or NUCs.

Amphibious Force, Pacific Fleet

Ship/Home port	Com/Decom	Disposition
Cayuga (LST-1186) Long Beach, CA	8 Aug 70/ 26 Aug 94	4 May 72/ Leased to Brazil, 30 Nov 1996, renamed NDCC *Mattoso Maia* (G-28)
Frederick (LST-1184) San Diego, CA	11 Apr 70/ 5 Oct 02	Sold to Mexico, 22 Nov 2002, renamed ARM *Usumacinta* (A-412)
Fresno (LST-1182) San Diego, CA	22 Nov 69/ 8 Apr 93	Disposed of as a target, 15 Sep 2014, during Fleet Exercise SINKEX-2014
Peoria (LST-1183) San Diego	21 Feb 70/ 28 Jan 94	Sunk as a target, 12 July 2004, during Exercise RIMPAC 2004
Racine (LST-1191) San Diego, CA	9 Jul 71/ 2 Oct 93	Sunk as a target, 12 July 2018, during Exercise RIMPAC 2018.
San Bernardino (LST-1189)	27 Mar 71/ 30 Sep 95	Transferred to Chile, 23 June 1999, renamed *Valdivia* (L-93)
Schenectady (LST-1185) San Diego, CA	13 Jun 70/ 15 Dec 93	Sunk as a target by aircraft, Nov 2004, during Exercise Resultant Fury
Sumter (LST-1181) Long Beach, CA	20 Jun 70/ 30 Sep 93	Leased to the Republic of China, ROCS *Chung Ping* (LST-233)
Tuscaloosa (LST-1187) San Diego, CA	24 Oct 70/ 18 Feb 94	Disposed of as a target during a SINKEX off Hawaii, date unknown
Amphibious Force, Atlantic Fleet		
Manitowoc (LST-1180) Little Creek, VA	24 Jan 70/ 30 Jun 93	Leased to the Republic of China, 10 July 1996, ROCS *Chung Ho* (LST-232)

Having introduced the World War II-vintage LSTs, and newer tank landing ships that served in Vietnam, we will now return to the action in Southeast Asia.

10

Inception of the River Patrol Force

> *GAME WARDEN was planned in December [1965] for operations in river mouths and estuaries of the Mekong Delta and the Rung Sat Special Zone. Objectives will be to prevent VC infiltration, interdict traffic and supplies at river crossings, and isolate the enemy in areas that are bounded by rivers and canals. By this effort substantial Navy support would be given to the Vietnamese Navy River Assault Groups.*
>
> *Forces will be composed of 100 31-foot fiberglass River Patrol Boats (PBR), 20 landing craft (LCPL) based at eight locations in the Delta, and three LST's anchored in principal river mouths. Operations are planned to be similar to MARKET TIME, but with the added hazard of continuous operations within weapon range of river banks. In-country logistic support will come from two major maintenance facilities at Nha Be and Can Tho, with minor maintenance available at the six other bases plus support from the three LST's.*
>
> —Vietnam War Highlights, "Naval Historical Summary January 1966 Highlights," Naval History and Heritage Command.

In early 1966, Rear Adm. Norvell G. Ward, USN, chief of the Naval Advisory Group, established a river patrol force intended to keep men, equipment, and food originating in the rich, densely populated Mekong Delta from reaching Viet Cong strongholds in the central highlands of South Vietnam. Designated Task Force 116, its area of operations was the major rivers of the Delta and the Rung Sat Special Zone (RSSZ), which included the major shipping channels to Saigon. The associated campaign was code named Operation GAME WARDEN.[1]

On 1 April 1966, Rear Admiral Ward became commander, Naval Forces Vietnam (ComNavFor), a newly created command with much greater responsibilities than the advisory group. Its establishment was necessary because of the large increase of naval forces and facilities in South Vietnam. Under Ward were the Naval Advisory Group, the Naval Support Activities in Saigon and Danang, the 30th Naval Construction Regiment, Task Force 115, and Task Force 116. General

Westmoreland exercised operational control over ComNavFor, while the new command was administratively under commander in chief, Pacific Fleet. ComNavFor turned over responsibility for Task Force 115 (Market Time) to Capt. Clifford L. Stewart, USN, on 16 April. The following month, Capt. Boyd B. Witham Jr., USN, assumed command of the River Patrol Force (Task Force 116) on 18 May, in a ceremony held at the base at Nha Be.[2]

Operation GAME WARDEN entered its fledgling stage in April 1966 as the first PBRs became operational and took up patrols of the waters of the Rung Sat Special Zone. This action followed the departure of the Marine Amphibious Force at the conclusion of JACKSTAY on 7 April. River patrols established during the operation, were maintained to deny the Viet Cong use of the major waterways in the RSSZ. As the boat crews received necessary indoctrination and training, construction of new bases in the Mekong Delta continued in preparation for the arrival of additional patrol units in forthcoming months.[3]

Map 10-1

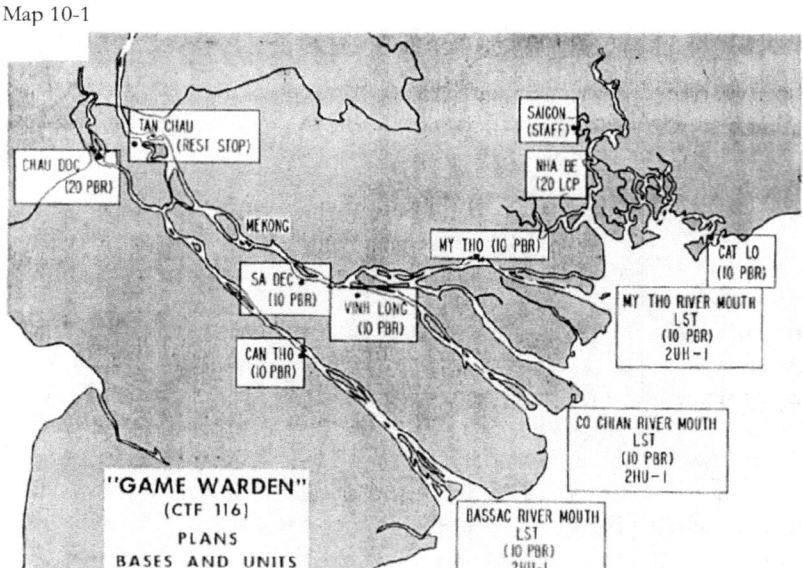

Planned GAME WARDEN bases and forces, including three tank landing ships.
Source: Vietnam War Highlights, "Naval Historical Summary February 1966 Highlights," Naval History and Heritage Command

Ten patrol stations in the Rung Sat were to be manned by five WPBs (cutters) of Coast Guard Squadron One, and four Navy PCFs (Swift boats). Other naval units were to temporarily provide assistance.

These included two LCPLs (large personnel landing craft), UH-1B (Seawolf) fire teams, and MSBs (minesweeping boats). The PBRs (river patrol boats) were to join when operationally ready. The patrols commenced on 6 April. Two days later, Vietnamese Navy units took over responsibility for two stations, freeing one WPB and one PCF for MARKET TIME patrols.[4]

Vietnamese River Assault Group (RAG) units—consisting of one "commandament," one "FOM," and one monitor—assumed patrols on the upper Soi Rap River. Other VNN units patrolled the eastern reaches of the Vam Co and Dong Tranh rivers.[5]

Photo 10-1

Vietnamese Navy commandament; a former LCM armed with .50-caliber machine guns, 20mm cannons, and an 81mm mortar.
National Archives photograph #USN 1104728

Photo 10-2

Vietnamese Navy "FOM" (France d'Outre Mer) river patrol boat.
Naval History and Heritage Command photograph #NH 93792

The PBRs of River Patrol Section 541 took up patrols on 16 April, which released two PCFs and two WPBs for MARKET TIME operations. Seven stations were then manned continually by U.S. units: two by PBRs, three by WPBs and two by PCFs. During the month, boats assigned the Soi Rap River patrol came under moderate to heavy small arms and automatic weapons fire from the banks. Most of the harassing fire occurred in a section near the mouth of the Vam Sat River—a known Viet Cong infiltration route terminal and the scene of considerable action during March and April. Shore fire was received on two occasions near the Soi Rap River mouth. Meanwhile, the Long Tau River patrol stations remained relatively quiet.[6]

On 26 April, twelve additional PBRs arrived at Cat Lo. These boats underwent shakedown cruises from the base at Cat Lo and from the tank landing ship *Floyd County* (LST-762). She had arrived in Vietnam two weeks earlier to become the second Inshore Support ship. River Division 51 was activated on 27 April aboard the *Tortuga* (LSD-26), in preparation for initial operations in the Mekong Delta in May. The new PBRs comprised subordinate River Section 512.[7]

Photo 10-3

Dock landing ship USS *Tortuga* (LSD-26) under way, circa the 1960s.
Naval History and Heritage Command photograph #NH 107634

Although crew performance during initial PBR operations was excellent, numerous problem areas arose in the boats themselves. Narrow vinyl beading on their hulls (which served as a fender when boarding and searching large junks, or alongside a support ship) proved insufficient to prevent damage to the side of the boats. Use of discarded helicopter tires as fenders corrected this shortcoming. Other necessary modifications included the removal of armor plating around the forward gun mount, to improve visibility and communications for the gunner and coxswain. M-72s (one-time-only antitank rockets) were carried aboard the boats, pending the installation of a 40mm grenade launcher. In a related improvement, .50-caliber machine guns were being installed to replace the after .30-caliber machine guns.[8]

Another first was achieved in April, when the ships engaged in naval gunfire support off the coast included newcomers from the Amphibious Force as well as destroyers and cruisers. The inshore fire support ship *Carronade* (IFS-1) and the rocket ship *St. Francis River* (LSMR-525) had recently arrived in the Western Pacific as members of Inshore Fire Support Division Ninety-three.[9]

Photo 10-4

USS *Carronade* (IFS-1) and USS *White River* (LSMR-536) off Danang. Naval History and Heritage Command photograph #L45-43.08.02

MINING OF SS *EASTERN MARINER* AT NHA BE

Photo 10-5

SS *Eastern Mariner* down by the stern, with a starboard list, after being mined in 1965. Courtesy of RAN, Sea Power Centre, Australia

In May 1966, GAME WARDEN operations continued in the Rung Sat Special Zone, and expanded into the Mekong Delta for the first time. Seawolves flew thirty-one reconnaissance, twenty-five rapid reaction, sixteen escort, and seven medical evacuation missions. During these operations, helicopter fire teams flying from *Tortuga* killed four enemy; destroyed four sampans, and damaged nineteen others; and destroyed five large Viet Cong structures.[10]

In early morning darkness on 26 May, Viet Cong swimmer-sappers infiltrated the port at Nha Be and sank a merchant vessel lying at anchor. The first indication of enemy action was a loud explosion resounding through the anchorage at 0150, followed by distress signals from a ship's fog horn. The base immediately went to General Quarters, and PBRs and units of VNN RAG 22 were sent to investigate. The PBRs reported the SS *Eastern Mariner* was settling by her stern with a starboard list. Of Panamanian registry, the merchant vessel carried a cargo of bagged cement. Her crew abandoned, and were brought to the base by the PBRs and RAG 22 units. There were no personnel casualties.[11]

Divers found a 12-foot by 10-foot hole in the starboard quarter of the sunken ship, and recovered remnants of nylon cord to which a mine had been attached. Few viewing the ruined vessel were probably aware of her storied Royal Australian Navy service in World War II. The coastal cargo ship (a product of Caledon Shipbuilding and Engineering Co Ltd, Dundee, Scotland) had been requisitioned by the Australian government on 10 October 1940 for conversion at Sydney and subsequent service as the RAN's only dedicated minelayer.[12]

As HMAS *Bungaree*, she emplaced defensive minefields from August 1941 to December 1943, as part of Australia and New Zealand

defenses against the very real possibility of a Japanese invasion. In total, she laid 9,289 moored mines in five general areas:
- 5,226 Mk XIV along the Great Barrier Reef off Queensland
- 1,468 Mk XIV and 593 Mk XVII at Noumea, New Caledonia
- 910 Mk XIV at Port Moresby, Papua (now Papua-New Guinea)
- 680 Mk XIV at New Zealand
- 412 XIV near Torres Strait (separating Australia and New Zealand)[13]

Following her naval service, *Bungaree* had been decommissioned on 7 August 1946, returned to her owners, and subsequently sold twice and renamed *Eastern Mariner* in 1960.[14]

Photo 10-6

HMAS *Bungaree* at Sydney, New South Wales, Australia. The future *Eastern Mariner* began life as a coastal cargo ship and, following requisitioning by the Australian government, and conversion, had served as an auxiliary minelayer in World War II. Australian War Memorial photograph 300494

Eastern Mariner was not the only target of swimmer-sappers the morning of 26 May. A second explosion occurred near another vessel, anchored about 350 yards away. No damage resulted. Inspection of her anchor chain revealed an attached nylon cord, believed to have tethered the mine. EOD divers discovered an unexploded mine attached to the chain of a third ship, and were able to remove it in time. Containing about 130 pounds of TNT, rigged to be electrically detonated by a double-timing device, the mine was affixed by metal hooks and nylon parachute cord. This arrangement, as intended, allowed it to drift with the current into position under the ship.[15]

The emplacement of munitions by swimmer-sappers prompted a quick reevaluation of anchorage security at Nha Be. Immediate actions taken included advising the masters of ships not to heave around on their anchor chains or turn their screws, preparatory to departure, until they had received an underwater inspection.[16]

MEKONG DELTA AND RUNG SAT DEVELOPMENTS

Patrol craft familiarization and training began in the Mekong Delta on 8 May, following the arrival of PBRs near Can Tho. A week later, two patrol boats received automatic weapons fire while distributing leaflets describing new curfew hours on the Bassac River. The boats cleared the area fifteen miles southwest of Can Tho with no casualties or damage. Returning later, they came under heavy, constant automatic weapons fire, which wounded two crewmen and lightly damaged both PBRs. Fish traps across the river had forced the boats to operate close to shore, and increased their vulnerability.[17]

A similar experience unfolded during the PBRs' first night action on 17 May, which was repeated several times during the month. The use of heavy shore fire by Viet Cong to cover the transport of supplies across rivers was a familiar tactic, but these incidents were the first involving U.S. Navy patrol boats on Mekong Delta waterways.[18]

The addition of sixteen PBRs in May 1966, brought the total number of the boats in country to forty-seven. However, the rapid tempo of operations in the RSSZ continued to tax crews and their boats. The PBRs ran twelve-hour patrols with an additional two or three hours spent transiting to and from patrol areas. Some of the scarce remaining time off-patrol each day, was devoted to maintenance, because most River Patrol Sections were required to perform their own. Operating from the support ships offered their own challenges. When even moderate seas were running, skilled boat handling was required to prevent damage to the patrol craft.[19]

The workload eased in June with the arrival of sixteen more PBRs (bringing the total to sixty-three in-county) and the assignment of two additional River Patrol Sections to the Mekong Delta. Patrol boats also took over the remaining stations in the Rung Sat assigned to Swift boats—releasing them for MARKET TIME duties.[20]

GAME WARDEN SUPPORT SHIPS

Five amphibious ships served as support ships in 1966. These were the dock landing ships *Belle Grove* (LSD-2), *Comstock* (LSD-19), and *Tortuga* (LSD-26), and tank landing ships *Floyd County* (LST-762) and *Jennings County* (LST-846). The duration of such assignments varied, because the "amphibs" were rotated to other duties, including Market Time and Special Landing Force operations.[21]

Belle Grove arrived at Chu Lai on 5 February 1966. Over the next two months, she maintained LCM landing craft, PBR river patrol boats, and UH-1B "Huey" helicopters in the Rung Sat Special Zone. She also served as a command center for coordinated Navy riverine patrols and Army helicopter sweeps against Viet Cong forces as part of Operation JACKSTAY. Those attacks, carried out in concert with B-52 bombing strikes, lasted from 26 March to 4 April 1966. In mid-April, *Belle Grove* coordinated the first PBR and helicopter patrols on the Long Tau River. After *Tortuga* relieved her at Vung Tau as armed-helo support ship, she departed for the Philippines on 19 April.[22]

Map 10-2

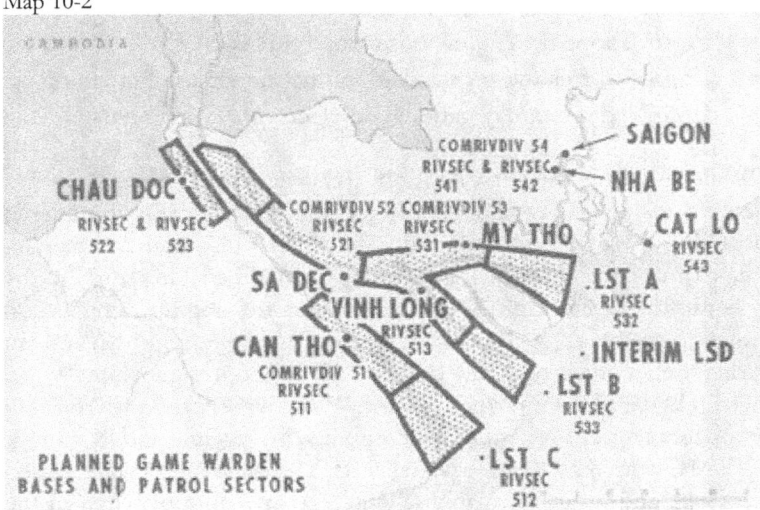

Diagram of planned River Division, and subordinate River Section operating areas, in the Mekong Delta and Rung Sat Special Zone. Support ship stations at the mouths of the My Tho River (LST A), Ham Luong River (Interim LSD), Co Chien River (LST B), and Bassac River (LST C) are also identified.
Source: Vietnam War Highlights, "Naval Historical Summary July 1966 Highlights," Naval History and Heritage Command

The first LST specially-configured to serve as mobile PBR/gunship bases, arrived in theater in late 1966. *Jennings County* reported to Chu Lai on 11 November from San Diego. The remaining three LSTs arrived in-county in 1967. The "Vietnam Service" column in the following table provides "ballpark" estimates of when the other ships reported for duty. The dates reflect the beginning of the eligibility period for the first Vietnam Service Medal earned by each LST, and the end of the period for their final one received.

Ship	Vietnam Service	Ship	Vietnam Service
Jennings County	7 Nov 66-12 Aug 70	*Hunterdon County*	5 Jul 67-31 Mar 71
Harnett County	12 Jan 67-21 Jul 70	*Garrett County*	29 Nov 67-2 Feb 71

The LSTs provided supply and maintenance facilities for PBRs (and other small boats), as well as some other services unavailable at shore bases. Modifications made to the tank landing ships in preparation for river patrol support of small boats and aircraft, included:

- A day and night landing area for UH-1 helicopters
- Refuel and rearm facilities for the gunships
- Four boat booms for mooring up to sixteen PBRs alongside
- A cargo boom to lift PBRs aboard for repairs
- Repair shops for engine, pump, and hull work
- Improved fresh water distillation due to increased manning
- Upgraded radio, navigation, and electronic equipment[24]

While awaiting the arrival of the *Jennings County*, *Harnett County*, *Hunterdon County*, and *Garrett County* in theater, interim LSDs shouldered support ship duties. *Tortuga* operated between Vung Tau and Saigon, helping to guard the entrances of shipping channels snaking through the Rung Sat to the capital city. She shifted to the Mekong Delta region on 12 June, to serve as a floating base for River Section 512 and an embarked detachment of Army Bell UH-1B helicopter gunships.[25]

The relatively heavily armed, 31-foot PBRs were fitted with one .50-caliber machine gun forward and a combined "over-and-under" mount (.50-cal. MG above an 81mm mortar) aft. The helicopters were armed with rockets and up to six machine guns. Army "choppers" from the 145th Aviation Detachment were replaced by Navy helicopters during *Tortuga*'s tour. Working together as a team in the verdant jungle, the patrol boats knifed through muddy, sandy-colored waters while the helicopters flew close cover overhead.[26]

GAME WARDEN FORCES STRENGTH IN JULY 1966

The total number of river patrol craft increased by another eight in July, bringing ComNavFor's riverine Navy strength to 71 PBRs, 12 MSBs, a SEAL team, and two helicopter fire teams from *Tortuga* (LSD-26). In addition to PBRs and helicopters, Task Force 116 included other units. Based at Nha Be, SEAL Team One engaged in direct combat with Viet Cong in the Rung Sat, while the twelve minesweeping boats of Mine Squadron Eleven Detachment Alfa toiled to keep the shipping channels passing through it open to Allied vessels.[27]

Photo 10-7

Minesweeping boat *MSB-49* operating on the Saigon River in July 1966. The three dayshapes (black balls forming a triangle) displayed on her mast signify that she is engaged in minesweeping operations.
National Archives photograph #USN 1118586

President Lyndon B. Johnson awarded the first Vietnam War-era Presidential Unit Citation to a unit of the U.S. Navy or Marine Corps on 9 October 1967. The recipient was not, as one might imagine, an aviation element flying strikes over North Vietnam or a group of special warfare experts embroiled in the war ashore. Instead, it went to the detachment of 57-foot wooden minesweeping boats, based at Nha Be. During the period cited, from 1 June 1966 to 18 February 1967, the boats and their crews faced great danger from river mines and Viet Cong ambush daily. They endured for the full thirty-mile segment of the Long Tau, from Nha Be through the infamous Rung Sat Special Zone, to the sea, while sweeping it clear of hostile ordnance.[28]

Photo 10-8

Navy SEALS engage in some target practice as their converted "Mike" boat carries them back to Nha Be, following a search-and-destroy operation in the jungle along one of the Mekong Delta's small waterways, September 1967.
National Archives photograph #K-40663

Known from before the French colonization of Vietnam as a refuge for the pirates and bandits that preyed upon river and coastal traffic, the area later became one of the strongholds of the Binh Xuyen gangsters (sometimes referred to as the "Vietnamese Mafia"). American servicemen commonly referred to the Rung Sat as the Forest of Assassins, because the Vietnamese word *rung* can be translated as "forest, jungle or woods" and *sat* as "assassin, killer or murderer."[29]

In *A Soldier Reports*, General William C. Westmoreland explains his rationale for ordering minesweeping of the waterway between the South China Sea and Saigon, as well as the Army's efforts to break the Viet Cong grip on the surrounding area:

> I was long concerned that the VC might sink a large vessel along the forty-mile course of the Saigon River to block the vital shipping channel between Saigon and the sea. The main channel ran through fifty square miles of mangrove swamps and thousands of tributary

waterways, a region known as the Rung Sat, which was an ideal base from which the VC could operate against shipping. One of the most savage pieces of terrain in the world, the Rung Sat has almost no ground that is not subject to inundation from a six-foot tidal variation. The houses of the few villages in the region are built on stilts.[30]

Daily sweeping for mines was both tedious and dangerous, particularly in the meandering restricted passages that cut through the Rung Sat Swamp. Here, boat crews, as well as Navy and merchant ships in passage, regularly faced death from mines command-detonated by observers hidden in heavy foliage along the banks, or from ambush by Viet Cong armed with rockets, 57mm and 75mm recoilless rifles, and automatic weapons. A former MSB crewman recalls witnessing two merchant vessels damaged by enemy mines during his initial duty aboard a minesweeping boat:

> We were the first group from Mine Squadron 11 to go to Nha Be. I was nineteen years old and the first trip down the Long Tau was scary.... I watched the *Eastern Mariner* sink at Nha Be after being blown up by the VC. Our boat, *MSB-16*, was one of the first on the scene at the SS *Baton Rouge Victory* [locale] after it was mined and beached.[31]

On 23 August 1966, three months after the mining of the *Eastern Mariner*, Viet Cong operating from bases in the Rung Sat mined, for the first time, a vessel proceeding upriver from Vung Tau to Saigon. Command-fired from the bank as the ship passed within the mine's kill radius, the explosion beneath the *Baton Rouge Victory* opened a sixteen-by-forty-five-foot hole in her port hull, killing seven crewmembers, all engineers. With water pouring in, the master put the vessel aground on the south bank, in order to prevent it from sinking and to keep the shipping channel open.[32]

RIVER CROSSING OF VC BATTALION INTERDICTED

While, it's only possible to provide a sampling of the heroics of PBR and Seawolf crews in a book primarily dedicated to amphibious ships, the following incident deserves special mention. In the fall of 1966, Lt. Comdr. Morton E. Toole, commander, River Division 53, set up a special patrol in the vicinity of Ngo Hiep Island. This action reflected his belief that the Viet Cong would be forced out of their operating areas in the Plain of Reeds by high water. The island lay fifteen miles west of

My Tho, a Delta town southwest of Saigon. Toole hoped to intercept the enemy at a well-established route into the Kien Hoa Province.[33]

The Plain of Reeds (a thirty-by-seventy-mile marshland due west of Saigon and north of the Mekong River) is generally flat, perennially inundated, and covered by a dense growth of aquatic grass and reeds ranging in height from three to twelve feet. The Viet Cong had long enjoyed hegemony over the region, because the difficult terrain made penetration by organized military units next to impossible. Patrol air cushion vehicles (PACVs) would be tried in this area in November, after less than spectacular evaluations in MARKET TIME and GAME WARDEN operations. The great noise produced by the hovercraft had alerted the enemy in other areas, but the Plain of Reeds, which offered much less concealment, seemed to be made for air-cushion vehicles.[34]

Photo 10-9

Crewmen of a PACV (patrol air cushion vehicle) and Vietnamese troops round up Viet Cong suspects in the Plain of Reeds near Moc Hoa, 21 November 1966. National Archives photograph #USN 1119446

On the evening of 31 October, PBRs *105* and *107* with Boatswain's Mate First James Elliott Williams in charge as patrol officer (and boat captain of the *105*), were on patrol in the area when a sampan with one occupant was sighted heading out of the Nam Thon River along the northern edge of Ngo Hiep Island. As *PBR-105*, covered by *PBR-107*, approached the sampan, it darted into the adjacent flooded paddies, and fired two rounds of small arms at the patrol boat. A second sampan, following the first, also fired at the PBRs, which returned fire with their .50-caliber machine guns. The two occupants of the sampan abandoned and were killed by machine gun rounds while trying to reach the shore.[35]

During the short firefight, a junk and several more sampans came into view on the other side of the island. Because of hightide and flood conditions, the crews of the PBRs had an unobstructed view over the low-lying feature. The patrol boats entered the Nam Thon, and came under heavy fire from its north bank and from two large junks in an inlet. Behind the junks were eight small sampans, with eight-to-ten green-uniformed men aboard each. Gunfire from the PBRs sank two of the sampans. As their survivors sought to reach the brush at river's edge, the remaining sampans took cover in dense woods, inundated by navigable waters, along its bank.[36]

As the PBRs withdrew along the southern edge of a small island in the Nam Thon, they were startled to find an armada of seventy-five sampans and seven junks. All of the craft had been abandoned, or were being so, by troops scampering ashore. The PBRs took fleeing Viet Cong under fire with .50-caliber and small arms, and requested assistance from the Vinh Long fire team. While awaiting the helicopters, the PBRs withdrew to the eastern edge of Ngo Hiep Island. Upon arrival of the fire team, the patrol boats deliberately drew enemy fire to pinpoint their positions for the gunships.[37]

As the fire team made its first pass overhead, the boats withdrew under heavy fire from about ten positions on the bank. *PBR-105* took a hit forward and aft, but suffered no serious damage or personnel casualties. As the PBRs moved away to give the helicopters a clear field of fire, the boats poured rounds into the junks. A firing run by the helicopters caused a secondary explosion aboard a junk, which reached an estimated height of 300 feet. The PBRs, firing on enemy troops retreating northward through waist-deep water, were joined by two other two-boat patrols. By engagement's end, eight PBRs, an LCM-6 from Naval Supply Activity Detachment, My Tho, and the fire team (two Navy helicopters) were on the scene.[38]

Nothing of intelligence value was found aboard sampans accessible to PBRs. Many of the small craft had drifted into brush in shallows denied the patrol boats. Debris, clothing, and some blood were floating in the area of the battle. Gunfire from the PBRs was responsible for twenty-eight sampans and eight junks sunk, and another three junks and three sampans captured. The LCM-6 towed the captured craft to My Tho. The fire team claimed fifteen sampans sunk, at least another seven damaged, and the ammunition-laden junk blown to bits. Helicopter reconnaissance reported the area was covered with burning sampans.[39]

There were no American casualties and only three hits to the boats. In addition to the two received by *PBR-105*, a bullet struck *PBR-107* forward, on her starboard side. The short action (which thwarted an estimated battalion-sized troop crossing) illustrated the value of a rapid, coordinated PBR/helicopter fire team response, against an enemy in the open, willing to engage in combat.[40]

In a ceremony at the Pentagon on 13 May 1968, Boatswain's Mate First Class James Elliott Williams, USN, received the Medal of Honor from Lyndon B. Johnson. As the president struggled to fasten the snaps at the back of the cravat (neck ribbon) of the Medal of Honor, he whispered in Johnson's ear, "Damn, Williams, you've got a big neck." (The medal citation, describing Williams' actions justifying receipt of the nation's highest and most prestigious personal military decoration for heroism in combat, may be found in Appendix E.)[41]

Photo 10-10

Boatswain Mate First Class James Elliott Williams, U.S. Navy, Medal of Honor recipient 13 May 1968.
Naval History and Heritage Command photograph L38-97.04.01

GAME WARDEN SUPPORT SHIP ROTATIONS

As river patrol boats and armed helicopters executed their dangerous tasking, amphibious ships continued to serve as floating bases for them. The dock landing ship *Comstock* relieved *Tortuga* of her duties on 11 September, and embarked River Patrol Section 512 and Helicopter Combat Support Squadron 1, Detachment 29. Efforts to interdict Viet Cong movements in the Mekong Delta, resumed immediately.[42]

Photo 10-11

USS *Comstock* (LSD-19), with a landing craft alongside, at Chu Lai, 24 June 1965. National Archives photograph #USN 1111760

Comstock was relieved by the tank landing ship *Jennings County* on 11 November, following arrival of this first specially configured GAME WARDEN LST in Vietnam. Some growing pains accompanied the employment of a different type of amphibious ship. Upon arriving off the mouth of the Bassac River on the 15th, *Jennings County* experienced difficulty in positioning herself, owing to heavy seas, high winds, and strong currents. The LST's initial attempt to anchor into the wind, failed because ship's head slewed 100 degrees off her anchor bearing, before the "bower" could be dropped. The stern anchor held on her third attempt, and the ship's roll steadied at 10-15 degrees.[43]

Attempts to launch PBRs the following day failed because of heavy seas. Continued difficulties in handling boats resulted in *Jennings County* shifting to Can Tho on 18 November. Other difficulties arose there. Steel-wheeled dollies and forklifts with hard rubber tires slipped on wet decks, dowsed by spray during constant rolling. After anchoring in a position to minimize rolling, strong winds from another direction created problems with boats on the lifting hook. PBR and helicopter handling appeared to be unmanageable at this location; favorable conditions for hauling boats precluded helicopter launching operations.[44]

GAME WARDEN ACTIVITIES AT YEAR'S END

In December 1966, enemy crossing attempts were disrupted by GAME WARDEN forces in the Soi Rap, Mekong (My Tho), and Ham Luong rivers. On one occasion, a PBR patrol proceeding up a confined canal, surprised a large force of Viet Cong. In the ensuing rapid engagement, fifteen enemy were killed and twenty-eight sampans destroyed.[45]

The year ended on an ominous note with the discovery, on 31 December, of a large Soviet moored-contact mine in the Long Tau River, Saigon's main shipping channel. At 0815 that morning, the boat captain of *MSB-52* sighted five contact horns exposed above the water. The associated unmoored red lead-coated mine was floating in the Long Tau, near the junction of the Nga Bay and Dua rivers.[46]

A Navy EOD team disarmed the "shipkiller" (which carried a 500-pound explosive charge) and took it to Nha Be. It resembled a Soviet MKB mine in every respect, except for the absence of a mercury safety switch. Russian lettering was found on the booster cover and on the arming and depth-setting devices. This was the first known occasion of a chemical-horn contact mine being discovered in inland waters.[47]

Photo 10-12

Russian MKB contact mine; the same type as found in the Long Tau. Courtesy of photographer Ronnie Newsome and custodian Jim Krebs

11

ARG Alfa's Landings in 1967

> *To conduct an amphibious operation to search out and destroy VC/NVA forces in the amphibious objective area or other operations as agreed upon with CG III MAF or his designated representative.*
>
> —Representative commander, Seventh Fleet mission description for a search-and-destroy operation to be executed by Marines embarked in Amphibious Ready Group Alfa. Such amphibious operations involved coordinated waterborne and heliborne assault landings. The acronym "CG III MAF" refers to commanding general, III Marine Amphibious Force.[1]

Photo 11-1

Marines of the 3rd Battalion, 9th Marine Regiment, move up a battle-scarred slope in the northern Ashau Valley, during Operation Dewey Canyon fought from 22 January to 18 March 1969. The leathernecks dubbed the North Vietnamese Army-held peak near the Laotian boarder, "Tiger Mountain."
Department of Defense Marine Corps photograph 3D-3-8055-69

The first assault mission of 1967 was Operation DECKHOUSE V, which took place from 6-15 January in IV Corps, the southernmost area of the Republic of Vietnam. The remainder of the amphibious landings in 1967, and for the duration of the war, were in I Corps. The below map is from USS *Eldorado*'s (AGC-11) Western Pacific 1967 cruise book. Qui Nhon lay inside the II Corps area. *Eldorado* participated in amphibious landings at the eight locations shown, northward up the coast. The Ashau Valley (west of the coastal city of Hue, along the border of Laos) was a key entry point for the North Vietnamese, moving men and materials along the Ho Chi Minh Trail into South Vietnam.

Map 11-1

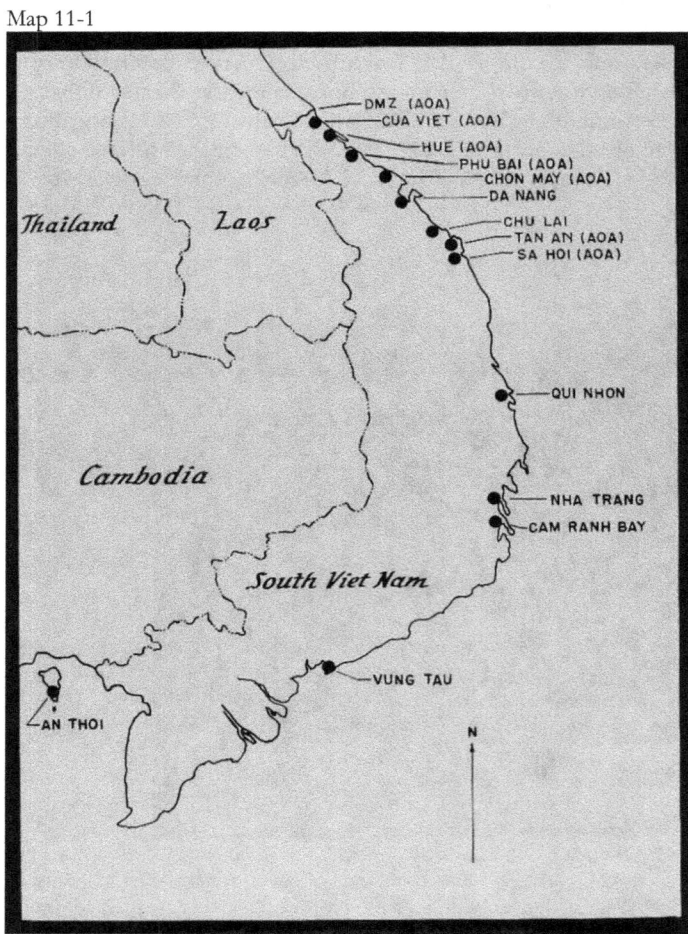

South Vietnam and surrounding areas

Bordering the Demilitarized Zone, I Corps saw heavy fighting almost continuously from 1956 to 1975. The northernmost tactical zone stretched south from the DMZ through the bases along Route 9 in Quang Tri Province, down through Thua Then Province (with the Ashau Valley) and Quang Nam Province (where the first Marines landed in 1965) to the Viet Cong-infested Quang Ngai Province.[2]

FORMATION OF A SECOND SLF

In early 1967, the Joint Chiefs of Staff authorized the formation of a second Special Landing Force. In response to this directive, Special Landing Force Alfa was formed at Okinawa on 1 March 1967 under the command of Col. James A. Gallo Jr., USMC. The new SLF (designated Task Group 79.4) consisted of a battalion (BLT 1/3 commanded by Lt. Col. Peter A. Wickwise, USMC) and a helicopter squadron (HMM-263 under Lt. Col. Edward K. Kirby, USMC).[3]

Task Group 79.5 (which had operated as a single SLF since 1965) was re-designated Special Landing Force Bravo. This chapter describes SLF Alfa's (embarked in Amphibious Ready Group Alfa) landings in 1967. A map from USS *Okinawa*'s 1967 cruise book identifies the eight operations in which the helicopter assault ship participated. Her first operation, BEAVER CAGE, took place from 28 April-12 May.[4]

Map 11-2

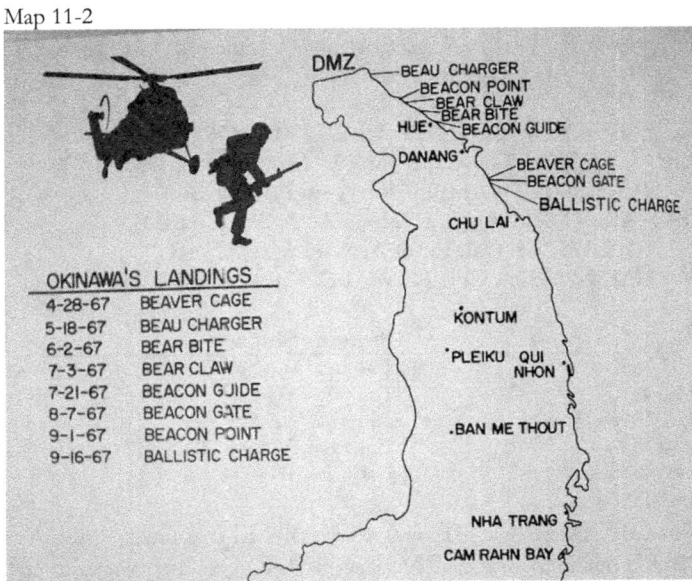

Landings in which the *Okinawa* took part in 1967
USS *Okinawa* (LPH-3) WestPac 1967 cruise book

OPERATION BEAVER CAGE

Photo 11-2

A Marine walking through a Vietnamese village during Operation BEAVER CAGE. Department of Defense Marine Corps photograph A371988

BEAVER CAGE (28 April-12 May 1967)
ARG Alfa (TG 76.4): Capt. Jack L. Lowentrout, USN
(Commander, Amphibious Squadron Nine)
SLF Alfa (TG 79.4): Col. James A. Gallo Jr., USMC
BLT 1/3: Lt. Col. Peter A. Wickwire, USMC
HMM-263: Lt. Col. Edward K. Kirby, USMC

ARG Units	Support Ships
Okinawa (LPH-3)	*Eldorado* (AGC-11)
Bayfield (APA-33)	*Sanctuary* (AH-17)
Seminole (AKA-104) (absent)	*St. Paul* (CA-73)
Point Defiance (LSD-31)	*Forest Royal* (DD-872)
Whitfield County (LST-1169)	*Henderson* (DD-785)[5]

The target for BEAVER CAGE was the rich and populous Que Son Valley (twenty-five miles south of Danang), which was important to the enemy as a source of food and manpower. The operation commenced in Quang Tin Province on 28 April with the landing of heliborne forces in Landing Zones Thrush and Oriole, and waterborne assault forces over Red Beach. The topography of the province was characterized by coastal plains and some low hills. Operations of SLF Alfa ashore were in conjunction with Operation UNION, already in progress.[6]

SLF Alfa had orders to conduct a search-and-destroy mission against VC/NVA troops in an area south of Hoi An (in southern Quang Tin Province) and/or other operations as agreed upon with the commanding general, III MAF, or his designated representative. The SLF landed its forces on schedule and by nightfall, was established ashore and prepared to conduct its mission at first light. Enemy forces believed to be in the area were the NVA 71st Battalion, the 72nd LF (Local Forces) Battalion, and the 74th, K51, and K50 LF Companies.[7]

The landing at Red Beach was unopposed, while the heliborne forces received light small arms-fire at landing zones. Enemy tactics in ensuing days included sniping and harassing fire, night probes of positions in conjunction with mortar attacks, firing from trenches in the nature of delaying action, and night attacks in strengths up to one reinforced platoon. Helicopters received light to moderate fire from automatic weapons and small arms when units were being extracted from landing zones, and two were forced down by hostile fire. Enemy losses during BEAVER CAGE were 181 VC killed (confirmed) and another 136 probable KIA, and 66 detainees.[8]

Due to the absence of a surgical team aboard the *Okinawa*, it was necessary to evacuate a majority of the Marine casualties directly to the hospital ship *Sanctuary*. The BLT team was backloaded on 12 May, and the operation officially terminated the following day.[9]

OPERATION BEAU CHARGER

> *The barrels are smooth, the barrels droop, we're out of powder, what's the scoop!!!!*
>
> —Message sent to the Seventh Fleet by Capt. Guy R. Griffiths, RAN, commanding officer, HMAS *Hobart*, at the end a long day spent with the crew at their battle stations, as her guns poured out rounds in support of Operation BEAU CHARGER.[10]

> *Just before and during the launching of the assault, a duel started between Navy fire support ships and NVA shore batteries. Although the NVA batteries hit no ships, 10 salvos bracketed the USS* Point Defiance *(LSD 31). After return fire silenced the shore batteries, the surface landing proceeded without further incident; there was no opposition.*

—From *U.S. Marines in Vietnam: Fighting The North Vietnamese 1967*, Telfer, Rogers and Fleming Jr. (Washington, DC: History and Museums Division, Headquarters Marine Corps, 1984)

Operation BEAU CHARGER was one of a series of simultaneous operations conducted in the DMZ buffer zone south of the Ben Hai River—to eliminate an enemy rocket and artillery buildup in the DMZ. The concept envisioned the movement of Special Landing Force Bravo into the HICKORY operation of 3rd Marine Division units by means of Operation BELT TIGHT. Special Landing Force Alfa was to operate east of the HICKORY and adjacent LAM SON 54 (South Vietnamese Army) areas under the aegis of BEAU CHARGER.[11]

On 18 May 1967 in support of the Operation BEAU CHARGER, eleven ships—nine of them surface combatants—joined Amphibious Ready Group Alfa near the Demilitarized Zone. The plan called for a search-and-destroy operation in the eastern area of the southern half of the DMZ in northern Quang Tri Province. This area was being used by the enemy to mount attacks against Marine outposts along the southern boundary of the DMZ.[12]

BEAU CHARGER (18-26 May 1967)
ARG Alfa (TG 76.4): Capt. Jack L. Lowentrout, USN
SLF Alfa (TG 79.4): Col. James A. Gallo Jr., USMC
BLT 1/3: Lt. Col. Peter A. Wickwire, USMC
HMM-263: Lt. Col. Edward K. Kirby, USMC

ARG Units	Support Ships
Okinawa (LPH-3)	*Eldorado* (AGC-11)
Bayfield (APA-33)	*Sanctuary* (AH-17)
Seminole (AKA-104) (rejoined on 25 May)	*Boston* (CAG-1)
Point Defiance (LSD-31)	*St. Paul* (CA-73)
Whitfield County (LST-1169)	*Allen M. Sumner* (DD-692)
	Edson (DD-946)
	Fechteler (DD-870)
	HMAS *Hobart* (D 39)
	Joseph Strauss (DDG-16)
	Mansfield (DD-728)
	Ozbourn (DD-846)[14]

Due to the proximity of enemy coastal defense batteries at Cap Mui Lay, assets from Task Unit 70.8.9 (the Naval Gunfire Support Force) were temporarily augmented by "Sea Dragon forces"—ships engaged in offensive operations in North Vietnamese waters. In direct support on D-Day, were the heavy cruisers *St. Paul* and *Boston*, and destroyers *Fechteler*, *Edson*, *Joseph Strauss*, and HMAS *Hobart*.[13]

Enemy batteries on Cap Mui Lay announced their intention to oppose the operation by opening fire on *St. Paul* at 0400 as she was moving into position. *St. Paul*, *Fechteler*, *Sumner*, *Strauss*, and *Hobart* commenced prelanding fire at 0600. As enemy rounds fell ten yards from the dock landing ship *Point Defiance* and fifty yards from her landing craft, the hostile gun position came under air and 8-inch gunfire attack. Enemy fire ceased at 0719 and *Point Defiance* resumed off-loading. Naval Gunfire support (NGFS) continued against assigned targets and counterbattery fire, although handicapped by the loss of the Naval Gunfire Liaison Officer who was killed early in the assault.[15]

The collective gunfire provided by the ships was the greatest concentration of firepower from the sea since the Korean War. Although successful in knocking out enemy positions, the operation identified the need for naval gunfire to reach further inland. This realization launched the first steps that would result in recommissioning of the battleship *New Jersey* (BB-62) on 6 April 1968.[16]

After counterbattery fire had silenced the enemy batteries, the amphibious landing proceeded smoothly, against no opposition. The helicopter-borne assault forces experienced a different reception. The designated landing area proved to be a "hot" zone, and only one platoon of Company A, the assault company, managed to land. Enemy forces closed in and the situation was very much in doubt. At 1100, elements of Company D and the rest of Company A, reinforced with tanks, joined up with the isolated assault platoon. The enemy withdrew only after air strikes began to hammer their positions.[17]

St. Paul and *Fechteler* were detached that day to return to Sea Dragon. *Boston* was directed to remain in general support of the III Marine Amphibious Force unless highly lucrative targets requiring 8-inch gunfire developed in the Sea Dragon area. *Strauss*, *Sumner*, and *Hobart* were detached on 19 May. The Amphibious Ready Group, with *Boston* and *Edson* supporting it, remained as operations continued ashore.[18]

Two days later, *Mansfield* relieved *Edson* on 21 May as the NGFS ship directly supporting BEAU CHARGER. *Ozbourn* relieved *Mansfield* the following day. Marine Corps search-and-destroy operations, sweeping to the south, to clear the area, continued. Early on the morning of 23 May, *Ozbourn* came under fire from Tiger Island. The next day, *Boston* and *Ozbourn* were taken under fire by guns estimated to be 100mm. After return fire by the two ships, the target was believed destroyed. *Edson* joined the others for NGFS support.[19]

On 25 May, the missile cruiser *Providence* participated in NGFS, as Vice Adm. John J. Hyland, commander, Seventh Fleet, arrived aboard her to visit units of the Amphibious Readiness Group and Special Landing Force (ARG/SLF) for briefings. Early in the afternoon the flagship came under enemy fire. Approximately forty rounds were observed. One direct hit damaged her SPS-8B radar antenna, but no personnel casualties resulted. *Providence* commenced evasive maneuvers and counterbattery fire as *Edson* and *Ozbourn* joined in the action. The three ships saturated the area and enemy fire ceased. Following re-embarkation of the special landing force aboard the amphibious ships, BEAU CHARGER was terminated in the early afternoon on 26 May.[20]

Commander, Amphibious Squadron Five, Capt. Philip S. McManus, USN, relieved ComPhibRon Nine as the ARG commander on 22 May, and other changes followed. *Duluth* (LPD-6) joined the ARG on 27 May, and *Bayfield* (APA-33) and *Whitfield County* (LST-1169) departed the following day. Planning for the next operation, BEAR BITE, began immediately upon the termination of BEAU CHARGER.[21]

Photo 11-3

USS *Providence* (CLG-6) firing her guns, location and date unknown.
USS *Providence* Western Pacific 1966-1968 cruise book

OPERATION BEAR BITE

BEAR BITE, a conventional LVT and helicopter assault, targeted Viet Cong operating along the coast twenty-five miles southeast of the DMZ in "The Street Without Joy" (*La Rue Sans Joie*) region. (Troops of the French Far East Expeditionary Corps had given this name to the stretch of Route 1 from Hue to Quang Tri during the First Indochina War.) The assault commenced at 0700 on 2 June, with the simultaneous landing of waterborne and heliborne forces over Blue Beach and into LZ Starling. The search-and-destroy mission took place near Hue, an ancient provincial capital of Vietnam. The area was thought to be an infiltration route used by North Vietnamese troops. The operation was concurrent with CUMBERLAND and CHOCTAW.[22]

BEAR BITE (2-12 June 1967)
ARG Alfa (TG 76.4) Capt. Philip S. McManus, USN
SLF Alfa (TG 79.4): Col. James A. Gallo Jr., USMC
BLT 1/3: Lt. Col. Peter A. Wickwire, USMC
HMM-263: Lt. Col. Edward K. Kirby, USMC

ARG Units	Support Ships
Okinawa (LPH-3)	*Eldorado* (AGC-11)
Duluth (LPD-6)	*Bigelow* (DD-942)
Seminole (AKA-104)	
Point Defiance (LSD-31)	
Hermitage (LSD-34)[23]	

Photo 11-4

Marines sweeping an area in search of enemy forces.
USS *Okinawa* (LPH-3) WestPac 1967 cruise book

The objective area originated along the seaward margin of the central coastal lowland and delta plain. Moving inland, gently rolling sandy beaches and sand dunes transitioned to marshes, swamps, lakes, and lagoons, then areas of rice fields with some dry land crops.[24]

The landings by waterborne and heliborne forces were unopposed. It was believed that guerrilla forces—one local company, P 14 LF Company (also known as C 113)—controlled the area. However, the possibility existed that an NVA main force battalion (VII NVA 806th) might be operating there. Enemy contact was light throughout the first day, with sporadic sniper fire encountered. Tunnels and punji traps were discovered and destroyed on the second day. Forty bunkers, and one hundred fighting holes with overhead covers, were destroyed the following day. BEAR BITE ended on 12 June, and amphibious forces backloaded.[25]

OPERATIONS BEAR CLAW AND BEACON GUIDE

> *It was known to local missionaries as "the Hill of Angels," but to the occupying Marines, Con Thien was a little piece of hell. Just two miles south of the Demilitarized Zone,... it was a barren, bulldozed plateau of red dirt 160 meters high and ringed with barbed wire, studded with artillery revetments and crisscrossed with trenches and sand bag-covered bunkers.*
>
> —Don North in his article "Tragic Valor of Marines at Con Thien."[26]

Operation BEAR CLAW was a planned amphibious landing in Quang Tri Province. Commander, Special Landing Force cancelled it in early morning on 3 July, upon receipt of orders alerting BLT 1/3 of an urgent need for their deployment to the 9th Marines TAOR (Tactical Area of Responsibility) at Con Thien. Their fellow Marines were in trouble, and BEAR CLAW would now involve heli-lift of the 1/3 to an area near the combat base in Quang Tri Province.[27]

Con Thien was one of two firebases associated with an electronic anti-infiltration barrier south of the DMZ, the so-called "McNamara Line." The purpose of the barrier was to detect North Vietnamese troops crossing it, coming south; whereupon, U.S. and allied forces could respond with air strikes and artillery bombardment. The 600-meter-wide barrier was anchored to the east by Firebase Gio Linh and westward by Con Thien. Secretary of Defense Robert McNamara had proposed the idea of the barrier in March 1966, at a meeting of the Joint Chiefs of Staff. The ill-conceived idea was approved, and construction began in April 1967, with Marines clearing and sowing the barrier with seismic and acoustic sensors and minefields.[28]

BEAR CLAW (3-18 July 1967)/BEACON GUIDE (21-30 July 1967)
ARG Alfa (TG 76.4)
SLF Alfa (TG 79.4): Col. John A. Conway, USMC
BLT 1/3: Lt. Col. Peter A. Wickwire, USMC (1-15 July)
Lt. Col. Alfred I. Thomas, USMC (16-31 July)
HMM-362: Lt. Col. Nick J. Kapetan, USMC

ARG Units	Support Ships
Okinawa (LPH-3)	*Eldorado* (AGC-11)
Duluth (LPD-6)	*Hopewell* (DD-681)
Hermitage (LSD-34)	*Harry E. Hubbard* (DD-748)
Seminole (AKA-104)	*Allen M. Sumner* (DD-692)
Tioga County (LST-1158)	*Walker* (DD-517)[29]

A glaring weakness of the McNamara Line was that it could be flanked on either side of the combat bases. Moreover, because the North Vietnamese side of the DMZ was off-limits to U.S. ground attack, NVA divisions employing 135mm artillery were free to target the bases and roving Marine patrols with deadly accuracy. The only reason Marines were at Con Thien was to protect a 160-meter hill which, if taken by the NVA, could facilitate hits on the key U.S. staging area at Dong Ha. The NVA artillery batteries were camouflaged and sheltered in caves in the northern hills of the DMZ. Enemy artillerymen would roll the 135mm guns out to fire, then return them to shelter. Although U.S. forces retaliated with artillery and air strikes, they were unable to stop the barrage taking a continual toll on Con Thien's defenders.[30]

NINTH MARINES SUFFER HEAVY CASUALTIES

The previous day, 2 July, two companies of the 1/9 (Alfa and Bravo) had launched Operation BUFFALO, a sweep in the area north of the base. As a result of faulty reconnaissance and inadequate observation, an undetected NVA force ambushed the Marines. Eighty-six members of Bravo Company were killed and another 176 wounded, leaving only 27 members to walk out of the battle unaided. An estimated 1,290 NVA were killed. Even so, it "was the worst single disaster to befall a Marine Corps rifle company during the Vietnam War."[31]

On 3 July, air strikes and Marine artillery fire were directed to the battle area in preparation for retrieval of the dead. Marine A-4 Skyhawk attack aircraft lay down suppressing fire, as two Marine battalions advanced to reach the bodies. The NVA were well aware of the U.S. Marines tradition of not leaving their dead behind. Consequently, before pulling out during the night, they left numerous booby traps behind to further bleed the Marines. The bodies, spread over a wide area of low bushes, had been rigged with grenades, and almost all had been mutilated or desecrated in some way.[32]

Following orders to proceed to the vicinity of the Cua Viet River, BEAR CLAW was launched on 3 July with helicopter insertion of BLT 1/3 in the vicinity of Con Thien. The mission assigned to SLF Alfa (during the continued engagement with the 90th NVA Regiment) was to tie in with the right flank of the 3/9 Marines, and sweep the area to recover the 1/9 casualties. HMM-362 lifted BLT 1/3, supplemented by CH-46 helicopters from SLF Bravo's HMM-164.[33]

The level of fighting had waned by the time BLT 1/3 joined the 3/9, and the night of 3 July was relatively quiet, as was the next day. The 5th opened with an early morning enemy mortar attack against Companies Alfa and Charlie, and exchanges of artillery and mortar fire punctuated most of the day. On the 6th, enemy rockets knocked out a tank, and savage fighting around it prevented the BLT from reaching it until late morning on 7 July.[34]

The following day, the BLT received orders to make an immediate withdrawal, a dangerous action under the circumstances. The battalion was in contact with the enemy; the withdrawal would occur over 600 meters of open ground in daylight; two of the attached tanks were crippled; and just as the withdrawal commenced, the enemy opened up with small arms, mortar, and artillery fire. In spite of these difficulties, the 1/3 was able to extract with only light casualties.[35]

The next four days involved patrolling the Con Thien perimeter. At the conclusion of BUFFALO on 14 July, BLT 1/3 had recovered the bodies of eleven fellow Marines from the 1/9. However, they paid a high cost to do so, battalion losses were eight killed and 179 wounded; Enemy losses in combat with the battalion were 424 NVA killed. The Special Landing Force was backloaded aboard ARG shipping on 17 July, and BEAR CLAW terminated the following day.[36]

OPERATION BEACON GUIDE

A change of command had taken place at sea a day earlier, on 16 July, in which Lt. Col. Alfred I. Thomas took over BLT 1/3 from Lieutenant Colonel Wickwire. BEACON GUIDE, a search-and-destroy mission in the coastal region eighteen miles southeast of Hue, commenced on 21 July. The operation was part of commander, Third Amphibious Force's continuing plan to maintain pressure on VC units in Coastal I Corps.[37]

At 0730 that morning, a heliborne force and waterborne force landed in LZ Quail and over Green Beach in Phu Loc district (Thua Thien Province) with no opposition encountered. On D+1, a recon patrol engaged 15-20 Viet Cong but withdrew and called artillery and mortar fire. No significant enemy contact was made over the next six days. Numerous weapon positions, fighting holes, billeting areas, and caves were discovered and destroyed, during which a small amount of equipment and explosives were found.[38]

On 29 July, BLT 1/3 landed by helicopter in the Phu Loc and Phu Tu districts of Thu Thien Province. The assault began with the landing of a blocking force in LZ Hawk, followed by other heliborne forces in LZ Sparrow against no opposition. Numerous punji traps were found and destroyed, and a sweep of the area uncovered "spider holes." This term referred to a shoulder-deep, protective hole (often covered by a camouflaged lid) in which a crouched soldier could stand and fire a weapon. Spider holes were also called spider traps, an allusion to the burrow with a trapdoor constructed by the trapdoor spider. A spider hole differed from a standard foxhole in that the latter was usually deeper, and designed to emphasize cover rather than concealment.[39]

Task Group 79.4 conducted an emergency amphibious withdrawal on 30 July and lay off the Cua Viet in response to a threat in the DMZ. No requirement to land developed, and the task group departed on 31 July for Danang, for a period of upkeep and rehabilitation.[40]

OPERATIONS BEACON GATE AND COCHISE

BEACON GATE was conducted 7-10 August in northeastern Quang Nam Province. It commenced with Marines landing over Blue Beach southeast of Hoi An, along the coastal boundary of Quang Nam and Quang Tin Provinces. The balance of BLT 1/3 was heli-lifted into LZ Crow after the beachhead was secured and a landing zone selected. The flat coastal lowlands were compartmented into rice cultivation with open sandy expanses, and villages scattered throughout the area. The Marines came ashore over loose, white sand. The approach to the landing beach had been obstructed by an island fourteen miles off the central portion of the beach and, closer in, islands, shoals, and rocks off its northwest portion.[41]

The enemy units that normally operated in the area were the V25 Local Force Battalion and the V4 Main Force (Sapper) Company. It had been reported by reliable sources that V4 Company was training the V25 Battalion in sapper tactics. The strength of these units was approximately 400 men. Elements of the Q12 and K51 Local Force Companies occasionally operated in the area, and there were indications that the 72nd Local Force Battalion had moved into the area prior to the operation.[42]

Photo 11-5

A Marine radioman of BLF 1/3 is silhouetted at sunrise as he takes a message during Operation BEACON GATE. Department of Defense Marine Corps photograph A650002

BEACON GATE (7-10 August 1967)/COCHISE (11-15 August 1967)
ARG Alfa (TG 76.4)
SLF Alfa (TG 79.4): Col. John A. Conway, USMC
BLT 1/3: Lt. Col. Alfred I. Thomas, USMC
HMM-362: Lt. Col. Nick J. Kapetan, USMC

ARG Units	Support Ships
Okinawa (LPH-3)	*Preston* (DD-795)[43]
Duluth (LPD-6)	
Hermitage (LSD-34)	
Tioga County (LST-1158)	

On D-Day, aerial observation sighted 20-30 enemy just east of the Truong Giang River, and close air support was called. The waterborne and heliborne forces both made unopposed landings. Sniper fire was encountered the first day, but no significant enemy contact was made. Bunkers, mines and surprise firing devices (booby traps) were found and destroyed. Over the next three days, additional bunkers and mines were encountered and destroyed, and some sniper fire was received. Enemy casualties were 16 KIA (confirmed), 4 KIA (probable), and 16 detainees.[44]

On the morning of 11 August, SLF Alfa shifted to operation control of the 1st Marine Division for Operation COCHISE. BLT 1/3 was heli-lifted to a landing zone about seven miles east of Que Son, and took up blocking positions. This action was in support of elements of the Fifth Marines, which were attacking from the east. Task Group 79.4's support of the battalion landing team ashore terminated on the 15th, when operational command was passed to commanding general, III Marine Amphibious Force. The ARG shipping departed the area the following day, en route to Subic Bay for a period of upkeep.[45]

BEACON POINT AND BALLISTIC CHARGE

Photo 11-6

A Marine 60mm mortarman carries his weapon on his shoulder while taking part in Operation BEACON POINT.
Department of Defense Marine Corps photograph A189426

Operation BEACON POINT was launched on 1 September near the border of Thua Thien Province, thirty miles northeast of the city of Hue. A southerly sweep of "The Street without Joy" was conducted to thwart Viet Cong attempts to use the area as a base of operations from which they could keep potential voters away from the polls during South Vietnam's first free election. The Marines encountered light sniper fire on several occasions, came under 60mm fire once, and found surprise firing devices, and caches of rice totaling 35 tons. Five helicopters were hit by small arms-fire and sustained minor damage.[46]

BEACON POINT (1-10 September 1967)/
BALLISTIC CHARGE (16-29 September 1967)
ARG Alfa (TG 76.4)
SLF Alfa (TG 79.4): Col. John A. Conway, USMC
BLT 1/3: Lt. Col. Alfred I. Thomas, USMC
HMM-362 (1-7 September 1967): Lt. Col. Nick J. Kapetan, USMC
HMM-163 (8-30 September 1967): Lt. Col. Walter C. Kelly, USMC

ARG Units	Support Ships
Okinawa (LPH-3)	*Robison* (DDG-12) – Beacon Point
Duluth (LPD-6)	*Waldron* (DD-699) – Beacon Point
Hermitage (LSD-34)	*Waldron* (DD-699) – Ballistic Charge
Tioga County (LST-1158)	*Hopewell* (DD-681) – Ballistic Charge
Belle Grove (LSD-2)	*Ernest G. Small* (DDR-838) – Ballistic Charge[47]
Winston (AKA-94)	

Photo 11-7

A Navy spotter aboard an Army "bird dog" selecting targets for USS *Robison*'s guns. USS *Robison* (DDG-12) Western Pacific 1967-1968 cruise book

In preparation for BEACON POINT, destroyers *Waldron* and *Robison* had delivered gunfire to the periphery of LZ Sparrow from L-40 to L-5. ("L-hour" refers to the time at which the first helicopter of the helicopter-borne assault wave touches down in the landing zone.

Thus, preparatory gunfire was delivered beginning forty hours before L-hour, and up to within five hours of it.) All gunfire was controlled by an airborne spotter. *Robison* was released from these duties as soon as the battalion's 105mm howitzer battery was ashore on D-Day. *Waldron* continued in direct support until the afternoon of D+2, when she was reassigned and given another NGFS mission.[48]

Operation BALLISTIC CHARGE involved a heliborne and surface assault a little southeast of Dai Loc, in Quang Nam Province.[49] The enemy units normally in the area were the V26 Local Force Company (a part of the V25 Local Force Battalion) and the Q12 Local Force Company. The V4 Main Company (sapper) was believed to still be using the area to train elements of the V25 in sapper tactics. Although the exact weapons in each unit was unknown, the enemy was known to have B40 and B90 rocket launchers and two 60mm mortars, in addition to automatic and semi-automatic weapons.[49]

On D-Day, 16 September, waterborne assault units landed unopposed over Red Beach, while heliborne units setting down in LZ Goose received small arms-fire. A rapid sweep to the north was followed by a detailed search-and-destroy sweep southward along the same track. Sniper fire was the only opposition.[50]

On D+1, Company B engaged an estimated fifteen Viet Cong, artillery fire was called, and the enemy broke contact. On D+2 and D+6, the enemy probed friendly night defensive positions and, in one instance, mortar fire from Marines was directed at an estimated twenty Viet Cong. On D+3, naval gunfire was called on five Viet Cong carrying a mortar. Three days later, helicopter assault forces received small arms-fire while landing in LZ Quail to serve as a reserve force for SHELBYVILLE. (Elements of BLT 1/3 participated in this operation from 22-28 September.) Concurrently, BLT 1/3 Company Alfa, tanks, the mortar battery, and LVTs withdrew to ships of the ARG/SLF, and BALLISTIC CHARGE ended on 29 September.[51]

BASTION HILL, MEDINA, FREMONT, AND GRANITE

BASTION HILL (10-31 October 1967)
ARG Alfa (TG 76.4)
SLF Alfa (TG 79.4): Col. John A. Conway, USMC
BLT 1/3: Lt. Col. Alfred I. Thomas, USMC
HMM-362: Lt. Col. Nick J. Kapetan, USMC
HMM-163: Maj. Frederick A. Rueckel, USMC (Acting CO)

ARG Units	ARG Units
Okinawa (LPH-3)	*Winston* (AKA-94)
Duluth (LPD-6)	*Fort Marion* (LSD-22)
Belle Grove (LSD-2)	*Washtenaw County* (LST-1166)[52]

BASTION HILL commenced on 10 October with helicopter insertion of BLT 1/3 from the *Okinawa* to the eastern edge of the MEDINA operating area. Its mission was to serve as a blocking force for the 1st Marines, engaged in Operation MEDINA in the rugged hills of the Hai Lang Forest south of Quang Tri City. The enemy's Base Area 101 lay within the forest, and elements of the 5th and 6th NVA Regiments operated in and around the region. MEDINA was part of a concerted effort to eliminate enemy base areas.[53]

The landing met no opposition. Except for one action between Company Charlie and a company of NVA regulars, in the early morning on 11 October, the battalion's contact with the enemy over the course of the operation involved scattered firefights, incoming mortar rounds, and grenade mines and booby traps.[54]

Following MEDINA, BLT 1/3 moved south to participate in LIBERTY II/FREMONT under the control of Marine commanders ashore. This operation sought to prevent the enemy from disrupting the South Vietnamese National Assembly elections. GRANITE began for the SLF with an early morning helicopter assault into the Hai Lang Forest to participate in a two-battalion search-and-destroy mission in the region of enemy Base Area 114. The 1st battalion, 4th Marines, and SLF Alfa's BLT 1/3 conducted GRANITE under the operational control of the 4th Marines. The battalion landing team never found the base area, but had no doubt of the presence of enemy troops in the forest. By the time, BLT 1/3 finished its sweep of the rugged terrain on 4 November, it had called in 59 fixed-wing sorties and 652 artillery fire missions during the preceding ten days.[55]

REMAINING OPERATIONS IN 1967

> *No fighting holes, bunkers, or fortifications of any kind were uncovered during the operation.... The area appeared to be quite pacified and the indigenous personnel were very friendly.*
>
> —Lt. Col. Richard Goodale, commander BLT 1/3, remarking on the ostensibly poor intelligence which triggered BALLISTIC ARCH.[56]

Some changes in ARG/SLF leadership and composition occurred that autumn. Commander, Amphibious Squadron Three (Capt. Thomas C. Harbert Jr., USN) and his squadron arrived in the Western Pacific in early November. Harbert assumed duties as commander, Amphibious Ready Group Alfa, on 15 November, with his broad pennant hoisted in *Iwo Jima*. *Iwo Jima* and *Cleveland* would be assigned to Amphibious Ready Group Alfa for over six months during Squadron Three's deployment. *Tulare*, *Comstock*, and *Whetstone* operated with ARG Alfa or Bravo for lesser periods. The high-speed transport *Cook* (APD-130) joined the squadron in February 1968.[57]

Amphibious Squadron Three's first undertaking was BALLISTIC ARCH, a helicopter and surface assault of Viet Cong-dominated villages on the northern coast of Quang Tri Province between the Cua Viet River and DMZ. After three days, operational control of BLT 1/3 passed to the Ninth Marines on 27 November for participation in KENTUCKY ashore. Operational command of the helicopter squadron was retained by the Special Landing Force, which provided air support to the 3rd Marine Division and BLT 1/3.[58]

BALLISTIC ARCH (24 November-29 December 1967)
ARG Alfa (TG 76.4) Capt. Thomas C. Harbert Jr., USN
SLF Alfa (TG 79.4): Col. John A. Conway, USMC
BLT 1/3: Lt. Col. Richard W. Goodale, USMC
HMM-361: Lt. Col. Daniel M. Wilson, USMC

ARG Units	Support Ships
Iwo Jima (LPH-2)	*Newport News* (CA-148)
Cleveland (LPD-7)	*Robison* (DDG-12)
Comstock (LSD-19)	*Goldsborough* (DDG-20)
Fort Marion (LSD-22)	*Collett* (DD-730)
Washtenaw County (LST-1166)	*New* (DD-818)
Tulare (AKA-112)	*Du Pont* (DD-941)
Wexford County (LST-1168)[59]	

These operations continued into December, as ARG shipping lay off the coast near the mouth of the Cua Viet, in support of the combat ashore. KENTUCKY was a search-and-destroy mission by the Ninth Marines in the vicinity of the southern border of the DMZ. The operation utilized three Marine battalions and was coordinated with an adjacent South Vietnamese Army operation.[60]

A change in battalion landing teams took place near month's end, as general offloading of BLT 1/3 was completed on 22 December, and embarkation of items of BLT 2/4 began and continued through year's end. Commander, Seventh Fleet, terminated BALLISTIC ARCH on the morning of 29 December 1967.[61]

12

1968 Tet Offensive

> *The Tet Offensive commenced on the night of 30-31 January 1968 with attacks by about 84,000 NVA [North Vietnamese Army] and VC [Viet Cong] troops against about 155 South Vietnamese cities, government, and military targets, including some U.S. targets such as the U.S. embassy in Saigon. Communist forces attacked 36 of the 44 provincial capitals in South Vietnam, and almost every military installation came under some form of mortar, rocket attack, or infantry assault.*
>
> —Excerpt from U.S. Naval History and Heritage Command article U.S. Navy Operations in Vietnam, January-March 1968.[1]

Photo 12-1

Republic of Vietnam President Nguyen Van Thieu declared 14 October 1968 as an official day of mourning for the victims of the "Tet 1968" Massacre, and joined mourners for the multi-faith rites at a mass burial ground south of Hue, Vietnam. U.S. Information Agency photograph #69-10-0049-E

On 29 January 1968 the Allies began the Tet-lunar new year expecting the customary 36-hour peaceful holiday truce. Such was not to be. Capitalizing on the lull in war posture, the North Vietnamese and Viet Cong launched a large-scale offensive on targets across South Vietnam. Assaults began in the northern and central provinces prior to dawn on 30 January, followed by more that night in Saigon and the Mekong Delta regions. Enemy forces attacked or fired upon scores of provincial capitals, autonomous cities, district capitals, and hamlets, and raided a number of military installations, including almost every airfield. The coordinated effort lasted three days. However, Saigon and Hue came under more intense and sustained attack.[2]

ARG/SLF ALFA AND BRAVO ASSUME NEW ROLES

The U.S. Seventh Fleet's amphibious force, permanently augmented by a second ARG/SLF after April 1967, had often been used to extend the allied flank at sea, reinforce front-line units, or land troops in the enemy's rear to take up blocking positions. Marines lifted ashore by helicopter or amphibious craft, provided ready, mobile, and powerful assistance. While ARG/SLF forces accounted for over 3,000 enemy killed in 1967, their support enabled other allied units to inflict even greater casualties on North Vietnamese Army and Viet Cong forces.[3]

During January 1968, the ARG/SLF Marines carried out four heliborne operations in I Corps. The enemy's massive Tet Offensive, launched on the 30th, resulted in the suspension of amphibious landings and long-term commitment ashore of the fleet's Marine forces. Over the next four months, ships of the ARGs served as havens for USN riverine combat and logistic craft deployed to the area. This sea-based support was crucial to Allied efforts in the northern reaches of South Vietnam. From June through the year's end, amphibious forces took part in nine I Corps operations, which decimated enemy forces fighting to hold Hue and the surrounding region.[4]

RIVER PATROL FORCE (TF 116) OPERATIONS

During the initial stages of the Tet Offensive, the Naval Supply Detachment at Vinh Long came under an intense Viet Cong attack. Initially, automatic weapons and small arms-fire was directed against the Vietnamese River Assault Group (RAG) base, the Navy villa and the detachment pier area. When mortar fire commenced, Naval Supply Activity personnel were relocated to the RAG base where a perimeter defense was established. As the enemy attack intensified, U.S. Navy personnel were evacuated to the *Garrett County* (LST-786).[5]

The tank landing ship had moved upriver from her normal station on the Co Chien to support friendly troops engaging the enemy. She also took aboard over 150 American, Korean, and Vietnamese civilians, as well as eight Irish nuns from a school overrun by Viet Cong. The evacuees were fed, made as comfortable as possible, and subsequently transferred to the light cargo ship *Mark* (AKL-22) and transported to Dong Tam. When Navy SEALs and an advance party of NavSuppAct Saigon Detachment personnel reoccupied the villa at Vinh Long, on 2 February, they found the Tactical Operations Center and adjacent storeroom completely destroyed by fire.[6]

Photo 12-2

USS *Mark* (AKL-12) on a South Vietnamese river in the Mekong Delta, 6 July 1966, operating in support of Navy small boat forces.
National Archives photograph #USN 1117682-B

By August 1968, the River Patrol Force, of which *Garrett County* was a part, would consist of five river divisions, each controlling two 10-boat sections that operated from combat bases along the major rivers, or from ships positioned on the rivers.

River Patrol Force Dispositions	River Patrol Squadron 5 Support Ships
River Division 51 Can Tho/Binh Thuy	*Garrett County* (LST-786)
River Division 52 Sa Dec (later Vinh Long)	*Harnett County* (LST-821)
River Division 53 My Tho	*Hunterdon County* (LST-838)
River Division 54 Nha Be River	*Jennings County* (LST-846)
Division 55 Danang[7]	

Elsewhere, river patrol force units were embroiled in some of the bitterest fighting seen in the Delta since GAME WARDEN operations were begun. The stalwart efforts of PBRs, helicopters, SEALs, and LSTs in support of friendly ground action contributed substantially to the high numbers of enemy casualties. Task Force 116 units engaged with the enemy on many fronts. Navy armed helicopters and PBRs played a major role in preventing the cities of Ben Tre and Mo Cay (in Kien Hoa Province) from being overrun by Viet Cong forces. During the first 48-hours of the Tet Offensive, the Seawolves of HAL-3 (Helicopter Attack, Light, Squadron Three) detachments 5 and 6, were practically the only air support available, and they provided around-the-clock air strikes for four days against intense ground fire.[8]

River patrol boats from Sections 531, 532, and 534 provided fire support, blocking forces, and medical evacuation for Ben Tre. On 5 February, *Harnett County* (LST-821) contributed firefighting equipment and a damage controlman to assist in extinguishing fires burning in the city. Elsewhere, LSTs engaged in repeated shore bombardments against enemy troop concentrations, as the ships transited rivers bringing their PBRs and helicopters to critical areas.[9]

INTERDICTION OF A VIET CONG CROSSING

Three days earlier, on 2 February, a PBR patrol on the Bassac River had detected a sampan and junk exiting a canal, fifteen miles southeast of Can Tho. As the PBRs pursued the craft, the junk capsized trying to evade, but the sampan managed to slip back into the canal. As the PBRs pursued it, automatic and small arms-fire erupted from at least twelve firing positions on both banks, followed by eight B-40 rockets from the south bank. Four PBRs arrived to assist, while two others took up a blocking position to the north to prevent a Viet Cong crossing. Navy Seawolves, an LCM(R) landing craft with 5-inch rockets, and *Jennings County* were also ordered into the area to put heavier fire on the enemy.[10]

The GAME WARDEN forces prevented another enemy crossing with the attendant loss of valuable rockets. A cargo of crates aboard the junk, containing sixty B-40 rockets, was captured. An additional crate of rockets and a bundle of uniforms sank, and were not recovered.[11]

GUNFIRE SUPPORT OF OPERATIONS ASHORE

Garrett County conducted shore bombardment on 20 February against an enemy troop concentration on the northern outskirts of the city of Phu Vinh, killing twenty and wounding twenty Viet Cong with 40mm cannon fire. The following day, *Hunterdon County*'s guns fired for nearly two hours in support of friendly troops about ten miles upriver from the mouth of the Ham Luong. Her saturation fire against various targets to the north of the river, included a hit on a Viet Cong platoon.[12]

MOBILE RIVERINE FORCE (TF 117) OPERATIONS

In early February, the Mobile Riverine Force came to the defense of several beleaguered Delta cities, and the enemy hit back. Shortly after midnight on 1 February, units of River Assault Division 91 were ambushed on the Ruong Stream, seven miles southeast of Sa Dec, by a heavily-bunkered enemy force. The location was the scene of the earlier 4-6 December Battle of Ruong Stream in which the Viet Cong had lost 266 men. As the riverine assault craft approached it, in anticipation of the possibility of an attack in the same area, the gunners on the artillery barges were ordered to level their 105mm howitzers and load them with deadly "Beehive" anti-personnel rounds.[13]

At twenty minutes past midnight, history repeated itself. The Viet Cong sprang their ambush, employing automatic weapons, rocket, and recoilless rifle fire from both banks of the 30-yard wide stream. The troop-laden ATCs, ASPBs, monitors, and artillery barges retaliated with overwhelming firepower at point-blank range. Boatswain Mate Second William M. Comer, a monitor boat captain, was the only U.S. casualty; enemy losses were undetermined.[14]

RAPID MOVEMENT TO VINH LONG PROVINCE

On 4 February, the Mobile Riverine Force received intelligence that two to three Viet Cong battalions were planning to lay siege to the city of Vinh Long that evening. RADS 92 and 111 embarked their troops and transported them down the Ba Rai Stream to the Mekong River. The craft received some enemy rocket and automatic weapons fire while in transit, but suffered no casualties.[15]

The 3/60th Infantry Battalion was landed at the fire support base near the junction of the Ba Rai Stream and Mekong River, and then airlifted into landing zones on the southwestern side of Vinh Long. Elements were also landed at Vinh Long Airfield to augment its security. Meanwhile, the riverine column transited the Co Chien River to Vinh Long, then proceeded up the Long Ho Stream, and RAD 91 landed the 3/47th south of the city to block enemy escape routes.[16]

Heavy contact with the enemy ensued, and the fighting continued throughout the night and until mid-afternoon on 5 February, when the enemy (believed to be elements of the Viet Cong 306th and 308th Main Force Battalions) broke contact. The bone-weary soldiers and boat crews then returned to the Mobile Riverine Base for their first rest after eight continuous days of intense operations.[17]

LIGHT CARGO SHIP *MARK* HIT BY ENEMY FIRE

At month's end, the light cargo ship *Mark* was hit by eleven rounds of recoilless rifle fire on 29 February, while proceeding east on the My Tho River, about three miles west of Dong Tam. Her crew were at battle stations (because of previous attacks on Naval Supply Center Activity, Saigon, craft in the same general area) and the ship was being escorted by three PBRs. In anticipation of an attack from the north bank, the river patrol craft were positioned on her portside.[18]

However, the attack came from the south bank of the river. One round hit *Mark* starboard side at the main deck, penetrated her hull and ruptured fire main piping and a fuel tank vent line. Shrapnel from another round pierced the galley, wounding twelve men in a repair party. The PBRs made firing runs on the river bank, causing two secondary explosions at enemy positions, and received recoilless rifle, automatic weapons, and small arms fire in return. Four other explosions followed an air strike on the same area by a helicopter fire team.[19]

The 180-foot *Mark* was a former unnamed freight supply ship (*FS-214*), built by Higgins Industries, New Orleans, Louisiana, for the U.S. Army in World War II. She saw action during the war, resupplying various units engaged in the Pacific Island Campaigns. The Navy acquired her on 30 September 1947. She was commissioned USS *Mark* (AG-143), a miscellaneous auxiliary, on 2 December 1947, and fifteen months later, re-designated a light cargo ship (AKL-12) on 13 March 1949. *Mark* was placed "out of commission in service" in 1956, but remained employed shuttling supplies and passengers between Subic Bay and Sangly Point, on the Cavite City peninsula.[20]

With the escalation of U.S. military involvement in Southeast Asia in 1963-64, her resupply missions were extended to include frequent trips to South Vietnam. As a result of increasing requirements, she was placed back in commission on 1 October 1965. *Mark* continued to operate from Subic Bay, but spent more and more time in Vietnam. In June 1966, she commenced full-time operations in the combat area, transporting vital supplies from Saigon and Vung Tau to units involved in GAME WARDEN and MARKET TIME operations.[21]

Mark was not the only ex-freight supply ship serving the U.S. Navy. Among the forty-five freight supply ships acquired by the sea service after World War II, nine received unit awards for combat duty in the Korean War or Vietnam War, or for service gathering intelligence. Summary information about the four ships, whose service coincided with the Vietnam War period, follows:

	Light Cargo Ships	
	Ex-*FS-214*	Ex-*FS-370*
Unit Awards	*Mark* (AKL-12)	*Brule* (AKL-28)
Combat Action Ribbons	2	2
Navy Unit Commendations	3	2
Vietnam Service Medals	14	11
Republic of Vietnam Meritorious Unit Citation, Gallantry	4	3

	Intelligence Gathering Ships	
	Ex-*FS-344*	Ex-*FS-345*
Unit Awards	*Pueblo* (AGER-2)	*Banner* (AGER-1)
Combat Action Ribbon	1	
Armed Forces Expeditionary Medal[22]	1	1

(Information about the hundreds of U.S. Army freight-supply ships and large tugs, and lesser numbers of coastal tankers and harbor tugs that served in World War II, may be found in my book, *MacArthur and Halsey's "Pacific Island Hoppers."* Those vessels were manned by Coast Guard, Merchant Marine, or Army crews.)

COMMANDER, NAVAL FORCES VIETNAM, URGES RAPID ACTIONS AGAINST A DISORGANIZED ENEMY

Enemy losses are now reported at about 44,000 KIA plus over 7,000 captured or detained all together equal to at least 100 VC/NVA Battalions.

Although captured documents and prisoners indicate the enemy plans to continue attacks and harassment he obviously must be hurting considerably. Now is the time to strike him. Now is the time to resort again to our basic philosophy of concentrate and clobber. Consider it preferable to eliminate one enemy unit than to take small attrition from several. Recommend where possible bait a trap and clobber the catch. The enemy is moving about. Recommend all units move to the offensive wherever practicable and where the means are not available scheme, urge and cajole others to do the same. This is a period when ingenuity and initiative can pay off – good luck.

—Commander, Naval Forces Vietnam message, sent on 28 February 1968 to naval forces under his command, recommending offensive actions to take advantage of a possible disorganized enemy who had suffered a disastrous defeat and enormous losses during the month.[23]

Photo 12-3

Chief of Naval Operations, Adm. Thomas H. Moorer, USN (at right), on a tour of Navy combat forces in Vietnam, is shown the remains of an enemy 122mm rocket by Rear Adm. Kenneth L. Veth, commander, Naval Forces Vietnam. During an early morning enemy attack on 7 June 1968, the rocket had exploded within thirty feet of the house occupied by Veth.
Naval History and Heritage Command photograph #NH 104913

TET PROVES TO BE TURNING POINT IN THE WAR

> *[I]t seems now more certain than ever that the bloody experience of Vietnam is to end in stalemate... [I]t is increasingly clear to this reporter that the only rational way out then will be to negotiate, not as victors, but as an honorable people who lived up to their pledge to defend democracy, and did the best they could.*
>
> —News anchorman Walter Cronkite in CBS (Columbia Broadcasting System) "Report from Vietnam: Who, What, When, Where, Why," which aired on 27 February 1968. The excerpt came at the end of the hour-long special, which Cronkite acknowledged was his subjective opinion.[24]

Although U.S. and South Vietnamese forces managed to hold off the attacks on more than 100 cities and outposts in South Vietnam, news coverage of the massive Tet Offensive shocked the American public and eroded support for the war effort. Despite heavy casualties, North Vietnam achieved a strategic victory, as the attacks marked a turning point in the Vietnam War and the beginning of the slow, painful American withdrawal from the region.[25]

13

Operation SEALORDS

Don't you people realize what's happening?... There is no longer a consensus of support for the war back in the United States. I have a letter in my pocket from the president [Lyndon B. Johnson] that tells me to turn the war over to the Vietnamese.... You tell me that we'll be all turned over by 1976. That's out of the question! The country will not sit still for that kind of commitment. The president wants to get the war turned over as soon as possible. We have to make that happen.

—Gen. Creighton W. Abrams Jr., commander, U.S. Military Assistance Command, Vietnam, addressing his chief advisors at a meeting on 2 November 1968.[1]

During the latter part of 1968, dramatic changes occurred in the conduct of the war, as a result of the enemy's bloody country-wide Tet Offensive of February and March and the follow-up attacks during the spring. The Johnson administration, convinced that the allied military effort was faring badly, and in recognition of increasing domestic opposition to the American role in the war, ordered the gradual withdrawal of U.S. forces from Southeast Asia. At the same time, the first significant attempt at peace talks came in May 1968 with an informal meeting between U.S. and North Vietnamese envoys in Paris. Five months later, Lyndon Johnson agreed to suspend all bombing sorties over North Vietnam, paving the way for formal peace negotiations.[2]

On 25 January 1969, five days after the inauguration of Richard M. Nixon as the 37th President of the United States, negotiators from Washington flew to Paris for peace meetings with representatives of North and South Vietnam and the National Liberation Front. The Paris peace talks would drag on for more than four years, plagued by setbacks and breakdowns in negotiations. The North Vietnamese demanded the withdrawal of American troops, the dissolution of the South Vietnamese government, and a return to the principles of the Geneva Accords; while the United States insisted that Hanoi recognize the sovereignty of South Vietnam.[3]

Richard Nixon had succeeded Lyndon Johnson amid much dissent and unrest throughout the nation, resulting from a long war that had taken many American lives. During his campaign, Nixon had pledged to get the United States out of Vietnam. Understanding the importance of negotiating from a position of strength, he now directed additional actions to expand, equip, and train Vietnamese military forces, steadily reduce American fighting troops, and give South Vietnam greater responsibility for fighting the war. The American military termed its part of the administration's "Vietnamization" of the war, the Accelerated Turnover to the Vietnamese (ACTOV) Program.[4]

Photo 13-1

Commencement of the Vietnam Peace talks on 25 January 1969. The U.S. delegation is in foreground with chief negotiator Henry Cabot Lodge, facing camera.
U.S. Information Agency photograph #69-526

THE SEALORDS CAMPAIGN

As United States forces began to train and equip the South Vietnamese military to assume complete responsibility for the war, they also worked to keep pressure on the enemy. From 1968 to 1971, the allies exploited the Communists' staggering losses during the Tet attacks by pushing the enemy's large main force units out to the border areas, extending their presence into Viet Cong strongholds, and consolidating control over population centers.[5]

Vice Adm. Elmo R. Zumwalt Jr., appointed commander, Naval Forces Vietnam, on 30 September 1968, was the architect of Operation SEALORDS. Promoted to vice admiral ahead of 130 other officers, he and his staff quickly devised a plan to isolate and destroy the weakened

Communist forces in the Mekong Delta. (Zumwalt would later become, at age forty-nine, the youngest officer ever to serve as chief of Naval Operations.) An acronym for Southeast Asia Lake, Ocean, River, and Delta Strategy, SEALORDS was a determined effort by U.S. Navy, South Vietnamese Navy, and allied ground forces to cut enemy supply lines from Cambodia and disrupt operations originating from base areas deep in the Delta.[6]

Photo 13-2

Adm. Elmo R. Zumwalt Jr., chief of Naval Operations (left), and Rear Adm. Robert S. Salzer, commander, Naval Forces Vietnam, chat aboard an aircraft following a visit to Nam Can Naval Base, South Vietnam. Salzer had relieved Vice Adm. Jerome H. King Jr. (Zumwalt's successor as ComNavForV) a month earlier, in April 1971.
Naval History and Heritage Command photograph USN 1148801

When Vice Admiral Zumwalt launched SEALORDS (Task Force 194) in October 1968, allied naval forces in South Vietnam were at peak strength. The U.S. Navy's Coastal Surveillance Force (Task Force 115) operated 81 Swift boats, 24 Coast Guard WPBs, and 39 other vessels. The River Patrol Force (Task Force 116) numbered 258 patrol and minesweeping boats; while the Riverine Assault Force (Task Force 117) marshalled 184 monitors, transports, and other armored craft. Supporting forces included U.S. Navy armed helicopters, fixed wing aircraft, and SEALs. Helicopter Attack Squadron Light (HAL) Three flew 25 armed helicopters—augmented by the 15 fixed-wing OV-10 Bronco aircraft of Attack Squadron Light (VAL) Four deployed to

Vietnam in March 1969. Rounding out these combat capabilities, five Navy SEAL platoons supported operations in the Delta.[7]

Photo 13-3

OV-10A Bronco of VAL-4 fires a Zuni rocket at a target in the Mekong Delta, 1969. Naval History and Heritage Command photograph #USN 1139900

Complementing the American naval forces were the Vietnamese Navy's 655 ships, assault craft, patrol boats, and other vessels. To focus the allied effort on the SEALORDS campaign, Zumwalt appointed his deputy, Capt. Robert S. Salzer, USN, as operational commander (or "First SEALORD") of the newly activated Task Force 194. The Game Warden, Market Time, and Riverine Assault Force operations continued, but were scaled down and their personnel and materiel resources increasingly devoted to SEALORDS.[8]

In addition to the allied forces cited, a few other units—or members of units—also participated in SEALORDS operations. As an example, personnel of the Royal Australian Navy's Clearance Diving Team Three, 4th Contingent, joined U.S. Navy EOD personnel on a few missions. The Aussies were part of the fourth sub-unit of CDT 3 to deploy, in succession, to Vietnam.

AUSTRALIAN CDT 3 FOURTH CONTINGENT

> *Although mine neutralization was the primary responsibility of the EODMUPAC teams, this was by no means a limiting factor in the wide range of operations in which they participated.... Clearing water obstacles while under heavy enemy fire so the Viet Cong sanctuaries could be entered by the Mobile Riverine Force, destroying enemy bunkers and caches, [and] risking life and limb*

in order that the enemy was forced into the open many times in frenzied efforts to curtail EOD, soon became a constant way of life for the EODMUPAC teams. On many combat operations where EOD was required, these teams unhesitatingly accompanied troops into enemy territory and oftentimes were directly responsible for the safe return of patrols where, without the quick and responsible actions of EOD personnel, the patrols would have been annihilated.

—Excerpt from a recommendation by commander, U.S. Naval Forces Vietnam, that Explosive Ordnance Disposal Mobile Unit, Pacific, be awarded a Presidential Unit Citation.[9]

Photo 13-4

Clearance Diving Team Three (4th Contingent) in Vietnam. Front row (L-R): ABCD Robert Spicer, LSCD David Rhook, and ABCD Colin Darling. Back row: POCD Robert Cox, POCD Barry Wilson, and Lt. Clement Littleton.
Courtesy of Donald (Scotty) Allan

In February 1969, two members of Royal Australian Navy Clearance Diving Team Three took part in a six-day operation along the Bo De River in the lower Mekong Delta. On the night of 3 February, Petty Officer Robert Cox and Leading Seaman David Rhook boarded USS *Washtenaw* at Vung Tau for a Task Force 115 operation in areas VQ and WQ. They were part of a team of five ordnance disposal personnel tasked with destroying Viet Cong bunker complexes, firing positions, fortifications, and targets of opportunity along the banks of rivers and canals.[10]

The demolition team was supported by:
- USS *Washtenaw County* (LST-1166)
- Five fast patrol craft ("Swift boats")
- Two "Cobra gunship" helicopters
- Forty "Mike Force" (indigenous troops led by members of U.S. Army special forces) for ground security[11]

Photo 13-5

USS *Washtenaw County* (LST-1166) at Subic Bay, 4 October 1969.
Naval History and Heritage Command photograph #K-78102

Cox and Rhook were part of the 4th Contingent of Royal Australian Navy Clearance Diving Team Three led by Lt. Clement Littleton, RAN, which deployed to Vietnam from 28 August 1968 to 26 February 1969. In November 1968, the Aussie clearance diving team at Vung Tau was attached to a nearby Mobile Riverine Group. On 13 January 1969, Petty Officer Barry Wilson and Able Seaman Robert Spicer participated in an amphibious operation to destroy enemy positions along a five kilometer stretch of river bank in southern An Xuyen Province. The divers demolished 65 bunkers, 13 huts, and a concrete revetment while under enemy sniper fire.[12]

Clearance Diving Team Three (Fourth Contingent)	
Lt. Clement J. Littleton, RAN	LSCD David N. Rhook, RAN
POCD Robert J. Cox, RAN	ABCD Colin Darling, RAN
POCD Barry W. Wilson, RAN	ABCD Robert H. Spicer, RAN

BROADER SEALORDS OPERATIONS

During the month of February 1969, combined SEALORDS forces operating in the Giant Slingshot, Border Interdiction, Search Turn, and Breezy Cove campaigns accounted for a total of 337 enemy killed and 27 captured. Friendly casualties were 20 killed and 86 wounded. South Vietnamese Riverine Assault Interdiction Division 72 (RAID 72) conducted nineteen patrols in February on rivers in An Xuyen Province. All river assault craft of CTG 194.7 (Riverine Strike Group) remained assigned to operational commanders with the exception of those craft undergoing overhaul. The operation in which Cox and Rhook took part was one of many that month.[13]

Map 13-1

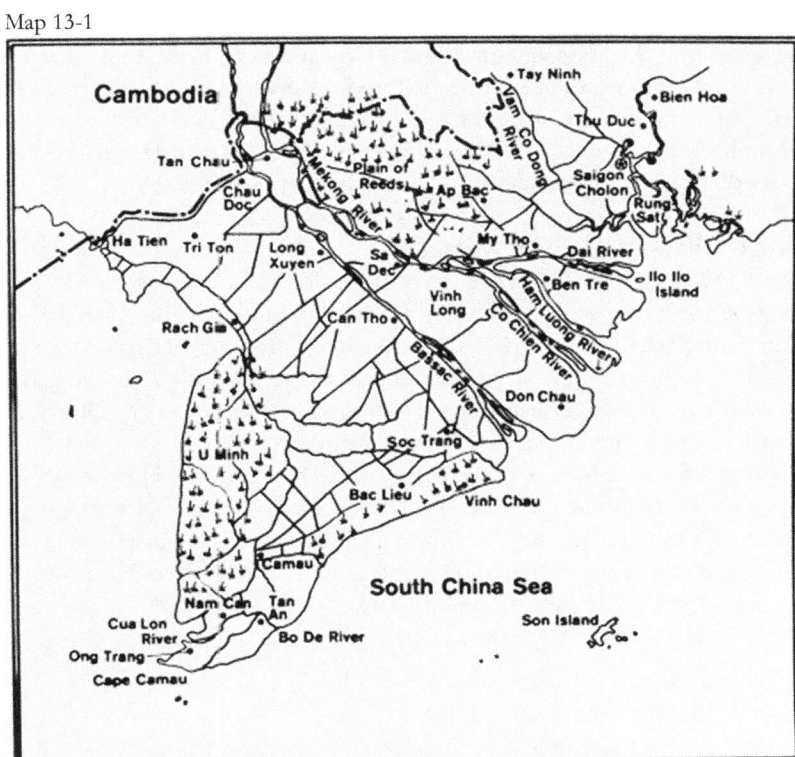

Mekong Delta, South Vietnam
Naval History and Heritage Command photograph #NH 96342

The six-day operation begun on 6 February, involved a sweep of the canals and river banks of the Bo De River in southern An Xuyen Province. While destroying Viet Cong fighting positions and clearing the banks, the task force frequently came under enemy fire. The muddy and slushy conditions made avoiding fire, or finding shelter while under fire, difficult. Even more so for the Australian divers, who were packing an additional twenty pounds of explosives, above what their American counterparts were carrying. (The latter individuals were older and more senior in rank, than their young Aussie compatriots.)[14]

On 11 February, Cox and Rhook were accompanying forty 'Mike Force' Irregulars when a patrol boat came under heavy enemy fire. By the time they arrived on scene, the boat had sunk and was resting on the shallow bottom of the canal. However, her crew were able to continue firing at the enemy, who were located in a complex bunker system on the bank. The Irregulars and two Australians attacked the underground shelter from inland, during which Cox was nearly hit by enemy fire while clearing a bunker. A thrown grenade killed the enemy, ending the short engagement. In subsequent actions, Cox rendered safe many enemy placed "claymore" mines and recovered several fragmentary grenades with instantaneous fuses. Leading Seaman Rhook sought out and neutralized mines dangerously perched in trees, 30 to 40 feet above the ground, apparently intended to serve as helicopter traps.[15]

UNIT AWARDS FOR VALOUR

The CDT 3 Fourth Contingent was awarded a U.S. Presidential Unit Citation for its participation in Operation SEALORDS, and a U.S. Navy Unit Commendation as part of Explosive Ordnance Disposal Unit, Pacific. Copies of these award citations may be found in Appendix B.

All five ordnance disposal personnel involved in the Bo De River operation were recommended for the Bronze Star Medal (with combat V device) for heroism. Comprising this diverse group were three U.S. Navy EOD members—a warrant officer, chief boatswain's mate (diver qualified), and chief mineman (diver qualified)—and from the RAN, a petty officer clearance diver, and leading seaman clearance diver.

- WO1 Henry W. Busseno, USN
- BMC(DV) Charlie Noland Jr., USN
- MNC(DV) Walter J. Dennison, USN
- POCD Robert J. Cox, RAN
- LSCD David N. Rhook, RAN[16]

A number of Foreign governments, particularly the United States, have formally recognized the contributions of Australian Clearance Divers over the past several decades. In some cases, awards were not allowed to be accepted, most notably in the Vietnam War. This appears due, at least in part, because members of the Australian military were not authorized to wear them. The attitude of top brass appears to have been, if they can't wear a medal or ribbon, why award it? The policy of not accepting foreign awards continued until 1995, when the Australian government changed its policy.[17]

The Bronze Star Medal award recommendation submitted by the officer in charge, Inshore Undersea Warfare Group One for Cox and Rhook was approved by commander, U.S. Navy Forces Vietnam, on 17 July 1969 and forwarded to the Secretary of the Navy. The Military Assistance Command Free World Military Assistance Office sent a copy of the correspondence to commander, Australian Force Vietnam two days later. The cover letter conveyed, "The attached recommendations for awards are forwarded for your consideration."

The award summary included in the recommendation for Leading Seaman Clearance Diver David Rhook follows. (That for Petty Officer Robert Cox was similar.)

> During a six day period from 06 thru 11 February 1969, LSCD RHOOK was a team member of Ordnance Disposal Personnel who completed a successful round of operations in support of Sea Lords missions and Mobile Strike Force sweeps in the lower Mekong Delta. In the majority of the missions, he was required to carry the added weight of 20 pounds of explosives besides regular battle gear on long ground sweeps through arduous terrain.
>
> He was personally involved in the dangerous and sensitive placement of demolition explosives and the added hazardous task of placing booby traps in enemy controlled territory. On 08 February, LSCD RHOOK personally placed numerous booby traps. On 11 February, he performed efficiently and professionally in an equal status with his allied shipmates. Also he personally sought out (with personal disregard) and rendered safe enemy claymore mines dangerously perched in trees, 30 to 40 feet above the ground in apparent helo traps (11 February).
>
> On this same date, LSCD RHOOK successfully assisted MSF troops in suppressing enemy small arms-fire while involved in one of the many demanding geographical changes, then continued with his work of assisting in the destruction of a large enemy bunker complex, in semi-darkness. Two (2) enemy KIA resulted from this action.
>
> All operations were conducted in extremely hazardous enemy territory in the face of personal harm and under actual combat conditions, however, LSCD RHOOK continually performed calmly, professionally, systematically and with great efficiency. The

operations were total successes even though some of the work was performed under heavy fire conditions involving small arms, B40 rocket and RPG [rocket-propelled grenade] fire. Throughout, LSCD RHOOK was highly enthusiastic and exhibited positive adaptability to discomfort and demanding workloads in hostile surroundings.[18]

SUBSEQUENT DUTIES FOR *WASHTENAW COUNTY*

The USS *Washtenaw County*, which supported the operation would, later in the war, be converted from tank landing ship to special minesweeper. This occurred in preparation for the clearance of American mines from Haiphong Harbor in 1973—a provision for the release of Allied prisoners of war by North Vietnam.

Photo 13-6

Special minesweeper USS *Washtenaw County* (MSS-2, formerly LST-1166) conducts a run in the main channel of Haiphong Harbor, North Vietnam, to demonstrate its safety for shipping after Operation End Sweep mine clearance activities, 20 June 1973. Naval History and Heritage Command photograph #NH 103693

14

Swimmer-Sapper Attack on the Motor Vessel *Heredia*

Photo 14-1

DeLong Pier at Vung Tau with the RAN bulk carrier HMAS *Jeparit* alongside.
Australian War Memorial photograph P03051.002

In the early hours of 23 May 1969, Royal Australian Navy Clearance Diving Team 3 (CDT 3) played a major role in thwarting a swimmer-sapper attack against ships berthed at the DeLong Pier in Vung Tau. The efforts of the Aussie divers helped prevent potential loss of life and vessel damage, and also resulted in the recovery of two modern Soviet BPM-2 limpet mines.[1]

DeLong Pier was so named because it was constructed of sections fabricated by the DeLong Corporation, which were easily towed to a site and quickly emplaced. The mobile pier had transformed Vung Tau into a major support base. Capable of offloading both shallow and deep draught vessels, Vung Tau had increased the flow of logistics throughout South Vietnam. Use of this same pier type had also made it possible to develop deep-draft ports and berths at Qui Nhon, Cam Ranh Bay, Vung Ro, and Danang.²

Map 14-1

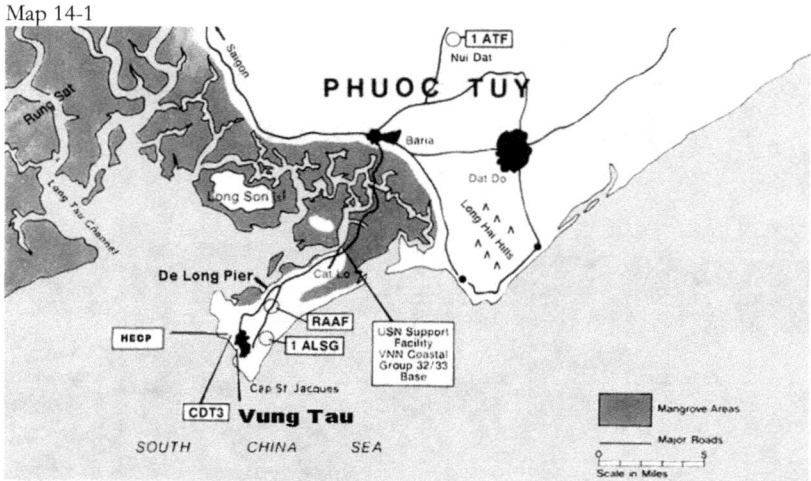

Allied military installations/units at Vung Tau included the Harbour Entrance Control Post (HECP), Clearance Diving Team 3 (CDT 3), Royal Australian Air Force air base (RAAF), and the 1st Australian Logistic Support Group (1 ALSG)

Although berthing ships alongside the pier, in lieu of unloading in an anchorage offshore, increased port productivity, it also made attacks by swimmer-sappers easier. Enemy swimmers still faced the possibility of detection by patrol boat or sentries on the pier or aboard ship, or death by concussion grenades randomly throw into the water to serve as a deterrent to their activities. However, it was easier to navigate underwater and affix explosives to a ship's hull in sheltered waters than doing so while battling stronger currents offshore.³

The port and anchorages offered many targets, and it was then known that Group 10 Viet Cong, reinforced by 126 North Vietnamese Navy Regiment sapper-swimmers, was based somewhere in the Rung Sat Special Zone, near Vung Tau. It must be highlighted that the same threat existed at many other locations in South Vietnam.⁴

A U.S. Navy study later found that there were 88 successful swimmer-sapper attacks against shipping in Vietnamese waters between January 1962 and June 1969, which killed more than 210 personnel and wounded 325 others. There was also considerable damage done to ships, including the sinking of USNS *Card* (T-AKV 40) while moored at Saigon, Vietnam, on 2 May 1964. Formerly an escort carrier, *Card* had been the first CVE to be awarded a Presidential Unit Citation. She earned it in World War II as the flagship of Task Unit 21.14—a hunter-killer group formed to destroy German U-boats in the North Atlantic.[5]

Commandos from the 65th Special Operations Group attached two explosive charges on the ship's starboard side, one near the bilge and the other at the engine compartment, just above the waterline. Lam Son Nao and Nguyen Phu Hung then set the timers and swam away. The ensuing explosions tore a huge hole in *Card*'s hull, killing five civilian crewmembers, and she sank in forty-eight feet of water—a propaganda coup for the Communists. The former CVE was refloated by Navy salvors on 19 May, and towed to the Philippines for repairs. She was returned to service on 11 December 1964.[6]

Photo 14-2

The cargo ship and aircraft ferry USNS *Card* (T-AKV 40) under way in 1966. Naval Photographic Center photograph #1120576

Only twenty enemy sappers were killed or captured for all the attacks against ships, which emphasized the advantageous payoff to the enemy of these type of operations.[7]

ATTACK AGAINST THE *HEREDIA*

On the night of 22 May 1969, a motorized-sampan reconnoitered the Vung Tau port area under the cloak of darkness, observing sentry positions and patrol boat patterns. This survey revealed that the port's lighting system posed little threat; the swimmer-sappers aboard the craft would not have to pass through an illuminated area while swimming to their objective. They waited until slack tide conditions, then entered the water near DeLong Pier—two with limpet mines and one with a locally-made explosive charge.⁸

The sappers swam toward the ships alongside the pier on the surface. They were not concerned with the possibility of small arms-fire or underwater explosions since their reconnaissance indicated that the sentries did not shoot at floating debris nor were grenades being used to any degree. A waning-crescent moon provided sufficient light for them to see their objective while, they believed, still allowing them to remain relatively safe from observation by sentries.⁹

This belief proved false. At around 0125, a sentry aboard USS *Hickman County* (LST-825) spotted two swimmers 75 yards astern of the tank landing ship, moving in a northerly direction with the incoming tide. The sentry opened fire with small arms as the sappers made for the pier in the vicinity of MV *Heredia*, berthed alongside the northern end. Two converted tankers at permanent moorings south of the pier were potentially lucrative targets, as they supplied electrical power for all the military installations and some civilian assets in Vung Tau and surrounding areas. However, MV *Heredia*, serving as an ammunitions ship with a cargo of almost 8,000 tons of explosives, was the target.¹⁰

Photo 14-3

USS *Hickman County* under way, date and location unknown.
National Archives photograph #USN 1046004

Hickman County's sentries, crewmen on watch on the main deck, then saw three swimmers with packages and opened fire again, while the ship increased readiness and called for EOD assistance. Two swimmers struck south toward the hard stand (a concrete area by the water for landing craft to beach). Anti-swimmer and signal lights were directed at them, and concussion grenades thrown into the water. The ship notified port control via radio, and army military police (MPs) arrived to investigate the shooting.[11]

The two swimmers were by now 150 yards to starboard heading toward the hard stand. A patrol boat pursuing them came within the line of fire; preventing further small arms-fire from the *Hickman County*, and the sentries' visual contact with the sappers was lost. The patrol boat captured one of the swimmers.[12]

CLEARANCE DIVING TEAM'S RESPONSE

Photo 14-4

Main Gate of the Harbor Entrance Control Post, circa 1968.
Courtesy of Albert Moore, Mobile Riverine Force Association

At 0130, a phone call was received at CDT 3's headquarters (and accommodation) at the Harbour Entrance Control Post (HECP), stating that swimmers had been positively sighted in the water off the end of the DeLong Pier. Within fifteen minutes, Chief Petty Officer Vic Rashleigh, and Able Seamen Jeff Garrett and Mike Ey arrived at the DeLong Pier. The officer in charge of the team, Lt. Allan Davis, was temporarily absent from the area. The other two members, Petty Officer John Brumley and Able Seaman Andy Sherlock, had left the HECP earlier to conduct a routine search of the anchor cables of ships in the anchorage off Vung Tau.[13]

Photo 14-5

Members of RAN Clearance Diving Team Three (5th Contingent) in 1969. Left to right: John R. Brumley, Andrew J. Sherlock, Michael H. Ey, Lt. Allan A. Davis, Jeffrey L. Garrett, and Albert V. Rashleigh.

Rashleigh, Garrett, and Ey found the area around the pier and ships in turmoil. U.S. Army military police were shooting at random, and throwing grenades and scare charges (hand-thrown explosives used to protect ships from divers) off the pier. Rashleigh restored order and cleared the pier of all but MPs and EOD personnel. It was learned that one swimmer had been captured and a nylon rope was visible, attached to a large tractor tire fender close to *Heredia*.[14]

Rashleigh decided to put a diver in the water. Security personnel were informed and use of scare charges and grenades was suspended. Well aware that enemy sappers were close, Garrett dived under the fender to discover a locally-made explosive charge the size of a four-gallon drum about twelve feet below the surface, suspended from the nylon line. Rashleigh and Ey pulled him out of the water and back onto the pier. After being briefed by Garrett, Rashleigh advised the MPs to clear the area of all personnel and the master of MV *Heredia* was warned to move his ship as soon as possible.[15]

As preparations were made to move the *Heredia*, a small explosion was heard. Rashleigh checked to see if grenades had been thrown in the water and on receiving a negative response, told Ey to investigate the charge. Ey entered the water from the bow of a patrol boat positioned between the *Heredia*'s stern and the pier and found the explosive charge had partially detonated. The container had burst open and he was able to recover some of the contents which appeared to be plastic explosive.[16]

Photo 14-6

Australian Clearance Diver Michael Ey, 1969.
Courtesy of Albert Moore, Mobile Riverine Force Association

Brumley and Sherlock joined the operation around 0230. Having learned of the attack, they cancelled the inspections they were to have carried out approximately three miles distant in the anchorage. The entire team commenced searching the pier structure and other vessels alongside the southern side of the pier.[17]

Motor Vessel *Heredia* was moved at 0310, after which the explosive charge attached to the pier was lifted clear of the water and onto the roadway. On inspection, the booster charges were found to be badly packed in American jam cans and had not detonated. The enemy had reached the target but were let down by a poor product. The bulk explosive was some 60-lbs of C4 plastic explosive and the booster 10-lbs of cast TNT. The mine had detonated, but failed to achieve a high order explosion due to a poor detonator-booster combination. Either the detonator was ineffective and/or the booster too stable to transmit the detonation wave into the bulk explosive.[18]

SECOND ENEMY SWIMMER CAPTURED

The captured swimmer was interrogated by an interpreter about the presence of other swimmers but admitted nothing. Around 0400, there was a new outbreak of shooting by MPs on the pier and a second swimmer was apprehended. He was a North Vietnamese Army sapper, wounded in the earlier shooting and found holding on to the pier, hoping to remain unseen in the darkness.[19]

Photo 14-7

Captured swimmer-sappers.
Courtesy of Hector Donohue

The team returned to the HECP at dawn to recharge diving equipment and resumed work around 0900. A sentry reported seeing a swimmer earlier near a large steel fender on the northern side of the pier, in the vicinity of where *Heredia* had been berthed. Ey dived in and found a Soviet BPM-2 limpet mine attached to the fender's underside. Visibility was poor. He could see the arming forks were intact on the dual firing fuses, but not ascertain if the safety pin was also intact on the antiremoval device fuse. A rubber flotation bag, still inflated, was strapped to the mine. He secured a rope to the limpet mine's carry handle and the patrol boat attempted to pull the mine free but the rope parted. Ey dived again to the mine and discovered that the third pin was in place. He pulled the mine off the fender and surfaced at the stern of the patrol boat. The limpet mine was taken on board and made safe by removing the three fuses.[20]

RECOVERY OF SOVIET LIMPET MINES

Photo 14-8

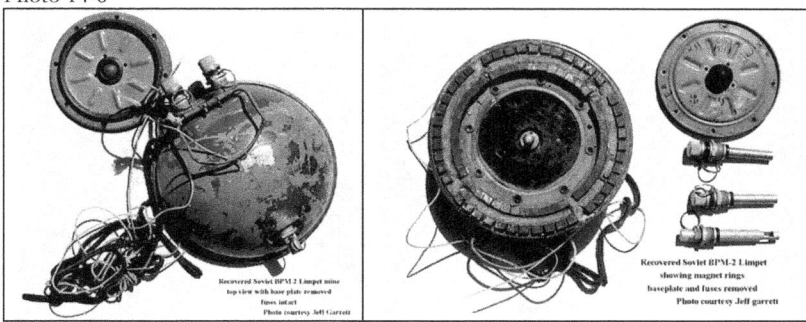

Photographs by Jeffrey L. Garrett of the recovered Soviet BPM-2 Limpet mine; the view on the left depicts the base plate removed and fuses intact, the one on the right shows the mine's magnetic rings and the fuses removed.
Courtesy of Hector Donohue

U.S. Navy salvage divers from Harbor Clearance Unit, Vung Tau, joined and assisted in the search of the general area in daylight, while the harbormaster closed the pier and prevented vessels moving in the area. No further limpet mines or explosive charges were found, and Rashleigh ceased efforts around midday. Further searches were made the following day, for another limpet mine the second swimmer would have carried, to no avail. It was found four days later, washed up on a beach eight kilometers away, still attached to its small flotation bladder.[21]

AWARDS FOR VALOUR

Chief Petty Officer Albert V. Rashleigh received the British Empire Medal, and Able Seaman Jeffrey L. Garrett a Mention in Despatches, for their actions in the early morning of 23 May 1969. Garrett and Ey, who entered the water, no doubt experienced a sense of disquiet while professionally performing their tasks and exhibiting great bravery. The fact that mines/charges had been deployed, that enemy sappers were still in the area, and working underwater at night with no visibility, made the diving task particularly difficult and hazardous. It was believed that the group of which the sappers were a part had been in the general area since December 1968.[22]

Photo 14-9

Garrett, Rashleigh and Ey, forty plus years later.
Courtesy of Hector Donohue

The recovery of two modern Soviet-made limpet mines provided valuable information. Although U.S. intelligence was aware of the BPM-2 limpet mine, this was the first time one in mint condition had been recovered. The CDT 3 team members removed the explosives and, together with a USN EOD team member (who was with CDT 3 as part of an Australian and United States exchange program), devised a render safe procedure, which was both safe and feasible. The established practice of sliding a metal shim under the mine proved impracticable and unsafe. Lieutenant Davis gave one mine to the U.S. Navy, which is held by the Naval Explosive Ordnance Disposal Technology Division Indian Head, Maryland, while the other was returned to Australia and is at the Diving School, HMAS Penguin, in Sydney Harbour.[23]

15

Final ARG/SLF Operations

Photo 15-1

Marines of the 26th Regiment come ashore by amphibious tractors on the Batangan Peninsula, South Vietnam, on 13 January 1969, to commence BOLD MARINER. NARA photograph A800449 (Reference Number: 127-GVB-60-A800449)

While Clearance Diving Team Three toiled to protect ships calling at Vung Tau (including supply LSTs delivering or loading cargo) from swimmer-sapper attack, Amphibious Ready Groups Alfa and Bravo spent much time off the South Vietnamese coast.

Since 1967, when Special Landing Force Bravo was established, the deployments of SLFs A and B had been arranged through coordination between commander, Seventh Fleet, and commander, U.S. Military Assistance Command Vietnam. Separate and alternating use of the two forces was envisioned. However, due to heightened levels of conflict (particularly in the I Corps Tactical Zone, beginning in the summer of 1967), commanding general, III Marine Amphibious Force often employed the SLFs concurrently.[1]

By mid-1968, the Special Landing Forces were being committed ashore more often, and remaining longer. The commanders of Task Force 79 (Seventh Fleet Marine Forces) and the 9th Marine Amphibious Brigade, which directly controlled the two SLFs, were under constant and conflicting pressures concerning the use of combat assets. The commonly held view of III MAF was that "any combat Marine not ashore and fighting was not being properly utilized." Hence the periods ashore grew longer and longer. With the SLFs ashore, the 7th Fleet's amphibious reserve (ARGs with landing forces embarked) was unavailable should a sudden crisis develop elsewhere—and it was hard for the Navy to justify the expense of keeping underutilized amphibious shipping off the Vietnamese coast.[2]

The existing, somewhat ad hoc, manning of the landing forces was corrected in 1969. Previously, any reinforced infantry battalion within III MAF, or medium helicopter squadron of the 1st Marine Air Wing, could be assigned to a tour with a special landing force. This changed in late 1968 under BGen. John E. Williams, commanding general of the 9th Marine Amphibious Brigade. Regimental Landing Team 26 (26th Marine Regiment, with 5th Marine Division supporting units) was reconstituted, and from it the SLFs drew their battalion landing teams. Similarly, HMM-164 and HMM-362 (replaced in May by HMM-265) were permanently assigned for duty with the landing forces.[3]

When not ashore, the SLFs were embarked in Amphibious Ready Groups Alfa and Bravo. Each ARG consisted of an amphibious assault ship (LPH), a dock landing ship (LSD), and a tank landing ship (LST). As necessary, additional ships were employed. A high-speed transport (AP) joined, if needed to carry UDT and Marine reconnaissance units. Either an amphibious transport dock (LPD), an attack transport (APA), or an attack cargo ship (AKA), to carry additional supplies, troops, and landing craft, could also be added.[4]

OPERATION BOLD MARINER

Amphibious Ready Groups Alfa and Bravo with Marines embarked, assembled off Quang Ngai Province in early January 1969, in preparation for BOLD MARINER—the largest amphibious operation since the Korean War. Under the command of General Williams, the brigade-size landing force, once ashore, would join with elements of the U.S. Army's Americal Division in an assault on the Batangan Peninsula. (This division had been activated on 27 May 1942, on the island of New Caledonia; the only division formed outside of United States territory during World War II. Its unique name was a contraction of "American, New Caledonian Division.") Located 18 kilometers south of Chu Lai, the peninsula's flat fertile lowlands and rolling hills harbored elements of the Viet Cong 38th Main Force Regiment, 48th Local Force Battalion, P-31st Local Force Company, and C-95th Sapper Company. From their well-entrenched positions on the peninsula, these enemy forces posed a threat to Quang Ngai City to the southwest.[5]

An amphibious demonstration—a show of force to mask the intended operational area—was conducted on Sunday, 12 January, off Mo Duc (40 kilometers south of Chu Lai). At 0700 the next morning, BLTs 2/26 and 3/26 landed on the northern side of the peninsula by air and landing craft. Concurrently, the Americal Division's Task Force Cooksey (comprised of elements of 46th Infantry and 1st Cavalry) and South Vietnam Army troops commenced Operation RUSSELL BEACH, to seal off the area's southern border. The battalion landing teams moved south and east, linking up with elements of the task force moving to the northeast. The combined force, supported by organic artillery and the battleship *New Jersey* (BB-62) offshore, then began sweeping eastward. This forced the enemy toward the sea, where the only avenues of escape were blocked by Navy and Coast Guard patrol boats.[6]

Photo 15-2

Infantrymen of the 2nd/26th Marines prepare to form an assault line on Hill 37, south of Chu Lai, during Operation BOLD MARINER.
Combat Information Bureau photograph 3M-3-0133-69

New Jersey had fired four prearranged missions on Sunday and that night, her secondary battery continued to put rounds into the Mo Duc area. At 0400 on 13 January, she moved northward to take up her fire support station for the actual landings off Batangan. With no request for additional gunfire forthcoming, she left at noon to proceed to Subic Bay for upkeep and rearming. The nine amphibious ships assigned to BOLD MARINER remained off the coast in support of ground operations ashore.[7]

Photo 15-3

Battleship USS *New Jersey* (BB-62) bombarding enemy targets near Tuyho, on South Vietnam's central coast, in March 1969.
Naval History and Heritage Command photograph

BOLD MARINER (13 January-9 February 1969)

ARG Alfa (TG 76.4)
SLF Alfa (TG 79.4): Col. John F. McHahon Jr., USMC
BLT 2/26: Lt. Col. William F. Sparks, USMC
HMM-362: Lt. Col. Jack E. Schlarp, USMC
ARG Bravo (TG 76.5)
SLF Bravo (TG 79.5): Col. Robert R. Wilson, USMC
BLT 3/26: Lt. Col. J. W. P. Robertson, USMC
HMM-164: Lt. Col. Richard T. Trundy, USMC

ARG Alfa Ships	ARG Bravo Ships
Okinawa (LPH-3)	*Tripoli* (LPH-10)
Duluth (LPD-6)	*Ogden* (LPD-5)
Ft. Marion (LSD-22)	*Monticello* (LSD-35)
Catamont (LSD-17)	*Seminole* (AKA-104)
Winston (AKA-94)[8]	

The only resistance encountered over the next several days (as Marine, Army, and 2nd ARVN Division units tightened the cordon around the peninsula) were brief exchanges with groups of enemy or individuals trying to flee under the cover of darkness. The Marines found extensive networks of mines and booby traps scattered throughout the area, as well as mazes of tunnels, connecting trenches, caves, and shelters. Each of these earthworks had to be searched and destroyed. Searches located numerous supply caches and training facilities. During one such on 19 January, Company Foxtrot of the 2/26 captured 102 Vietnamese; fifty-six of whom were males of military age. Subsequent interrogation revealed they were members of the C-95th Sapper Company, and their apprehension represented the largest unit captured up to that point in the war.[9]

Photo 15-4

Combat engineer Sgt. R. L. Slemons (attached to the 26th Marine Regiment) prepares a charge on the end of a pole, which he will use to blow an enemy tunnel complex. Defense Department photograph Marine Corps SLF-5-0135-69

After sealing off the Batangan Peninsula by land, sea, and air, the combined force methodically screened over 12,000 Vietnamese. The process identified 256 Viet Cong troops, including the captured sappers. Viet Cong casualties during BOLD MARINER numbered 239 killed.[10]

SPECIAL LANDING FORCE OPERATIONS CEASE

Following the spectacular success of BOLD MARINER, amphibious operations tapered off, then essentially ended upon withdrawal of the 3rd Marine Division from Vietnam. There would be fourteen SLF operations in 1969, and thirteen in 1968, as compared to twenty-five in 1967. In May 1969, following unproductive operations in February and March, amphibious forces landed on Barrier Island south of Hoi An and killed or captured 178 enemy soldiers.[11]

Four other actions between May and August on the I Corps coast resulted in almost as many Marine as enemy casualties, primarily because of the numerous mines and booby traps in the operational areas. On 7 September, the ARG/SLF team launched the final operation of the year, DEFIANT STAND, another strike against the enemy on Barrier Island. This time, the one U.S. Marine and two South Korean Marine battalions involved killed 293 Viet Cong and captured 121 weapons at a cost of fifty-nine allied casualties.[12]

During the remainder of 1969, the Seventh Fleet Amphibious Force was fully occupied with the withdrawal of the 3rd Marine Division from South Vietnam. By year's end, in keeping with the Vietnamization policy, Washington withdrew both ARG/SLFs from South Vietnamese waters, placing them in an alert status. Thereafter, Joint Chiefs of Staff authorization was required to initiate combat landings in South Vietnam. Throughout 1970 and 1971 the fleet's amphibious forces were prepared for the evacuation of Americans from the mainland and other contingencies, but such need did not arise.[13]

16

"Vietnamization" Begins

They are tigers in every respect. Tales of their courage are legend. The episodes they have brought off are almost unbelievable.

—Vice Adm. Elmo R. Zumwalt Jr., commander, U.S. Naval Forces, Vietnam, speaking (in 1969) in tribute of his "Brown Water" sailors. The Mobile Riverine Force, of which these men were a part, was stood down during the latter part of that year.

Photo 16-1

President Richard M. Nixon reviews the Vietnam situation with senior advisors on 12 July 1969, at the White House. From left are: Dr. Henry Kissinger; Attorney General John Mitchell; Vice President Spiro Agnew; Adm. John McCain, commander of the U.S. forces in the Pacific; Gen. Creighton Abrams Jr., commander of the U.S. forces in Vietnam; Richard Helms, director of the CIA; Philip Habib, of the U.S. delegation to the Paris peace talks; Ellsworth Bunker, U.S. Ambassador to Vietnam; Secretary of State William P. Rogers; President Nixon; Secretary of Defense Melvin R. Laird; and Gen. Earle Wheeler, chairman of the Joint Chiefs of Staff.
U.S. Information Agency photograph #69-3361

In autumn 1969, the Mobile Riverine Force was disestablished. This action followed an announcement by President Nixon at the Midway Island Conference on 8 June (at which he and Republic of Vietnam President Nguyen Van Thieu met for the first time to discuss reducing the American presence in Vietnam) that 25,000 American servicemen would depart South Vietnam by the end of August. Concurrent with this pronouncement, the U.S. Navy, in June, decommissioned River Assault Squadrons Nine and Eleven and turned over a total of 64 assault craft to the Vietnamese Navy.[1]

The sixty-four boats, plus twenty-five river craft turned over earlier in February 1969, and twenty new ASPBs delivered directly to the Vietnamese Navy in June 1968, brought to 109 the total number of river craft then operated by the Vietnamese Navy River Assault and Interdiction Force (RAID). The two oilers (refuelers) listed in the table were modified ATCs.

Assault Craft turned over to the Vietnamese Navy in June 1969

CCB	Monitor	ATC	ASPB	Oilers
4	7	35	36	2[2]

The U.S. Army Second Brigade, U.S. Ninth Infantry Division, began phasing out of Mobile Riverine Force operations in July and August. The entire division began withdrawing in summer 1969, except for its Third Brigade, which remained behind as a separate unit under the Twenty-fifth Infantry Division until October 1970.[3]

Vice Admiral Zumwalt termed the Navy part of "Vietnamization," ACTOV (Accelerated Turnover to the Vietnamese). River Division 574 was turned over to the Vietnamese Navy on 11 August at Nha Be, marking the first ACTOV program transfer of a PBR division. Two weeks later the Army-Navy Mobile Riverine Force was phased out of existence, with the disestablishment of River Flotilla One, River Support Squadron Seven, and Task Force 117 on 25 August.[4]

TURNOVER OF AMPHIBIOUS SHIPS

The Vietnamese Navy had earlier received its fourth tank landing ship on 1 July 1969, during ceremonies at Guam. Rear Adm. Philip P. Cole, commander, U.S. Naval Forces Marianas, representing the United States, presented the ex-*Coconino City* to Commodore Tran Van Chon, chief of Naval Operations, Republic of Vietnam. A total of six tank landing ships were transferred to South Vietnam; three—*Marion County*, *Maricopa County*, and *Cayuga County*—previously in 1962-1963.

Photo 16-2

Commodore Tran Van Chon, chief of Naval Operations of the Republic of Vietnam Navy, (left) and (to his left) Adm. Thomas H. Moorer, chief of Naval Operations, inspect some of the Vietnamese sailors who would take over river patrol operations from the U.S. Navy, circa September 1969.
Naval History and Heritage Command photograph #NH 104916

Date	Tank Landing Ship	VNN Ship
12 Apr 62	*Marion County* (LST-975)	RVNS *Cam Ranh* (HQ-500)
12 Jul 62	*Maricopa County* (LST-938)	RVNS *Danang* (HQ-501)
17 Dec 63	*Cayuga County* (LST-529)	RVNS *Thi Nai* (HQ-502)
1 Jul 69	*Coconino County* (LST-603)	RVNS *Vung Tau* (HQ-503)
8 Apr 70	*Bulloch County* (LST-509)	RVNS *Qui Nhon* (HQ-504)
8 Apr 70	*Jerome County* (LST-848)	RVNS *Nha Trang* (HQ-505)5

Bulloch County and *Jerome County* became the *Qui Nhon* and *Nha Trang*, respectively, in a formal ceremony in San Diego on 8 April 1970. Commodore Tran Van Chon accepted the ships for the Vietnamese Navy. The VNN's latest acquisitions were to remain in San Diego for approximately six weeks for training of their (14 officer, 206 man) crews, before departing for South Vietnam.6

The former *Marion County*, *Cayuga County*, and *Jerome County* later escaped to the Philippines in April 1975, before Saigon fell to North Vietnamese forces. (This subject is taken up in the final chapter of the book.) These ships served in the Philippine Navy as BRP *Zamboanga Del Sur* (LT-86), BRP *Cotabato Del Sur* (LT-87), and BRP *Agusan Del Sur* (LT-54), respectively. The ex-*Maricopa County* and *Coconino County* were captured and taken into the Vietnam People's Navy, *Maricopa County* as

PRVS *Tran Khanh Du* (HQ-501). The fate of the ex-*Bulloch County* is unknown.[7]

Two patrol craft tenders and a landing craft repair ship turned over to the Vietnamese Navy, were also able to escape to the Philippines. The *Harnett County* and *Garrett County* (former tank landing ships) served in the Philippine Navy as BRP *Sierra Madre* (LT-57) and BRP *Kalinga Apayao* (LT-516). *Satyr*, a tank landing ship converted to landing craft repair ship in World War II, served as BRP *Yakal* (AR-617).

Date	USN Patrol Craft Tender	VNN Ship
12 Oct 70	*Harnett County* (AGP-821)	RVNS *My Tho* (HQ-800)
23 Apr 71	*Garrett County* (AGP-786)	RVNS Can Tho (HQ-801)
	Landing Craft Repair Ship	**VNN Ship**
30 Sep 71	*Satyr* (ARL-23)	RVNS *Vinh Long* (HQ-802)[8]

TURNOVER OF U.S. COAST GUARD VESSELS

Photo 16-3

Seaplane tender USS *Bering Strait* (AVP-34) off Houghton, Washington, 12 July 1944. National Archives photograph #19-N-72076

Although coverage of the activities of U.S. Coast Guard patrol boats and cutters is not within the scope of this book, it's worthwhile to note that thirty-three such vessels were turned over to the Vietnamese Navy. Twenty-six 82-foot *Point*-class patrol boats of Coast Guard Squadron One (Divisions 11, 12, and 13) were transferred in 1969 and 1970. Four

311-foot cutters of Squadron Three were turned over in 1971, and three same type cutters, comprising Squadron Two, in 1972.

Coast Guard Squadron One: Commissioned 27 May 1965
(82-foot *Point*-class patrol boats)

Date	USCG Patrol Boat	VNN Ship
16 May 69	*Point League* (WPB-82304)	RVNS *Le Phuoc Duc* (HQ-700)
16 May 69	*Point Garnet* (WPB-82310)	RVNS *Le Van Nga* (HQ-701)
15 Sep 69	*Point Clear* (WPB-82315)	RVNS *Huynh Van Duc* (HQ-702)
11 Nov 69	*Point Gammon* (WPB-82328)	RVNS *Nguyen Dao* (HQ-703)
17 Nov 69	*Point Comfort* (WPB-82317)	RVNS *Dao Thuc* (HQ-704)
9 Dec 69	*Point Ellis* (WPB-82330)	RVNS *Le Ngoc Thanh* (HQ-705)
11 Dec 69	*Point Slocum* (WPB-82313)	RVNS *Nguyen Ngoc Thach* (HQ-706)
11 Dec 69	*Point Hudson* (WPB-82322)	RVNS *Dang Van Hoanh* (HQ-707)
12 Jan 70	*Point White* (WPB-82308)	RVNS *Le Dinh Hung* (HQ-708)
14 Feb 70	*Point Dume* (WPB-82325)	RVNS *Truong Tien* (HQ-709)
14 Feb 70	*Point Arden* (WPB-82309)	RVNS *Pham Ngoc Chau* (HQ-710)
14 Feb 70	*Point Glover* (WPB-82307)	RVNS *Dao Van Dang* (HQ-711)
21 Feb 70	*Point Jefferson* (WPB-82306)	RVNS *Le Ngoc An* (HQ-712)
16 Mar 70	*Point Kennedy* (WPB-82320)	RVNS *Huynh Van Ngan* (HQ-713)
16 Mar 70	*Point Young* (WPB-82303)	RVNS *Tran Lo* (HQ-714)
27 Mar 70	*Point Partridge* (WPB-82305)	RVNS *Bui Viet Thanh* (HQ-715)
29 Apr 70	*Point Caution* (WPB-82301)	RVNS *Nguyen An* (HQ-716)
29 Apr 70	*Point Welcome* (WPB-82329)	RVNS *Nguyen Han* (HQ-717)
26 May 70	*Point Banks* (WPB-82327)	RVNS *Ngo Van Quyen* (HQ-718)
26 May 70	*Point Lomas* (WPB-82321)	RVNS *Van Dien* (HQ-719)
16 Jun 70	*Point Grace* (WPB-82323)	RVNS *Ho Dang La* (HQ-720)
16 Jun 70	*Point Mast* (WPB-82316)	RVNS *Dam Thoai* (HQ-721)
14 Jul 70	*Point Orient* (WPB-82319)	RVNS *Nguyen Kim Hung* (HQ-722)
14 Jul 70	*Point Grey* (WPB-82324)	RVNS *Huynh Bo* (HQ-723)
15 Aug 70	*Point Cypress* (WPB-82326)	RVNS *Ho Duy* (HQ-724)
15 Aug 70	*Point Marone* (WPB-82331)	RVNS *Truong Ba* (HQ-725)[9]

Coast Guard Squadron Three:
Commissioned at Pearl Harbor, Hawaii, 24 April 1967
(310-foot *Casco*-class high endurance cutters;
ex-USN *Barnegat*-class seaplane tenders)

Date	USCG Cutter/ USS Seaplane Tender	Vietnamese Navy Ship/ Philippine Navy Usage
1 Jan 71	*Bering Strait* (WHEC-382)/ USS *Bering Strait* (AVP-34)	RVNS *Tran Quang Khai* (HQ-02)/ BRP *Diego Silang* (PF-9)
1 Jan 71	*Yakutat* (WHEC-380)/ USS *Yakutat* (AVP-32)	RVNS *Tran Nhat Duat* (HQ-03)/ Philippine Navy, spare parts
21 Dec 71	*Castle Rock* (WHEC-383)/ USS *Castle Rock* (AVP-35)	RVNS *Tran Binh Trong* (HQ-05)/ BRP *Francisco Dagohoy* (PF-10)
21 Dec 71	*Cook Inlet* (WHEC-384)/ USS *Cook Inlet* (AVP-36)	RVNS *Tran Quoc Toan* (HQ-06)/ Philippine Navy, spare parts[10]

Six of the seven cutters of Squadrons Two and Three turned over to the Vietnamese—*Absecon, Bering Strait, Castle Rock, Chincoteague, Cook Inlet,* and *Yakutat*—were former U.S. Navy World War II *Barnegat*-class small seaplane tenders. The other cutter was the former *Wachapreague,* one of four *Barnegat*s reclassified while still under construction as AGPs (motor torpedo boat tenders). The former cutters of Squadron Three identified in the table—*Tran Quang Khai, Tran Nhat Duat, Tran Binh Trong,* and *Tran Quoc Toan*—escaped to the Philippines in April 1975 and were taken into the Philippine Navy.[11]

Coast Guard Squadron Two
(310-foot *Casco*-class high endurance cutters; ex-USN *Barnegat*-class seaplane tenders)

In the spring of 1972, the three cutters of Coast Guard Squadron Two—*Absecon, Chincoteague,* and *McCulloch*—departed Norfolk, Virginia, bound for the Western Pacific. Their crews were comprised mainly of USCG Reserve members. After arriving at the U.S. Navy base at Apra Harbor, Guam, the ships were decommissioned, turned over to the U.S. Navy, and then transferred to South Vietnam.

Date	USCG Cutter/ USS Seaplane Tender	Vietnamese Navy Ship/ Philippine Navy Usage
15 Jul 72	*Absecon* (WHEC-374) USS *Absecon* (AVP-23)	RVNS *Pham Ngu Lao* (HQ-15)/ captured by North Vietnam
21 Jun 72	*Chincoteague* (WHEC-375)/ USS *Chincoteague* (AVP-24)	RVNS *Ly Thuong Kiet* (HQ-16)/ BRP *Andres Bonifacio* (PF-7).
21 Jun 72	*McCulloch* (WHEC-386)/ USS *Wachapreague* (AGP-8)	RVNS *Ngo Quyen* (HQ-17)/ BRP *Gregorio del Pilar* (PF-8)[12]

The former *Chincoteague* and *McCulloch* escaped to the Philippines. Unable to do so, ex-*Absecon* was captured by North Vietnamese forces.

Cambodian Incursion

Many intelligence analysts at the time believed that the Cambodian incursion dealt a stunning blow to the communists, driving main force units away from the border and damaging their morale, and in the process buying as much as a year for South Vietnam's survival. However, the incursion gave the antiwar movement in the United States a new rallying point. News of the incursion set off a wave of antiwar demonstrations, including one at Kent State University that resulted in the killing of four students by Army National Guard troops and another at Jackson State in Mississippi that resulted in the shooting of two students when police opened fire on a women's dormitory. The incursion also angered many in Congress, who felt that Nixon was illegally widening the scope of the war; this resulted in a series of congressional resolutions and legislative initiatives that would severely limit the executive power of the president.

—Excerpt from the article, U.S.-South Vietnamese forces launch Cambodian "incursion," by History.com editors.[1]

On the morning of 9 May 1970, a joint American and Vietnamese task force pushed up the Mekong River into Cambodia. Numbering about 140 vessels, it was the largest task force formed during the war. Its mission was to gain control of the Mekong from the Cambodian border to the capital city Phnom Penh, and assist in the evacuation of refugees as required. Concurrently, Vietnamese and American ships set up a blockade along the Cambodian coast to prevent enemy infiltration by sea. The naval operation was part of a larger incursion by American and Vietnamese Army forces into Cambodia to strike at well-established North Vietnamese sanctuaries there.[2]

The immediate objective of the naval aspect of the operation, code named TRAN HUNG DAO XI, was to gain control of the Neak Luong Ferry, a strategic point where Highway 1 crossed the river. The Viet Cong held the town, and embarked VNN Marines were to take control of the crossing from the enemy. Once Neak Luong was secured, a VNN portion of the task force was to continue up the Mekong to

Phnom Penh to deliver food and supplies, and to evacuate refugees. The American advisors were to go only as far as Neak Luong, beyond which Vietnamese naval forces would be solely responsible for the remaining portion of the operation.³

Rear Adm. Herbert Spencer Mathews Jr., "First SEALORD" and deputy Commander, U.S. Naval Forces Vietnam, was in command of the American portion of the operation. The task organization follows:

TRAN HUNG DAO XI Joint USN/VNN Task Group

USN/VNN	Unit	Title	Commander
USN	TG 194.0	Group Commander	First SEALORD
VNN	TU 194.0.1	Amphibious Assault Unit	CATF 211
VNN	TE 194.0.1.1	Assault Element A-RAIDs 70 and 71 and 5th Bn. VNMC	CTG 211.1
VNN	TE 194.0.1.2	Assault Element B-RAIDs 72 And 73 and 1st Bn. VNMC	CTG 211.2
VNN	TE 194.0.1.3	Assault Element C-RAIDs 74 And 75 and 4th Bn. VNMC	CTG 211.3
USN	TE 194.0.1.4	River Security Element – RID 42	
USN	TU 194.0.2	Fast Raider/Fire Support/River Security Unit	ComCosRon One
USN	TE 194.0.2.1	PCF Element – 8 Swift boats	
	TE 194.0.2.2	ASPB Element – 8 ASPBs	
VNN	TE 194.0.2.3	PCF Element – 15 Swift boats	
USN	TU 194.0.3	Air Support Unit One	HAL-3
USN	TE 194.0.3.1	Helo Air Support Element One	HAL-3 Det 8
USN	TE 194.0.3.2	Helo Air Support Element Two	HAL-3 Det 9
USN	TE 194.0.3.3	Helo Air Support Element Three	HAL-3 Det 5
USN	TU 194.0.4	Air Support Unit Two	VAL-4
USN	TU 194.0.5	Logistics Unit – RAG 21/33	4th Riverine Area commander
USN	TU 194.0.6	PBR Unit (river patrol boats) – RIVDIV 593 and RPG 55	ComRivDiv 593
USN	TU 194.0.7	Flagship/Staging Unit – *Benewah*, *Askari*, *Hunterdon County*, *YRBM-16*, *YRBM-21*	CO, USS *Benewah*
VNN	TU 194.0.8	Refugee Lift Unit	VNN Fleet Command⁴

Bn:	Battalion
CosRon One:	Coastal Squadron One
HAL-3:	Helicopter Attack, Light, Squadron Three
RAID:	Riverine Assault Interdiction Division
RID:	River Interdiction Division
RIVDIV:	River Division
VAL-4:	Light Attack Squadron Four

Map 17-1

Southern portion of South Vietnam, and adjacent area of Cambodia
Naval History and Heritage Command photograph #NH 96337

STRIKE ASSAULT BOATS ADD EXTRA FIREPOWER

Comprising Task Unit 194.0.2, under Comdr. Lawrence Richard Jefferis, USN (commander, Coastal Squadron One), were ten STABS (strike assault boats) functioning as the Fast Raider/Fire Support/River Security Unit. These boats constituted half of Strike Assault Boat Squadron Twenty (StabRon 20)—an initiative of Admiral Zumwalt. Impressed by the sixteen LSSCs (light SEAL support craft) that Grafton Boat Company built for the SEALS, he wanted a small, quiet, high-speed craft that could be airlifted by helicopter into remote areas to deliver quick deadly attacks on unsuspecting enemy targets.[5]

Photo 17-1

A strike assault boat carrying out a patrol near the Cambodian border, 20 June 1970. National Archives photograph #USN 1146259

A contract was issued to Grafton Boat Company, Grafton, Illinois, in 1969 for the construction of twenty-two aluminum-hulled boats. Grafton modified the 24-foot SEAL LSSC design, installing two Chevrolet 325hp gasoline engines with MerCruiser III stern drives and propellers instead of water jets. To increase survivability, each STAB was Styrofoam-filled from bow to stem to prevent capsizing if holed. A damaged boat would sink to the gunwale and no farther. These changes increased the length of the STAB to 26 feet 2 inches. The 7 ½-ton boats could make a top speed of 40-45 knots and, with their miniscule 2-foot draft, ply extremely shallow waters.[6]

Well-armed for their size, the boat's normal armament was two M60 (7.62mm) machine guns aft, or one M60 on a forward pintle mount and either two M60s aft or one M60 and one Mk 20 automatic grenade launcher (firing 40mm grenades). "Occasionally, .50-caliber machine guns were substituted for one or both of the M60s forward."[7]

Twenty of these boats served in Vietnam hence the name of their parent command, Strike Assault Boat Squadron Twenty. The other two boats remained at the Naval Inshore Operations Training Center, Mare Island Naval Station, Vallejo, California, where the officers and crews of the boats received their training.[8]

Comdr. John Kirk Ferguson, USN, commanded StabRon 20. His twenty boats arrived in Vietnam in early January 1970, delivered to Dong Tam, South Vietnam, by *Tioga County* (LST-1158). From there, they transited the Mekong River north to An Long, where the *Benewah* (mother-ship for the STABs and squadron personnel) was anchored. The STABS were the fastest boats in the Brown Water Navy and their crews delighted in outrunning Swift boats and LSSCs and running circles around the PBRs in the Mekong River.[9]

FLAGSHIP/STAGING UNIT

Photo 17-2

Repair, Berthing and Messing Barge *YRBM-16* mined at Ben Tre, South Vietnam. Salvage operations were carried out by Harbor Clearance Unit One.
Naval History and Heritage Command photograph #NH 74177

The five vessels comprising Task Unit 194.0.7 were responsible for supporting the flotilla of USN and VNN riverine craft and United States and Vietnamese aircraft participating in the operation.

Flagship/Staging Unit (Task Unit 194.0.7)

Tank landing ship	*Hunterdon County* (LST-838)	Lt. Comdr. Warren Howard Fischer, USN
Landing Craft Repair Ship	*Askari* (ARL-30)	Lt. Comdr. Albert Peter, Festag Jr., USN
Self-propelled Barracks Ship	*Benewah* (APB-35)	Lt. Comdr. Billy Ralph Tilger, USN[10]
Repair, Berthing and Messing Barge	*YRBM-16*	
Repair, Berthing and Messing Barge	*YRBM-21*	

YRBM-16 had been mined at Ben Tre, South Vietnam, two-and-a-half years earlier, resulting in five men aboard her killed in action, and two wounded. Berthing barges housing large numbers of soldiers were a prime target for enemy swimmer-sappers. In the early hours of 24 November 1967, the barge (anchored at the junction of the Ham Luong and Ben Tre River in support of Operation GAME WARDEN) suffered an underwater explosion, which ripped an 18- by 17-foot hole in her hull below the waterline. A resultant fire, fed by fuel escaping a ruptured tank, raged out of control for several hours, completely gutting the engineering and shop spaces before finally being extinguished.[11]

Hunterdon County, on station at the mouth of the Ham Luong, came to the aid of the stricken barge, and provided assistance in putting out the fire, which burned for fifteen hours. The light salvage lift craft *YLLC-4* (with Harbor Control Unit One personnel embarked) rushed to the scene from Dong Tam and provided emergency power and firemain pressure. Following the explosion, *YRBM-16* settled nine feet by the stern due to flooding of her engine room, stowage spaces, and adjacent living compartments. The most serious flooding was confined to these spaces and contained. Divers later found the remains of five crewmembers in the after berthing compartment.[12]

On the morning of 25 November, the harbor tug *Kalispell* (YTB-784), escorted by two ASPBs, PBRs, and *Hunterdon County*, towed the disabled barge to Dong Tam for emergency repairs. Following the offloading of all ammunition, provisions, fuel, lube oil, and PBR spare parts, the lightened *YRBM-16* was beached on 30 November, stern first on the My Tho river bank south of Dong Tam. Taking advantage of the ten-foot tidal range, temporary underwater hull repairs were made to permit an ocean tow to the ship repair facility at Subic Bay.[13]

EVE OF THE OPERATION

TRAN HUNG DAO XI proved anti-climactic for the U.S. Navy forces involved in the operation. Arnold E. Resnicoff, *Hunterdon County*'s communications officer, later briefly described her service during his tour; the trepidation felt by some on the eve of the incursion into Cambodia; and finding that most of the Viet Cong troops had abandoned the area prior to arrival of the task force at Neak Luong:

> When I left NROTC for an 8-week school in San Diego (to prepare me for my assignment as communications officer and assistant operations officer), I thought I would be reporting to USS *Hunterdon County* there, after the school. Instead, I soon learned that HC had been in Vietnam for years. It was one of four WWII LSTs converted for riverine warfare, to participate in Operation Game Warden but also in Operation Market Time. We were part of TF 116.
>
> Three of the four LSTs were in the Mekong and Bassac rivers at any given time, while the fourth was in overhaul, either in Subic Bay, Philippines, or Yokosuka, Japan. So the year I was on board HC, I was actually in the rivers for 10 months and then one month in each of those ports for overhaul.
>
> When we were ordered into Cambodia as part of the Cambodia Operation, we all expected heavy fighting, and we were terrified. Body bags were delivered to our ship, and of course that added to the terror. It seems to me that a chaplain rode into Cambodia with us, which added to our fear. In any event, when we crossed the line into Cambodia, we took no fire at all for the time we were there, and we did not fire our guns, either. We were told the Viet Cong had cleared out because they knew our forces were coming.
>
> We did break all kinds of records in terms of refueling and re-arming helicopters—and we were doing that not only for Navy helos (like Seawolves) but also US Army and Air Force helos, and Vietnamese helos as well. We also acted as command ship and supply ship for the PCF "swift boats" and PBR small boats, as we had been doing in the rivers inside Vietnam, along with our rearming and resupplying the helicopters.[14]

There was good reason to be wary of river entry into Cambodia. Allied forces had begun operations in the border area of Cambodia in early May, in response to North Vietnamese Army/Viet Cong troops pushing Cambodian forces back all along the border. After capturing Neak Luong, the enemy had continued to mount pressure on border and coastal towns in an apparent attempt to isolate Cambodia. During the first week in May, Communist China had severed relations with the government of Cambodia and recognized the exiled government under Sihanouk.[15]

This action followed a coup against the former Cambodian leader. Prince Norodom Sihanouk was on a trip to Moscow and Beijing in March 1970 when General Lon Nol launched a successful coup d'état. Abandoning Sihanouk's policy of neutrality in the war, Nol established close ties with the United States and South Vietnam, permitting their forces to operate in Cambodian territory. Meanwhile, Sihanouk took up residency in Beijing as the titular head of a government-in-exile.[16]

ENTRY INTO CAMBODIA

Opposition to the task force was very light at Neak Luong. The ferry, defended by a single Viet Cong company, was captured after a short fight. Larger forces previously present there, had withdrawn before the assault. Some 2,000 refugees waiting at the ferry landing were evacuated south of the border. On 11 May, the refugee lift unit, with the approval of the Cambodian government, proceeded up the Mekong River to Phnom Penh. This unit was composed of the following VNN vessels:

- Tank landing ships *Cam Ranh* HQ-500 (ex-*Marion County* LST-975) and *Vung Tau* HQ-503 (ex-*Coconino County* LST-603)
- Medium landing ships *Lam Giang* HQ-402 (ex-USS *LSM-226*) and *Tien Giang* HQ-405 (ex-USS *LSM-313*)
- Armed hospital ship *Hat Giang* HQ-400 (ex-USS *LSM-355*)
- Fifteen PCFs (Task Element 194.0.2.3)
- Ten LCM-8s[17]

The U.S. advisors debarked before the vessels left the Neak Luong Ferry en route to the Cambodian capital. The lift of refugees from Phnom Penh and Kampong Cham (a city on the Mekong in southeast Cambodia) was entirely a Vietnamese operation. By 18 May, 19,750 refugees had been evacuated with thousands more awaiting evacuation in the capital city. Although the American component withdrew from Cambodia by 29 June, the Vietnamese continued to guard the Mekong and evacuate to South Vietnam over 82,000 ethnic Vietnamese jeopardized by the conflict.[18]

YEOMAN'S WORK OF *HUNTERDON COUNTY*

The *Hunterdon County* (LST-838) entered Cambodian waters on 12 May, the first commissioned USN vessel to do so. Designed to stage, refuel, and rearm gunship helicopters, she was also capable of supplying, maintaining, and repairing river patrol craft, serving as a mobile communication center, and providing gunfire support. In Cambodia, she serviced as many as forty aircraft a day; rearmed automatic weapons; resupplied folding fin 2.75-inch air-to-ground rockets; and refueled the helicopters. These "birds" included Navy "Seawolves," Army "Cobras," and helicopters of the Vietnamese Air Force. *Hunterdon County* also supplied fuel and food to allied river craft and patrol boats. She left Cambodian waters on 6 June for the Philippines, for thirty days of repair and replenishment.[19]

Hampshire County (LST-819) made three trips into Cambodia. On one occasion, she ventured to within fifteen miles of Phnom Penh while transferring ammunition to *Hunterdon County*.[20]

UNITED STATES SUPPORT FOR CAMBODIA

Following the Cambodian incursion and the withdrawal of U.S. ground forces from Cambodia in June, President Nixon committed the United States to a policy of shoring up the regime of Lon Nol with funds and equipment. On 23 July, Nixon issued Presidential Determination 71-2, which reallocated approximately $40 million of Military Assistance Program funds from other countries to Cambodia.[21]

TRANSFER OF OPERATIONS TO THE VIETNAMESE

The generally good performance of the Vietnamese Navy during the Cambodia incursion resulted in the transfer of additional operational responsibilities to the Vietnamese. The barrier along the Cambodian border had been turned over to the Vietnamese Navy in March 1970, which renamed the operation Tran Hung Dao I. In May, Giant Slingshot and Sea Tiger had become Tran Hung Dao II and Tran Hung Dao VII. In July, the Vietnamese Navy assumed sole responsibility for the Ready Deck operation, which was designated Tran Hung Dao V. That same month, the U.S. Navy ceased combat activity on the Cua Viet and Hue rivers, and then transferred the last combatant vessels of Task Force Clearwater to the Vietnamese.[22]

A final turnover of river craft at the end of 1970 would enable the Vietnamese Navy to take charge of the Search Turn, Barrier Reef, and Breezy Cove efforts in the Mekong Delta. Except for continued support by HAL-3 and VAL-4 aircraft and SEAL detachments, the U.S. Navy's role in the SEALORDS campaign ended in April 1971.[23]

VNN Operations as of 30 June 1970

USN	VNN	USN	VNN
None	Tran Hung Dao I	Sea Tiger	Tran Hung Dao VII
Giant Slingshot	Tran Hung Dao II	None	Tran Hung Dao VIII
Sea Float	Tran Hung Dao III	Barrier Reef	Tran Hung Dao IX
Solid Anchor	Tran Hung Dao IV	Breezy Cove	Tran Hung Dao X
Ready Deck	Tran Hung Dao V	None	Tran Hung Dao XI[24]
Search Turn	Tran Hung Dao VI		

TOO MUCH, TOO SOON

> *In the turbulent months since I relieved Admiral Zumwalt on 15 May 1970, the Navy in Vietnam had undergone an almost complete transition from an operating force to an advisory organization... Despite the inevitable problems which had accompanied the transition, I have been deeply gratified at the performance of U.S. Navymen in Vietnam. In the final tally, progress has meaning only in terms of how well we have assisted the Vietnamese Navy toward the ability to continue, on their own, the fight against the enemy. In these terms, I believe we can view the past with quiet pride.*

—Vice Adm. Jerome H. King Jr., USN, upon his relief on 5 April 1971 by Rear Adm. Robert S. Salzer, USN, as commander, U.S. Naval Forces Vietnam and chief, Naval Advisory Group, MACV.[25]

> *Before the ACTOV [Accelerated Turnover to the Vietnamese] program our navy numbered about 10,000. In two years it increased to 40,000. We increased the navy four times in two years... We didn't have enough time to train the people.*

—Capt. Hoang Co Minh, VNN deputy Chief of Staff.[26]

The Vietnamese Navy grew from 18,000 men in autumn 1968 to 32,000 men at the end of 1970. This dramatic change reflected the rapid but measured withdrawal from South Vietnam of U.S. naval forces. Naval Force Vietnam strength dropped from a peak of 38,083 personnel in September 1968 to 16,757 at the end of 1970.[27]

18

Swimmer-Sapper Attack on USS *Meeker County*

In 1965 Landing Ship Squadron Three was as it had been for years. It was based in San Diego and divided into two divisions. The first division had four big LSTs- the 1156 class. The second division had four of the smaller 542-class LSTs and a separate division commander. But that all changed when the Navy decided to reactivate the last of the LSTs that they had in mothballs. There were 17 of them and they were assigned to Squadron Three. For a short time, then, the squadron had 25 ships. But they took the first 8 away and of the 17 they converted 4 to be Riverine Craft Support ships. About the same time, they changed the Squadron's home port to Guam, Marianas Islands. Later, the Squadron picked up a fourteenth ship [San Joaquin County] that had been moored to the pier at Iwakuni, Japan, for years on a special mission.

—Capt. Peter H. Orvis, USN (Retired), former commander,
Landing Ship Squadron Three, describing the formation
of the squadron for duty in the Vietnam War.[1]

Blanco County *was awarded a Meritorious Unit Commendation for achieving the highest average cargoes for an LST: 1,338 tons per load, on many trips through the Mekong Delta and (with the added thrust of six landing craft mechanized pulling abreast) over the sand bar into the Cua Viet River adjacent to the misnamed Demilitarized Zone bordering on North Vietnam. River operations were conducted under constant aerial surveillance and nocturnal illumination by falling flares. Landings were under cover of artillery barrage and in perimeters secured by aerial strafing. Two sister ships,* Clarke County *(LST 601) at Cua Viet and* Mahnomen County *(LST 912) near Chu Lai, were lost around this time in similar operations and the 10,000-ton aircraft ferry* USNS Card *(T-AKV-49) was sunk by enemy action in the Saigon River. My ship had no fatalities, but the operations could be deadly. On two days during my time, three heavy losses occurred: November 1, 1968 when 26 were killed on the* Westchester County *(LST 1167) in the Mekong Delta, and February 27, 1969 when 13 were killed on* Utility Landing Craft 1500 *at Danang. Except for the sinking of the civilian-manned* Card, *I don't think any of these events made the news.*

—Lawrence P. Blumette, Supply and Disbursing Department Head aboard the USS *Blanco County* (LST-344) from March 1968 to October 1969. *Mahnomen County* ran aground at Chu Lai during a typhoon on 30 December 1966, and was unsalvageable. *Clarke County* suffered damage to her port side, as a result of broaching at Duc Pho in November 1967, and was later returned to service.[2]

Photo 18-1

Tank landing ship USS *Meeker County* (LST-980) at anchor, circa 1950s. Naval History and Heritage Command photograph #NH 84878

On 27 June 1970, USS *Meeker County* (LST-980) was berthed at DeLong Pier, the only alongside facility for shipping at Vung Tau. The tank landing ship was a unit of Landing Ship Squadron Three, operating from Danang. The squadron was smaller than it had been earlier in the war, as a result of the loss of one ship to typhoon-induced damage, and downsizing associated with "Vietnamization."[3]

ACTIVITIES OF LANDING SHIP SQUADRON THREE

From July 1969 to 1 December 1970, when Landing Ship Squadron Three was decommissioned, its units were assigned to Naval Support Activities Saigon and Danang for combat-resupply missions on the rivers of South Vietnam. LandShipRon 3 had begun to experience the beginning stages of inactivation a year earlier when, in July 1969, the *Coconino County* was turned over to the South Vietnamese Navy, and the *San Joaquin County* changed operational control to commander, U.S. First Fleet, for eventual decommissioning.[4]

The First Fleet had its origin in World War II as Admiral Raymond Spruance's Central Pacific Force. His command was re-designated the Fifth Fleet on 26 April 1944. Following the war, it became the First

Task Fleet on 1 January 1947, and was later renamed the First Fleet on 11 February 1950. First Fleet would be disestablished near the end of the Vietnam War. Combined with ASW (Anti-submarine Warfare) Forces Pacific, it became the Third Fleet on 1 February 1973.[5]

During the summer of 1969, eight of the squadron's LSTs—*Clarke County*, *Hampshire County*, *Holmes County*, *Iredell County*, *Outagamie County*, *Park County*, *Pitkin County*, and *Snohomish County*—participated in operations in Vietnam. In October, *Clarke County* and *Iredell County* were transferred to the operational control of commander, Service Force, Pacific Fleet; and *Litchfield County* and *Sedgwick County* were placed "out-of-commission, in reserve" at Guam. This left the squadron with eight ships. Squadron composition as of 1 July 1970 follows. A ninth ship, *Page County*, joined on 1 August 1970.

Landing Ship Squadron Three (1 July 1970)

Ship	Commanding Officer
Hampshire County (LST-819)	Lt. David P. Richardson, USN
Holmes County (LST-836)	Lt. D. Q. Pearson, USN
Meeker County (LST-980)	Lt. Comdr. James C. Van Slyke Jr., USN
Outagamie County (LST-1073)	Lt. Comdr. Steven L. Turner Jr., USN
Park County (LST-1077)	Lt. Comdr. Glynn Q. Lane Jr., USN
Pitkin County (LST-1082)	Lt. Joseph E. Callahan, USN
Snohomish County (LST-1126)	Lt. Comdr. John P. Kelly, USN
Sutter County (LST-1150)	Lt. Robert H. Riley, USN
Page County (LST-1076) (1 Aug 1970)	Lt. Comdr. John P. Kelly, USN[6]

In July 1970—subsequent to the incident described in this chapter—*Snohomish County* was decommissioned at Guam. Shortly after, the squadron gained *Page County* on 1 August, manned by *Shohomish County*'s crew, which had relieved *Page County*'s crew. LandShipRon 3 lost four ships in September; another two—*Hampshire County* and *Meeker County*—were lost when they completed inactivation, and two more, *Sutter County* and *Outagamie County*, upon "chopping" (transferring) to the First Fleet for eventual inactivation.[7]

SWIMMER-SAPPER ATTACK ON *MEEKER COUNTY*

At approximately 0220 on 28 June 1970, an armed sentry aboard the *Meeker County* noticed a nylon line tied to a pier fender under the ship's starboard bow, leading down into the water. (The LST was starboard side to the pier, with the sentry posted on the main deck at the bow.) Two minutes later, an enemy swimmer surfaced near the fender, then immediately submerged following sentry-directed gunfire.[8]

Within a short time, an unarmed sentry on the fantail sighted a swimmer on the surface, fifty feet off the *Meeker County*'s port side, swimming on his back away from the ship. The sentry alerted others and located some grenades. By then, the swimmer was some 100 feet away and beyond reach of the grenades, and was soon lost from sight. The ship went to General Quarters and the nylon rope was raised to pier level, hauled tight and secured. (It's not obvious why, after sightings of swimmers, someone, presumably untrained, handled a line likely to have a mine affixed to the other end.)[9]

CLEARANCE DIVING TEAM MEMBERS ARRIVE

Photo 18-2

Clearance Diving Team Three (Seventh Contingent) in 1970. Front row, L-R: Chief Petty Officer John F. C. Dollar; Lt. Ross S. Blue, with Fred the monkey; and Petty Officer John Kershler. Back row: Able Seaman Gerald Kingston; Leading Seaman John A. Aldenhoven; and Leading Seaman Russell L. Steer. The inset photo is of Able Seaman Bogdan K. Wojcik, who was killed in a vehicle accident on 22 June 1970. Comdr. Edward W. (Jake) Linton, RAN (Retired) collection

At 0250, the duty officer aboard *Meeker County* requested EOD support from Clearance Diving Team Three, located at the Harbor Entrance Control Post (HECP). The officer in charge, Lt. Ross Blue, and two of his team—Petty Officer John Kershler and Able Seaman Gerald (Jock)

Kingston—arrived at the ship twenty minutes later. While Blue was being briefed by Lt. Comdr. James Van Slyke Jr., USN (*Meeker County*'s commanding officer), Kershler and Kingston inspected the nylon line. Seeing it (new and bright white) leading under the ship, Kershler realised the potential danger it suggested and decided to dive immediately.[10]

He made his way along the rope for about thirty feet and found a black plastic package the size of a large brief case. Fishing floats were secured to its side, making it neutrally buoyant and easy to maneuver in the water. The charge was positioned about three feet under the engine room, slung between the nylon line leading forward and another line leading aft and tied to the port rudderpost. Kershler estimated the charge was about 45 pounds of explosive.[11]

On surfacing, Kershler advised Blue on what he had found and the urgency of the situation in that the charge could explode at any time. Blue ordered a nearby U.S. Army military police riverine patrol boat to take hold of the line affixed to the pier, while Kershler dived back down to the charge and cut the aft support line. At about 0340, the boat hauled out to the ship's port side, drawing the charge under and clear of *Meeker County*. Clearing the threat within thirty minutes of arriving on scene was testimony to the professionalism of the team members.[12]

Blue took over control of the boat, shortened the tow to forty feet to ensure the charge would not strike the bottom, and ordered a search of the ship's waterline in his absence. He then proceeded about a half mile to seaward and secured the charge to an empty barge clear of the main shipping channel. The barge was marked with an additional buoy, and the Army boat ordered to keep the area clear. The plan was to wait for high water at 0950, move the charge to a mud bank and wait a further five hours before examining the ordnance closely.[13]

Meanwhile, back at *Meeker County*, Kingston had found a snorkel, and Kershler completed his waterline search of the ship around 0415, while a search of the pier and minor vessels alongside was begun. At 0430, Kershler and Kingston were using a boat to search the waterline of *Caney* and *Sebee*. (Berthed at mooring dolphins south of the pier, the U.S. Army generation ships provided electrical power to Vung Tau and surrounds.) Kershler was informed by a crewman that he had seen two men on the nearby mud flats. Illumination of it proved fruitless. Kershler and Kingston completed their searches at 0530, and returned to the HECP to collect more diving equipment.[14]

On their return, they were offered breakfast which was interrupted at 0715 by a report from the military police boat that the charge had detonated of its own accord, producing a 15-meter-high-plume of water. No damage resulted. Kershler and Kingston began a search at 0745 of the other ships in the vicinity, as well as one on the sea bed near *Meeker County* for possible attackers' bodies. All searches were completed by 1010 with nothing found, and the team returned to their base.[15]

But for the alertness of a sentry—aided by a bright white nylon line, easy to see at night—the attack would have succeeded. The sappers were believed dropped from a sampan near the pier, and swam underwater using their snorkels, toward the target. While the charge was neutrally buoyant, the two lines would have been heavy and made the approach more difficult. Notwithstanding, the two arrived at *Meeker County* undetected and suspended the charge under her. This would have been tough without diving equipment, and require close co-operation as one secured his line underwater aft, while the other swam up the ship's side and under the forward section before hauling the line taut. Their escape inland through the mangrove swamp, after first crossing the mud flats, is testimony to their stamina, water skills, and drive.[16]

Two weeks later, Lieutenant Blue received a letter from Vice Adm. Jerome H. King Jr., commander Naval Forces Vietnam, commending the members of Clearance Diving Team Three for their efforts. It read:

> I desire to express my sincere appreciation for the exceptionally alert and professional response which you and your men, Petty Officer (Clearance Disposal) J. KERSHLER and Able-Bodied Seaman (Clearance Disposal) G. KINGSTON, displayed in the early morning hours of 28 June 1970 in removing an enemy water mine from USS *MEEKER COUNTY*, at Vung Tau, Republic of Vietnam. Although sufficient time had elapsed for the mine to detonate, you and your men unhesitatingly dived and successfully removed the mine with full knowledge of the risks involved.
>
> The actions of the Royal Australian Navy Clearance Diving Team THREE in this emergency situation bear testimony to outstanding professionalism and courage of the highest order. Well done![17]

A copy of the letter may be found in Appendix F. The fact that Kershler and Kingston should have been identified as Petty Officer (Clearance Diver) and Able Seaman (Clearance Diver) attests that no Australian input spurred the issuance of it.

19

Final U.S. Involvement in Vietnam – 1971 to 1973

Following the several-years-long turnover of its riverine, coastal and logistics craft to the Vietnamese Navy, the U.S. Navy continued a phased transfer of the associated shore maintenance, training, and logistics commands. This effort was completed on 29 March 1973 with the departure of all remaining U.S. Navy and Marines forces, except embassy personnel, from Vietnam. In the interim, the war continued in Southeast Asia.[1]

U.S. MINING OF HAIPHONG HARBOR

On 8 May 1972, three Marine A-6 and six Navy A-7 attack aircraft from the carrier *Coral Sea* (CVA-43) mined the river approaches to Haiphong Harbor through which passed most of North Vietnam's imported war material and all of its fuel. The decision to mine was motivated by the need to deny North Vietnamese forces invading South Vietnam the logistical means to sustain their offensive against the cities of Quang Tri, Pleiku, An Loc, Hue, and Danang, which had been attacked or threatened.[2]

In succeeding days and months, carrier aircraft laid thousands more mines in the principal ports of Haiphong, and "reseeded" the approaches to complete the operation. For the remainder of 1972, twenty-seven Sino-Soviet merchant ships remained trapped in Haiphong and none of the nations would risk steaming their ships through the American minefield to enter port. The offensive mining campaign, in conjunction with air attacks on North Vietnam's land supply line, curtailed the supply of munitions to Communist forces mounting the "Easter Offensive" in South Vietnam. The U.S. LINEBACKER II or "Christmas bombing" campaign of Hanoi and North Vietnam, begun 18 December 1972, finally persuaded Hanoi to seriously negotiate an end to the prolonged conflict.[3]

Peace talks, begun in Paris that past October, between Henry A. Kissinger and Le Duc Tho, acting on behalf of the United States and the Democratic Republic of Vietnam, respectively, had stalled due to charges and countercharges, as alluded to by the entertainer Bob Hope during his annual Vietnam Christmas tour in 1972. He greeted Marines at Danang with, "Wonderful to be working for your leftovers!" There were, at this point in the drawdown of American military forces, only a relatively small number of Navy and Marine Corps personnel remaining in Vietnam. Hope quickly added: "You guys are lucky because you get to go home, not like our representatives at the Paris Peace Talks.[4]

On 15 January 1973, President Nixon announced the end of offensive operations against North Vietnam. The Paris Peace Accords ending the conflict were signed twelve days later, followed by the phased withdrawal of the remaining American troops over the next two months. Eight months earlier, the president's revelation of the mining of North Vietnamese ports by American aircraft on 11 May 1972 had been followed by an article in the *Washington Evening Star* that stated, "Nixon says mines will go when POWs are free."[5]

Thereafter, minesweepers, low among Navy priorities after their long service as MARKET TIME patrol ships, rapidly became a topic of vital service. The coastal minesweepers previously based at Sasebo (which had also taken part in MARKET TIME operations) had returned to the United States for transition to the Naval Reserve Force, while the number of larger ocean minesweepers (MSOs) deploying from Long Beach, California, to the Western Pacific had declined from twenty in 1970 to five in 1972. All but the five active MSOs assigned to Mine Flotilla One at Guam were slated for transfer to the Naval Reserve, inactivation, or scrapping.[6]

The Navy believed, before it laid the mines, that it might be ultimately responsible for clearing them as a provision of future peace negotiations, and this presumption proved valid. Under the terms of the Paris Peace Accords, the United States became responsible for neutralizing the mines. The follow-on activity of minesweeping helicopters and ocean minesweepers to render the approaches and harbors of North Vietnam safe was code named Operation END SWEEP. Lasting from 6 February to 18 July 1973, the effort would be the U.S. Navy's largest mine countermeasures operation since October 1950, when 3,000 North Korean mines, spread over a 400-square mile field, had prevented an armada of allied ships from landing troops at Wonsan for almost a week.[7]

OPERATION END SWEEP

Coincident with the signing of the Paris Peace Accords, the ocean minesweepers *Engage* (MSO-433), *Force* (MSO-445), *Fortify* (MSO-446) and *Impervious* (MSO-449) left Subic for the Tonkin Gulf on 27 January. END SWEEP, under Rear Adm. Brian McCauley, USN, commenced on 6 February with the four MSOs sweeping the areas in which the amphibious ships (LPHs and LPDs) carrying minesweeping helicopters were to anchor—protected by the guided-missile destroyer *Worden* (DLG-18) and destroyer *Epperson* (DD-719). During the initial sweeping, when the amphibious ships were still in Subic, the *Worden* served as flagship for McCauley and as an alternate site for meeting the North Vietnamese. The admiral was commander, Mine Warfare Force, and commander Task Force Seventy-Eight.[8]

Photo 19-1

Ocean minesweeper USS *Force* (MSO-445) off Oahu, Hawaii, 18 October 1971. Naval History and Heritage Command photograph #NH 84418

The amphibious ships *New Orleans*, *Ogden*, and *Dubuque* arrived in Haiphong on 23 February, carrying Navy Helicopter Squadron HM-12 augmented by three Marine CH-53s and other Marine support helos. Airborne minesweeping began on the afternoon of 27 February with two missions flown in the Haiphong main shipping channel. The CH-53 helicopters had been modified at Subic to tow the Magnetic Orange Pipe minesweeping device employed against magnetic mines. That night, because of difficulties over the second POW exchange, Task Force 78 was withdrawn. Within twelve hours the issues were resolved, and the task force was ordered back into North Vietnamese waters.[9]

By this time, two Marine Airborne Mine Countermeasures units had joined *Inchon* and *Cleveland* and sweeping in the Haiphong area resumed on 6 March. Because of difficulty with the North Vietnamese, who wanted all efforts devoted to sweeping the Haiphong main channel, sweeping in the two other northern international ports of Hon Gai and Cam Pha was not started until two weeks later. From then until completion, helicopters swept daily in Haiphong, Hon Gai, and Cam Pha. (Summary information about the five amphibious ships follow, including eligibility periods for Vietnam Service Medals.) The ocean minesweepers continued to sweep the deep-water approaches to these three ports.[10]

Task Force 78 Amphibious Assault and Transport Dock Ships

Ships	Dates	Commanding Officer
New Orleans (LPH-11)	22 Feb-28 Mar 73	Capt. Robert Wilhelm Carius, USN
Ogden (LPD-5)	22 Feb-28 Mar 73	Capt. Ralph Eugene Neiger, USN
Dubuque (LPD-8)	23-28 Feb 73	Capt. Cecil Joe Kempf, USN
Inchon (LPH-12)	27 Feb-28 Mar 73	Capt. John Keith Thomas, USN
Cleveland (LPD-7)	27 Feb-28 Mar 73	Capt. Robert E. Kirksey Jr., USN

Photo 19-2

A CH-53 helicopter tows a magnetic orange pipe minesweeping device during sweep operations in Haiphong Harbor, 20 June 1973.
National Archives photograph #USN 711574

Minesweeping helicopters had many limitations not shared by the ocean minesweepers. They could not sweep in inclement weather or at night, nor sweep to as great water depths as the ships. However, their crews were much safer than those of MSOs during the performance of minesweeping duties. A mine detonated by a device pulled by a low-flying helicopter would not blast the aircraft out of the sky, while the explosion of a magnetic mine close aboard might well damage or sink a minesweeping ship. For this reason, the Navy used helicopters—towing a Mk-105 magnetic sled, the Mk-104, and the AMK-2G acoustic devices, the MOP (magnetic orange pipe) or the triple MOP (three in tandem)—to conduct precursory sweeps before sending in the MSOs. Helicopters also swept shallow waters that precluded ship operations.[11]

Photo 19-3

The special minesweeper USS *Washtenaw County* (MSS-2, formerly *LST-1166*) carrying out operations in Haiphong Harbor during Operation End Sweep, 20 February 1973. Naval History and Heritage Command photograph #USN 711573

The surface minesweeping force grew to ten ocean minesweepers, used principally in the deep-water approaches and as helicopter control ships. In addition, a surface support force was made up of two destroyers, two fleet tugs (later reduced to one), a submarine rescue ship, a tank landing ship (LST) for MSO support, and a specially configured LST—the USS *Washtenaw County*. *Washtenaw County* transited the Haiphong channel after sweeping had been completed in order to demonstrate confidence in the thoroughness of the sweep. The "guinea pig" performed pressure mine and check sweeping, and made several passages through the main Haiphong Channel to demonstrate the effectiveness of mine clearance efforts, with the last runs on 20 June 1973.[12]

On 17 April 1973, because of difficulties in Laos and Cambodia, the force was once again withdrawn. The period of inactivity lasted until 13 June when the Paris Joint Communique was signed, implementing the agreement and protocols of 27 January on ending the war and restoring peace in Vietnam. Having completed sweeping in the Haiphong area, the task force moved south to the Hon Lai coastal area. Final sweeping in this area was performed on 5 July and, after the North Vietnamese refused to allow sweeping of the remainder of the fields, the task force left Vietnamese waters on 18 July 1973.[13]

Photo 19-4

Two American prisoners of war released by Hanoi, arriving at Clark Air Force Base, Philippines, in February 1973. They are Col. Robinson Risner, USAF (waving), and Capt. James Stockdale, USN.
National Archives and Records Administration photograph #USN 1155662

20

Operation FREQUENT WIND

This action closes a chapter in the American experience. I ask all Americans to close ranks, to avoid recrimination about the past, to look ahead to the many goals we share, and to work together on the great tasks that remain to be accomplished.

—Statement by American President Gerald Ford on 29 April 1975 as Operation Frequent Wind commenced, the evacuation by airlift of American and "at risk" South Vietnamese personnel from Saigon, ending over twenty years of U.S. involvement in Vietnam.[1]

Photo 20-1

South Vietnamese refugees arrive by helicopter aboard a U.S. Navy aircraft carrier or amphibious ship as part of Operation Frequent Wind, the final evacuation of Saigon, South Vietnam, 29-30 April 1975.
Official U.S. Marine Corps photograph

In the final year of the Vietnam War, a series of offensives by the North Vietnamese led to the fall of Saigon, the South Vietnamese capital, on 30 April 1975. North Vietnamese troops entered the deserted streets of Saigon just hours after the last Americans were evacuated, airlifted by Marine helicopters to U.S. Navy ships waiting off the coast. As those ships were steaming away from Vietnam, Comdr. Paul Jacobs, USN, the commanding officer of the destroyer escort USS *Kirk* (DE-1087), received a mysterious order to head back to Vietnam. This directive came from Rear Adm. Donald B. Whitmire, USN, commander of the evacuation mission, Operation FREQUENT WIND.[2]

In preceding days, with the fall of Saigon imminent, the U.S. Navy had formed Task Force 76 off the coast of South Vietnam, a massive assembly of aircraft and ships that became the largest helicopter evacuation in history. FREQUENT WIND was the final phase in the evacuation of thousands of Vietnamese who had ardently supported U.S. efforts to stop the Communist takeover of South Vietnam and a dwindling number of American civilians still remaining in Vietnam.

Task Force 76: USS *Blue Ridge* (LCC-19) (command ship)
Movement Transport Groups

TG 76.4 (Alfa)	TG 76.5 (Bravo)	TG 76.9 (Charlie)
USS *Okinawa* (LPH-3)	USS *Dubuque* (LPD-8)	USS *Anchorage* (LSD-36)
USS *Vancouver* (LPD-2)	USS *Durham* (LKA-114)	USS *Denver* (LPD-9)
USS *Thomaston* (LSD-28)	USS *Frederick* (LST-1184)	USS *Duluth* (LPD-6)
USS *Peoria* (LST-1183)		USS *Mobile* (LKA-115)[3]

The task force would be joined by the carriers *Hancock* and *Midway* (carrying Marine and Air Force CH-53 and HH-53 helicopters); the Seventh Fleet flagship *Oklahoma City*, and other surface combatants for naval gunfire, escort, and area defense; additional amphibious ships; and the cargo ship USNS *Sgt. Andrew Miller*.

Seventh Fleet flagship: USS *Oklahoma City* (CLG-5)

Aircraft Carriers	Surface Combatants	Surface Combatants
USS *Hancock* (CV-19)	USS *Bausell* (DD-845)	USS *Kirk* (FF-1087)
USS *Midway* (CV-41)	USS *Cochrane* (DDG-21)	USS *Richard B. Anderson* (DD-786)
Cargo Ship	USS *Cook* (FF-1083)	USS *Rowan* (DD-782)
USNS *Sgt. Andrew Miller* (T-AK-242)	USS *Gurke* (DD-783)	USS *Worden* (DLG-18)
Amphibious Ships		
USS *Barbour County* (LST-1195)		
USS *Mount Vernon* (LSD-39)		
USS *Tuscaloosa* (LST-1187)[4]		

Photo 20-2

U.S. Navy ships of Task Force 76 staged off Vung Tau, Vietnam in the South China Sea for the start of Operation Frequent Wind, 29 April 1975. Official U.S. Marine Corps photograph A7718475

FREQUENT WIND was carried out 29-30 April, during which 71 American military helicopters extracted more than 7,800 evacuees from the Defense Attaché Office and U.S. Embassy. Such was the speed of the operation and the number of people involved that the ships became overwhelmed with evacuees and the helicopters that brought them. Out of necessity, orders were given to jettison surplus helicopters over the sides of the ships to make room for more to land.[5]

Photo 20-3

South Vietnamese Air Force UH-1 Huey helicopters landing aboard the aircraft carrier USS *Midway* (CV-41) during Operation FREQUENT WIND.
USS *Midway* 1975-76 cruise book

Photo 20-4

A South Vietnamese helicopter is pushed over the side of the amphibious assault ship USS *Okinawa* (LPH-3) during Operation Frequent Wind, April 1975.
Official U.S. Marine Corps photograph

The first of the helicopters that participated in the evacuation had carried U.S. Marines to form defensive perimeters at a landing zone at Tan Son Nhut Air Base near Saigon, and at the U.S. Embassy. When the last helicopter departed Vietnam, it radioed, "Swift 22 is airborne with eleven passengers. Ground-security force is aboard."[6]

Vietnamese refugees were taken to Clark Air Base and the naval base at Subic Bay in the Philippines, Andersen AFB in Guam, and Wake Island. In Operation NEW ARRIVALS, Military Airlift Command transports and commercial airliners transported tens of thousands of refugees from the Pacific island camps to reception centers in the continental United States. Refugees landed at one of several military bases, including Fort Chaffee, Arkansas; Camp Pendleton, California; and Eglin AFB, Florida. To reduce the refugee population on Guam, which was becoming increasingly vulnerable as the typhoon season approached, the Department of Defense opened a fourth reception center at Fort Indiantown Gap, Pennsylvania.[7]

ESCAPE OF THE SOUTH VIETNAMESE NAVY

> *We're going to have to send you back to rescue the Vietnamese navy. We forgot 'em. And if we don't get them or any part of them, they're all probably going to be killed.*
>
> —Directive to Comdr. Paul H. Jacobs, commanding officer of the destroyer escort USS *Kirk* (DE-1087) from Rear Adm. Donald B. Whitmire, commander of Operation FREQUENT WIND, embarked aboard the command ship *Blue Ridge* (LCC-19).[8]

> *The average age of my crew was 23. They were young and new to the Navy and were trained for war, but the situation quickly turned into a humanitarian effort. We had to take care of a large amount of people by providing them food, shelter, and medical care.*
>
> —Capt. Paul Jacobs, USN (Retired) describing unique challenges his crew faced during evacuation of the South Vietnamese Navy to Subic Bay, Philippine Islands, in May 1975.[9]

During FREQUENT WIND, as Seventh Fleet ships monitored on radar screens U.S. helicopters loaded with evacuees flying seaward to them, hordes of unknown air contacts began appearing. South Vietnamese Army and Air Force Hueys, packed with refugees, were following the American aircraft, in an effort to escape Vietnam as well. Lt. Comdr. Raymond W. Addicott, the USS *Cook*'s (DE-1083) executive officer, later recalled that the image on the radar scope "looked like a swarm of bees," explaining, "I went topside on the bridge and the sky was just full of helicopters. It was an amazing sight." In addition to the

Marine and Air Force helicopters evacuating people from Saigon, there were also hundreds of Vietnam Air Force (VNAF) Bell UH-1 Iroquois helicopters (better-known as "Hueys") flown by south Vietnamese pilots who had fled with their friends, neighbors, and relatives in tow.[10]

The carriers *Midway* and *Hancock* along with the *Blue Ridge* attracted the initial wave, but eventually, smaller ships such as the *Cook* and sister ship *Kirk* had to take on refugees. The 415-foot USS *Kirk* (DE-1087) quickly began to land aircraft on her relatively small flight deck. A *Knox*-class destroyer escort, she had been commissioned at Long Beach, California, on 9 September 1972 (too late for war duty) and assigned to Destroyer Squadron 23 in San Diego.[11]

Photo 20-5

Destroyer escort USS *Kirk* (DE-1087) off Oahu, Hawaii, on 9 February 1973. Naval History and Heritage Command photograph #NH 78236-KN

Kirk had sailed from San Diego in early March 1975, beginning her second Western Pacific deployment since commissioning. During this cruise, she and her crew of 250 sailors had participated in the evacuation of Phnom Penh, Cambodia, in early April. Cambodia fell before Vietnam, and Operation EAGLE PULL, of which *Kirk* had been a part, proved to be a quick, orderly extraction of fewer than 300 Americans. The *Kirk* then proceeded south with *Cook* and the carrier *Midway* and entered Singapore on 16 April for a welcomed visit to that exotic port.

Soon, liberty was summarily cancelled, the crews abruptly recalled, and the three ships ordered north to join the evacuation force off the coast of Vietnam.[12]

First one and then two helicopters were on the *Kirk*'s deck. With several more approaching, Comdr. Paul H. Jacobs, her commanding officer, gave the order to start pushing aircraft over the side once the men, women, and children were safely aboard to make room for more. Then the unthinkable happened, a twin-rotor CH-47 Chinook, the largest helicopter in the South Vietnamese inventory, appeared. As the flight deck crew tried to wave off the massive helicopter, its pilot, with utmost prowess, hovered over the fantail while the refugees jumped or were dropped into the waiting arms of sailors. After everyone was safely aboard, the pilot moved a short distance off *Kirk*'s starboard quarter. Hovering within inches of the sea, he slowly rolled the Chinook over on its right side, and escaped the crash unharmed by diving out the left door in mid-roll. Both main rotors disintegrated on impact, and shattered shards of the blades flew across *Kirk*, splashing into the sea well off her port side. The captain's gig and motor whaleboat were standing by and rescued the pilot in short order. By day's end, the DE had landed thirteen aircraft safely without any mishaps.[13]

The refugees were transferred to the Military Sealift Command freighter SS *Green Port* the following morning. The destroyer escort was without refugees, but that wouldn't last long. That night, Jacobs received orders from Rear Admiral Whitmire, sending the *Kirk* by herself to an island off the Vietnamese mainland. Whitmire also informed Jacobs that he would be taking orders from a civilian. Late that afternoon, *Kirk* received orders to rendezvous with the *Blue Ridge*, for a boat transfer of "an important person." That person turned out to be Richard L. Armitage, emissary of the Department of Defense (and future Deputy Secretary of State under Colin Powell in the George W. Bush Administration).[14]

A former naval officer, Armitage had served in the Vietnam War as an advisor, and this experience and acquired fluency in Vietnamese made him useful to the foreign service community after the war. Leaving active duty as a lieutenant commander in 1973, he had joined the State Department. He had been working in Vietnam as of late, planning the extraction of as many South Vietnamese Navy ships as possible. *Kirk* was to deliver Armitage to the South Vietnamese Navy's flagship, RVNS *Tran Nhat Duat* (HQ-03), off Con Son Island, east of the southern tip of Vietnam, early the next morning.[15]

After arrival aboard *Kirk*, Armitage was escorted to the wardroom where he met with Jacobs and Capt. Donald P. Roane, USN, commander, Destroyer Squadron 23, who was embarked aboard the *Kirk*. Roane remarked, 'Young man, I'm not used to having strange civilians come aboard my ship in the middle of the night and give me orders.' Armitage (who'd just turned 30 that week) responded, 'I am equally unaccustomed, sir, to coming aboard strange ships in the middle of the night and giving you orders. But steam to Con Son.' So, the *Kirk* set a course for the largest island in the Con Dao archipelago, off southern Vietnam.[16]

Map 20-1

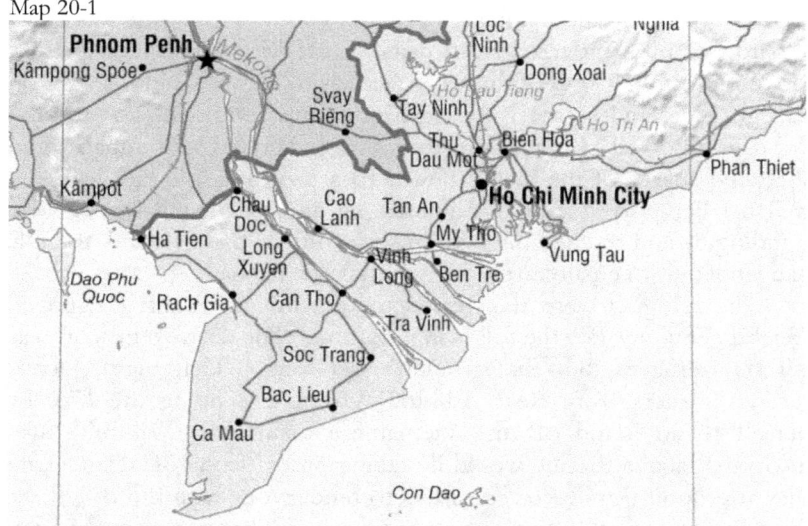

Con Dao Archipelago (Ho Chi Minh City was formerly known as Saigon.)

At dawn on 1 May, *Kirk* was greeted by the somber sight of the remnants of the Vietnamese Navy: ships and boats of all sizes and descriptions, either anchored, drifting, or slowly steaming in the vicinity of Con Son Island. Some were empty and had been abandoned, but thirty-two ships considered seaworthy for the 1,000-mile open-ocean transit to the Philippines were overloaded with refugees. Aboard the flotilla were more than thirty thousand Vietnamese men, women, and children, and the entire fleet was well within striking range of North Vietnamese MiGs that were suspected to be operating freely out of the captured Tan Son Nhut airfield. Armitage's task was to quickly move the vulnerable ships and precious human cargo east to the Philippines, with *Kirk* initially the lone U.S. ship, responsible for providing security and engineering support to the damaged and floundering ships, and feeding and providing medical care.[17]

Kirk's engineers repaired what they could on seaworthy vessels and transferred people from the ships that would be left behind. The flotilla of 32 navy ships and 2 fishing vessels sailed the next morning, under escort by the *Kirk*. The *Cook* rendezvoused *Kirk* and the Vietnamese fleet to form a five-mile-long convoy that would safely lead the ships to Subic Bay. They were joined by the amphibious ships *Barbour County*, *Denver*, *Mobile*, and *Tuscaloosa*; salvage ship *Deliver* (ARS-23); stores ship *Vega* (AF-59); fleet tugs *Abnaki* (ATF-96) and *Lipan* (ATF-85); and the ammunition ship *Flint* (AE-32). Proceeding only as fast as the slowest ship (about 5 knots), *Cook* and *Kirk* brought the flotilla safely into Subic Bay on 7 May 1975, saving an estimated 30,000 evacuees.[18]

Photo 20-6

Former South Vietnamese and Cambodian Navy ships at Subic Bay, Philippines, 31 May 1975. They are (l-r): Vietnamese ships: *HQ-471*, *Dong Da II* (07), *Chi Lang II* (08), *Chi Linh (11)*; Cambodian Ships: *P112*, *E312*.
National Archives photograph #K-109092

Earlier, the *Kirk*'s commanding officer had received some bad news as the flotilla approached the Philippines. President Ferdinand Marcos had been one of the first to recognize the Communist rulers now in control of a single Vietnam, and Jacobs was told the ships should go back. The Philippine government wasn't going to allow the flotilla in, because its ships now belonged to the North Vietnamese, and they didn't want to offend the new country. Armitage and Capt. Kiem Do, deputy chief of staff for the South Vietnamese Navy, quickly came up with a solution that Marcos would have to accept. Do explained:

> We will raise the American flag and lower the Vietnamese flag as a sign of transfer [of] the ship back to the United States, because during the war those ships are given to the Vietnamese government as a loan, if you want, from the United States, to fight the Communists. Now the war is over, we turn them back to the United States.[19]

There was a frantic search to find sufficient American flags, and two personnel from the *Kirk* were sent aboard each Vietnamese ship to take command after a formal flag ceremony. Rick Sautter, one of the *Kirk* officers who took command of a Vietnamese ship, recalled about the occasion, "That was the last vestige of South Vietnam. And when those flags came down and the American flags went up, that was it. Because a Navy ship is sovereign territory and so that was the last sovereign territory of the Republic of Vietnam." (A listing of these ships may be found in Appendix G.)[20]

UNIT AWARDS FOR THE EVACUATION OF SAIGON

The below listed surface combatant ships received the Armed Forces Expeditionary Medal (AE), Humanitarian Service Medal (HS), and Meritorious Unit Commendation (MUC) or Navy Unit Commendation (NUC) for Operation FREQUENT WIND. The asterisks denote awards for Operation EAGLE PULL—an earlier evacuation by air of Phnom Penh, Cambodia, on 12 April 1975.[21]

Amphibious Ships	AE Medal	HS Medal	MUC/NUC
Anchorage (LSD-36)	29-30 Apr 75	29-30 Apr 75	22-30 Apr 75
Barbour County (LST-1195)	29-30 Apr 75	20-30 Apr 75	22-30 Apr 75
Blue Ridge (LCC-19)	11-13 Apr 75* 29-30 Apr 75	12 Apr 75* 29-30 Apr 75	30 Mar-15 Apr 75*
Denver (LPD-9)	29-30 Apr 75	29-30 Apr 75	29-30 Apr 75
Dubuque (LPD-8)	11-13 Apr 75* 29-30 Apr 75	12 Apr 75* 29-30 Apr 75	30 Mar-15 Apr 75* 22-30 Apr 75
Duluth (LPD-6)	29-30 Apr 75	29-30 Apr 75	29-30 Apr 75
Durham (LKA-114)	11-13 Apr 75* 29-30 Apr 75	12 Apr 75* 29-30 Apr 75	30 Mar-15 Apr 75* 22-30 Apr 75
Frederick (LST-1184)	11-13 Apr 75* 29-30 Apr 75	12 Apr 75* 29-30 Apr 75	30 Mar-15 Apr 75* 22-30 Apr 75
Mobile (LKA-115)	29-30 Apr 75	29-30 Apr 75	29-30 Apr 75

Mount Vernon (LSD-39)	29-30 Apr 75	29-30 Apr 75	29-30 Apr 75
Peoria (LST-1183)	11-13 Apr 75* 29-30 Apr 75	12 Apr 75* 29-30 Apr 75	12 Apr 75* 29-30 Apr 75
Thomaston (LSD-28)	11-13 Apr 75* 29-30 Apr 75	12 Apr 75* 29-30 Apr 75	12 May 75* 29-30 Apr 75
Tuscaloosa (LST-1187)	29-30 Apr 75	29-30 Apr 75	
Vancouver (LPD-2)	11-13 Apr 75* 29-30 Apr 75	12 Apr 75* 29-30 Apr 75	12 May 75* 29-30 Apr 75
Aircraft Carrier			
Hancock (CV-19)	11-13 Apr 75* 29-30 Apr 75	12 Apr 75* 29-30 Apr 75	12 Apr 75* 29-30 Apr 75
Surface Combatants			
Bausell (DD-845)	29-30 Apr 75	29-30 Apr 75	22-30 Apr 75
Cochrane (DDG-21)	29-30 Apr 75	29-30 Apr 75	22-30 Apr 75
Cook (FF-1083)	11-13 Apr 75* 29-30 Apr 75	12 Apr 75* 20-30 Apr 75	12 Apr 75*
Gurke (DD-783)	29-30 Apr 75	29-30 Apr 75	22-30 Apr 75
Kirk (FF-1087)	11-13 Apr 75*	12 Apr 75*	12 Apr 75* 22 Apr-7 May 75
Oklahoma City (CLG-5)	29-30 Apr 75	29-30 Apr 75	22-30 Apr 75
Richard B. Anderson (DD-786)	29-30 Apr 75	29-30 Apr 75	22-30 Apr 75
Rowan (DD-782)	29-30 Apr 75	29-30 Apr 75	22-30 Apr 75

Photo 20-7

The city of Phnom Penh as seen from a CH-53 helicopter as it comes in to make a landing for the evacuation of personnel during Operation EAGLE PULL. Defense Department Marine Corps photograph A150857

Photo 20-8

Painting *Welcome to Sunny Saigon* by James Scott, circa 1967. With the fall of Saigon in April 1975, United States involvement in Vietnam came to an end.
Naval History and Heritage Command accession #88-160-EC

21

The *Mayaguez* Incident

On May 12, 1975 at approximately 1410 hours the vessel was challenged by Cambodian gunboat P128. At 1420 hours reduced to maneuvering speed and gunboat fires antiaircraft machine guns across starboard bow.... 1435 [hours] vessel boarded by 7 armed men carrying AK 47s, shoulder held rocket launchers, and grenade launchers.

—Entry made by Charles T. Miller, master of the SS *Mayaguez*, in the ship's log book, regarding her capture by Khmer Rouge forces.[1]

We were just coming off the evacuations of Phnom Penh and Saigon, so my battalion (1st Battalion 9th Marines) was not inserted into the battle on Koh Tang island. However, since the battalion that went in - 2nd Battalion 9th Marine Regiment was just getting formed up on Okinawa with new additions from the mainland, select elements from 1/9 were 'volunteered' to reinforce the companies. They went alphabetical and I was not selected. However, two from my company (Charlie) that were - one being a corpsman - were killed.

Bottom line, it was a real charlie foxtrot [former military personnel will be familiar with this 2-letter phonetic alphabet reference.] The 'green' troops sent in hadn't really trained together as a unit due to their recent arrival from the States, and Air Force helicopter pilots (from their US military base in Thailand) were bringing Marines into a hot LZ - with no experience in such operations. There was faulty intel regarding the 41 Merchant Mariners and where they were actually located. Even worse, political leaders back in DC were of the mindset that the US Gov't was going to 'draw a red line in the sand' and show the world that we (US) were not weak as a result of the fall of South Vietnam.

—Former Marine David Zebley, remarking on the ill-advised and hurried preparations, and loss of life (41 casualties), associated with the recovery of SS *Mayaguez* and her crew.[2]

On 12 May 1975, about a month after the fall of Phnom Penh in Cambodia to Communists, Khmer Rouge forces seized the American container-ship SS *Mayaguez* (en route from Hong Kong to Sattahip, Thailand) off the Cambodian coast. The ship's captain, Charles T. Miller, and his 39-man crew were forced to proceed to anchor off nearby Koh Tang Island (also known as Poulo Wai) in the Gulf of Thailand.³

Photo 21-1

Two Khmer Rouge gunboats alongside the container-ship SS *Mayaguez*, 15 May 1975. U.S. Air Force photograph (http://www.henninger.com/Mayaguez/stills.htm)

AIR FORCE RESCUE OPTION ILL-PLANNED

President Gerald Ford's National Security Council (NSC) was determined to end the crisis decisively, believing that the fall of South Vietnam less than two weeks earlier, and the forced withdrawal of the United States from Cambodia (EAGLE PULL) and South Vietnam (FREQUENT WIND), had severely damaged America's reputation. The NSC also wished to avoid another *Pueblo* incident, where the failure to promptly use military force to halt the capture of a U.S. intelligence ship by North Korea had led to an eleven-month hostage situation.⁴

A plan developed by Lt. Gen. John J. Burns, and his U.S. Seventh Air Force staff at Korat Royal Thai Air Force Base, to retake the *Mayaguez*, using an assault force of seventy-five volunteers from the Air Force 56th Security Police Squadron, never came to fruition. During the flight of five HH-53 Jolly Green Giant and seven CH-53 transport helicopters to U-Tapao Royal Thai Navy Airfield for staging, one of the CH-53s crashed due to mechanical failure, killing all twenty-three airmen aboard. The embarked assault force members and five-man crew were the first casualties of the *Mayaguez* rescue operation. Following this tragedy, the NSC cancelled the operation. It was judged that deck-loaded containers aboard the ship could not bear the weight of the helicopters setting down, and men rappelling from them would be exposed to gunfire.[5]

NAVY/MARINE CORPS PREPARATIONS

On 13 May, Vice Adm. George P. Steele, commander, Seventh Fleet, ordered the carrier *Coral Sea* (CV-43), en route to Australia, to the area. The guided missile destroyer *Henry B. Wilson* (DDG-7), destroyer escort *Harold E. Holt* (DE-1074), and stores ship *Vega* (AF-59) were similarly to proceed at high speed from the Philippine Sea toward *Mayaguez*'s last known location. These ships were expected to be on station on 15 May, but none carried troops. Commander, III Marine Amphibious Force assigned D Company 1/4 Marines in the Philippines as the unit that would retake *Mayaguez*. Second Battalion, 9th Marines (BLT 2/9) were to rescue the ship's crew, believed to be on the island of Koh Tang.[6]

Commanded by Lt. Col. Randall W. Austin, BLT 2/9 was involved in a training exercise on Okinawa when it received orders on the night of 13 May to return to camp and prepare for departure by air at dawn. That morning, 14 May, the Marines boarded Air Force C-141 Starlifters at Kadena Air Base to fly to Thailand.[7]

While preparations were being made, President Ford instructed Secretary of State Henry Kissinger to urge the People's Republic of China to persuade the Khmer Rouge to release *Mayaguez* and her crew. The use of an intermediary was necessary because the U.S. had no diplomatic contact with the Khmer Rouge regime in Cambodia. Early on the morning of 14 May, the Khmer Rouge loaded *Mayaguez*'s crew onto a fishing vessel, which, along with another fishing vessel left Koh Tang Island following two gunboats on a heading for Kampong Som.[8]

With a diplomatic solution appearing unlikely, the NSC decided to proceed with a simultaneous attack by Marines to retake *Mayaguez* and attack Koh Tang, together with air attacks against Cambodian shipping and bombing mainland targets. Gen. David C. Jones, acting chairman of the Joint Chiefs of Staff, presented the NSC with a range of military options. Rescue planning was complicated because it was believed that some of *Mayaguez*'s crew were still on the ship, some on Koh Tang, and others on the fishing boat bound for Kampong Som (formerly Sihanoukville) on the mainland.[9]

Upon arrival of the fishing boat at Kampong Som in late morning on 14 May, the local Khmer Rouge commander (apparently fearing attack by U.S. forces) refused to accept responsibility for the *Mayaguez*'s crew. Turned away, the boat proceeded further down the coast, and anchored off the island of Koh Rong Sanloem. Several hours earlier, the 1/4 Marines had arrived at U-Tapao at 0545, and were on standby for a helicopter assault on *Mayaguez*. Following receipt of the news of the fishing boat's arrival at Kampong Som, the assault was cancelled. That afternoon, BLT 2/9 began arriving at U-Tapao.[10]

The rescue plan was finalized that night. Six hundred Marines from BLT 2/9 (Golf and Echo Companies), carried aboard five CH-53 Knives and three HH-53 Jolly Greens, were to seize and hold Koh Tang. Two helicopters would make a diversionary assault on the west beach, while the other six carried out the main assault on the wider east beach. The East Beach Force would move to the nearby compound where *Mayaguez*'s crew was believed to be held, and then link up with the West Beach Force.[11]

Harold E. Holt was to arrive on station at dawn on 15 May, for a ship-to-ship boarding of *Mayaguez* one hour after the assault on Koh Tang began. In preparation, fifty-seven Marines from Delta Company (1/4 Marines), volunteers from the Military Sealift Command to get the merchant vessel under way, an explosive ordnance disposal team, and a Cambodian linguist were to be brought aboard the destroyer escort by three HH-53s.[12]

Photo 21-2

Painting of USS *Harold E. Holt* (DE-1074) by Lee W. Swenson, circa 1975. Naval History and Heritage Command accession #92-035-M

Henry B. Wilson was assigned to support the Koh Tang operation. After retaking *Mayaguez*, *Holt* would be deployed in a blocking position between Koh Tang and the Cambodian mainland to intercept and engage any Khmer reaction forces. Naval aircraft from the *Coral Sea* were to strike targets on the Cambodian mainland to prevent interference with the rescue.[13]

ASSAULT ON KOH TANG ISLAND

On the morning of 15 May, eight helicopters carrying almost 200 Marines left U-Tapao for Koh Tang, where they believed the *Mayaguez*'s crew was being held. Minutes before the first helos landed, President Ford received word that the Cambodians had released the ship and its crew. However, the rescue mission was already under way for the young Marines who had not completed training on Okinawa, much less been in combat. The only breaks in the jungle canopy sufficient for the helicopters to land were small beaches on the east and west sides of Koh Tang's northern tip. When Khmer Rouge commander Em Som heard the faint thump of helicopter blades in the distance, his men locked and loaded anti-aircraft guns, large machine guns, rocket-propelled grenades, and small arms, and waited in fortified bunkers for the Americans' arrival.[14]

Photo 21-3

The wreckage of U.S. Air Force CH-53 helicopters (Knife 23 and Knife 31) shot down on Koh Tang's east beach, during combat with Khmer Rouge forces on 15 May 1975. U.S. Air Force photograph (www.phnompenhpost.com/post-weekend/hell-revisited)

The Khmer Rouge held their fire until the first helo, approaching west beach, was less than 100 feet off the ground. Then bullets began to rip through the HH 53's fuselage. Although the Marines were able to disembark, the helicopter was so badly shot up, it crashed a mile offshore after taking off. As soon as the Marines stepped onto the beach, black-clad soldiers were shooting at them from less than 50 meters away. The situation was not any better on the east beach, where two helos had already been shot down by the Cambodians.[15]

The Marines on the west beach were undergoing a trial-by-fire and running out of ammunition. When a chopper filled with reinforcements managed to land, young Marines felt a sense of relief when their senior NCO, Fofo "Staff Sergeant T" Tuitele walked down the ramp. Then nineteen-year-old Al Bailey later recounted that "he stepped out of the helicopter and was like, 'Let me get this shit under control.' It was a walk in the park to him, he was ready to conduct business."[16]

Tuitele calmed the Marines on the west beach and spread them out into a defensive perimeter. Noticing an enemy machine gun position on a ridge at the north end of the beach (that was raining down fire, making it impossible for helicopters to land), he stated, "I'm going to take care of this problem," and disappeared into the jungle. "Within 15 minutes the machine gun position was silenced," wrote Bailey and, "about another 20-25 minutes later, I heard more gun fire to my 11 o'clock position and then silence."[17]

By noon, the Khmer Rouge were running out of ammunition and, they retreated into the forest, while the Americans soldiers occupied their bunkers. As the Marines prepared for a long night, they learned that helicopters were on their way to take them off the island. Air Force pilots and PJs (pararescuemen) packed each helicopter with twice the normal combat load. When the final chopper was ready to take off, the Marines on board told the Air Force crew that a three-man machine gun team covering their flank was still on the beach.[18]

At 2000, the radio aboard the AC 130 Airborne Battlefield Command and Control Center aircraft came to life. Air Force Sergeant Robert Veile was the last to talk to the Marines, forced to convey that "nobody was coming back for them."[19]

RETURN OF *MAYAGUEZ*'S CREW

While the fighting on Kho Tang was at its most intense, a Thai fishing vessel approached the destroyer *Henry B. Wilson* with white flags waving. Aboard was the crew of the *Mayaguez*. Apparently, earlier air strikes, which sank a number of Cambodian gunboats, had changed the minds of Khmer Rouge leaders regarding the best use of the hostages. Instead of continued captivity, they were released. Following this action, the Marines on Kho Tang were ordered to disengage and withdraw.[20]

WITHDRAWAL UNDER ENEMY FIRE

Despite having no previous warning, the Marines were ready to depart, having gathered their wounded into one area and devised a withdrawal plan. After each helicopter lift reduced the number of Marines, the remaining ones would shrink their perimeter and fortify defenses before arrival of the next helicopter. The Khmer Rouge resumed offensive action as Air Force helicopters moved through heavy fire to withdraw U.S. forces. The last of 203 Marines were not evacuated until after dark. Unfortunately, darkness and the confusion caused by the deafening noise of helicopter rotor blades and enemy gunfire, resulted in three Marines being inadvertently left behind.[21]

Photo 21-4

USS *Henry B. Wilson* (DDG-7) under way in the Pacific, October 1969. Naval History and Heritage Command photograph #USN 1142937

During the helicopter extraction, *Henry B. Wilson* stood by offshore as her gig assisted in the recovery of twenty Marines and five airmen (the crew and embarked troops of a downed helicopter) isolated on the eastern beach. Her armed small boat also moved around the northern tip of the island to a position near the western shore, and laid down suppression fire in the area of Staff Sergeant Tuitele's position on the northern perimeter of the western zone.[22]

Earlier that evening, rounds from the *Wilson*'s 5-inch guns had sunk one, and possibly two gunboats which had been harassing the Marines and their air cover. In total, she fired 157 rounds while involved in extraction of Marines by boat.[23]

RETAKING OF THE CONTAINER SHIP *MAYAGUEZ*

Rear Adm. Samuel H. Moore, commander Military Sealift Command, had asked for volunteers from MSC ships in Subic Bay to accompany the Marine boarding party, during recapture of the *Mayaguez* to help get her under way. Captain Raymond Iacobacci of the USNS *Greenville Victory* found six members of his crew willing to undertake a dangerous assignment. The Marines were to overpower Khmer Rouge soldiers thought to be aboard *Mayaguez*, allowing the MSC crewmen to prepare and sail the ship to safety.

USNS *Greenville Victory* Volunteers	
Clinton Harriman, First Officer	Michael Saltwick, 2nd Asst. Engineer
Karl Lonsdale, Third Officer	Hermino Rivera, Fireman Watertender
Robert Griffin, Yeoman Storekeeper	Epifanio Rodriguez, Oiler[24]

In early morning darkness on 15 May, the Marines, an Army linguist, six volunteer USAF bomb disposal experts, six sailors from the USS *Duluth*, and the MSC mariners boarded three helicopters at 0300, bound for the *Harold E. Holt*. The CH-53s were too large to set down on her helicopter pad, so the men in one helicopter clambered down rope ladders; others disembarked using cargo ramps as the helicopters touched down only their rear wheels.[25]

Photo 21-5

Members of Company D, 1st Battalion, 4th Marines board the *Mayaguez* wearing gas masks, because the ship was bombed with tear gas munitions by USAF A-7D aircraft. U.S. Department of Defense Marine Corps photograph A706262

Air Force planes dropped tear gas on the *Mayaguez* to help quell any opposition, and once *Holt* was alongside the merchant ship, the Marines boarded her wearing gas masks. They found no one present. About 0800, the MSC mariners went aboard. They quickly got the emergency diesel generator running and at 0820, Marines hoisted the American flag aloft. The volunteers rigged tow lines and cut the anchor chain with an acetylene torch. At 1045, *Holt* took the *Mayaguez* in tow, while the MSC engineers worked to get steam up.[26]

Photo 21-6

USS *Harold E. Holt* (DE-1074) with the SS *Mayaguez* in tow, 15 May 1975.
Marine Corps Historical Collection photograph

The crew of *Mayaguez* was subsequently returned aboard, and by 1700, the container ship was proceeding under her own power and with no further need of assistance. Accordingly, Captain Miller transferred the remaining fifteen members of the 1st Battalion, 4th Marines, which had been serving as a security force, to the *Henry B. Wilson*.[27]

AFTERMATH

We lost 41 and saved 40. What kind of trade is that? That's what bothers me still. It didn't have to happen like that. It all sounded good on paper, but it was a disaster.

—Retired Master Sgt. Fofo Tulifua Tuitele, whose actions as a senior, combat-hardened Marine and scout sniper saved the lives of many fellow Marines during fighting on Koh Tang Island.[28]

The sad part of the Mayaguez *is that we had sufficient force coming up with the Seventh Fleet, after it had been turned around from the evacuation of Vietnam stand down, to seize Southern Cambodia. I begged for another day or two, rather than commit forces piecemeal as we did .... The idea that we could use U.S. Air Force air police and Air Force helicopters as an assault force appears to me as ridiculous today as it did then.*

—Vice Adm. George P. Steele, USN, commander Seventh Fleet (who, on 13 May, had dispatched the four Navy ships nearest the crisis to the waters off Kampong Som, Cambodia's main port), commenting on the *Mayaguez* Incident.[29]

The casualties suffered in recovering SS *Mayaguez* and her crew totaled forty-one Marines, sailors, and airmen killed; and forty-nine wounded. The fourteen Marines killed included LCpl. Joseph N. Hargrove, PFC Gary C. Hall, and Pvt. Danny G. Marshall, the missing members of the same machine gun team who were later declared dead. The bulk of the Air Force casualties occurred before commencement of the operation, when a CH-53 helicopter crashed, killing all twenty-three aboard.

- 14 Marines killed and 41 wounded
- 2 Navy corpsmen killed and 2 wounded
- 25 Air Force personnel killed and six wounded[30]

UNIT AWARDS

Navy Unit Commendation

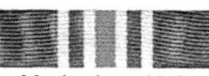
Meritorious Unit Commendation

Armed Forces Expeditionary

Ship	Period	Commanding Officer
Coral Sea (CV-43)	AE 15 May 75 MUC 15 May 75	Capt. Thomas S. Rogers Jr., USN
Harold E. Holt (DE-1074)	AE 15 May 75 NUC 15 May 75	Comdr. Robert A. Peterson, USN
Henry B. Wilson (DDG-7)	AE 15 May 75 NUC 15 May 75	Comdr. John M. Rodgers, USN
Vega (AF-59)	AE 15 May 75	Comdr. Ralph E. Brown Jr., USN

MERCHANT MARINERS HONORED

I'm glad to have been able to do something for my country, and I wouldn't hesitate to volunteer in the future.

—Hermino Rivera in accepting his medal.[31]

Merchant Marine Distinguished Service

Navy Distinguished Civilian Service

The six *Greenville Victory* crewmen—Robert Griffin, Clinton Harriman, Karl Lonsdale, Hermino Rivera, Epifanio Rodriguez, and Michael Saltwick—were awarded the Merchant Marine Distinguished Service and Navy Distinguished Civilian Service Medals.[32]

Postscript

Clearance Diving Team Three
Vietnam 1966-1971
Commodore Hector Donohue AM RAN (Rtd)

To see danger and face it calls for its own character of resolve. To seek to find danger in order to protect others, and to conduct that search in waters that shut out all sight, calls for a very unique character of human resolve. And that is precisely what distinguished those who served with the RAN Clearance Diving Team in Vietnam. They were a very unique body of men and they contributed in a very unique way to the record of service of the RAN. In all their activities constant courage was to be found. And here too was to be found that great stimulant in human affairs – humour. This indeed was mateship at its very best.

—Sir James Killen (former Australian Minister of Defence) in his foreword to Lex McAulay's book, *In the Ocean's Dark Embrace*.[1]

Statistics aside, it is impossible to quantify the achievements of CDT 3 in South Vietnam 1967-71. There is no doubt this small band of Australians was known and respected for professional ability wherever the men operated. Man for man, there probably was no more effective unit deployed during the war in Vietnam, on either side.

—Lex McAulay, *In the Ocean's Dark Embrace*.

Clearance Diving Team Three (CDT 3) is the designation assigned to Royal Australian Navy CD Teams raised for a special purpose. In 1966 the first CDT 3 was formed as a result of a decision to deploy a team to Vietnam. A total of eight contingents of the team, deployed to Vietnam from February 1967 to May 1971 when the final team returned to Australia and disbanded. A ninth contingent had trained but did not deploy.

CDT 3 was formed for a second time in 1980 to support the Special Air Service in its Counter Terrorism role. Later, this Team would be assigned the title of the Special Duties Unit (SDU) of CDT Four, which is based in Western Australia.

CDT 3 was formed for the third time in January 1991 to support joint operations in the Middle East. A team of 23 personnel was despatched to Bahrain. The team entered Kuwait by land on 5 March and was involved, along with divers from other navies, in clearing several Kuwaiti ports, a naval base and a number of beaches. The team returned to Australia on 11 May and disbanded. Subsequently a small number of clearance divers have been attached to RAN ships deploying to the Middle East.

CDT 3 re-formed in January 2003 for another deployment to the Middle East as part of Australia's contribution to the Iraq War. The team was the largest ever deployed which, at the height of its operation, consisted of 32 men. They left Australia 22 February and staged through Bahrain, with the main party crossing into Iraq by road on 24 March. They cleared the port of Umm Qasr which was essential to allow the coalition to bring humanitarian aid into southern Iraq. While some of the team cleared the inland port of Khawar AZ Zubayr to the north, another detachment deployed to the Al Faw Peninsula and cleared ordnance from the tidal flats. The team departed Iraq on 12 May, arrived in to Australia at the end of May and was disbanded.

CDT 3 THE BEGINNING

In late 1966, the Australian Government directed the Department of Defence to consider an increased force commitment to the war in Vietnam. From the naval perspective, the provision of one of the new Guided Missile Destroyers (DDG), recently arrived from the U.S. and fully compatible with the U.S. Navy logistical system, was straight forward. The U.S. had also made it clear that a clearance diving team able to undertake explosive ordnance disposal duties would be welcome, and was quickly endorsed, given the significant training dividend such a deployment would bring, and the fact that such a capability was immediately available.

The decision to send clearance divers to Vietnam was welcomed by the U.S. at the highest level, as evidenced in a secret White House memorandum from Special Assistant for National Security Affairs, Walt Rostow, to U.S. President Lyndon B. Johnson on 16 December 1966 stating: 'Mr. President, Good news. The Australians have decided to send 500 more men to Vietnam, plus a fighter squadron of 8 fighter bombers, plus a ship, plus six frogmen that Westy [General Westmoreland] wants for harbor clearance. It is being held very tight because they must detach some of them from Malaysia and have not yet talked to the British.'

Clearance Diving Team 3 (CDT 3) was quickly formed and by late 1966 had commenced training for service in Vietnam. Following both Governments' endorsement to the RAN involvement, an Australian Defence team went to Saigon in early January 1967 to negotiate the detailed military working arrangements with CincPacFlt staff. These were quickly agreed and ultimately signed on 12 April by the RAN Chief of Naval Staff, Vice Admiral Sir Alan McNicoll and Commander in Chief Pacific Fleet, Admiral Roy L Johnson. CDT 3 deployed in advance of the formal agreement in February 1967.

Photo Postscript-1

US Ambassador, Mr. Walter L. Rice, with members of CDT 3 1st Contingent, after presenting USN Meritorious Unit Commendation award at HMAS Penguin, September 1969.
Comdr. Edward W. (Jake) Linton, RAN (Retired) collection

In all, eight CDT 3 contingents were deployed between February 1967 and May 1971, totaling 8 officers and 41 sailors. Each team rotated through the war zone at approximately seven-month intervals. The formation of CDT 3 is summarised in the Preface which includes the names of the Officer in Charge for each contingent and awards earned by team members.

VUNG TAU

CDT 3 was placed under the overall command and administrative control of the Commander Australian Forces, Vietnam, while operational control was vested in the Commander, U.S. Military Assistance Command Vietnam, exercised through the ComNavForV. Coastal and riverine shipping were a prime target for the North Vietnam and Viet Cong Forces, and control of the inland waterways, especially the Mekong Delta, was strongly contested. CDT 3 would come under the command of Task Force 115, the Coastal Surveillance Force known as Operation Market Time, through Task Group 115.9, the Harbour Defence Group. The Team was allocated to the Harbour Defence Unit in Vung Tau (one of five) containing a Harbour Entrance Control Post (HECP), a harbour patrol element, and an EOD team. The function of the EOD team, in conjunction with the HECP and harbour patrol craft, was to conduct daily inspection of ships at anchor and disarm any ordnance encountered. The overall defence of shipping against attack was designated Operation Stable Door.

The first contingent was initially employed in Saigon with the USN EOD team to settle in and undergo local indoctrination courses. At the end of February, they deployed to Vung Tau and moved in to one of the bunkers in the HECP. These had been built by the French many years earlier and although bare, were solid. The CDT 3 bunker or 'cave' as it was known, was progressively developed over the years and became famous for its luxurious appointments.

When not employed in their primary task of Stable Door operations, the team undertook many tasks including disposing of damaged ordnance at Vung Tau air field and the local military bases, and providing demolition and diving support as required.

The second contingent arrived in August and was quickly made aware they were in a war zone when later that month Able Seaman David C. Tromp was wounded by a sniper during an opposed amphibious insertion north of Vung Tau. He was medevacked, but soon returned to duty.

In October 1967, CDT 3 was fully integrated into the USN EOD Mobile Unit Pacific (EODMUPAC) organisation in South Vietnam and designated by the U.S. military as EODMUPAC Team 21, which was subsequently changed to EODMUPAC Team 35. Its responsibility widened to include part of the Mekong Delta.

Soon after the arrival of the fourth contingent in August 1968, arrangements were made to initiate a program of 'in country' exchanges of EOD personnel between units. This exchange provided a much wider experience for the team, as the nature of tasks varied in each area.

Photo Postscript-2

Diving operations by CDT 3 on a crashed C-123 aircraft off the Ca Mau Peninsula, May 1968. The officer in charge, Lt. William D. H. Lees, is on the right. Comdr. Edward W. (Jake) Linton, RAN (Retired) collection

The teams were on call 24 hours a day, seven days a week, for the entire length of their tours. To achieve this high rate of availability, most teams implemented an internal roster, which in any 24-hour period had two personnel ready to deploy at immediate notice, two on standby as backup, and two on stand down. Occasionally, four or five team members were deployed together on the one operation.

Operational activity increased as the U.S. commanders became aware of the team's capabilities. They were often called to assist in salvage operations in Coastal Zone 3 when the handling of ordnance was involved. This particularly applied to crashed aircraft and sunken Market Time patrol craft. From mid-1968 the team began to support the 'Brown Water War' and accompanied Vietnamese units and their U.S. naval advisors into Viet Cong occupied areas clearing booby traps and using their demolition skills to destroy log barriers, bunkers and tunnels. Team members worked alongside U.S. Navy Seals, U.S. Army, U.S. Air Force, Marine and Navy EOD, U.S. Army Rangers, U.S.

Cavalry (air & armoured), the Australian Army Training Team, U.S. Advisors, and South Vietnamese Army and Navy units.

Photo Postscript-3

CDT 3 members together with U.S. and Army of the Republic of Vietnam (ARVN) personnel attaching Mark 8 demolition hose charges to wooden stakes driven into the river bed by the Viet Cong to interrupt local traffic, February 1970.
Comdr. Edward W. (Jake) Linton, RAN (Retired) collection

COUNTERING THE SWIMMER-SAPPER

CDT 3 was involved in two significant swimmer/saboteur attacks in Vung Tau Harbour in May 1969 and June 1970. The two incidents involving MV *Heredia* and USS *Meeker County* are covered in Chapters 14 and 18.

SUPPORT FOR OFFENSIVE OPERATIONS

From mid-1968, the team received requests for EOD assistance in offensive operations. Members of CDT 3 supported Task Force 115 operations in January and February 1969 to destroy bunker complexes in An Xuyen Province, as described in Chapter 13.

From late 1969, increasingly EOD support for offensive operations became the higher priority task allocated to the team. Special operations were undertaken with the Vietnamese armed forces, clearing barriers along the approaches to enemy positions and allowing the ARVN or Special Forces to mount ambushes and reconnaissance patrols against known or suspected enemy-held areas. Altogether the sixth team was involved in 22 offensive operations in the Delta, all conducted in areas held by the enemy and, on most occasions, involving enemy fire of varying intensity.

These operations intensified in 1970 and team members were often under enemy fire while engaged in the destruction of bunker complexes, tunnels, trenches, observation posts and log barricades erected by the VC in the rivers and waterways of South Vietnam.

In June 1970, Able Seaman Bogdan K. Wojcik from the seventh contingent was fatally injured in a motor vehicle accident, the only fatal CD casualty of the war.

MOVE TO DANANG

In August 1970, after being relieved at Vung Tau by South Vietnamese Navy personnel, the 7th team and their equipment were airlifted to the northern city of Danang in I Corps, Military Region 1, where the war was more intense. The team would regularly deploy to the 'badlands' along the DMZ which saw them often in a hot war situation when in contact with the North Vietnamese Army.

With the move, the nature of the tasks changed. The first major task was the clearance of the Dong Ha ammunition storage area. Dong Ha is located in the province of Quang Tri, 24 km south of what was then the Demilitarized Zone (DMZ) which divided North and South Vietnam. A large Logistic base was set up to support U.S. operations and included an ammunition storage area of 90 acres. In 1968, the base was attacked by VC and North Vietnamese forces. The ammunition area exploded in a vast chain of interlocking blasts which left a carpet of dangerous unexploded ordnance covering the entire area. Shells of 155mm calibre and 105mm, as well as 40mm grenades and anti-personnel mines, were the main items to deal with. Attempts to clean up the area resulted in casualties to U.S. forces. Work was suspended and the site left to bake in the 40°C of the dry season, and to soak in the monsoonal rain of the wet.

The problem of course would not go away, and in March 1970 a special EOD unit was formed to clear the area. Personnel from the U.S.

Navy, Army, Air Force and Marines, and members of CDT 3 participated; about 12 at any given time was all that could be spared. The clearance began on 24 March 1970.

The task was tedious and constantly dangerous. Much of the ordnance was partially buried and needed careful removal. The anti-personnel mines which numbered in the thousands were especially concerning. Called 'birds,' these were an air dropped bomblet, requiring a pressure of about 4oz to detonate them. In temperatures of 40°C the area was systematically combed with ordnance being passed from man to man along a line and then placed in designated 'safe areas;' it was then evaluated as unstable and for disposal, or safe and therefore reusable.

Every few days the unstable ammunition was trucked to a demolition range and destroyed under controlled conditions. Work under those conditions was limited to 30 minutes as concentration faded and a 10-minute rest period followed. Bored ARVN troops would take pot shots at the EOD Teams from time to time despite threats of a most serious nature from the Marine officer in charge of the operation.

Photo Postscript-4

EOD Teams clear unstable ordnance from Dong Ha, May 1970.
Comdr. Edward W. (Jake) Linton, RAN (Retired) collection

The camp was mortared on two occasions during CDT 3's period there, and in these 'stand to' conditions everyone manned the perimeter till the 'stand down' word was given.

The clearance was completed on 7 May 1970. In all, 1025 tonnes of unstable ammunition was destroyed and ammunition valued at U.S. $1,587,000.00 was salvaged for future use. Dong Ha was considered to be the most hazardous area cleared in Vietnam.

All EOD personnel who participated were awarded the U.S. Army Commendation Medal. Five were awarded to the CDT 3 personnel involved.

The eighth and final contingent relieved its predecessor in October 1970 and served its entire tour based out of Camp Tien Sha in Danang, assuming responsibility for Naval EOD in the whole of Military Region I up to the Demilitarized Zone (DMZ).

Shortly after the eighth contingent arrived, Chief Petty Officer John F. C. Dollar and Leading Seaman John A. Aldenhoven of contingent seven together with two members from the relief team, Chief Petty Officer John J. Gilchrist and Able Seaman Brian J. Furner were involved in an operation on Cam Thanh Island with the Jungle Surveillance Group. The party came under fire from three sides and were pinned down for some two hours until helicopter gunships extracted the group. Aldenhoven and Furner assisted the wounded to cover when the ambush was first sprung, and crossed open ground under fire to recover weapons and ammunition.

Routine calls for assistance from ships in Danang Harbour and military authorities continued, but operations in support of U.S. Naval Coastal Groups increased. The team was employed on booby trap clearance for USN Surveillance Groups, which infiltrated into disputed areas by day, and implanted sensitive acoustic sensors to monitor human movements at night. During the final months much time was devoted to salvaging ammunition from stranded ships and the ships themselves.

Further enemy sapper activity in the Cua Viet River resulted in CDT 3 support in keeping the river open. There were some 20 separate mining incidents with evidence of several other attempts to disrupt shipping. Two ammunition barges were damaged by limpet mines in addition to a MCM (mine countermeasures) vessel sunk. CDT 3 recovered three pressure mines as well as two VC sappers killed by scare charges.

Photo Postscript-5

North Vietnamese pressure mines recovered by CDT 3 from the Cua Viet River, March 1971.
Comdr. Edward W. (Jake) Linton, RAN (Retired) collection

Photo Postscript-6

ABCD Anthony L. Ey passing a 2.75" rocket he recovered under water to CPOCD John J. Gilchrist, at Danang, November, 1970.
Comdr. Edward W. (Jake) Linton, RAN (Retired) collection

In April 1971 CDT 3 was relieved of its responsibilities and the eighth contingent departed Danang and left Saigon for Australia 5 May. It was the end of CD involvement in the war.

IN RETROSPECT

When the first contingent arrived in Vietnam, they really had no idea of what to expect. They arrived in Vietnam wearing white Navy uniforms and carried no weapons. However, the next day they were armed, dressed in jungle greens and immediately in action. Early teams felt that their broadly based 'jack of all trades' skills were being under-utilized. The diving teams had a lot to offer but the Americans were, at that stage, unaware of the high level and depth of CD training. This under-utilization was to change as the US Command became increasingly aware of the extreme versatility and positive 'can do easy' mind-set of the Australian divers. In fact, the U.S. authorities began to regard the CDs as 'can do anything' troops.

Certainly by the time the eighth contingent arrived in country the Americans were employing the Australian divers as their 'Immediate response team' to any EOD/diving/salvage incident, which was 'outside the square.' This had the sailors responding to calls for assistance from every corner of Military Region 1. They were treated with the utmost respect and wanted for nothing in terms of equipment, transportation, weapons, ammunition and victuals. In fact, they were amazed at the ease with which they could obtain virtually anything they wanted from the U.S. system. The Australian system was a completely different story.

The Vietnam experience was invaluable to the development of clearance diving techniques in the RAN, and the lessons learnt in the first experience of guerrilla warfare were fast incorporated into branch doctrine and training.

Though EOD was the continuing theme of the daily work of the eight contingents, the great variety of duties performed—of which perhaps the special operations in Viet Cong-occupied territory were the most noteworthy—brought out the value of RAN clearance diving training, and the versatility of the men of the clearance diving branch. Vietnam was to be the testing ground for the CD Branch and it confirmed that the selection and training process was turning out men made of the 'right stuff.'

Over its four and a half years' service in Vietnam, the eight teams searched 7,573 ships and removed 78 explosive devices from them, undertook 153 other major diving tasks, destroyed 353 tonnes of heavy ordnance, and destroyed over 42,000 items of unsafe ammunition. Members also participated in 68 special operations.

Appendix A: Amphibious Ship Unit Awards

Self-propelled Barracks Ship (4 ships, 26 awards/6.5 average per ship)

Ship	CR	PUC/MUC/NUC
USS *Benewah* (APB-35) 5 CR, 2 PUC, 1 MUC, 4 NUC	21 Mar 68 15 Apr 68 3 Nov 68 16 Jul 69 17 Aug 70	PUC 29 Jan-4 Mar 68 PUC 25 Jan-2 Mar 69 MUC 25 Aug-16 Nov 69 NUC 19 Jun-19 Dec 67 NUC 12-16 Jan 68 NUC 5 Mar 68-24 Jan 69 NUC 1 Jul 70-26 Feb 71
USS *Colleton* (APB-36) 1 CR, 2 PUC, 2 NUC	31 May 68	PUC 29 Jan-4 Mar 68 PUC 25 Jan-19 Jun 69 NUC 19 Jun-18 Dec 67 NUC 5 Mar 68-24 Jan 69
USS *Mercer* (APB-39) 4 CR, 1 PUC, 1 NUC	Spring 1969 Spring 1969 Spring 1969 Spring 1969	PUC 25 Jan-5 Jul 69 NUC 31 Jul 68-24 Jan 69
USS *Nueces* (APB-40) 1 CR, 1 PUC, 2 NUC	2 Mar 69	PUC 25 Jan-5 Jul 69 NUC 3 Aug 68-24 Jan 69 NUC 5 May 70-30 Jun 71

Landing Craft Repair Ship (5 ships, 31 awards/6.2 average per ship)

Ship	CR	PUC/MUC/NUC
Askari (ARL-30) 5 CR, 2 PUC, 5 NUC	8-14 Mar 68 22 Mar 68 30 Apr 68 18 Jan 69 3 Mar 69	PUC 29 Jan-4 Mar 68 PUC 6 Dec 68-31 Mar 69 NUC 19 Jun 67-16 Jan 68 NUC 5 Mar 68-24 Jan 69 NUC 1 Jul-31 Aug 70 NUC 4 Nov 70-30 Jul 71 NUC 1 Jul-31 Aug 71
Indra (ARL-37) 1 NUC		NUC 10 Jun-15 Oct 68
Krishna (ARL-38) 1 CR, 4 NUC	5 Jul 70	NUC 14 Jun 65-1 Jun 66 NUC 2 Jun 66-23 Sep 68 NUC 24 Sep 68-1 Jul 69 NUC 5 May 70-30 Jun 71
Satyr (ARL-23) 1 PUC, 4 NUC		PUC 25 Jan-21 Apr 69 NUC 10 Jul 68-24 Jan 69 NUC 5 May-26 Sep 70 NUC 16 Dec 70-30 Jun 71 NUC 1 Jul-30 Sep 71

288 Appendix A

Sphinx (ARL-24)   5 Nov 68   PUC 25 Jan-19 Jun 69
5 CR, 1 PUC, 2 NUC   21 Jan 69   NUC 9 Jun 68-24 Jan 69
    18 Jun 69   NUC 28 Aug 70-13 May 71
    21 Nov 70
    23 Nov 70

Inshore Fire Support Ship (4 ships, 22 awards, 5.5 average per ship)

Ship	CR	MUC/NUC
Carronade (IFS-1)	23 Apr 66	MUC 2 Sep 68-31 Jan 70
3 CR, 1 MUC, 2 NUC	18 Mar 68	NUC 19 Apr 66-31 May 67
	9 Jun 68	NUC 1 Jun 67-1 Sep 68
Clarion River	15-17 Jun 67	MUC 2 Sep 68-31 Jan 70
(LSMR-409/LFR-409)	12 Aug 68	NUC 19 Apr 66-31 May 67
2 CR, 1 MUC, 2 NUC		NUC 1 Jun 67-1 Sep 68
St. Francis River	5-6 Jan 67	MUC 2 Sep 68-31 Jan 70
(LSMR-525/LFR-525)	30 Oct 68	NUC 19 Apr 66-31 Mar 67
2 CR, 1 MUC, 2 NUC		NUC 1 Jun 67-1 Sep 68
White River	17 Feb 67	MUC 2 Sep 68-31 Jan 70
(LSMR-536/LFR-536)	3 Nov 67	NUC 19 Apr 66-31 May 67
3 CR, 1 MUC, 2 NUC	5 May 69	NUC 1 Jun 67-1 Sep 68

High Speed Transport (3 ships, 13 awards, 4.3 average per ship)

Ship	CR	MUC/NUC
Cook (APD-130)	21 Apr 65	MUC 29-31 Jul 66
4 CR, 2 MUC	23 Apr 65	MUC 16-30 Aug 66
	12 Mar 69	
	1 Jul 69	
Diachenko (APD-123)	18 Mar 68	MUC 14-25 Sep 66
1 CR, 3 MUC, 1 NUC		MUC 6-16 Jan 67
		MUC 16 Feb-3 Mar 67
		NUC 24 May-3 Dec 65
Weiss (APD-135) 1 CR, 1 NUC	26 Mar 66	NUC 24 Jan-9 Feb 69

Tank Landing Ship (63 ships, 250 awards, 4.0 average per ship)

Ship	CR	PUC/MUC/NUC
Blanco County (LST-344)	1-2 Jan 67	NUC 1 Jul 66-31 Mar 68
1 CR, 1 NUC		
Bulloch County (LST-509) 1 MUC		MUC 1 Jul 66-31 Mar 68
Caddo Parish (LST-515)	22-23 Apr 68	MUC 1 Sep 68-1 May 69
4 CR, 2 MUC, 1 NUC	6 Mar 69	MUC 2 May-1 Nov 69
	9 Mar 69	NUC 2 Nov 69-21 Nov 70
	20-21 Mar 69	
Caroline County (LST-525)	24 Feb 68	MUC 1 Jul 66-31 Mar 68
1 CR, 1 MUC, 1 NUC		NUC 11 Oct-13 Nov 68
Cayuga (LST-1186) 1 CR	24 May 72	
Chase County (LST-532)		
Chesterfield County (LST-551)		
Clarke County (LST-601)	17 Nov-	MUC 1 Jul 66-31 Mar 68
1 CR, 2 MUC	1 Dec 67	MUC 18 Nov 69-24 Apr 70

Coconino County (LST-603) 4 CR, 2 MUC	29 Jul 67 10 Jan 68 3 Sep 68 17 Feb 69	MUC 1 Jul 66-31 Mar 68 MUC 10 Nov-8 Dec 68
Desoto County (LST-1171) 1 MUC		MUC 16 Sep-2 Oct 70
Floyd County (LST-762) 3 CR, 1 MUC	2 Jun 68 26 Aug 68 2 Sep 68	MUC 1 Apr-11 Oct 68
Frederick (LST-1184) 2 MUC		MUC 30 Mar-15 Apr 75 MUC 22-30 Apr 75
Fresno (LST-1182)		
Garrett County (LST-736) 2 CR, 1 PUC, 6 NUC	29 Mar 68 23 Jan 69	PUC 31 Jan-29 Feb 68 NUC 10 Nov 66-30 Jan 68 NUC 1 Mar-30 Sep 68 NUC 1 Oct-2 Dec 68 NUC 3 Mar-6 Aug 69 NUC 10 Sep-31 Dec 69 NUC 6 Sep 70-27 Jan 71
Hampshire County (LST-819) 2 CR, 1 PUC, 1 NUC	7-15 Jan 67 23 May 70	PUC 25 Jan-19 Apr 69 NUC 22 Apr-27 Jun 70
Harnett County (LST-821) 6 CR, 2 PUC, 4 NUC	13 Jun 67 29 Dec 67 23 Dec 68 29 Jan- 1 Feb 69 15 Mar 69 24 Mar 69	PUC 31 Jan-29 Feb 68 PUC 12 Dec 68-30 Apr 69 NUC 10 Nov 66-30 Jan 68 NUC 1 Mar-30 Sep 68 NUC 1 Oct-31 Dec 69 NUC 20 Feb-30 Jun 70
Henry County (LST-824) 2 CR	29-30 Jan 68 6 Feb 68	
Hickman County (LST-825) 3 CR, 2 MUC	12 May 68 30 May 68 23 May 69	MUC 1 Sep 68-1 May 69 MUC 2 May-1 Nov 69
Holmes County (LST-836) 1 CR, 3 NUC	30 Oct 68	NUC 19 Jun-17 Aug 67 NUC 26 Jan-3 Mar 71 NUC 2 Apr-10 May 71
Hunterdon County (LST-838) 3 CR, 2 PUC, 8 NUC	29 Aug 67 12 Mar 68 12 Sep 68	PUC 20-29 Feb 68 PUC 10 Oct-5 Dec 68 NUC 10 Nov 66-30 Jan 68 NUC 1 Mar-30 Sep 68 NUC 6 Dec 68-6 Apr 69 NUC 11 May-16 Oct 69 NUC 5 May-30 Jun 70 NUC 19 Jul-1 Aug 70 NUC 2 Aug 70 NUC 1 Jan-19 May 71
Iredell County (LST-839) 4 CR, 1 PUC, 1 MUC, 1 NUC	6-8 Feb 68 21 Feb 68 10 Mar 68 18 Mar 70	PUC 25 Jan-15 Feb 69 MUC 5 Dec 69-24 Apr 70 NUC 11 Nov-31 Dec 68

290 Appendix A

Jennings County (LST-846)	12 Mar 67	PUC 31 Jan-29 Feb 68
5 CR, 2 PUC, 8 NUC	22 Mar 67	PUC 18 Oct-5 Dec 68
	11 Apr 67	NUC 10 Nov 66-30 Jan 68
	12 Jun 67	NUC 1 Mar-30 Sep 68
	25 June 67	NUC 1-17 Oct 68
		NUC 6 Dec 68-4 Mar 69
		NUC 5 Apr-11 Sep 69
		NUC 17 Oct-31 Dec 69
		NUC 1 Jul 70-30 Apr 71
		NUC 4 Jan-30 Jun 71
Jerome County (LST-848)	18 Mar 68	PUC 29 Jan-18 Feb 68
1 CR, 1 PUC, 1 MUC		MUC 29 Nov 67-1 Jun 68
Kemper County (LST-854)	3 Mar 66	NUC 19-25 Jun 67
1 CR, 1 NUC		
Litchfield County (LST-901)	24 Feb 68	MUC 1 Jul 66-31 Mar 68
1 CR, 1 MUC, 1 NUC		NUC 11 Jul-11 Aug 68
New London County (LST-1066)		
Luzerne County (LST-902)	18 Feb 68	MUC 1 Sep 68-1 May 69
4 CR, 2 MUC	22 Feb 68	MUC 2 May 69-24 Apr 70
	4 Mar 68	
	3 Mar 69	
Madera County (LST-905)	4 Jun 68	MUC 1 Sep 68-1 May 69
3 CR, 2 MUC	19 Aug 69	MUC 29 May-15 Nov 69
	3 Nov 69	
Mahnomen County (LST-912) 1 CR	20 Jan 67	
Manitowoc (LST-1180)		
Meeker County (LST-980)	2 Mar 68	MUC 1 Jul 66-31 Mar 68
4 CR, 1 MUC, 1 NUC	23 May 68	NUC 27 Jun-21 Nov 70
	14 Oct 68	
	28 Jun 70	
Monmouth County (LST-1032)		MUC 1 Sep 68-1 May 69
2 MUC, 1 NUC		MUC 2 May 69-24 Apr 70
		NUC 25 Apr-21 Nov 70
Nye County (LST-1067) 1 CR	9 Jul 66	
Outagamie County (LST-1073)		
Page County (LST-1076)	21 Aug 68	MUC 7 Jun-30 Nov 68
7 CR, 2 MUC, 1 NUC	25 Aug 68	MUC 28 Dec 69-24 Apr 70
	12-13 Sep 68	NUC 25 Apr-31 May 70
	22 Sep 68	
	28 Sep 68	
	5 Oct 68	
	26 Feb 70	
Park County (LST-1077)	1 Nov 68	MUC 1 Jul 66-31 Mar 68
1 CR, 1 MUC, 5 NUC		NUC 2 Aug-4 Sep 68
		NUC 22 Sep-12 Nov 68
		NUC 24 Dec 70-26 Jan 71
		NUC 28 Feb-2 Apr 71
		NUC 10 May-30 Jun 71
Peoria (LST-1183)		MUC 12 Apr 75
1 MUC, 1 NUC		NUC 29-30 Apr 75

Amphibious Ship Unit Awards

Ship	Date(s)	Award Period(s)
Pitkin County (LST-1082) 1 MUC, 3 NUC		MUC 1 Jul 66-31 Mar 68 NUC 2-24 Jun 68 NUC 11 Oct-19 Nov 68 NUC 5 May-24 Dec 70
Polk County (LST-1084)		
Pulaski County (LST-1088)		
Racine (LST-1191)		
San Bernardino (LST-1189)		
San Joaquin County (LST-1122) 1 MUC		MUC 1 Apr 68-30 Jun 69
Schenectady (LST-1185) 1 CR	27 Jun 72	
Sedgwick County (LST-1123) 2 CR, 1 PUC, 2 MUC	5 Mar 68 11 Mar 68	PUC 23 Apr-6 May 69 MUC 1 Jul 66-16 Feb 68 MUC 5-31 Mar 68
Snohomish County (LST-1126) 1 CR	17 Nov 68	
St. Clair County (LST-1096) 2 CR, 1 NUC	23-24 Jul 68 30 Jul 68	NUC 3 Sep-12 Oct 68
Stone County (LST-1141) 1 CR	5 Mar 68	
Summit County (LST-1146)		
Sumner County (LST-1148) 1 CR, 1 MUC	25 Jun 68	MUC 2 Jun-30 Nov 68
Sumter (LST-1181)		
Sutter County (LST-1150) 1 MUC, 1 NUC		MUC 1 Jul 66-31 Mar 68 NUC 16 Nov-17 Dec 68
Terrell County (LST-1157) 1 PUC, 3 MUC, 1 NUC		PUC 1 Jan-3 Feb 69 MUC 1 Aug 65-31 Mar 68 MUC 18 Jun-4 Aug 67 MUC 1 Apr 68-31 Mar 69 NUC 25 Jun-28 Oct 69
Tioga County (LST-1158) 1 CR	16 Feb 66	
Tom Green County (LST-1159) 5 CR, 3 MUC, 4 NUC	3 Jul 67 15 Apr 68 28 Dec 68 21 Jan 69 16 Jun 69	MUC 1 Aug 65-31 Mar 68 MUC 18 Jun-8 Jul 67 MUC 1 Apr 68-31 Mar 69 NUC 1 Apr-25 May 68 NUC 28 Dec 68-24 Jan 69 NUC 3 Nov-16 Dec 70 NUC 4 Apr-10 May 71
Tuscaloosa (LST-1187) 1 MUC		MUC 1-7 May 75
Vernon County (LST-1161) 3 CR, 1 PUC, 5 MUC, 4 NUC	21 Nov 66 9-12 Jun 68 25 Jan 69	PUC 28 Feb-25 Mar 69 MUC 1 Aug 65-31 Mar 68 MUC 1 Apr-22 May 68 MUC 22 Jun-24 Jul 68 MUC 14 Oct 68-31 Mar 69 MUC 2 Mar-15 Dec 72 NUC 19-25 Jun 67 NUC 23 May-21 Jun 68 NUC 25 Jul-13 Oct 68 NUC 2 Oct-5 Nov 70

Ship	Commissioned	Awards
Washoe County (LST-1165) 1 CR, 1 PUC, 2 MUC, 1 NUC	2 Apr 66	PUC 18 Oct-5 Dec 68 MUC 1 Aug 65-31 Mar 68 MUC 1 Apr 68-31 Mar 69 NUC 28 Jul-28 Aug 69
Washtenaw County (LST-1166) 1 CR, 3 PUC, 4 MUC, 3 NUC	14 Mar 68	PUC 29 Jan-4 Mar 68 PUC 5-23 Feb 69 PUC 1-31 Mar 69 MUC 1 Aug 65-31 Mar 68 MUC 1 Apr-16 Jun 68 MUC 3-20 Sep 69 MUC 2 Mar-15 Dec 72 NUC 17 Jun-20 Jul 68 NUC 10 Nov-2 Dec 68 NUC 23 Feb-6 Apr 71
Westchester County (LST-1167) 3 CR, 2 MUC, 4 NUC	9 Sep 66 11 Dec 67 31 Oct- 1 Nov 68	MUC 1 Aug 65-31 Mar 68 MUC 1 Apr-20 Sep 68 NUC 20 Aug 67-16 Jan 68 NUC 21 Sep-5 Nov 68 NUC 30 Jul-2 Oct 70 NUC 18-30 Jun 71
Wexford County (LST-1168) 3 CR, 1 MUC	17 Sep 65 20 Oct 65 8 Nov 70	MUC 15 Nov 67-22 May 68
Whitfield County (LST-1169) 4 CR, 1 PUC, 5 MUC	24 Jul 68 10 Jan 69 30 Apr 69 18 Jun 69	PUC 8 May-5 Jul 69 MUC 1 Aug 65-31 Mar 68 MUC 1 Apr-17 Jul 68 MUC 25 Sep-30 Nov 68 MUC 25 Jan-31 Mar 69 MUC 2 Mar-15 Dec 72
Windham County (LST-1170) 1 CR, 1 PUC, 4 MUC, 3 NUC	17 Jan 66	PUC 25 Mar-10 May 69 MUC 1 Aug 65-31 Mar 68 MUC 1 Apr-19 Jun 68 MUC 27 Jul 68-31 Mar 69 MUC 2 Mar-15 Dec 72 NUC 20 Jun-26 Jul 68 NUC 28 Aug-1 Oct 69 NUC 18 Dec 70-23 Feb 71

Amphibious Assault Ship, Helicopter (8 ships, 26 awards, 3.2 average)

Ship	CR	MUC/NUC
Boxer (LPH-4) 1 NUC		NUC 26-30 Apr 65
Inchon (LPH-12) 1 MUC		MUC 13 May-3 Jun 74
Iwo Jima (LPH-2) 1 CR, 4 MUC	3 May 68	MUC 29 Jul 66-6 Mar 67 MUC 15 Nov 67-22 May 68 MUC 1 Jun-20 Sep 69 MUC 12-14 Apr 74
New Orleans (LPH-11)		

Okinawa (LPH-3) 1 CR, 3 MUC, 3 NUC	18 May 67	MUC 28 Apr-31 Oct 67 MUC 25 Mar-6 Apr 68 MUC 12 Apr 75 NUC 12-24 Jan 69 NUC 5-20 May 69 NUC 29-30 Apr 75
Princeton (LPH-5) 1 CR, 3 MUC	25 Mar 67	MUC 23 Mar-2 Aug 66 MUC 6 Mar-27 May 67 MUC 4 May-1 Jun 69
Tripoli (LPH-10) 3 CR, 1 MUC, 2 NUC	3 Jul 67 28 Aug 67 20 Oct 67	MUC 18 Jun-4 Aug 67 NUC 16 May-1 Dec 67 NUC 12 Jan-9 Feb 69
Valley Forge (LPH-8) 2 MUC		MUC 30 Aug 65-9 Apr 66 MUC 7 Sep-1 Dec 66

Amphibious Transport Dock (7 ships, 20 awards, 2.8 average per ship)

Ship	CR	MUC/NUC
Cleveland (LPD-7) 2 CR, 2 MUC	22 Dec 67 14 Nov 72	MUC 15 Nov 67-22 May 68 MUC 1 Jun-20 Sep 69
Denver (LPD-9) 1 CR, 2 NUC	24 May 72	NUC 22 Jun-26 Jul 72 NUC 29-30 Apr 75
Dubuque (LPD-8) 2 MUC		MUC 30 Mar-15 Apr 75 MUC 22-30 Apr 75
Duluth (LPD-6) 1 CR, 1 MUC, 3 NUC	24 May 72	MUC 28 May-15 Nov 67 NUC 12-24 Jan 69 NUC 5-20 May 69 NUC 29-30 Apr 75
Juneau (LPD-10)		
Ogden (LPD-5) 2 CR, 1 MUC, 1 NUC	3 Jul 67 6 Jul 67	MUC 18 Jun-4 Aug 67 NUC 12 Jan-9 Feb 69
Vancouver (LPD-2) 1 MUC, 1 NUC		MUC 12 Apr 75 NUC 29-30 Apr 75

Amphibious Force Command Ship (4 ships, 7 awards, 1.7 average)

Ship	CR	MUC/NUC
Blue Ridge (LCC-19) 1 CR, 1 MUC, 1 NUC	27 Jun 72	MUC 30 Mar-15 Apr 75 NUC 29-30 Apr 75
Eldorado (AGC-11) 1 MUC, 1 NUC		MUC 8 Feb-30 Jul 67 NUC 12-25 Jan 69
Estes (AGC-12) 1 MUC		MUC 6-16 Jan 67
Mount McKinley (AGC-7) 1 MUC		MUC 30 Jul 67-21 Feb 68

Dock Landing Ship (18 ships, 27 awards, 1.5 average per ship)

Ship	CR	MUC/NUC
Alamo (LSD-33) 1 CR, 2 MUC	26 Mar- 7 Apr 66	MUC 29-31 Jul 66 MUC 15 Nov 67-22 May 68
Anchorage (LSD-36) 1 CR, 1 MUC	24 May 72	MUC 22-30 Apr 75
Belle Grove (LSD-2)		

294   Appendix A

Ship	CR	MUC/NUC
Cabildo (LSD-16) 1 CR	28 Feb-11 Mar 67	
Carter Hall (LSD-3) 1 CR	13 Dec 66	
Catamount (LSD-17) 1 NUC		NUC 12-24 Jan 69
Colonial (LSD-18) 1 MUC		MUC 31 Aug-20 Sep 69
Comstock (LSD-19) 1 MUC		MUC 15 Nov 67-22 May 68
Epping Forest (LSD-4)		
Fort Marion (LSD-22) 1 MUC, 1 NUC		MUC 15 Nov 67-22 May 68 NUC 5-20 May 69
Gunston Hall (LSD-5) 1 MUC		MUC 20 Aug 69-5 Mar 70
Hermitage (LSD-34) 1 CR, 1 MUC	6 Jul 67	MUC 26 May-29 Nov 67
Monticello (LSD-35) 2 CR, 2 MUC, 1 NUC	3 Jul 67 6 Jul 67	MUC 18 Jun-4 Aug 67 MUC 1 Oct 72-15 Apr 73 NUC 12 Jan-9 Feb 69
Oak Hill (LSD-7)		
Point Defiance (LSD-31) 2 CR	18 Apr 67 27 Jun 72	
Thomaston (LSD-28) 2 MUC, 1 NUC		MUC 29 Jul-6 Mar 67 MUC 12 May 75 NUC 29-30 Apr 75
Tortuga (LSD-26) 1 NUC		NUC 5-20 May 69
Whetstone (LSD-27) 1 MUC		MUC 1 Jun-20 Sep 69

Amphibious Cargo Ship (12 ships, 14 awards, 1.2 average per ship)

Ship	CR	MUC/NUC
Charleston (LKA-113)		
Durham (LKA-114) 2 MUC		MUC 30 Mar-15 Apr 75 MUC 22-30 Apr 75
Mathews (AKA-96)		
Merrick (AKA-97) 1 CR	28 Feb-11 Mar 67	
Mobile (LKA-115) 1 CR, 1 MUC, 1 NUC	27 Jun 72	MUC 1-7 May 75 NUC 29-30 Apr 75
Seminole (AKA-104) 1 CR, 1 NUC	18 May 67	NUC 12 Jan-9 Feb 69
Skagit (AKA-105)		
St. Louis (LKA-116) 1 CR	24 May 72	
Tulare (AKA-112) 1 MUC, 1 NUC		MUC 16 Nov-18 Dec 67 NUC 19 Dec 67-29 Jan 68
Union (AKA-106)		
Washburn (AKA-108) 1 MUC		MUC 1 Jun-20 Sep 69
Winston (AKA-94/LKA-94) 2 NUC		NUC 12-24 Jan 69 NUC 5-20 May 69

Attack Transport (15 ships, 8 awards, 0.5 average per ship)

Ship	CR	MUC/NUC
Bayfield (APA-33) 2 CR	28 Feb-11 Mar 67 18 May 67	
Bexar (APA-237) 1 NUC		NUC 9 May-25 Jul 68

Calvert (APA-32)		
Cavalier (APA-37)		
George Clymer (APA-27)		
Henrico (APA-45) 1 MUC		MUC 6-16 Jan 67
Lenawee (APA-195)		
Magoffin (APA-199)		
Montrose (APA-212) 1 CR	25 May 67	
Navarro (APA-215) 1 MUC		MUC 1 Jan 67-23 Mar 68
Okanogan (APA-220)		
Paul Revere (APA-248) 1 MUC		MUC 7 Aug-11 Nov 67
Pickaway (APA-222) 1 MUC		MUC 29-31 Jul 66
Renville (APA-227)		
Talladega (APA-208)		

Source: Master List of Unit Awards and Campaign Medals, OPNAVNOTE 1650 N09B1 of 9 March 2001

Appendix B: Royal Australian Navy CDT 3 Unit Awards

By virtue of the authority vested in me as President of the United States and as Commander-in-Chief of the Armed Forces of the United States, I have today awarded

THE PRESIDENTIAL UNIT CITATION (NAVY)

FOR EXTRAORDINARY HEROISM TO

COMMANDER TASK GROUP 194.0
(Units Participating in Operation SEA LORDS)

For extraordinary heroism and outstanding performance of duty from 18 October to 5 December 1968 while engaged in armed conflict against enemy forces in the Republic of Vietnam. Commander Task Group 194.0 initiated and prosecuted the first of several interdiction campaigns to sever enemy lines of communication and resupply and to establish the legal government in areas previously held by the enemy. The naval units engaged in Operation SEA LORDS consistently displayed the striking power and professionalism which were to mark this and following campaigns. Tasked with routing a myriad of enemy forces from their previous sanctuaries, personnel of Commander Task Group 194.0 ventured courageously into little-known canals and back-water areas, fighting valiantly through countless intense enemy rocket and automatic weapons attacks. The naval units, through their persistent and aggressive strikes against enemy strongholds, were eminently successful in their campaign to interdict enemy resupply routes and base areas throughout the lower Mekong Delta region. The courage, professionalism, and dedication displayed by the officers and men of Commander Task Group 194.0 reflected credit upon themselves and were in keeping with the highest traditions of the United States Naval Service.

Richard Nixon

THE SECRETARY OF THE NAVY
WASHINGTON

The Secretary of the Navy takes pleasure in presenting the MERITORIOUS UNIT COMMENDATION to

ROYAL AUSTRALIAN NAVY CLEARANCE DIVING TEAM THREE

for service as set forth in the following

CITATION:

For meritorious achievement while conducting defense and surveillance operations in the harbors of Vung Tau, Cam Ranh Bay, Qui Nhon, and Nha Trang, in the Republic of Vietnam during the period 19 February through 30 June 1967. As a part of the Inshore Undersea Warfare Group ONE, Western Pacific Detachment, the Royal Australian Navy Clearance Diving Team THREE displayed well-coordinated effort and exemplary performance of duty during the planning and establishment phase of the counterinsurgency operations. Although operating in an environment where the United States Navy had virtually no past experience, detachment personnel were instrumental in denying enemy forces freedom of movement within assigned harbors. Harbor Defense units detected, boarded, and searched large numbers of suspect junks and craft, contributing significantly to the curtailment of acts of sabotage and the flow of enemy supplies. Through their initiative, versatility, reliability, and professional competence, the officers and men of the Royal Australian Navy Clearance Diving Team THREE reflected great credit upon themselves and the Royal Australian Navy, and upheld the highest traditions of the naval service.

Paul R. Ignatius

Secretary of the Navy

THE SECRETARY OF THE NAVY
WASHINGTON

The Secretary of the Navy takes pleasure in presenting the NAVY UNIT COMMENDATION to

UNITED STATES NAVY COASTAL SURVEILLANCE FORCE
(TASK FORCE 115)

for service set forth in the following

CITATION:

For exceptionally meritorious service from 1 January 1967 to 31 March 1968 in connection with the interdiction of enemy forces and supplies into the Republic of Vietnam. Maintaining a close vigil over 1,200 miles of coastline and more than 50,000 licensed watercraft, United States Navy Coastal Surveillance Force (Task Force 115) created one of the most effective coastal barriers in naval history. Although constantly subjected to enemy fire, the task force successfully fulfilled its missions in support of the counterinsurgency effort in Vietnam. Nine large-scaled enemy attempts to infiltrate arms, ammunition, and supplies were interdicted and defeated by Task Force 115 and vast quantities of insurgent war materials were destroyed or captured. In addition to conducting almost daily naval gunfire support missions which inflicted extensive damage and destruction upon the enemy, task force units completed over seventy search and rescue missions; carried out hundreds of psychological missions and medical civic action programs; and medically evacuated numerous injured or wounded civilian and military personnel. One particularly significant mission undertaken by Task Force 115 was the training of Vietnamese Navy personnel, which resulted in greatly improved morale and professional abilities within the Vietnamese Navy. The task force also developed a multifaceted operation, without precedent in modern naval annals, to counter enemy insurgency. The outstanding professionalism, courage, and dedication displayed by the officers and men of the Coastal Surveillance Force reflected great credit upon themselves and were in keeping with the highest traditions of the United States Naval Service.

John H. Chafee
Secretary of the Navy

Note: Units eligible include: 115.9.1 Harbor Defense Unit Vung Tau

THE SECRETARY OF THE NAVY
WASHINGTON, D.C. 20350

The Secretary of the Navy takes pleasure in presenting the NAVY UNIT COMMENDATION to

EXPLOSIVE ORDNANCE DISPOSAL MOBILE UNIT, PACIFIC

for service as set forth in the following

CITATION:

For exceptionally meritorious service from 1 January 1968 to 31 December 1970 in providing explosive ordnance disposal support to United States and other Free World Military Assistance Forces engaged in armed conflict against enemy forces in the Republic of Vietnam. During this period, Explosive Ordnance Disposal Mobile Unit, Pacific (EODMUPAC) provided explosive ordnance disposal support for more than two hundred combat operations. In addition to locating and rendering safe anti-personnel mines and booby traps under strange environmental conditions and often in the face of hostile fire, EODMUPAC teams conducted daily underwater searches of military and merchant ships in many of the deep water ports throughout the Republic of Vietnam. The teams successfully located, rendered safe, and removed sapper-placed water mines from six merchant ships and two units of the mobile riverine bases; rendered safe and removed eight command or time-delay mines from bridges and twenty-eight mines, including ten floating contact mines, from various harbors and waterways; successfully removed armed rounds which had penetrated the hulls of ships or riverine force boats without exploding; and cleared, or assisted in the clearance of sixteen ammunition dumps that had been hit by incoming rounds or otherwise damaged by fire. Although not a part of their primary mission, EODMUPAC teams destroyed several thousand enemy bunkers and numerous arms or supply caches. By their exceptional level of professional competence, disregard for personal safety, and unswerving devotion to duty, the officers and men of Explosive Ordnance Disposal Mobile Unit, Pacific upheld the highest traditions of the United States Naval Service.

J. William Middendorf
Secretary of the Navy

THE SECRETARY OF THE NAVY
WASHINGTON, D. C. 20350

The Secretary of the Navy takes pleasure in presenting the NAVY UNIT COMMENDATION to

COMMANDER TASK FORCE 115.9/INSHORE UNDERSEA WARFARE GROUP ONE, WESTERN PACIFIC DETACHMENT

for service as set forth in the following

CITATION:

For exceptionally meritorious service while carrying out its mission of protecting all friendly shipping in the harbors of Vung Tau, Cam Ranh Bay, Nha Trang, and Qui Nhon in the Republic of Vietnam against swimmer/sapper mining attempts, interdiction of enemy supply routes, and disruption of black-market operations during the period 1 June 1969 to 25 November 1970. While operating as a part of Coastal Surveillance Force, personnel of Task Force 115.9/Inshore Undersea Warfare Group ONE, Western Pacific Detachment displayed an exemplary coordinated effort during the planning and training phases of the turning over to the Vietnamese Navy the assets and responsibilities of Harbor Defense. This was accomplished while enemy forces were continuously denied freedom of movement within assigned harbors. Large numbers of suspected junks and craft were boarded and searched which contributed significantly toward curtailing acts of sabotage and the flow of enemy supplies. The initiative, versatility, reliability, and professional competence displayed by the officers and men of Task Force 115.9/Inshore Undersea Warfare Group ONE, Western Pacific Detachment during this period were in keeping with the highest traditions of the United States Naval Service.

William Middendorf
Secretary of the Navy

Note: Units eligible include: Royal Australian Navy Clearance Diving Team 3 assigned to Unit ONE, Vung Tau

Appendix C: Navy Unit Citation for Mobile Support Base LSTs

The Secretary of the Navy takes pleasure in commending

USS *GARRETT COUNTY* (LST-786), USS *HARNETT COUNTY* (LST-821), USS *HUNTERDON COUNTY* (LST-838) AND USS *JENNINGS COUNTY* (LST-846)

for service as set forth in the following

CITATION:
For exceptionally meritorious service from 10 November 1966 to 30 January 1968 and from 1 March 1968 to 30 September 1968 in connection with operations against enemy aggressor forces in Southeast Asia. Participating as a unit of Commander Task Force 116 (Operation Game Warden), Task Unit 76.8.3 served as a mobile support base for river patrol boats (PBR's) and UH-1B (Seawolf) helicopter gunships in support of friendly forces ashore along the rivers of the Mekong Delta in the Republic of Vietnam. The four ships comprising Task Unit 76.8.3 have spent in excess of 1,800 ship days on station, conducted more than 11,000 helicopter launches and landings (all accident free), originated nearly 6,400 PBR patrols, fired 475 gunfire support missions, coordinated 2,300 PBR/helicopter operations, and expended over 12,000,000 rounds of various types of ammunition. Additionally, Task Unit 76.8.3 pursued a vigorous civic action program, providing tangible benefits to the Vietnamese people such as medical assistance and clothing, and thereby enhancing United States efforts in Southeast Asia. The professionalism, initiative, and dedication displayed by the officers and men of Task Unit 76.8.3 reflect great credit upon themselves and the United States Naval Service.

All personnel attached to and serving with Task Unit 76.8.3 during the above-designated period, or any part thereof, are hereby authorized to wear the Navy Unit Commendation Ribbon.

John H. Chafee
Secretary of the Navy

Appendix D: Presidential Unit Citations Awarded LSTs

The President of the United States takes pleasure in presenting the
PRESIDENTIAL UNIT CITATION to
The United States Navy Element of the
MOBILE RIVERINE FORCE (TASK FORCE 117)

For exceptionally meritorious and heroic service from 29 January to 4 March 1968 while engaged in armed conflict against communist insurgent (Viet Cong) forces in the Republic of Vietnam. Throughout the Tet (Lunar New Year) Offensive, the Mobile Riverine Force (MRF) was locked in nearly continuous combat as the enemy lay siege to or threatened to attack every large population center and military installation in the Delta. During this hectic, 35-day campaign, the MRF played a vital role in driving the enemy out of My Tho and Vinh Long, the most severely ravaged of all the Delta cities, and in preventing enemy forces from launching sustained attacks on Can Tho, Binh Thuy, Sa Dec, Cai Be, Cai Lay, the Army Base at Dong Tam, and many other less-populated areas. In every battle, MRF personnel, both individually and collectively, although often matched against forces of much greater size than their own, displayed outstanding courage and professionalism in subduing the Viet Cong challenge. Navy crewmen embarked in Monitors, Command and Communication Boats, Assault Support Patrol Boats, and Armored Troop Carriers were frequently ambushed at point-blank range from concealed positions along both banks of the narrow, jungle-enshrouded Delta streams. In each instance, they succeeded in suppressing the enemy fire before maneuvering their assault craft out of ambush areas. Together, the MRF Army/Navy team successfully met the challenge posed by the Tet Offensive, probably saving the Delta from being overrun by insurgent forces. The gallantry, professionalism, courage under fire, and devotion to duty displayed by the officers and men of the United States Navy Element of the Mobile Riverine Force were in keeping with the highest traditions of the United States Naval Service.

Richard Nixon

The President of the United States takes pleasure in presenting the
PRESIDENTIAL UNIT CITATION to the
I CORPS RIVER PATROL GROUP

For extraordinary heroism in action from 31 January to 29 February 1968 while conducting river patrols and convoy escorts on the Perfume River (Song Huong) between Hue and Tan My, Republic of Vietnam. During a major enemy attack on the city of Hue, River Patrol Boats (PBRs) of the I Corps River Patrol Group provided suppressive fire against large enemy forces on both banks of the river to permit helicopters to conduct urgent medical evacuation and ammunition resupply missions. In the course of the battle for the city, the enemy made a major effort to cut the waterborne supply route from the sea to Hue. Enemy ambushes, launched from entrenched positions on the river banks, brought the convoys, which were escorted by PBRs, under intense fire from automatic weapons, recoilless rifles, mortars, and rocket-propelled grenades. Despite lack of armor and restricted maneuvering room, personnel of the I Corps River Patrol Group courageously maneuvered their units between the enemy fire and the supply craft to provide suppressive fire and to draw the enemy fire away from vital suppliers. Each day, crewmen of the Patrol Group performed their dangerous tasks with the full knowledge that they would be heavily engaged by the enemy at certain locations along the banks, and subjected to sniper fire at any point along their route. Through their superior dedication and motivation and indomitable courage displayed by the officers and men of the I Corps River Patrol Group in the face of a determined enemy campaign to cut the supply route to Hue, were in keeping with the highest traditions of the United States Naval Service.

Richard Nixon

By virtue of the authority vested in me as President of the United States and as Commander-in-Chief of the Armed Forces of the United States, I have today awarded

THE PRESIDENTIAL UNIT CITATION (NAVY)

FOR EXTRAORDINARY HEROISM TO

COMMANDER TASK GROUP 194.0
(Units Participating in Operation SEA LORDS)

For extraordinary heroism and outstanding performance of duty from 18 October to 5 December 1968 while engaged in armed conflict against enemy forces in the Republic of Vietnam, Commander Task Group 194.0 initiated and prosecuted the first of several interdiction campaigns to sever enemy lines of communication and resupply and to establish the legal government in areas previously held by the enemy. The naval units engaged in Operation SEA LORDS consistently displayed the striking power and professionalism which were to mark this and following campaigns. Tasked with routing a myriad of enemy forces from their previous sanctuaries, personnel of Commander Task Group 194.0 ventured courageously into little-known canals and back-water areas, fighting valiantly through countless intense enemy rocket and automatic weapons attacks. The naval units, through their persistent and aggressive strikes against enemy strongholds, were eminently successful in their campaign to interdict enemy resupply routes and base areas throughout the lower Mekong Delta region. The courage, professionalism, and dedication displayed by the officers and men of Commander Task Group 194.0 reflected credit upon themselves and were in keeping with the highest traditions of the United States Naval Service.

Richard Nixon

By virtue of the authority vested in me as President of the United States and as Commander-in-Chief of the Armed Forces of the United States, I have today awarded

THE PRESIDENTIAL UNIT CITATION (NAVY)

FOR EXTRAORDINARY HEROISM TO

COMMANDER TASK GROUP 194.9
(Units Participating in Operation GIANT SLINGSHOT)

For extraordinary heroism and outstanding performance of duty from 6 December 1968 to 31 March 1969 while engaged in armed conflict against enemy forces in the Republic of Vietnam. Commander Task Group 194.9 initiated and prosecuted a determined interdiction offensive against the ingress of enemy personnel and war material from Southeast Cambodia into the upper Mekong Delta region of the Republic of Vietnam. The naval units engaged in Operation GIANT SLINGSHOT, including the Riverine Warfare and River Patrol Forces who supplied support, consistently distinguished themselves by their countless deeds of valiant service while carrying out patrols along the narrow, enemy-infested Vam Co, Vam Co Dong, and Vam Co Tay rivers. Operating with limited logistic support under austere and dangerous conditions, personnel of Commander Task Group 194.9 countered intense rocket and automatic weapons barrages at point-blank range with unshakable determination. As a result of their intrepidity and resolution, the enemy threat was significantly diminished and vital routes of resupply were severed. The quantity of captured enemy war material reached staggering proportions, and the ever-increasing number of enemy casualties attested to the effectiveness of ingeniously developed individual and group offensive tactics. The selfless dedication and inspiring professional performance of the officers and men of Commander Task Group 194.9 reflected credit upon themselves and were in keeping with the highest traditions of the United States Naval Service.

Richard Nixon

By virtue of the authority vested in me as President of the United States and as Commander-in-Chief of the Armed Forces of the United States, I have today awarded

THE PRESIDENTIAL UNIT CITATION (NAVY)

FOR EXTRAORDINARY HEROISM TO

USS HARNETT COUNTY (LST-821)

USS HARNETT COUNTY distinguished herself by extraordinary heroism in actions against hostile forces in the Republic of Vietnam during the period 12 December 1968 to 30 April 1969. Although landlocked and immobile some twenty-five miles from the sea, and consequently a lucrative target for a resourceful and determined enemy, USS HARNETT COUNTY nonetheless succeeded in providing excellent secondary support to the combat units of the riverine forces involved in one of the most successful river campaigns of the conflict. The ship's performance was superb in every phase of her diverse actions. Supporting both United States and Vietnamese naval units, HARNETT COUNTY provided tactical and naval operations centers that were models of efficiency and materially aided the entire operation of the Vam Co Dong River portion of Operation GIANT SLINGSHOT. Included among the many services which HARNETT COUNTY rendered were those in connection with communications, supply, repair, security, fueling and rearming for helicopter gunships, medical evacuation station, and harassment and interdiction fire. Through her invaluable support efforts, HARNETT COUNTY contributed materially to the success of riverine forces in accounting for numerous enemy casualties and the capture of vital guns and equipment. Despite long dangerous hours, difficult heavy labor under the most trying conditions, night sessions at battle stations while awaiting enemy attack, fierce enemy rocket barrages, personnel and material casualties, and the ever-present danger of mines, the morale and esprit de corps of her officers and men never faltered. Their extraordinary performance and selfless dedication throughout this period were in keeping with the highest traditions of the United States Naval Service.

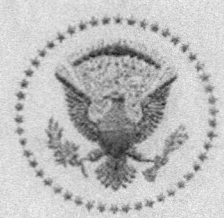

By virtue of the authority vested in me as President of the United States and as Commander-in-Chief of the Armed Forces of the United States, I have today awarded

THE PRESIDENTIAL UNIT CITATION (NAVY)

FOR EXTRAORDINARY HEROISM TO

TASK FORCE 115
(Units Participating in Operation SWIFT RAIDER)

For extraordinary heroism and outstanding performance of duty during operations against enemy forces in the Republic of Vietnam from 6 December 1968 to 31 March 1969. Conducting devastating raids into enemy strongholds and sanctuaries located in and about river mouths, inlets, coves and canals of coastal South Vietnam, men of SWIFT RAIDER forces were highly successful in harassing and severing enemy lines of supply and communications. The lightning attacks carried out by SWIFT RAIDER units confronted hostile forces in the most serious challenge for control of IV Corps and the Cua Dai River in the history of the Vietnamese conflict. Time and again, friendly patrol craft on swift and daring raids penetrated enemy strongholds in the face of concentrated hostile fire to inflict extensive personnel and material casualties. Enemy vessels were intercepted and destroyed, thus denying him freedom of waterways he formerly controlled. By their outstanding courage, professionalism, and inspiring dedication throughout this period, the officers and men of the units of Task Force 115 participating in Operation SWIFT RAIDER reflected great credit upon themselves and upheld the highest traditions of the United States Naval Service.

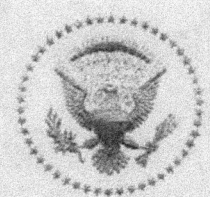

By virtue of the authority vested in me as President of the United States and as Commander-in-Chief of the Armed Forces of the United States, I have today awarded

THE PRESIDENTIAL UNIT CITATION (NAVY)

FOR EXTRAORDINARY HEROISM TO

The United States Navy Element of the
MOBILE RIVERINE FORCE (TASK FORCE 117)

For extraordinary heroism and outstanding performance of duty from 25 January through 5 July 1969 while engaged in armed conflict against enemy forces in the Mekong Delta region of the Republic of Vietnam. With enemy forces planning to launch a large-scale, winter-spring offensive against Saigon and other cities of the upper Mekong Delta, the ships and assault craft of Task Force 117 provided waterborne mobile support to United States Army, Vietnamese Army, and Vietnamese Marine Corps troops. By riverine assault operations preempting enemy offensive operations, the Force made a significant contribution to thwarting the threat to Saigon and the Mekong Delta. Surprise attacks and routine fire fights on the narrow streams and canals were an almost daily occurrence, while rocket and mining attacks against the Mobile Riverine Bases were an ever-present danger. The courage and determination of Task Force 117 personnel contributed significantly to the successful completion of each Force objective. The skill, fortitude, perseverance, and sustained outstanding performance of the officers and men of the United States Navy element of the Mobile Riverine Force reflected great credit upon themselves and were in keeping with the highest traditions of the United States Naval Service.

Richard Nixon

Appendix E: BM1 James E. Williams Medal of Honor Citation

The President of the United States of America, in the name of Congress, takes pleasure in presenting the Medal of Honor to Boatswain's Mate First Class James Elliott Williams, United States Navy, for conspicuous gallantry and intrepidity at the risk of his life above and beyond the call of duty in action on the Mekong River, Republic of Vietnam, 31 October 1966. Petty Officer First Class Williams was serving as Boat Captain and Patrol Officer aboard River Patrol Boat (PBR) 105, River Section 531, My Tho Detachment, accompanied by another patrol boat when the patrol was suddenly taken under fire by two enemy sampans. Petty Officer First Class Williams immediately ordered the fire returned, killing the crew of one enemy boat and causing the other sampan to take refuge in a nearby river inlet. Pursuing the fleeing sampan, the U.S. patrol encountered a heavy volume of small arms fire from enemy forces, at close range, occupying well-concealed positions along the river bank. Maneuvering through this fire, the patrol confronted a numerically superior enemy force aboard two enemy junks and eight sampans augmented by heavy automatic weapons fire from ashore. In the savage battle that ensued, Petty Officer First Class Williams, with utter disregard for his safety exposed himself to the withering hail of enemy fire to direct counter-fire and inspire the actions of his patrol. Recognizing the overwhelming strength of the enemy force, Petty Officer First Class Williams deployed his patrol to await the arrival of armed helicopters In the course of his movement his discovered an even larger concentration of enemy boats. Not waiting for the arrival of the armed helicopters, he displayed great initiative and boldly led the patrol through the intense enemy fire and damaged or destroyed 50 enemy sampans and seven junks. This phase of the action completed, and with the arrival of the armed helicopters, Petty Officer First Class Williams directed the attack on the remaining enemy force. Now virtually dark, and although Petty Officer First Class Williams was aware that his boats would become even better targets, he ordered the patrol boats' search lights turned on to better illuminate the area and moved the patrol perilously close to shore to press the attack. Despite a waning supply of ammunition the patrol successfully engaged the enemy ashore and completed the rout of the enemy force. Under the leadership of Petty Officer First Class Williams, who demonstrated unusual professional skill and indomitable courage throughout the three hour battle, the patrol accounted for the destruction or loss of 65 enemy boats and inflicted numerous casualties on the enemy personnel. His extraordinary heroism and exemplary fighting spirit in the face of grave risks inspired the efforts of his men to defeat a larger enemy force, and are in keeping with the finest traditions of the U.S. Naval Service.

Appendix F: Commander, Naval Forces Vietnam Letter to CDT 3

DEPARTMENT OF THE NAVY
U S NAVAL FORCES, VIETNAM
FPO SAN FRANCISCO 96626

FF5-16/00:sn
1650
Ser

1 JUL 1970

From: Commander U. S. Naval Forces, Vietnam
To: Lieutenant R. S. BLUE, RAN, Officer in Charge Explosive Ordnance Disposal Mobile Unit Pacific Team THIRTY FIVE
Via: Major General C. B. FRAZIER, CBE, Commander Australian Forces, Republic of Vietnam

Subj: Letter of appreciation

1. I desire to express my sincere appreciation for the exceptionally alert and professional response which you and your men, Petty Officer (Clearance Disposal) J. KERSHLER and Able-Bodied Seaman (Clearance Disposal) G. KINGSTON, displayed in the early morning hours of 28 June 1970 in removing an enemy water mine from USS MEEKER COUNTY, at Vung Tau, Republic of Vietnam. Although sufficient time had elapsed for the mine to detonate, you and your men unhesitatingly dived and successfully removed the mine with full knowledge of the risks involved.

2. The actions of Royal Australian Navy Clearance Diving Team THREE in this emergency situation bear testimony to outstanding professionalism and courage of the highest order. Well done!

J. H. KING, JR.

Copy to:
Chief of Naval Staff
Australian Commonwealth Naval Board
Canberra, C.T.
Commander Amphibious Force, U. S. SEVENTH Fleet
Commanding Officer, USS MEEKER COUNTY (LST 980)

Appendix G: VNN Ships that Escaped to the Philippines

Hull#	Ship Name/Formerly	Hull#	Ship Name/Formerly
HQ-01	RVNS *Tran Hung Dao*/ USS *Camp* (DE-251)	HQ-330	RVNS *Loi Cong*/ USS *LSI(L)-699*
HQ-02	RVNS *Tran Quang Khai*/ USCGC *Bering Strait* (WAVP-382)	HQ-400	RVNS *Hat Giang*/ USS *LSM-335*
HQ-03	RVNS *Tran Nhat Duat*/ USCGC *Yakutat* (WAVP-380)	HQ-401	RVNS *Han Giang*/ USS *LSM-110*
HQ-05	RVNS *Tran Binh Trong*/ USS *Castle Rock* (AVP-35)	HQ-404	RVNS *Huong Giang*/ USS *Oceanside* (LSM-175)
HQ-06	RVNS *Tran Quoc Toan*/ USCGC *Cook Inlet* (WAVP-384)	HQ-470	RVNS *HQ-470*/ USS *YOG-80*
HQ-07	RVNS *Dong Da II*/ USS *Crestview* (PCE-895)	HQ-471	RVNS *HQ-471*/ USS *YOG-33*
HQ-08	RVNS *Chi Lang II*/ USS *Gayety* (AM-239)	HQ-474	RVNS *HQ-474*/ USS *YOG-131*
HQ-11	RVNS *Chi Linh*/ USS *Shelter* (AM-301)	HQ-500	RVNS *Cam Ranh*/ USS *Marion County* (LST-975)
HQ-12	RVNS *Ngoc Hoi*/USS *Brattleboro* (PCE(R)-852)	HQ-502	RVNS *Thi Nai*/ USS *Cayuga County* (LST-529)
HQ-14	RVNS *Van Kiep II*/USS *Amherst* (PCE(R)-853)	HQ-505	RVNS *Nha Trang*/ USS *Jerome County* (LST-848)
HQ-16	RVNS *Ly Thoung Kiet*/ USCGC *Chincoteague* (WAVP-375)	HQ-618	RVNS *Hon Troc*/ USS *PGM-83*
HQ-17	RVNS *Ngo Quyen*/ USCGC *McCulloch* (WAVP-386)	HQ-702	RVNS *Huynh Van Duc*/ USCGC *Point Clear* (WPB-82315)
HQ-228	RVNS *Doan Ngoc Tang*/ USS *LSSL-9*	HQ-800	RVNS *Huynh Van Cu*/ USS *Harnett County* (LST-821)
HQ-229	RVNS *Lu Phu Tho*/ USS *LSSL-101*	HQ-801	RVNS *Can Tho*/ USS *Garrett County* (LST-786)
HQ-230	RVNS *Nguyen Ngoc Long*/ USS *LSSL-96*	HQ-802	RVNS *Vinh Long*/ USS *Satyr* (ARL-23)
HQ-231	RVNS *Nguyen Duc Bong*/ USS *LSSL-129*		Fishing Trawler #1
HQ-329	RVNS *Thien Kich*/ USS *LSI(L)-872*		Fishing Trawler #2[2]

Bibliography/Chapter Notes

Bosiljevac, Timothy L. Thesis: *The Teams in 'Nam: U.S. Navy UDT/SEAL Operations of the Vietnam War*. Emporia, Ks: Emporia State University, 1987.

Bruhn, David D. *Eyes of the Fleet: The U.S. Navy's Seaplane Tenders and Patrol Aircraft in World War II*. Berwyn Heights, Md: Heritage Books, 2016.

—*MacArthur and Halsey's "Pacific Island Hoppers": The Forgotten Fleet of World War II*. Berwyn Heights, Md: Heritage Books, 2014.

—*On the Gunline: U.S. Navy and Royal Australian Navy Warships off Vietnam, 1965-1973*. Berwyn Heights, Md: Heritage Books, 2019.

—*Wooden Ships and Iron Men: The U.S. Navy's Coastal and Inshore Minesweepers, and the Minecraft That Served in Vietnam, 1953-1976*. Westminster, Md: Heritage Books, 2011.

Cloninger Jr., James M. Thesis: *Analysis of Communist Vietnamese Special Operations Forces during the Vietnam War and the Lessons that can be applied to Current and Future U.S. Military Operations*. Monterey, Ca: Naval Postgraduate School, 2005.

Couhat, Jean Labayle. *Combat Fleets of the World 1976/77*. Annapolis, Md: Naval Institute, 1976.

Cutler, Thomas J. *Brown Water, Black Berets*. Annapolis, Md: Naval Institute, 1988.

Dunham, George R., David A. Quinlan, *U.S. Marines in Vietnam: The Bitter End, 1973-1975*. Washington, DC: History and Museums Division, Headquarters, U.S. Marine Corps, 2009.

Goldman, David, Erin Mahan, Edward C. Keefer. *Foreign Relations of the United States, 1969-1976, Vol. VII Vietnam July 1970-January 1972*. Washington, DC: U.S. Department of State, 2010.

Marolda, Edward J. *By Sea, Air, and Land: An Illustrated History of the U.S. Navy and the War in Southeast Asia*. Washington, DC: Naval Historical Center, 1994.

—*The Approaching Storm: Conflict in Asia, 1945-1965*. Washington, DC: Naval History and Heritage Command, 2009

Marolda, Edward J., R. Blake Dunnavent. *Combat at Close Quarters Warfare on the Rivers and Canals of Vietnam*. Washington, DC: Naval History and Heritage Command, 2015.

McAulay, Lex. *In the Ocean's Dark Embrace: Royal Australian Navy Clearance Diving Team 3 (USN EODMUPAC Team 21 & 35) Vietnam 1967-71*. Maryborough, Australia: Banner Books, 1997.

Mooney, James L. *Dictionary of American Naval Fighting Ships, Vol. VII*. Washington, DC: Office of the Chief of Naval Operations, 1981.

Shulimson, Jack. *U.S. Marines in Vietnam: An Expanding War 1966*. Washington, DC: History and Museums Division, Headquarters, U.S. Marine Corps, 1982.

Shulimson, Jack, Leonard A. Blasiol, Charles R. Smith, David A. Dawson,

U.S. Marines in Vietnam: The Defining Year 1968. Washington, DC: History and Museums Division, Headquarters U.S. Marine Corps, 1997.

Shulimson, Jack, Charles M. Johnson. *U.S. Marines in Vietnam: The Landing and the Buildup 1965*. Washington, DC: History and Museum Division, Headquarters, U.S. Marine Corps, 1978.

Smith, Charles R. *U.S. Marines in Vietnam, High Mobility and Standdown 1969*. Washington DC: History and Museums Division, Headquarters, U.S. Marine Corps, 1988.

Stillwell, Paul. *Battleship New Jersey: An Illustrated History*. Annapolis, Md: Naval Institute, 1986.

Telfer, Gary L., Lane Rogers, Keith Fleming Jr., *Marines in Vietnam: Fighting the North Vietnamese 1967*. Washington, DC: History and Museum Division, Headquarters, U.S. Marine Corps, 1984.

Turner, Mike, Hector Donohue, *Australian Minesweepers at War*. Canberra, Australia: Sea Power Centre – Australia, 2018.

Watkins, G. C., E. R. Jahn. *Countering the Swimmer/Sapper*. San Francisco, Ca: Commander US Naval Forces, Vietnam, Operations Analysis Branch, 1970

Wetterhahn, Ralph, *The Last Battle: The Mayaguez Incident and the end of the Vietnam War*. New York: Carroll and Graf Publishers, 2001.

PREFACE NOTES:

[1] "Commander, Amphibious Squadron 3" (https://www.public.navy.mil/surfor/cpr3/Pages/ourShip.aspx: accessed 10 May 2019).

[2] "Amphibious Landings in South Vietnam" (https://www.globalsecurity.org/military/ops/vietnam2-amphibious.htm: accessed 20 December 2018).

[3] USS *Valley Forge* (LPH-8) Western Pacific 1965-1966 cruise book.

[4] "Amphibious Landings in South Vietnam."

[5] Ibid.

[6] Ibid.

[7] Was Jesse Ventura a SEAL or a UDT guy? "SEALs certainly are different. We don't wear skivvies" by Bill Salisbury, *The San Diego Reader*, December 2, 1999.

[8] "Amphibious Landings in South Vietnam."

[9] "USS *Perch*: SOF Submarine" by Dwight Jon Zimmerman (https://www.defensemedianetwork.com/stories/uss-perch-sof-submarine/3/: accessed 21 December 2018).

[10] G. C. Watkins and E. R. Jahn, "Countering the Swimmer/Sapper" (San Francisco, CA: Commander US Naval Forces, Vietnam, Operations Analysis Branch, 1970), 5.

[11] "Official History of Clearance Diving Team 3 Vietnam" (http://www.gunplot.net/main/content/offical-history-clearance-diving-team-3-vietnam: accessed 15 March 2019).

[12] "Official History of Clearance Diving Team 3 Vietnam;" "Histories for Inshore Undersea Warfare Group One, Units 1-5"

(https://navy.togetherweserved.com/usn/servlet/tws.webapp.WebApp?cmd=PublicDisplayUnitInfo&type=UnitInfoExt&ID=575: accessed 15 March 2019).
[13] "Histories for Inshore Undersea Warfare Group One, Units 1-5."
[14] "Naval Operations in Vietnam" by Jozef Straczek (http://www.navy.gov.au/history/feature-histories/naval-operations-vietnam: accessed 15 March 2019).
[15] "CDT Vietnam 69-70 Brown Water War" by J. H. Farrell, *Australian & NZ Defender* (https://web.archive.org/web/20030403051334/http://australiandefender.com.au/stories/cdtnam.pdf: accessed 16 March 2019).
[16] "Naval Operations in Vietnam" by Jozef Straczek.
[17] "Official History of Clearance Diving Team 3 Vietnam."
[18] Ibid.
[19] Ibid.
[20] Ibid.
[21] Ibid.
[22] Ibid.
[23] Ibid.
[24] "Official History of Clearance Diving Team 3 Vietnam;" "CDT Vietnam 69-70 Brown Water War" by J. H. Farrell.
[25] Ut supra.
[26] "Vietnam Service 1962-1973" (https://www.history.navy.mil/content/history/nhhc/browse-by-topic/heritage/banners/battle-streamers/vietnam-service.html: accessed 18 June 2019).

CHAPTER 1 NOTES:
[1] "NVA/VC Sappers" by W. W. Turnbow (https://www.academia.edu/28036224/NVA_VC_SAPPERS: accessed 27 December 2018).
[2] "USS *Westchester County*: Attacked During the Vietnam War" by Gene Frederickson, *Vietnam Magazine*, August 1998; *Westchester County*, *DANFS*.
[3] "USS *Westchester County*: Attacked During the Vietnam War."
[4] Ibid.
[5] Ibid.
[6] "Sapper Attack: The Elite North Vietnamese Units" by Arnold Blumberg, *Vietnam Magazine*, 1 February 2017.
[7] Ibid.
[8] Commander Naval Forces Vietnam Monthly Summary, December 1970.
[9] Ibid.
[10] James M. Cloninger Jr., Thesis: *Analysis of Communist Vietnamese Special Operations Forces during the Vietnam War and the Lessons that can be applied to Current and Future U.S. Military Operations*, June 2005 Naval Postgraduate School Monterey, California, 2005.
[11] Ibid.

[12] Ibid.
[13] "USS *Westchester County*: Attacked During the Vietnam War."
[14] Ibid.
[15] Ibid.
[16] Ibid.
[17] Ibid.
[18] Ibid.
[19] Ibid.
[20] Ibid.
[21] Ibid.
[22] Ibid.
[23] Ibid.
[24] Ibid.
[25] Ibid.
[26] "USS *Westchester County*: Attacked During the Vietnam War;" "History," USS *Westchester County* LST 1167 Association
(http://www.lst1167.com/history.htm: accessed 31 December 2018).
[27] "USS *Westchester County*: Attacked During the Vietnam War."
[28] Ibid.
[29] Ibid.
[30] "History," USS *Westchester County* LST 1167 Association.
[31] "USS *Westchester County* (LST-1167)"
(http://www.navsource.org/archives/10/16/161167.htm: accessed 1 November 2019).
[32] "USS *Westchester County*: Attacked During the Vietnam War."
[33] "USS *Westchester County* (LST-1167)"
(http://virtualwall.org/units/lst1167.htm: accessed 27 December 2018).

CHAPTER 2 NOTES:
[1] "History of The USS *Benewah* (APB-35)" by Albert Moore
(http://www.mrfa.org/us-navy/us-navy-mobile-riverine-force/benewah-apb-35/: accessed 5 January 2019).
[2] Ibid.
[3] Ibid.
[4] Ibid.
[5] Ibid.
[6] "High Speed Transport… Destroyers?" by Keith Patton
(https://thenavalist.com/home/2017/11/15/high-speed-transport-destroyers: accessed 4 January 2019).
[7] Ibid.
[8] *Krishna, DANFS*.
[9] *Askari, DANFS*.
[10] "Ship Reportedly Readied To Monitor Nicaragua" by Fred Hiatt, *The Washington Post*, 9 February 1985.

[11] "Operation Sandstone 1948" (http://nuclearweaponarchive.org/Usa/Tests/Sandston.html: accessed 25 December 2018).
[12] Ibid.
[13] "LPH-2 *Iwo Jima* class" (https://fas.org/man/dod-101/sys/ship/lph-2.htm: accessed 6 January 2019).
[14] Jean Labayle Couhat, *Combat Fleets of the World 1976/77* (Annapolis, Md: Naval Institute, 1976), 513.

CHAPTER 3 NOTES:
[1] David D. Bruhn, *Wooden Ships and Iron Men: The U.S. Navy's Coastal and Inshore Minesweepers, and the Minecraft That Served in Vietnam, 1953-1976* (Westminster, Md: Heritage Books, 2011), 111.
[2] Ibid, 111-112.
[3] Ibid, 112.
[4] Ibid, 112.
[5] Ibid, 112.
[6] Ibid, 113.
[7] Ibid, 113.
[8] Ibid, 113-114.
[9] Ibid. 114.
[10] Ibid, 114.
[11] Ibid, 122-123.
[12] Ibid, 123

CHAPTER 4 NOTES:
[1] Edward J. Marolda, *The Approaching Storm: Conflict in Asia, 1945-1965* (Washington, DC: Naval History and Heritage Command, 2009), 76.
[2] Edward Marolda, *By Sea, Air, and Land: An Illustrated History of the U.S. Navy and the War in Southeast Asia* (Washington, DC: Naval Historical Center, 1994), Chapter 3: The Years of Combat, 1965-1968; *Vancouver, DANFS*.
[3] Marolda, *By Sea, Air, and Land*, Chapter 3: The Years of Combat, 1965-1968.
[4] USS *Eldorado* (AGC-11) Western Pacific 1965-1966 cruise book
[5] "US Marines Land at Danang" (https://www.history.com/this-day-in-history/u-s-marines-land-at-da-nang); "Amphibious Landings in South Vietnam" (https://www.globalsecurity.org/military/ops/vietnam2-amphibious.htm: both accessed 20 December 2018).
[6] Marolda, *By Sea, Air, and Land*, Chapter 3: The Years of Combat, 1965-1968.
[7] "In Danang, Where U.S. Troops First Landed, Memories Of War Have Faded" (https://www.npr.org/sections/parallels/2015/05/02/403597845/in-Danang-where-u-s-troops-first-landed-memories-of-war-have-faded: accessed 17 December 2018).

CHAPTER 5 NOTES:

[1] Jack Shulimson and Charles M. Johnson, *U.S. Marines in Vietnam: The Landing and the Buildup 1965* (Washington, DC: History and Museum Division, Headquarters U.S. Marine Corps, 1978), 193-194.
[2] Ibid, 194.
[3] Ibid.
[4] "Operation Starlite" (https://www.marines.mil/Community-Relations/Commemorations/Operation-Starlite/: accessed 22 December 2018).
[5] "Ben Palermo remembers Vietnam, Operation Starlite 50 years after" (https://www.marines.mil/News/News-Display/Article/614176/ben-palermo-remembers-vietnam-operation-starlite-50-years-after/: accessed 22 December 2018).
[6] "Operation Starlite."
[7] Ibid.
[8] *Vernon County*, DANFS.
[9] *Vernon County*, DANFS; "Operation Starlite."
[10] *Vernon County*, DANFS.
[11] Shulimson and Johnson, *U.S. Marines in Vietnam: The Landing and the Buildup 1965*, 196.
[12] Ibid.
[13] Ibid.
[14] Ibid.
[15] Ibid, 197.
[16] Ibid.
[17] Ibid.
[18] Ibid, 197-198.
[19] Ibid, 198.
[20] Ibid, 198-200.
[21] Ibid, 200.
[22] "September 30th Movement" (https://www.britannica.com/event/September-30th-Movement: accessed 23 December 2018).
[23] Shulimson and Johnson, *U.S. Marines in Vietnam: The Landing and the Buildup 1965*, 200.
[24] Ibid, 200-201.
[25] Ibid, 201.
[26] Ibid.
[27] Ibid.
[28] Ibid, 202.
[29] Ibid.
[30] Ibid.
[31] Ibid, 202-203.
[32] Bosiljevac Thesis, *The Teams in 'Nam: U.S. Navy UDT/SEAL Operations of the Vietnam War*, 21 December 1987.
[33] Ibid.

[34] Ibid.
[35] "Harvest Moon" by Frank Beardsley (https://www.mca-marines.org/leatherneck/harvest-moon: accessed 23 December 2018).
[36] Ibid.
[37] Ibid.
[38] Ibid.
[39] Ibid.
[40] Ibid.
[41] Ibid.
[42] Ibid.
[43] Ibid.
[44] Ibid.
[45] Ibid.
[46] Ibid.
[47] Ibid.
[48] Ibid.
[49] Shulimson and Johnson, *U.S. Marines in Vietnam: The Landing and the Buildup 1965*, 203.
[50] Ibid.
[51] Ibid.

CHAPTER 6 NOTES:
[1] Jack Shulimson, *U.S. Marines in Vietnam: An Expanding War 1966* (Washington, DC: History and Museums Division, Headquarters, U.S. Marine Corps, 1982), 297
[2] Ibid, 297.
[3] "USS *Skagit* and Operation Double Eagle Quang Ngai Province, Vietnam January 28, 1966" (http://www.ussskagit.org/DE.html: accessed 22 February 2019).
[4] Shulimson, *U.S. Marines in Vietnam: An Expanding War 1966*, 297; "Operation Double Eagle, Operation Masher, Operation Thang Phong II, Operation Lien Ket-22, Operation White Wing" (https://www.100megsfree2.com/jjscherr/scherr/double-eagle.htm: accessed 22 February 2019).
[5] Bosiljevac Thesis, *The Teams in 'Nam: U.S. Navy UDT/SEAL Operations of the Vietnam War*, 21 December 1987.
[6] Ibid.
[7] "Operation Double Eagle, Operation Masher, Operation Thang Phong II, Operation Lien Ket-22, Operation White Wing."
[8] Ibid.
[9] United States Naval Operations Vietnam, Highlights; February 1966 (https://www.history.navy.mil/content/history/nhhc/research/archives/digitized-collections/vietnam-war/united-states-naval-operations-vietnam-highlights-february-1966.html: accessed 22 February 2019); "Operation Double Eagle, Operation Masher, Operation Thang Phong II, Operation Lien Ket-22, Operation White Wing."

[10] United States Naval Operations Vietnam, Highlights; February 1966; Marolda, *By Sea, Air, and Land*, Chapter 3: The Years of Combat, 1965-1968.
[11] Shulimson, *U.S. Marines in Vietnam: An Expanding War 1966*, 299-300.
[12] Ibid, 300.
[13] USS *Princeton* (LPH-5) Far East 1966 cruise book.
[14] Vietnam War Highlights, March 1966 (https://www.history.navy.mil/content/history/nhhc/research/archives/digitized-collections/vietnam-war/highlights-march-1966.html: accessed 23 February 2019).
[15] Vietnam War Highlights, March 1966; *Washoe County*, *DANFS*.
[16] Bosiljevac Thesis, The Teams in 'Nam: U.S. Navy UDT/SEAL Operations of the Vietnam War, 21 December 1987.
[17] Ibid.
[18] Shulimson, *U.S. Marines in Vietnam: An Expanding War 1966*, 301-302.
[19] Vietnam War Highlights, March 1966.
[20] Ibid.
[21] Commander Landing Ship Squadron One, Command History for 1966, 22 December 1967.
[22] Shulimson, *U.S. Marines in Vietnam: An Expanding War 1966*, 303; Bosiljevac Thesis, The Teams in 'Nam: U.S. Navy UDT/SEAL Operations of the Vietnam War, 21 December 1987.
[23] Shulimson, *U.S. Marines in Vietnam: An Expanding War 1966*, 303; Vietnam War Highlights, April 1966 (https://www.history.navy.mil/content/history/nhhc/research/archives/digitized-collections/vietnam-war/highlights-april-1966.html#amphibious_operations: accessed 23 February 2019).
[24] Shulimson, *U.S. Marines in Vietnam: An Expanding War 1966*, 303.
[25] Ibid.
[26] Vietnam War Highlights, June 1966 (https://www.history.navy.mil/content/history/nhhc/research/archives/digitized-collections/vietnam-war/highlights-june-1966.html#deckhouse_map: accessed 23 February 2019); Bosiljevac Thesis, The Teams in 'Nam: U.S. Navy UDT/SEAL Operations of the Vietnam War, 21 December 1987.
[27] Vietnam War Highlights, June 1966; Shulimson, *U.S. Marines in Vietnam: An Expanding War 1966*, 304.
[28] Vietnam War Highlights, July 1966 (https://www.history.navy.mil/content/history/nhhc/research/archives/digitized-collections/vietnam-war/highlights-july-1966.html: accessed 25 February 2019); Shulimson, *U.S. Marines in Vietnam: An Expanding War 1966*, 305.
[29] Vietnam War Highlights, July 1966.
[30] Vietnam War Highlights, July 1966; Bosiljevac Thesis, The Teams in 'Nam: U.S. Navy UDT/SEAL Operations of the Vietnam War, 21 December 1987.
[31] Vietnam War Highlights, July 1966.
[32] Ibid.

[33] USS *Vancouver* (LPD-2) Second Cruise Book
[34] Shulimson, *U.S. Marines in Vietnam: An Expanding War 1966*, 305; USS *Vancouver* (LPD-2) Second Cruise Book; Bosiljevac Thesis, The Teams in 'Nam: U.S. Navy UDT/SEAL Operations of the Vietnam War, 21 December 1987.
[35] Commanding Officer, Battalion Landing Team 1-26, Combat After Action Report for Operation DECKHOUSE III, Phase I and Phase II/Operation TOLEDO, 2 September 1966; Bosiljevac Thesis, The Teams in 'Nam: U.S. Navy UDT/SEAL Operations of the Vietnam War, 21 December 1987.
[36] Ut supra.
[37] "Vietnam War 1962-73" (http://www.defence.gov.au/army/ahu/HISTORY/vietnam_war.htm: accessed 12 March 2019); Hector Donohue correspondence of 25 May 2019.
[38] "Battalion History" (http://6rarassociation.com/bnhistory.htm); "Vietnam Veterans Day 15 August 2008" by Libby Stewart (https://www.awm.gov.au/articles/blog/vietnam-veterans-day: both accessed 25 May 2019); Hector Donohue correspondence of 25 May 2019.
[39] Ut supra.
[40] Hector Donohue correspondence of 25 May 2019.
[41] "Vietnam Veterans Day 15 August 2008" by Libby Stewart.
[42] "The RAN HFV Story" by Kim Dunstan (https://www.faaaa.asn.au/heritage-ran-helicopter-flight-vietnam/: accessed 17 March 2019).
[43] "RAN Helicopter Flight Vietnam History" (http://www.navy.gov.au/history/ran-helicopter-flight-vietnam-history: accessed 17 March 2019).
[44] Ibid.
[45] Commodore Hector Donahue, RAN (Retired); "RAN Helicopter Flight Vietnam History."
[46] "RANHFV Awarded Unit Citation for Gallantry" (https://www.faaaa.asn.au/ranhfv-awarded-unit-citation-gallantry/: accessed 17 March 2019).
[47] Commanding Officer, Battalion Landing Team 1-26, Combat After Action Report for Operation DECKHOUSE III, Phase I and Phase II/Operation TOLEDO, 2 September 1966; Bosiljevac Thesis, The Teams in 'Nam: U.S. Navy UDT/SEAL Operations of the Vietnam War, 21 December 1987.
[48] Commanding Officer, Battalion Landing Team 1-26, Combat After Action Report for Operation DECKHOUSE III, Phase I and Phase II/Operation TOLEDO, 2 September 1966; Bosiljevac Thesis, The Teams in 'Nam: U.S. Navy UDT/SEAL Operations of the Vietnam War, 21 December 1987; Vietnam War Highlights, July 1966.
[49] Bosiljevac Thesis, The Teams in 'Nam: U.S. Navy UDT/SEAL Operations of the Vietnam War, 21 December 1987; "Surface Action: Submarine Support Special Ops" by John B. Dwyer, *Soldier of Fortune* magazine, May 1987.

328 Bibliography/Notes

[50] Ut supra.
[51] Ut supra.
[52] Ut supra.
[53] Commanding Officer, Battalion Landing Team 1-26, Combat After Action Report for Operation DECKHOUSE III, Phase I and Phase II/Operation TOLEDO, 2 September 1966; Bosiljevac Thesis, The Teams in 'Nam: U.S. Navy UDT/SEAL Operations of the Vietnam War, 21 December 1987.
[54] Commanding Officer, Battalion Landing Team 1-26, Combat After Action Report for Operation DECKHOUSE III, Phase I and Phase II/Operation TOLEDO, 2 September 1966.
[55] Bosiljevac Thesis, The Teams in 'Nam: U.S. Navy UDT/SEAL Operations of the Vietnam War, 21 December 1987; "Surface Action: Submarine Support Special Ops" by John B. Dwyer.
[56] Ut supra.
[57] Ut supra.
[58] Commanding Officer, Battalion Landing Team 1-26, Combat After Action Report for Operation DECKHOUSE IV/PRAIRIE, 26 September 1966.
[59] Ibid.
[60] *Perch, DANFS*; Bosiljevac Thesis, The Teams in 'Nam: U.S. Navy UDT/SEAL Operations of the Vietnam War, 21 December 1987.
[61] Commanding Officer, Special Landing Force, Combat After Action Reports, Operations DECKHOUSE IV and PRAIRIE, 30 September 1966.
[62] *Vancouver, DANFS*; Commanding Officer, Battalion Landing Team 1-26, Combat After Action Report for Operation DECKHOUSE IV/PRAIRIE, 26 September 1966.
[63] *Thomaston, DANFS*; Commanding Officer, Marine Medium Helicopter Squadron 363, After Exercise Report, Operation Deckhouse IV and Operation Prairie; submission of, 26 September 1966; USS *Vancouver* LPD-2 Second Cruise Book.
[64] Commanding Officer, Special Landing Force, Combat After Action Reports, Operations DECKHOUSE IV and PRAIRIE, 30 September 1966.
[65] Ibid.
[66] Commanding Officer, Battalion Landing Team 1-26, Combat After Action Report for Operation DECKHOUSE IV/PRAIRIE, 26 September 1966.
[67] Shulimson, *U.S. Marines in Vietnam: An Expanding War 1966*, 305-306.

CHAPTER 7 NOTES:
[1] Gary L. Telfer, Lane Rogers, and Keith Fleming Jr., *Marines in Vietnam Fighting the North Vietnamese 1967* (Washington, DC: History and Museum Division, Headquarters, U.S. Marine Corps, 1984), 150.
[2] Ibid.
[3] Ibid.
[4] Ibid, 150-151.

[5] Telfer, Rogers, and Fleming Jr., *Marines in Vietnam Fighting the North Vietnamese 1967*, 151; Commander, U.S. Naval Forces, Vietnam, Monthly Historical Supplement, January 1967.
[6] "Operation Deckhouse V, 6-15 January 1967" (http://www.echo23marines6569.org/OperationDeckhouseV.html: accessed 24 April 2019).
[7] *Washtenaw County*, *DANFS*; Commander, U.S. Naval Forces, Vietnam, Monthly Historical Supplement, January 1967.
[8] Telfer, Rogers, and Fleming Jr., *Marines in Vietnam Fighting the North Vietnamese 1967*, 151.
[9] Ibid, 151-152.
[10] Ibid, 151-152.
[11] Edward J. Marolda and R. Blake Dunnavent, *Combat at Close Quarters Warfare on the Rivers and Canals of Vietnam* (Washington, DC: Naval History and Heritage Command, 2015), 2
[12] Ibid, 3.
[13] "Mobile Riverine Force Task Force – 117" (https://www.mrfa.org/us-navy/us-navy-mobile-riverine-force/task-force-117/: accessed 27 March 2019).
[14] "Mobile Riverine Force Task Force – 117;" Marolda and Dunnavent, *Combat at Close Quarters Warfare on the Rivers and Canals of Vietnam*, 3; Commander, U.S. Naval Forces, Vietnam, Monthly Historical Supplement, January 1967.

CHAPTER 8 NOTES:

[1] ComNavForV Monthly Historical Supplement, January 1967.
[2] Ibid.
[3] "River Assault Force (Vietnam)" (https://www.mrfa.org/us-navy-army/riverine-assault-force-vietnam/: accessed 30 March 2019).
[4] "Mobile Riverine Force Task Force – 117" (https://www.mrfa.org/us-navy/us-navy-mobile-riverine-force/task-force-117/: accessed 27 March 2019).
[5] "River Assault Force (Vietnam)."
[6] "River Assault Force (Vietnam);" ComNavForV Monthly Historical Supplement, January 1967.
[7] "River Assault Force (Vietnam)."
[8] "River Assault Force (Vietnam);" Bruhn, *Wooden Ships and Iron Men: The U.S. Navy's Coastal and Inshore Minesweepers, and the Minecraft That Served in Vietnam, 1953-1976*, 157.
[9] Bruhn, *Wooden Ships and Iron Men*, 188.
[10] "River Assault Force (Vietnam)."
[11] Bruhn, *Wooden Ships and Iron Men*, 209-210.
[12] ComNavForV Monthly Historical Supplement, June 1967; "Recollections of Commander Anthony R. DeMarco, USN (Ret) who served as a historian with Naval Forces, Vietnam, during 1967-1968" (https://www.history.navy.mil/content/history/nhhc/research/library/oral-

histories/post-1946/navy-combat-field-historian-in-vietnam.html: accessed 31 March 2019).
[13] ComNavForV Monthly Historical Supplement, June 1967.
[14] ComNavForV Monthly Historical Supplement, June 1967; Bruhn, *Wooden Ships and Iron Men*, 1.
[15] ComNavForV Monthly Historical Supplement, June 1967.
[16] Ibid.
[17] Ibid.
[18] Ibid.
[19] Ibid.
[20] Ibid.
[21] Ibid.
[22] Ibid.
[23] ComNavForV Monthly Historical Supplement, July 1967.
[24] Ibid.
[25] Ibid.
[26] Ibid.
[27] Ibid.
[28] Ibid.
[29] Ibid.
[30] Ibid.
[31] Ibid.
[32] Ibid.
[33] Ibid.
[34] Ibid.
[35] ComNavForV Monthly Historical Supplement, August 1967.
[36] Ibid.
[37] Ibid.
[38] Ibid.
[39] Ibid.
[40] Ibid.
[41] Ibid.
[42] Ibid.
[41] Bruhn, *Wooden Ships and Iron Men*, 163.
[42] Ibid.
[43] Ibid.
[44] "The Brown Water Navy in Vietnam" by Robert H. Stoner (http://warboats.org/StonerBWN/The%20Brown%20Water%20Navy%20in%20Vietnam_Part%202.htm: accessed 28 April 2019).
[45] Bob Kermen correspondence of 1 May 2019.
[46] ComNavForV Monthly Historical Supplement, October 1967.
[47] Ibid.
[48] Ibid.
[49] Ibid.
[50] Ibid.
[51] ComNavForV Monthly Historical Supplement, November 1967.

[52] Ibid.
[53] Ibid.
[54] Ibid.
[55] Ibid.
[56] Ibid.
[57] Ibid.
[58] Ibid.
[59] Bruhn, *Wooden Ships and Iron Men*, 169; ComNavForV Monthly Historical Supplement, December 1967.
[60] Bruhn, *Wooden Ships and Iron Men*, 168.
[61] Ibid.
[62] Ibid, 169.
[63] Ibid.
[64] ComNavForV Monthly Historical Supplement, December 1967.

CHAPTER 9 NOTES:
[1] "Tank Landing Ships (LST)," James L. Mooney, *Dictionary of American Naval Fighting Ships, Vol. VII* (Washington, DC: Office of the Chief of Naval Operations, 1981), 569-731
(https://www.hazegray.org/danfs/amphib/lst.htm: accessed 1 April 2019).
[2] Ibid.
[3] Ibid.
[4] Ibid.
[5] Ibid.
[6] Ibid.
[7] *Caddo Parish, DANFS*.
[8] Ibid.
[9] Commander Landing Ship Squadron Two, Command History; forwarding of, 25 August 1966.
[10] *Caddo Parish, DANFS*.
[11] Commander Landing Ship Squadron Two, Command History; forwarding of, 25 August 1966; Commander Landing Ship Squadron Two, OPNAV Report 5750.1, 21 March 1967.
[12] Ut supra.
[13] Commander Landing Ship Squadron Two, OPNAV Report 5750.1, 21 March 1967.
[14] Commander Landing Ship Squadron Two, OPNAV Report 5750.1, 21 March 1967; *Mahnomen County, DANFS*; Commander Landing Ship Squadron Two, Command History, 23 April 1968.
[15] Commander Landing Ship Squadron Two, Command History, 23 April 1968.
[16] Ibid.
[17] "Gary Bagwell Letters"
(https://www.lib.lsu.edu/sites/default/files/sc/findaid/3279.pdf: accessed 4 April 2019); *Caddo Parish, DANFS*; Commander Landing Ship Squadron Two, Command History, 3 February 1969.

[18] *Caddo Parish*, *DANFS*; Commander Landing Ship Squadron Two, Command History, 3 March 1970.
[19] Alan Halldorson correspondence with author.
[20] Commander Landing Ship Squadron Two, Command History, 3 March 1970.
[21] "John R. Swofford's recollections of his time on the *Iredell County*" (https://www.mrfa.org/us-navy/us-navy-mobile-riverine-force/iredell-county-lst-839/: accessed 4 April 2019).
[22] Commander Landing Ship Squadron Two, Final Command History, 26 June 1970.
[23] Ibid.
[24] Commander Landing Ship Squadron Two, Final Command History, 26 June 1970; *Luzerne County*, *DANFS*.
[25] "Nixon authorizes invasion of Cambodia, April 28, 1970" by Andrew Glass (https://www.politico.com/story/2015/04/this-day-in-politics-april-28-1970-117377: accessed 9 April 2019).
[26] "USS *Hunterdon County* (LST-838) - Service History - Vietnam War, 1966–1974" (http://www.liquisearch.com/uss_hunterdon_county_lst-838/service_history/vietnam_war_1966%E2%80%931974: accessed 8 April 2019).
[27] "History of the USS *Hampshire County* (LST-819)" by William Posson (https://www.mrfa.org/us-navy/us-navy-mobile-riverine-force/hampshire-county-lst-819/: accessed 8 April 2019).
[28] "Squadron Nine History Page" (http://lstsquadron9.com/index-3.html: accessed 5 April 2019).
[29] Commander Landing Ship Squadron Nine, Command History; submission of, 5 March 1971.
[30] *Washoe County*, *Westchester County*, *DANFS*.
[31] *Westchester County*, *DANFS*.
[32] Commander Landing Ship Squadron Nine, 1967 Command History; forwarding of, 5 April 1968; Commander Landing Ship Squadron One, Command History for 1967, 23 January 1968.
[33] Ut supra.
[34] Commander Landing Ship Squadron Nine, Command History; submission of, 5 March 1971.
[35] Ibid.
[36] Ibid.
[37] Lawrence P. Blumette description of duty aboard USS *Blanco County* (https://www.mrfa.org/us-navy/us-navy-mobile-riverine-force/blanco-county-lst-344/: accessed 5 April 2019).
[38] Commander, Landing Ship Squadron Three, Command History; forwarding of (OPNAV Report Symbol 5750-1), 15 February 1967.
[39] Ibid.
[40] Ibid.
[41] Ibid.

[42] Commander, Landing Ship Squadron Three, Command History; forwarding of, 8 September 1968.
[43] Commander, Landing Ship Squadron Three, Command History; forwarding of, 2 September 1969.
[44] Ibid.
[45] Commander, Landing Ship Squadron Three, Command History; forwarding of, 2 September 1969; Commander, Landing Ship Squadron Three, Command History; forwarding of, 28 November 1970.
[46] Commander, Landing Ship Squadron Three, Command History; forwarding of, 28 November 1970.
[47] Commander Landing Ship Squadron One, Command History for 1966, 22 December 1967.
[48] Ibid.
[49] Commander, Landing Ship Squadron Three, Command History; forwarding of, 2 September 1969.

CHAPTER 10 NOTES:

[1] Vietnam War Highlights, "Naval Historical Summary February 1966 Highlights," Naval History and Heritage Command (https://www.history.navy.mil/research/archives/digitized-collections/vietnam-war.html: accessed 26 April 2019.
[2] Vietnam War Highlights, Naval Historical Summary March, April, and May 1966 Highlights, Naval History and Heritage Command.
[3] Commander, U.S. Naval Forces, Vietnam, Historical Summary April 1966, 27 May 1966.
[4] Ibid.
[5] Ibid.
[6] Ibid.
[7] Ibid.
[8] Ibid.
[9] Ibid.
[10] Commander, U.S. Naval Forces, Vietnam, Historical Summary May 1966.
[11] Ibid.
[12] Commander, U.S. Naval Forces, Vietnam, Historical Summary May 1966; "HMAS *Bungaree*" (http://www.navy.gov.au/hmas-bungaree: accessed 27 April 2019).
[13] Mike Turner and Hector Donohue, *Australian Minesweepers at War* (Canberra, Australia: Sea Power Centre – Australia, 2018), 70.
[14] "HMAS *Bungaree*."
[15] Commander, U.S. Naval Forces, Vietnam, Historical Summary May 1966.
[16] Ibid.
[17] Ibid.
[18] Ibid.
[19] Ibid.
[20] Vietnam War Highlights, "Naval Historical Summary June 1966 Highlights," Naval History and Heritage Command.

[21] "The Brown Water Navy in Vietnam" by Robert H. Stoner.
[22] *Belle Grove, DANFS.*
[23] *Jennings County, DANFS.*
[24] "The Brown Water Navy in Vietnam" by Robert H. Stoner.
[25] *Comstock, DANFS.*
[26] *Tortuga, DANFS.*
[27] Vietnam War Highlights, "Naval Historical Summary July 1966 Highlights," Naval History and Heritage Command.
[28] Bruhn, *Wooden Ships and Iron Men: The U.S. Navy's Coastal and Inshore Minesweepers, and the Minecraft That Served in Vietnam, 1953-1976*, 1.
[29] Ibid, 1-2.
[30] Ibid.
[31] Ibid, 3.
[32] Ibid, 4.
[33] Commander, U.S. Naval Forces, Vietnam, Monthly Historical Summary, October 1966, 16 December 1966; http://www.davidsearswrites.com/?cat=3: accessed 29 April 2019)
[34] Thomas J. Cutler, *Brown Water, Black Berets* (Annapolis, Md: Naval Institute, 1988), 188-189.
[35] Commander, U.S. Naval Forces, Vietnam, Monthly Historical Summary, October 1966, 16 December 1966.
[36] Ibid.
[37] Ibid.
[38] Ibid.
[39] Ibid.
[40] Ibid.
[41] Cutler, *Brown Water, Black Berets*, 204.
[42] *Comstock, DANFS.*
[43] Commander, Naval Forces Vietnam, Monthly Historical Summary, November 1966, 23 January 1967.
[44] Ibid.
[45] Commander, Naval Forces Vietnam, Monthly Historical Summary, December 1966, 15 February 1967.
[46] Ibid.
[47] Ibid.

CHAPTER 11 NOTES:
[1] Commanding Officer, Task Group 79.4, Combat After Action Report, Operation Ballistic Charge/Shelbyville, 11 October 1967.
[2] "I Corps" (https://namwartravel.com/i-corps/: accessed 5 May 2019).
[3] Telfer, Rogers, and Fleming Jr., *Marines in Vietnam Fighting the North Vietnamese 1967*, 150-151, 158; Commanding Officer, Special Landing Force Alfa, Command Chronology for the period 1 to 31 March 1967, 10 April 1967.
[4] Telfer, Rogers, and Fleming Jr., *Marines in Vietnam Fighting the North Vietnamese 1967*, 156.

[5] Commanding Officer, Special Landing Force Alfa, Command Chronology for the period 1 April – 13 May 1967, submission of, 28 May 1967.
[6] Commanding Officer, Special Landing Force Alfa, Combat After Action Report, Operation Beaver Cage/Union, 28 May 1967; Telfer, Rogers, and Fleming Jr., *Marines in Vietnam Fighting the North Vietnamese 1967*, 158.
[7] Commanding Officer, Special Landing Force Alfa, Combat After Action Report, Operation Beaver Cage/Union, 28 May 1967.
[8] Ibid.
[9] Ibid.
[10] "Operation Beau Charger - Battle of the Ben Hai River Task Group 76.4 - 18 to 19 May 1967" (http://www.dd-692.com/beau.htm: accessed 12 October 2018).
[11] Telfer, Rogers, and Fleming Jr., *Marines in Vietnam Fighting the North Vietnamese 1967*, 159
[12] "H-009-3: Significant U.S. Navy Operations and Events in Vietnam Through 1967" (https://www.history.navy.mil/content/history/nhhc/about-us/leadership/director/directors-corner/h-grams/h-gram-009/h009-3.html: accessed 12 October 2018); *Seminole, DANFS*; "Operation Beau Charger - Battle of the Ben Hai River Task Group 76.4."
[13] "Operation Beau Charger - Battle of the Ben Hai River Task Group 76.4."
[14] Commanding Officer, Task Group 79.4, Command Chronology for the period 14-31 May 1967, submission of, 10 June 1967.
[15] "Operation Beau Charger - Battle of the Ben Hai River Task Group 76.4."
[16] "H-009-3: Significant U.S. Navy Operations and Events in Vietnam Through 1967."
[17] "Operation Beau Charger - Battle of the Ben Hai River Task Group 76.4."
[18] Ibid.
[19] Ibid.
[20] Ibid.
[21] Commanding Officer, Task Group 79.4, Command Chronology for the period 14-31 May 1967, submission of, 10 June 1967.
[22] Commanding Officer, Task Group 79.4, Combat After Action Report, Operation Bear Bite, 1 August 1967; USS *Okinawa* (LPH-3) WestPac 1967 cruise book; Telfer, Rogers, and Fleming Jr., *Marines in Vietnam Fighting the North Vietnamese 1967*, 162.
[23] Commanding Officer, Task Group 79.4, Command Chronology for the period 1 to 30 June 1967, 2 August 1967.
[24] Commanding Officer, Task Group 79.4, Combat After Action Report, Operation Bear Bite, 1 August 1967.
[25] Ibid.
[26] "Tragic Valor of Marines at Con Thien" by Don North (https://www.commondreams.org/views/2016/05/29/tragic-valor-marines-con-thien: accessed 14 May 2019).

[27] Ibid.
[28] Ibid.
[29] Commanding Officer, Task Group 79.4, Command Chronology for period 1 to 31 July 1967, 5 September 1967; Commanding Officer, Task Group 79.4, Combat After Action Report, Operation Beacon Guide, 3 August 1967.
[30] "Tragic Valor of Marines at Con Thien" by Don North.
[31] Ibid.
[32] Ibid.
[33] Telfer, Rogers, and Fleming Jr., *Marines in Vietnam Fighting the North Vietnamese 1967*, 163.
[34] Ibid, 164.
[35] Ibid.
[36] Commanding Officer, Task Group 79.4, Command Chronology for period 1 to 31 July 1967, 5 September 1967; USS *Okinawa* (LPH-3) WestPac 1967 cruise book; Telfer, Rogers, and Fleming Jr., *Marines in Vietnam Fighting the North Vietnamese 1967*, 164.
[37] Commanding Officer, Task Group 79.4, Command Chronology for period 1 to 31 July 1967, 5 September 1967; Commanding Officer, Task Group 79.4, Combat After Action Report, Operation Beacon Guide, 3 August 1967; Telfer, Rogers, and Fleming Jr., *Marines in Vietnam Fighting the North Vietnamese 1967*, 167.
[38] Commanding Officer, Task Group 79.4, Command Chronology for period 1 to 31 July 1967, 5 September 1967; Commanding Officer, Task Group 79.4, Combat After Action Report, Operation Beacon Guide, 3 August 1967.
[39] Ut supra.
[40] Ut supra.
[41] Commanding Officer, Task Group 79.4, Command Chronology for period 1 to 31 August 1967, 17 September 1967; Commanding Officer, Task Group 79.4, Combat After Action Report, Operation Beacon Gate/Cochise, 7 September 1967; Telfer, Rogers, and Fleming Jr., *Marines in Vietnam Fighting the North Vietnamese 1967*, 168.
[42] Commanding Officer, Task Group 79.4, Command Chronology for period 1 to 31 August 1967, 17 September 1967; Commanding Officer, Task Group 79.4, Combat After Action Report, Operation Beacon Gate/Cochise, 7 September 1967.
[43] Ut supra.
[44] Ut supra.
[45] Commanding Officer, Task Group 79.4, Command Chronology for period 1 to 31 August 1967, 17 September 1967; Commanding Officer, Task Group 79.4, Combat After Action Report, Operation Beacon Gate/Cochise, 7 September 1967; Telfer, Rogers, and Fleming Jr., *Marines in Vietnam Fighting the North Vietnamese 1967*, 169.
[46] USS *Okinawa* (LPH-3) WestPac 1967 cruise book; Commanding Officer, Task Group 79.4, Combat After Action Report, Operation Beacon Point, 8

October 1967; Telfer, Rogers, and Fleming Jr., *Marines in Vietnam Fighting the North Vietnamese 1967*, 170.
[47] Commanding Officer, Task Group 79.4, Command Chronology for period 1 to 30 September 1967, 16 October 1967.
[48] Commanding Officer, Task Group 79.4, Combat After Action Report, Operation Beacon Point, 8 October 1967.
[49] Commanding Officer, Task Group 79.4, Combat After Action Report, Operation Ballistic Charge/Shelbyville, 11 October 1967; Telfer, Rogers, and Fleming Jr., *Marines in Vietnam Fighting the North Vietnamese 1967*, 171.
[50] Ibid.
[51] Ibid.
[52] Commanding Officer, Task Group 79.4, Command Chronology for period 1 to 31 October 1967, supporting documents forwarding of, 11 January 1968.
[53] Telfer, Rogers, and Fleming Jr., *Marines in Vietnam Fighting the North Vietnamese 1967*, 172.
[54] Ibid.
[55] Commanding Officer, Task Group 79.4, Combat After Action Report, Operation Bastion Hill/Medina/Fremont/Granite, 10-30 Sep 67, 1 December 1967; Telfer, Rogers, and Fleming Jr., *Marines in Vietnam Fighting the North Vietnamese 1967*, 173.
[56] Telfer, Rogers, and Fleming Jr., *Marines in Vietnam Fighting the North Vietnamese 1967*, 180.
[57] "Commander, Amphibious Squadron 3" (https://www.public.navy.mil/surfor/cpr3/Pages/ourShip.aspx: accessed 10 May 2019).
[58] Commanding Officer, Task Group 79.4, Command Chronology for period 1 to 30 November 1967, 26 December 1967.
[59] Commanding Officer, Task Group 79.4, Command Chronology for period 1 to 31 December 1967, 20 January 1968.
[60] Commanding Officer, Task Group 79.4, Combat After Action Report, Operation Ballistic Arch/Kentucky, 21 January 1968.
[61] Ibid.

CHAPTER 12 NOTES:
[1] "U.S. Navy Operations in Vietnam, January–March 1968" (https://www.history.navy.mil/content/history/nhhc/about-us/leadership/director/directors-corner/h-grams/h-gram-017/h-017-1.html: accessed 19 October 2018).
[2] "Vietnam War Campaigns" (https://history.army.mil/html/reference/army_flag/vn.html: accessed 19 October 2018).
[3] Marolda, *By Sea, Air, and Land*, Chapter 3: The Years of Combat, 1965-1968.
[4] Ibid.

[5] Commander, U.S. Navy Forces, Vietnam, Monthly Historical Supplement, February 1968, 29 June 1968.
[6] Ibid.
[7] Marolda, *By Sea, Air, and Land*, Chapter 3: The Years of Combat, 1965-1968.
[8] Commander, U.S. Navy Forces, Vietnam, Monthly Historical Supplement, February 1968, 29 June 1968.
[9] Ibid.
[10] Ibid.
[11] Ibid.
[12] Ibid.
[13] Ibid.
[14] Ibid.
[15] Ibid.
[16] Ibid.
[17] Ibid.
[18] Ibid.
[19] Ibid.
[20] "U.S. Army Coastal Freighters (F, FS) Built During WWII" (http://shipbuildinghistory.com/smallships/armyfreighters.htm: accessed 21 May 2019); *Mark*, *DANFS*.
[21] "History of the USS *Mark* (AKL-12)" (https://www.mrfa.org/us-navy/us-navy-mobile-riverine-force/mark-akl-12/: accessed 21 May 2019).
[22] David D. Bruhn, *MacArthur and Halsey's "Pacific Island Hoppers": The Forgotten Fleet of World War II* (Berwyn Heights, Md: Heritage Books, 2014), 260-261.
[23] Commander, U.S. Navy Forces, Vietnam, Monthly Historical Supplement, February 1968, 29 June 1968.
[24] "Did the news media, led by Walter Cronkite, lose the war in Vietnam" (https://www.washingtonpost.com/national/did-the-news-media-led-by-walter-cronkite-lose-the-war-in-vietnam/2018/05/25/a5b3e098-495e-11e8-827e-190efaf1f1ee_story.html?utm_term=.da9a56dfd832: accessed 2 December 2018).
[25] "Tet Offensive" (https://www.history.com/topics/vietnam-war/tet-offensive: accessed 2 December 2018).

CHAPTER 13 NOTES:
[1] Bruhn, *Wooden Ships and Iron Men: The U.S. Navy's Coastal and Inshore Minesweepers, and the Minecraft That Served in Vietnam, 1953-1976*, 195.
[2] Marolda, *By Sea, Air, and Land*, Chapter 4: Winding Down the War, 1968 – 1973.
[3] "Vietnam War Peace Talks" (https://alphahistory.com/vietnamwar/vietnam-war-peace-talks/: accessed 23 May 2019)
[4] Bruhn, *Wooden Ships and Iron Men: The U.S. Navy's Coastal and Inshore Minesweepers, and the Minecraft That Served in Vietnam, 1953-1976*, 197.

[5] Marolda, *By Sea, Air, and Land*, Chapter 4: Winding Down the War, 1968 – 1973.
[6] Marolda, *By Sea, Air, and Land*, Chapter 4: Winding Down the War, 1968 – 1973; "Elmo R. Zumwalt Jr., Admiral Who Modernized the Navy, Is Dead at 79" by Richard Goldstein (https://www.nytimes.com/2000/01/03/us/elmo-r-zumwalt-jr-admiral-who-modernized-the-navy-is-dead-at-79.html: accessed 23 May 2019).
[7] Marolda, *By Sea, Air, and Land*, Chapter 4: Winding Down the War, 1968 – 1973; "VAL-4 "Black Ponies" (https://www.blackpony.org/: accessed 24 May 2019).
[8] Marolda, *By Sea, Air, and Land*, Chapter 4: Winding Down the War, 1968 – 1973.
[9] Commander, U.S. Naval Forces, Vietnam, Presidential Unit Citation for Explosive Ordnance Disposal Mobile Unit, Pacific; recommendation for, 21 April 1971.
[10] Untitled document provided by Donald (Scotty) Allan, CDT 3 historian.
[11] Ibid.
[12] Cutler, *Brown Water, Black Berets*, 286-288; Unpublished account by John Kennett, who is compiling an Awards history of all RAN Clearance Divers in consultation with RANCDA Historian Donald (Scotty) Allan.
[13] U.S. Naval Forces Vietnam, Monthly Historical Summary, February 1969.
[14] Unpublished account by John Kennett, who is compiling an Awards history of all RAN Clearance Divers in consultation with RANCDA Historian Donald (Scotty) Allan.
[15] Ibid.
[16] Award recommendation from Officer in Charge, Inshore Undersea Warfare Group One, to Commander, U.S. Naval Forces, Vietnam, dated 6 March 1969.
[17] Ibid.
[18] Ibid.

CHAPTER 14 NOTES:

[1] "The Swimmer/Sapper Attack at Vung Tau 23 May 1969" by Hector Donohue and Jake Linton, *NOC Newsletter* Number 111, December 2017.
[2] Ibid.
[3] Ibid.
[4] Ibid.
[5] "The Swimmer/Sapper Attack at Vung Tau 23 May 1969" by Donohue and Linton; "Commando recalls sinking of US aircraft carrier" (https://vietnamnews.vn/society/269334/commando-recalls-sinking-of-us-aircraft-carrier.html#dtLjzg4Y7ImALo6j.97: accessed 17 March 2019).
[6] "Commando recalls sinking of US aircraft carrier."
[7] "The Swimmer/Sapper Attack at Vung Tau 23 May 1969" by Donohue and Linton.
[8] Ibid.

[9] Ibid.
[10] Ibid.
[11] Ibid.
[12] Ibid.
[13] Ibid.
[14] Ibid.
[15] Ibid.
[16] Ibid.
[17] Ibid.
[18] Ibid.
[19] Ibid.
[20] Ibid.
[21] Ibid.
[22] Ibid.
[23] Ibid.

CHAPTER 15 NOTES:

[1] Charles R. Smith, *U.S. Marines in Vietnam, High Mobility and Standdown 1969* (Washington DC: History and Museums Division, Headquarters, U.S. Marine Corps, 1988), 297.
[2] Ibid.
[3] Ibid, 298-299.
[4] Ibid, 299-300.
[5] Ibid, 300.
[6] Ibid, 300-301.
[7] Paul Stillwell, *Battleship New Jersey: An Illustrated History* (Annapolis, Md: Naval Institute, 1986), 226; *Tripoli*, *DANFS*.
[8] Commander, Task Group 79.4, Command Chronology for period 1-31 Jan. 1969, 22 February 1969.
[9] Smith, *U.S. Marines in Vietnam, High Mobility and Standdown 1969*, 301.
[10] Marolda, *By Sea, Air, and Land*, Chapter 4: Winding Down the War, 1968 – 1973.
[11] Jack Shulimson, Leonard A. Blasiol, Charles R. Smith, and David A. Dawson, *U.S. Marine Corps U.S. Marines in Vietnam The Defining Year 1968* (Washington, DC: History and Museums Division, Headquarters U.S. Marine Corps, 1997), 639; Marolda, *By Sea, Air, and Land*, Chapter 4: Winding Down the War, 1968 – 1973.
[12] Marolda, *By Sea, Air, and Land*, Chapter 4: Winding Down the War, 1968 – 1973.
[13] Shulimson, Blasiol, Smith, and Dawson, *U.S. Marine Corps U.S. Marines in Vietnam The Defining Year 1968*, 639; Marolda, *By Sea, Air, and Land*, Chapter 4: Winding Down the War, 1968 – 1973.

CHAPTER 16 NOTES:

[1] Bruhn, *Wooden Ships and Iron Men: The U.S. Navy's Coastal and Inshore Minesweepers, and the Minecraft That Served in Vietnam, 1953-1976*, 208-209.

[2] Commander U.S. Naval Forces, Vietnam, U.S. Naval Forces, Vietnam Monthly Historical Summary for June 1969, forwarding of, 7 August 1969.
[3] Bruhn, *Wooden Ships and Iron Men: The U.S. Navy's Coastal and Inshore Minesweepers, and the Minecraft That Served in Vietnam, 1953-1976*, 208-209.
[4] Ibid.
[5] Commander U.S. Naval Forces, Vietnam, U.S. Naval Forces, Vietnam Monthly Historical Summary for July 1969; forwarding of, 15 October 1969; "Tank Landing Ship (LST)," NavSource (http://www.navsource.org/archives/10/16/16idx.htmNavSource: accessed 7 June 2019).
[6] Commander U.S. Naval Forces, Vietnam, U.S. Naval Forces, Vietnam Monthly Historical Summary for April 1970, 13 June 1970.
[7] "These Are the Voyages" by Tom Marcinko, December 2016 (https://www.phoenixmag.com/2016/12/01/these-are-the-voyages/: accessed 31 May 2019).
[8] "Tank Landing Ship (LST)," NavSource; *Satyr, DANFS*.
[9] "WPB-82301 *Point* class" (https://web.archive.org/web/20111002154115/http://www.harpoondatabases.com/encyclopedia/Entry2010.aspx); "The United States Coast Guard in South East Asia During the Vietnam Conflict" by Eugene N. Tulich (https://media.defense.gov/2018/Jan/11/2001864980/-1/-1/0/VTN-TULICH-USCG-OFFICIAL-HISTORY.PDF; "USCG in Vietnam Chronology" (https://media.defense.gov/2018/Jan/11/2001864982/-1/-1/0/USCGVIETNAMCHRONOLOGY.PDF: all accessed 30 May 2019).
[10] "Bering Strait - 1971 and beyond" (http://www.uscgcberingstrait.com/bering-strait---1971-and-beyond.html); "USCG in Vietnam Chronology" (https://media.defense.gov/2018/Jan/11/2001864982/-1/-1/0/USCGVIETNAMCHRONOLOGY.PDF: all accessed 31 May 2019).
[11] David D. Bruhn, *Eyes of the Fleet: The U.S. Navy's Seaplane Tenders and Patrol Aircraft in World War II* (Berwyn Heights, Md: Heritage Books, 2016), 22.
[12] "USCGC Absecon (WHEC-374)" (http://www.navsource.org/archives/09/43/4323.htm: accessed 29 May 29, 2019). There is agreement between Navy and Coast Guard references, and the authoritative *Jane's Fighting Ships*, that *Chincoteague* became *Ly Thuong Kiet*; but not whether her hull number was HQ-16.

CHAPTER 17 NOTES:
[1] U.S.-South Vietnamese forces launch Cambodian "incursion" (https://www.history.com/this-day-in-history/u-s-south-vietnamese-forces-launch-cambodian-incursion: accessed 9 June 2019).
[2] Commander U.S. Naval Forces Vietnam, U.S. Naval Forces, Vietnam Monthly Historical Summary for May 1970, 15 July 1970; Cutler, *Brown Water, Black Berets*, 353-354.
[3] Ut supra.

[4] Commander U.S. Naval Forces Vietnam, U.S. Naval Forces, Vietnam Monthly Historical Summary for May 1970, 15 July 1970.
[5] "Strike Assault Boat Squadron Twenty STABRON20 Overview" by Ken Burkett (http://www.warboats.org/stabron20.htm: accessed 10 June 2019).
[6] "Strike Assault Boat Squadron Twenty STABRON20 Overview" by Ken Burkett; "Strike Assault Boat Squadron Twenty (STABRON 20)" by John Kirk Ferguson (http://www.warboats.org/Stabron20/STABPDF/STABRON20FullHistory.pdf: accessed 9 June 2019).
[7] Ferguson, "Strike Assault Boat Squadron Twenty (STABRON 20)."
[8] Burkett, "Strike Assault Boat Squadron Twenty STABRON20 Overview."
[9] Ferguson, "Strike Assault Boat Squadron Twenty STABRON20 Overview;" Burkett, "Strike Assault Boat Squadron Twenty (STABRON 20)."
[10] Commander U.S. Naval Forces Vietnam, U.S. Naval Forces, Vietnam Monthly Historical Summary for May 1970, 15 July 1970.
[11] Commander U.S. Naval Forces, Vietnam, U.S. Naval Forces, Vietnam Monthly Historical Supplement; forwarding of, 23 March 1968.
[12] Ibid.
[13] Ibid.
[14] Rabbi Arnold E. Resnicoff correspondence of 10 June 2019.
[15] Commander U.S. Naval Forces Vietnam, U.S. Naval Forces, Vietnam Monthly Historical Summary for May 1970, 15 July 1970.
[16] "Lon Nol president of Cambodia" (https://www.britannica.com/biography/Lon-Nol); "The March 1970 Coup d'Etat" (http://countrystudies.us/cambodia/23.htm: both accessed 12 June 2019).
[17] Commander U.S. Naval Forces Vietnam, U.S. Naval Forces, Vietnam Monthly Historical Summary for May 1970, 15 July 1970.
[18] Commander U.S. Naval Forces Vietnam, U.S. Naval Forces, Vietnam Monthly Historical Summary for May 1970, 15 July 1970; Commander U.S. Naval Forces, Vietnam, U.S. Naval Forces, Vietnam Monthly Historical Summary for June 1970, 23 August 1970; Marolda, *By Sea, Air, and Land*, Chapter 4: Winding Down the War, 1968-1973.
[19] "USS *Hunterdon County*: First into Cambodia," Volume 22, Number 12 Amphibious Force Pacific Fleet June 19, 1970 (http://www.resnicoff.net/ship_story.html: accessed 9 June 2019).
[20] "History of the USS *Hampshire County* (LST-819)" by William Posson (https://www.mrfa.org/us-navy/us-navy-mobile-riverine-force/hampshire-county-lst-819/: accessed 8 April 2019).
[21] David Goldman, Erin Mahan, Edward C. Keefer, *Foreign Relations of the United States, 1969-1976, Vol. VII Vietnam July 1970-January 1972* (Washington, DC: U.S. Department of State, 2010), 1.
[22] Marolda, *By Sea, Air, and Land*, Chapter 4: Winding Down the War, 1968-1973.
[23] Ibid.

[24] Commander U.S. Naval Forces, Vietnam, U.S. Naval Forces, Vietnam Monthly Historical Summary for June 1970, 23 August 1970.
[25] Bruhn, *Wooden Ships and Iron Men: The U.S. Navy's Coastal and Inshore Minesweepers, and the Minecraft That Served in Vietnam, 1953-1976*, 228.
[26] Ibid.
[27] Marolda, *By Sea, Air, and Land*, Chapter 4: Winding Down the War, 1968-1973.

CHAPTER 18 NOTES:

[1] "USS *Litchfield County* (LST-901)" (https://www.usslitchfieldcounty.com/peter-orvis-speech-at-2009-reunion.html: accessed 21 March 2019). Text of LANSHIPRON-3 commander Peter Orvis' speech delivered at the 2009 reunion.
[2] "History of The USS *Blanco County* (LST-344)" (https://www.mrfa.org/us-navy/us-navy-mobile-riverine-force/blanco-county-lst-344/: accessed 24 May 2019).
[3] *Blanco County*, *DANFS*.
[4] Commander Landing Ship Squadron Three, Command History; forwarding of, 28 November 1970.
[5] "Commander First Fleet" (https://www.history.navy.mil/research/library/research-guides/lists-of-senior-officers-and-civilian-officials-of-the-us-navy/commander-first-fleet.html: accessed 24 May 2019).
[6] Commander Landing Ship Squadron Three, Command History; forwarding of, 28 November 1970.
[7] Ibid.
[8] Ibid.
[9] Account by Hector Donohue, based on the official report submitted by Lt. Ross Blue, and discussions with John Kershler regarding the incident.
[10] Ibid.
[11] Ibid.
[12] Ibid.
[13] Ibid.
[14] Ibid.
[15] Ibid.
[16] Ibid.
[17 Based on a passage from an article by Hector Donohue on the incident, to be published in a local Australian defence journal.

CHAPTER 19 NOTES:

[1] Bruhn, *Wooden Ships and Iron Men: The U.S. Navy's Coastal and Inshore Minesweepers, and the Minecraft That Served in Vietnam, 1953-1976*, 227.
[2] Ibid, 228-229.
[3] Ibid, 229.
[4] Ibid, 229-230.
[5] Ibid, 230.

[6] Ibid.
[7] Ibid.
[8] David D. Bruhn, *On the Gunline: U.S. Navy and Royal Australian Navy Warships off Vietnam, 1965-1973* (Berwyn Heights, Md: Heritage Books, 2019), 211, 213.
[9] "February 6, 1973: Navy Task Force 78 Begins Operation End Sweep" (https://www.navalhistory.org/2013/02/07/february-6-1973-navy-task-force-78-begins-operation-end-sweep: accessed 13 June 2019); Bruhn, *On the Gunline*, 211, 213.
[10] "February 6, 1973: Navy Task Force 78 Begins Operation End Sweep."
[11] Bruhn, *On the Gunline*, 211-212.
[12] Ibid, 213.
[13] Ibid, 214.

CHAPTER 20 NOTES:

[1] "April 1975 No room for helicopters with the close of the Vietnam War, Operation Frequent Wind" by Amanda Uren (https://mashable.com/2015/05/04/operation-frequent-wind/#x2.uImn9_8q7); "Vietnam Evacuation: Operation Frequent Wind" by Daniel L. Haulman (https://media.defense.gov/2012/Aug/23/2001330098/-1/-1/0/Oper%20Frequent%20Wind.pdf: both accessed 9 November 2018).
[2] Ibid.
[3] "Operation Frequent Wind: April 29-30, 1975" (https://www.navalhistory.org/2010/04/29/operation-frequent-wind-april-29-30-1975: accessed 2 November 2018).
[4] Ibid.
[5] "April 1975 No room for helicopters with the close of the Vietnam War, Operation Frequent Wind" by Amanda Uren; "Vietnam Evacuation: Operation Frequent Wind" by Daniel L. Haulman.
[6] "Frequent Wind Delivered Thousands to Freedom" (http://www.navalaviationmuseum.org/history-up-close/frequent-wind-delivered-thousands-to-freedom/: accessed 9 November 2018).
[7] "Vietnam Evacuation: Operation Frequent Wind" by Daniel L. Haulman.
[8] "At War's End, U.S. Ship Rescued South Vietnam's Navy" (https://www.npr.org/2010/09/01/129578263/at-war-s-end-u-s-ship-rescued-south-vietnam-s-navy: accessed 2 November 2018).
[9] "USS *Kirk* Saigon Evacuation Documentary Premiers at Smithsonian Institute" (https://www.navy.mil/submit/display.asp?story_id=57186: accessed 9 November 2018).
[10] *Cook, DANFS*; "USS *Kirk* Saigon Evacuation Documentary Premiers at Smithsonian Institute."
[11] "USS *Kirk* Saigon Evacuation Documentary Premiers at Smithsonian Institute;" "How to Steal a Navy and Save 30,000 Refugees" by Don North (http://www.historynet.com/how-to-steal-a-navy-and-save-30000-refugees-in-the-process.htm: accessed 9 November 2018).
[12] "How to Steal a Navy and Save 30,000 Refugees;" "Frequent Wind" (http://www.kirk1087.org/frequent-wind/: accessed 10 November 2018).

[13] "USS *Kirk* Saigon Evacuation Documentary Premiers at Smithsonian Institute;" "Frequent Wind."
[14] "At War's End, U.S. Ship Rescued South Vietnam's Navy" by Joseph Shapiro and Sandra Bartlett"
(http://vnafmamn.com/USS_kirk_VNmission.html: accessed 10 November 2018); "Frequent Wind"
[15] "How to Steal a Navy and Save 30,000 Refugees;" "Frequent Wind."
[16] Ut supra.
[17] "Frequent Wind."
[18] *Cook*, *DANFS*; "At War's End, U.S. Ship Rescued South Vietnam's Navy."
[19] "At War's End, U.S. Ship Rescued South Vietnam's Navy" by Joseph Shapiro and Sandra Bartlett."
[20] Ibid.
[21] Chief of Naval Operations, Master List of Unit Awards and Campaign Medals, 9 March 2001.

CHAPTER 21 NOTES:
[1] George R. Dunham and David A. Quinlan, *U.S. Marines in Vietnam: The Bitter End, 1973-1975* (Washington, DC: History and Museums Division, Headquarters, U.S. Marine Corps, 2009), 238.
[2] David Zebley correspondence of 16 June 2019.
[3] "USS *Harold E. Holt* DE-1074"
(https://www.history.navy.mil/content/history/nhhc/our-collections/art/exhibits/communities/100th-anniversary-cno/admiral-james-l-holloway-iii/uss-harold-e--holt-de-1074.html); "Instances of Use of United States Armed Forces Abroad, 1798-2004" by Richard F. Grimmett (https://www.history.navy.mil/content/history/nhhc/research/library/online-reading-room/title-list-alphabetically/i/use-of-armed-forces-abroad-1798-2004.html: both accessed 15 June 2019).
[4] Ralph Wetterhahn, *The Last Battle: The Mayaguez Incident and the end of the Vietnam War* (New York: Carroll and Graf Publishers, 2001), 36-39.
[5] Ibid, 76-79.
[6] Wetterhahn, *The Last Battle: The Mayaguez Incident and the end of the Vietnam War*, 43-45, 61-62, 113; Dunham and Quinlan, *U.S. Marines in Vietnam: The Bitter End, 1973-1975*, 239.
[7] Wetterhahn, *The Last Battle: The Mayaguez Incident and the end of the Vietnam War*, 63-66.
[8] Ibid, 39, 91.
[9] Ibid, 100.
[10] Ibid, 104-112.
[11] Wetterhahn, *The Last Battle: The Mayaguez Incident and the end of the Vietnam War*, 120-121; Dunham and Quinlan, *U.S. Marines in Vietnam: The Bitter End, 1973-1975*, 245.
[12] Wetterhahn, *The Last Battle: The Mayaguez Incident and the end of the Vietnam War*, 122.
[13] Ibid, 123-124.

[14] "Leave No Man Behind: The Truth About the *Mayaguez* Incident" by Peter Maguire (https://thediplomat.com/2018/06/leave-no-man-behind-the-truth-about-the-mayaguez-incident/: accessed 15 June 2019).
[15] Ibid.
[16] Ibid.
[17] Ibid.
[18] Ibid.
[19] Ibid.
[20] "*Mayaguez* Incident" (https://www.u-s-history.com/pages/h1949.html: accessed 15 June 2019); Dunham and Quinlan, *U.S. Marines in Vietnam: The Bitter End, 1973-1975*, 252.
[21] "*Mayaguez* Incident;" Dunham and Quinlan, *U.S. Marines in Vietnam: The Bitter End, 1973-1975*, 260.
[22] Ibid, 260.
[23] Ibid, 260-261.
[24] "Capture and Release of SS *Mayaguez* by Khmer Rouge forces in May 1975" (http://www.usmm.org/mayaguez.html: accessed 15 June 2019).
[25] Ibid.
[26] Ibid.
[27] Ibid.
[28] "Leave No Man Behind: The Truth About the *Mayaguez* Incident" by Peter Maguire.
[29] Dunham and Quinlan, *U.S. Marines in Vietnam: The Bitter End, 1973-1975*, 239.
[30] Ibid, 262-263.
[31] "*Mayaguez* Incident."
[32] Ibid.

POSTSCRIPT NOTES:
[1] Lex McAulay, *In the Ocean's Dark Embrace: Royal Australian Navy Clearance Diving Team 3 (USN EODMUPAC Team 21 & 35) Vietnam 1967-71* (Maryborough, Australia: Banner Books, 1997).
[2] McAulay, *In the Ocean's Dark Embrace*, 180.

Index

Abrams Jr., Creighton W., 199, 225
Addicott, Raymond W., 257
Agnew, Spiro, 225
Aldenhoven, John Adrian, xli, 244, 283
Armitage, Richard L., 259-262
Armstrong, Marshall B., 94, 97
Austin, Randall W., 267
Australia/Australian
  Army
    1st Australian Logistics Support Group, 210
    1st Australian Task Force, xxxvi, 83, 87
      1st Armoured Personnel Carrier Squadron, 83
      1 Field Regiment, Special Air Service Regiment (SASR), 83-84
    Battle of Long Tan, xxxvi, 83-85
  Royal Australian Navy
    Clearance Diving Team
      One and Two (CDT 1 and 2), xli
      Three (CDT 3), xviii, xxiii, xxxvii-xliii, 202-218, 244-246, 275-285, 297-302, 315
    Diving School, HMAS Penguin (in Sydney Harbour), xlii, 218, 277
    Helicopter Flight Vietnam, xxxvi, 85-87
  Sydney, 158-159, 218
Bailey, Barrie J., xlii
Ball P. (Reverend), xliii
Bannister, Howard W., 119
Beyerle, Garland T., 94
Blackburn Jr., Paul B., 53, 64
Blue, Ross S., xl, 244-246
Blumette, Lawrence P., 146, 242
Bodley, Charles H., 49
Boe, Nils William, 83, 92, 98
Bowman, Leslie V., 12
Branin, John W., 8-11
Brenneman, Richard A., 76
Brown, Edward J., 134
Brown Jr., Ralph E., 274
Brumley, John R., 214-215
Brunot, Richard, 40
Buell, Thomas Chapin, 69
Bunker, Ellsworth, 225
Burnett, John R., 57-59, 65, 67, 76

Burns, John J., 266
Burns, Robert J., xl
Busseno, Henry W., 206
Callahan, Cornelius P., 147
Callahan, Joseph E., 243
Cambodia, 5, 38, 40-41, 87, 101, 125, 135, 142-143, 201, 231-239, 252, 258-273, 308
　Battambang Province, 40
　Khmer Rouge, xlvi, 265-272
　Kampong Cham, 238
　Kampong Som (formerly Sihanoukville), 267-268, 273
　Koh Rong Sanloem Island, 267
　Koh Tang Island (also known as Poulo Wai), 265-273
　Neak Luong, 231-238
　Phnom Penh, xlvi, 143, 231-232, 238-239, 258-269
Carius, Robert Wilhelm, 250
Carlson, William Clifford, 82
Carter, J., 85
Carter, Jackie C., 12
Carterette, Robert Theodore, 69
Cartwright, Richard C., 12
Chambliss, Joe E., 69
Chon, Tran Van, 226-227
Christensen, Jack Andrew, 82
Christensen Jr., Charles Stahl, 69
Churchill, Winston, 39, 129-130
Cintron-Mendez, Wilfredo, 12
Coffman, Harold L., 71
Cole, Philip P., 226
Comer, William M., 195
Conway, John A., 181-189
Cook, Ernest F., 12
Cox, Robert J., xlii, 203-207
Cronkite, Walter, 198
Cruse, Carl Mann, 83, 92, 98
D'Argenlieu, Thierry, 39
Dai, Bao, 39-41
Dale, Chester D., 12
Darling, Colin, xlii, 203-204
Davis, Allan A., xl, 213-214, 218
Day, James L., 94, 97
Dennison, Walter J., 206
Diem, Ngo Dinh, 41-42
Dillon, Alfred John, 98
Do, Kiem, 262
Dollar, John F. C., xlii, 244, 283

Index   349

Donald, Alexander, xxxviii, xli
Downey, Louis Aloysius, 70
Duffy, Keith W., 12
Dugan Jr., Timothy Parks, 98
Dunning, Timothy C., 12
Dyer Jr., George Thomas, 69
Dykers Jr., Tom, 89-90
Ekman, Roger Edgar, 69
Ewers, Norman G., 49, 53, 57
Ey, Michael H., 214-215
Ey, Anthony L., 284
Fell, David G., 12
Ferguson, John Kirk, 235
Festag Jr., Albert Peter, 236
Fields, Lewis J., 53, 57, 64
Fischer, Warren Howard, 236
Fischer Jr., Harry Frederick, 92
Folta Jr., George William, 69
Ford Jr., Gerald R., xlii, 253, 266-269
Funke, Thomas G., 12
Gallagher Jr., Thomas James, 69
Garrett, Jeffrey L., xlii, 213-218
Giap, Vo Nguyen, 39-41
Gallo Jr., James A., 173-179
Goodale, Richard W., 189
Griffin, Robert, 272, 274
Griffiths, Guy R., 175
Habib, Philip, 225
Hall, Gary C., 274
Halldorson, Alan, xxvii-xxviii, 137, 139
Hamm, Gerald E., 12
Hanifin, Robert T., 53, 55, 64
Hansen, Norman Thomas, 69
Hansen Jr., Herman, 71
Harbert Jr., Thomas C., 189
Hargrove, Joseph N., 274
Harriman, Clinton, 272, 274
Helms, Richard, 225
Henderson, Melvin D., 52-53
Herbert, Thomas, 67
Heuer, Edward Herman, 70
Higgins Jr., Edward Mathew, 82
Horn, William K., 64
Houghtaling, Floyd W., 12
Hung, Nguyen Phu, 211
Hyland, John J., 64, 178

Iacobacci, Raymond, 271
Ibanez, Aristotoles D., 12
Jacobs, Paul H., xlv, 254-261
Jefferis, Lawrence Richard, 233
Jensen, Richard, 8
Johnson, Lyndon B., 46-47, 84, 134, 163, 168, 199-200, 276
Johnson, Roy L., 49, 53, 58, 64, 82, 277
Jones, David C., 267
Jose, Paul D., 12
Juarez, Robert, 69
Kai-shek, Chiang, 39
Kapetan, Nick J., 181-188
Kelley, Vincent F., 69
Kelly, John P., 243
Kelly, Walter C., 186
Kember, Phillip C., vli
Kempf, Cecil Joe, 250
Kenney, Harry J., 12
Kermen, Robert J., 109, 111, 123
Kershler, John, xlii, 244-246
King Jr., Jerome H., 201, 240, 246
Kingston, Gerald, xlii, 244-246
Kirby, Edward K., 173-179
Kirby, Jack, 85
Kirksey Jr., Robert E., 250
Kissinger, Henry A., 225, 247, 267
Knapp, Paul J., 66
Krulak, Victor H., 52, 57, 71
Lauffenberg, H. J. 75, 150
Laird, Melvin R., 225
Lane Jr., Glynn Q., 243
Lamb, Derwin T., 75, 150
Lees, William D. H., xl, 279
Leonard, Jerry S., 12
Lincoln, Abraham, xxvii
Linton, Edward W., xxiii, xl, xliii
Littleton, Clement J., xl, xlii, 203-204
Lodge, Henry Cabot, 200
Lonsdale, Karl, 272, 274
Love Jr., John Jefferson, 69
Lowentrout, Jack L., 174, 176
Maddocks, William J., 67-68
Madson, Richard Oscar, 69
Maher, Eugene Hugh, 70
Mangol, Frederick N., 92
Marcos, Ferdinand, 261-262

Marshall, Danny G., 274
Mathews Jr., Herbert Spencer, 232
McCain, John, 225
McCauley, Brian, 248-249
McDonald, David L., 45
McDowell Jr., William Robert, 69
McGough, James D., 80
McHahon Jr., John F., 222
McManus, Philip S., 178-179
McPartlin Jr., Charles E., 47
Metzler, Donald Moderl, 92
Miller, Charles T., 265, 273
Miller, Joseph A., 12
Minh, Ho Chi, 1, 37-40
Minh, Hoang Co, 240
Mitchell, John, 225
Momyer, William W., 100
Monti, Anthony A., 82, 90
Moore, Albert, 13
Moore, Samuel H., 271
Moore, W. R., 85
Moorer, Thomas H., 44-45, 198, 227
Muir, Joseph E., 51
Nao, Lam Son, 211
Neiger, Ralph Eugene, 250
Niedermair, John C., 130
Nixon, Richard M., xlv, 142, 199-200, 225-226, 231, 239, 248, 305, 306, 308
Noland Jr., Charlie, 206
O'Connor, Dennis K., 12
O'Neil, John W., 98
Operation
  BALLISTIC CHARGE, 185-187
  BASTION HILL, 188
  BARRIER REEF, 239-240
  BEACON GATE, 183-184
  BEACON GUIDE, 180-182
  BEACON HILL, 29
  BEACON POINT, 185-186
  BEAR BITE, 178-180
  BEAR CLAW, 180-182
  BEAU CHARGER, 175-178
  BEAVER CAGE, 173-175
  BELT TIGHT, 176
  BLUE MARLIN, 59
  BOLD MARINER, 219-224
  BREEZY COVE, 205, 239-240

BUFFALO, 181-182
CHOCTAW, 179
COCHISE, 183-185
CONCORDIA, 115-118
CORONADO, 108-128
CUMBERLAND, 179
DAGGER THRUST, xxxvi, 32, 54-64
DECKHOUSE, xxxi, 28, 78-99, 147, 172
DEFIANT STAND, 224
DEWEY CANYON, 171
DOUBLE EAGLE, 65-70, 147
EAGLE PULL, xxvi, xlv-xlvi, 258-266
END SWEEP, 27, 208, 248-251
FREMONT, 188
FREQUENT WIND, xxvi, xlv-xlvi, 253-266
GAME WARDEN (Task Force 116), 101, 114, 130-132, 141-146, 153-170, 194, 196, 202, 236-237, 297
GIANT SLINGSHOT, 111, 205, 239-240, 308
GRANITE, 188
GREAT BEND, 114-115, 121
HARVEST MOON, 60-64
HASTINGS, 80
HICKORY, 176
JACKSTAY, xxxiii, 72-76, 150, 154, 161
LIBERTY, 188
LINEBACKER, 247
MARKET TIME (Task Force 115), xv, xviii, xxxvi, xliii, 49, 54, 77, 98-101, 132, 143-166, 196, 202, 237, 248, 278-279
MEDINA, 188
NATHAN HALE, 78-79
NEW ARRIVALS, 257
OSAGE, 76
PASSAGE TO FREEDOM, 18, 42
PIRANHA, 59
PRAIRIE, 90-92
READY DECK, 239-240
RUSSELL BEACH, 221
SANDSTONE, 18-19
SEA FLOAT, 240
SEALORDS, xvii, xviii, 133, 199-206, 240
SEA TIGER, 239-240
SEARCH TURN, 205, 239-240
SHELBYVILLE, 187
SOLID ANCHOR, 240
STABLE DOOR, xxxviii, xl, 278
STARLITE, 50-53, 59, 64

SWIFT RAIDER, xlii, 133
TOLEDO, 82
Orvis, Peter H., 147, 241
Palermo, Benjamin, 50
Peters, Rodney W., 12
Peterson, Robert A., 274
Platt, Jonas M., 68-69
Porter, Melvin B., 57
Powell, Colin, xxvii
Rashleigh, Albert V., xlii, 213-218
Resnicoff, Arnold E., 237
Reynolds, Thomas E., 147
Rhook, David N., xLi, 203-208
Richardson, David F., 243
Riley, Robert H., 243
Risner, Robinson, 252
Rivera, Hermino, 272, 274
Roane, Donald P., 250
Robertson, J. W. P., 222
Rodgers, John M., 274
Rodriguez, Epifanio, 272, 274
Rogers, William P., 225
Rogers Jr., Thomas S., 274
Roosevelt, Franklin D., 130
Rosenberg, Edwin Miller, 98
Rueckel, Frederick A., 188
Rundle, Cary F., 12
Russell, Rick, 8
Saltwick, Michael, 272, 274
Salzer, Robert S., 127, 201-202, 240
Sautter, Rick, 262
Schlarp, Jack E., 222
Schnurrer, Reinhard J., 12
Scott, David A., 49, 56
Seiple, Ron, 88-90
Sharp, U.S.G., 49, 56, 77, 105
Shaw, Arthur, 69
Shepard, Berger M., 120
Sherlock, Andrew J., 214-215

Ships and Craft
  Australian
    Brisbane, Perth, Sydney, Vendetta, 85
    Bungaree, 158-159
    Hobart, 85, 175-177,
    Jeparit, 209
  Cambodian

E312, P112, 261
P128, 265
Panamanian, *Eastern Mariner* (former *Bungaree*), 158-165
South Vietnamese
  Cam Ranh, 227, 238, 317
  Chi Lang II, Chi Linh, Dong Da II, HQ-471, 261, 317
  Commandament, FOM (France d'Outre Mer), 155
  Hat Giang, 238, 317
  Lam Giang, Tien Giang, 238
  Qui Nhon, 148, 227
  Tran Nhat Duat, 229, 230, 259, 317
  Vung Tau, 227, 238
United States
  Army, *Caney, Sebee*, 245
  Coast Guard
    cutters
      Absecon, 230
      Bering Strait, Castle Rock, Chincoteague, Cook Inlet, McCulloch, Yakutat, 228-230, 317
    patrol boats
      Pt. Arden, Pt. Banks, Pt. Caution, Pt. Clear, Pt. Comfort, Pt. Cypress, Pt. Dume, Pt. Ellis, Pt. Gammon, Pt. Garnet, Pt. Glover, Pt. Grace, Pt. Grey, Pt. Hudson, Pt. Jefferson, Pt. League, Pt. Lomas, Pt. Marone, Pt. Mast, Pt. Orient, Pt. Partridge, Pt. Slocum, Pt. Welcome, Pt. White, Pt. Young, 229
      Pt. Kennedy, 98, 229
  Merchant Marine/Military Sea Transportation Service
    Baton Rouge Victory, 165
    General A. W. Brewster, 43
    Green Port, 259
    Greenville Victory, 271-274
    Mayaguez, xxvi, xlv-xlvi, 265-274
    Sgt. Andrew Miller, 254
  Navy
    amphibious
      amphibious assault ship, helicopter (LPH)
        Boxer, 26, 292
        Inchon, 27, 250, 292
        Iwo Jima, 26-28, 49, 53-56, 82-83, 92, 97-98, 189, 292
        New Orleans, 27, 249-250, 292
        Okinawa, 27, 173-188, 222, 254-256, 293
        Princeton, xxxiii, 26, 66, 69-80, 293
        Tripoli, xxix, 27, 222, 293
        Valley Forge, 26, 56, 61-69, 293
      amphibious cargo ship/attack cargo ship (AKA/LKA)
        Charleston, Mathews, St. Louis, 32-33, 294

Index   355

    Durham, 33, 254, 262, 294
    Merrick, 33, 74, 294
    Mobile, 33, 254, 261-262, 294
    Montague, 43
    Seminole, 34, 174-181, 222, 294
    Skagit, 34, 66-69, 294
    Tulare, 34, 189, 294
    Union, 34, 46, 294
    Washburn, 34, 294
    Winston, 33, 186, 188, 222, 294
amphibious force command ship (AGC/LCC)
    Blue Ridge, xlv, 24-25, 254-262, 293
    Eldorado, 24-25, 46, 58, 172-181, 293
    Estes, 25, 55, 293
    Mount McKinley, 18, 25, 46-47, 293
amphibious transport dock (LPD)
    Cleveland, 29, 189, 250, 293
    Denver, 29, 254, 261-262, 293
    Dubuque, 29, 249-254, 262, 293
    Duluth, 29, 178-188, 222, 254, 262, 272, 293
    Juneau, 29, 293
    Ogden, 29, 222, 249-250, 293
    Vancouver, 28, 46, 82-83, 92, 98-99, 254, 263, 293
attack transports (APA)
    Bayfield, 35, 43, 174-178, 294
    Bexar, Calvert, Cavalier, George Clymer, Lenawee, Magoffin, Okanogan, Renville, 35, 295
    Henrico, 35, 46, 98-99, 295
    Menard, 43
    Montrose, 35, 56, 65, 69, 295
    Navarro, 35, 69, 295
    Paul Revere, 36, 65, 69, 295
    Pickaway, 18, 35, 72-80, 295
    Talladega, 35, 49, 51-56, 295
barracks ship, self-propelled (APB)
    Benewah, 2-3, 13-15, 105-106, 112, 116, 232-236, 287
    Colleton, 14-15, 105-106, 116, 287
    Mercer, Nueces, 15, 287
barracks craft, non-self-propelled (APL)
    APL-26, 106-109
dock landing ship (LSD)
    Alamo, 31, 72-80, 293
    Anchorage, 29, 32, 254, 262, 293
    Belle Grove, 30, 161, 186, 188, 293
    Cabildo, Colonial, 31, 294
    Carter Hall, 30, 294

356 Index

    Catamount, 31, 69, 294
    Comstock, 18, 31, 161, 169, 189, 294
    Epping Forest, Gunston Hall, Oak Hill, 30, 294
    Fort Marion, 31, 69, 188-189, 294
    Hermitage, 31, 179-186, 294
    Monticello, 31, 56, 65, 69, 222, 294
    Mount Vernon, 254, 263
    Point Defiance, 31-32, 49, 53-56, 174-179, 294
    Thomaston, 28, 31, 82, 91-99, 254, 263, 294
    Tortuga, 31, 156-169, 294
    Whetstone, 31, 189, 294
  high speed transport (APD)
    Alex Diachenko, xxxvi, 17, 55, 91-92, 288
    Cook, xxix, xxxvi, 16-17, 78-82, 189, 288
    Weiss, xxxvi, 17, 69, 74, 288
  inshore fire support ship (LFR)
    Carronade, xxix, 22-23, 145, 157, 288
  landing craft repair ship (ARL)
    Askari, xxix, 2, 10, 17-18, 106, 120, 232, 236, 287
    Indra, Krishna, 17-18, 287
    Satyr, 17-18, 228, 287, 317
    Sphinx, xxix, 17-18, 288
  landing ship, medium (rocket) (LFR)
    Clarion River, 23, 78-79, 145, 288
    St. Francis River, 23, 92, 97-98, 145, 157, 288
    White River, xxix, 23, 79-82, 145, 157, 288
  medium landing ships *LSM-226, LSM-313, LSM-355*, 238
  tank landing ship (LST)
    LST-516 (later renamed *Calaveras County*), 42
    Barbour County, 254, 261-262
    Blanco County, 20, 128, 146-149, 241-242, 288
    Bulloch County, 20, 147-149, 227-228, 288
    Caddo Parish, xxvii-xxix, 20, 134-140, 288
    Caroline County, 20, 147-149, 288
    Cayuga County, 21, 152, 226-227, 288, 317
    Chase County, 20, 134-139, 288
    Chesterfield County, 20, 134-139, 288
    Clarke County, 20, 136-141, 147-149, 241-243, 288
    Coconino County, xxix, 20, 95-98, 147-149, 226-227, 238, 242, 289
    Floyd County, xxix, 20, 147-149, 156, 161, 289
    Frederick, 21, 152, 254, 262, 289
    Fresno, 21, 152, 289
    Garrett County, xliv, 20, 101, 130, 133, 141-147, 162, 192-194, 228, 289, 297, 317
    Hampshire County, 20, 133-134, 143-149, 239, 243, 289
    Harnett County, xxix, xliv, 20, 130-133, 141-147, 162, 193-194, 228,

Index 357

289, 297, 317
Henry County, 20, 74, 150-151, 289
Hickman County, xxix, 20, 134-139, 212-213, 289
Holmes County, 20, 145-146, 151, 243, 289
Hunterdon County, xxiv, xxix, xliv, 21, 130-133, 141-147, 162, 193-194, 232-239, 289, 297
Iredell County, xxvii, xxix, 21, 133-151, 243, 289
Jennings County, xxix, xliv, 21, 98, 130-133, 141-147, 161-162, 169, 193-194, 290, 297
Jerome County, 21, 129, 133, 151, 227, 290, 317
Kemper County, 21, 105, 147-150, 290
Litchfield County, 21, 147-150, 243, 290
Luzerne County, xxix, 21, 134-141, 290
Madera County, xxix, 21, 134-139, 290
Mahnomen County, 20, 134-139, 241-242, 290
Manitowoc, 21, 152, 290
Maricopa County, 226-227
Marion County, 226-227, 238, 317
Meeker County, xxix, 20, 147-150, 241-246, 280, 290
Monmouth County, 20, 134-141, 290
New London County, 21, 134-139, 290
Newport, 131-132
Nye County, 20, 134-139, 290
Outagamie County, 20, 151-152, 243, 290
Page County, xxix, 20, 136-150, 243, 290
Park County, 20, 145-150, 243, 290
Peoria, 22, 152, 254, 263, 290
Pitkin County, 20, 128, 145-150, 243, 291
Polk County, 20, 129, 147-150, 291
Pulaski County, 20, 134-139, 291
Racine, 21, 152, 291
San Bernardino, 21, 152, 291
San Joaquin County, 20, 151-152, 241-242, 291
Schenectady, 21, 152, 291
Sedgwick County, 20, 133-134, 147-150, 243, 291
Snohomish County, 21, 147-150, 243, 291
St. Clair County, 21, 150-152, 291
Stone County, 21, 139, 147-152, 291
Summit County, 21, 151-152, 291
Sumner County, 21, 151-152, 291
Sumter, 22, 152, 291
Sutter County, 21, 147-150, 243, 291
Terrell County, 21, 133, 143-145, 291
Tioga County, 21, 69, 147-150, 181-186, 235, 291
Tom Green County, xxix, 21, 69, 143-146, 291
Tuscaloosa, 21, 152, 254, 261, 263, 291

Vernon County, xxix, 21, 51, 133-134, 143-146, 291
Washoe County, 21, 74, 133, 143-150, 292
Washtenaw County, xxxi, 21, 97-98, 133, 143-146, 188-189, 203-208, 251, 292
Westchester County, xviii, xxi, xxix, xxxvii, xlvi, 1-14, 21, 69, 125, 137, 143-146, 241, 292
Wexford County, xxix, 21, 129, 151-152, 189, 292
Whitfield County, xxix, 21, 103-104, 125, 133-134, 143-146, 174-178, 292
Windham County, 21, 69, 133-134, 143-146, 292
utility landing craft *LCU-1500*, 241
riverine craft
armored troop carrier (ATC)
ATC-91-3, ATC-91-10, 122
ATC-111-7, 125
ATC-112-4, 116, 118
ATC-112-7, xxi, 109, 111
ATC-152-1, xx
ATC(H) R-92-2, 119-120
assault support patrol boats (ASPB), 105-108, 122, 195, 226, 232, 236
monitor
M-91-1, 102
M-91-2, M-91-10, M-112-1, 119
M-111-2, 122
river patrol boats, *PBR-105, PBR-107*, 166-168
auxiliary/service force
Abnaki, Flint, Lipan, 261
Banner, Brule, 197
Card, 210-211, 241
Current, 140
Elkhorn, Safeguard, 70
Jason, xxxix
Kalispell, 106, 118, 236
Mark, 193-197
Pueblo, 197, 266
Reclaimer, 74
Repose, xxxiii-xxxiv, 69-70,
Sanctuary, xxxiii, 174-176
Vega, 261, 267, 274
Winnemucca, 106, 118
YLLC-4, 236
YRBM-16, YRBM-21, 232-236
combatant
aircraft carrier
Coral Sea, 247, 267-268, 274
Hancock, 74, 254, 258, 263

Midway, 254-258
battleship *New Jersey*, 177, 221-222
cruisers
  Boston, 176-177
  Canberra, 93,
  Newport News, 189
  Oklahoma City, 69, 80-81, 92, 254, 263
  St. Paul, 79, 82, 92-94, 174-177
  Topeka, 69
destroyers/frigates
  Allen M. Sumner, 176-177, 181
  Barry, 69
  Basilone, 79
  Bausell, 254, 263
  Bigelow, 179
  Cochrane, 254, 263
  Collett, 189
  Cook, 254-263
  Du Pont, 189
  Edson, 176-178
  Epperson, 249
  Ernest G. Small, 55, 186
  Fechteler, 176-177
  Forest Royal, 174
  Frank Knox, 53
  Goldsborough, 189
  Gurke, 254, 263
  Harold E. Holt, 267-274
  Harry E. Hubbard, 181
  Henderson, 174
  Henry B. Wilson, 267-274
  Hopewell, xxvii, 181, 186
  Hull, 92, 94
  John W. Thomason, 77, 79, 82
  Joseph Strauss, 176-177
  Kirk, xlv, 254-263
  Leonard F. Mason, 55
  Lofberg, 80
  Mansfield, 176-177
  New, 189
  O'Brien, 69
  Orleck, 70
  Ozbourn, 176-178
  Preston, 184
  Richard B. Anderson, Rowan, 254, 263
  Robison, Waldron, 186-187

Walker, 77, 181
Worden, 249, 254
minesweepers
Engage, Force, Fortify, Impervious, 248
Leader, 133
Woodpecker, xxxix
minesweeping boats
MSB-16, 165
MSB-49, 163
MSB-52, 170
submarines
Grayback, xxxv
Perch, xxxv-xxxvi, 59-67, 88-91
Tunny, xxxv-xxxvi, 91

Shotter, Michael T. E., xl
Sihanouk, Norodom, 40, 238
Simmons, Kendall Washburn, 69, 92
Slemons, R. L., 223
Smith, Harry, 85
Smith, Thomas H., 12
Som, Em, 269
Sommerville, Daniel A., 76
Soviet Union
   BPM-2 limpet mine, xxviii, 209, 216-218
   MKB contact mine, 170
Sparks, William F., 222
Spicer, Robert H., xlii, 203-204
Steele, George P., 267, 273
Steer, Russell L., xlii, 244
Stephens Jr., Franklin Taylor, 82, 92
Stewart, Clifford L., 154
Stockdale, James, 252
Sullivan, John S., 9-11
Swofford, John R., 139
Thailand
   Korat Air Force Base, 266
   Royal Thai Army Volunteer Regiment, 125
   Sattahip, 265
   U-Tapao Navy Air Base, 266-269
Thi, Lam Quang, 50
Thieu, Nguyen Van, 191, 226
Tho, Le Duc, 247
Thomas, Alfred I., 181-188
Thomas, John Keith, 250
Thorpe, Gordon Lewis, 70
Tiderman, Otto Darby, 69

Tien, Nguyen, 48
Tilger, Billy Ralph, 236
Timmes, Francis Xavier, 98
Toole, Morton E., 155-166
Torcivia, Anthony R., 12
Tse-Tung, Mao, 37
Tromp, David Charles, 278
Troutman Jr., Burl Abraham, 69
Tru, Le Huu, 51
Truman, Harry S., 39
Trundy, Richard T., 222
Tuitele, Fofo Tulifua, 270-273
Turner Jr., Steven L , 243
United States
  Air Force
    Clark Air Force Base, 252, 257
    Seventh Air Force, 99, 266
    56th Security Police Squadron, 266
  Army
    1st Cavalry Division, 54, 78-79, 221
    2nd/35th Artillery Battalion, 84
    9th Infantry Division, 2, 12, 87, 104, 106, 109, 226
      2nd Brigade, 106, 112, 118, 226
      3rd Brigade, 106, 226
      3rd/60th ("River Raiders") Infantry Battalion, 2, 12, 121, 195
      11th Ranger Battalion, 60
      47th Infantry, 115-127, 195
      173rd Airborne Brigade, 82
    145th Aviation Detachment, 162
  Coast Guard
    Squadron
      One, 154, 228-229
      Two, Three, 229-230
  Marine Corps
    1st Air Naval Gunfire Liaison Company, xxxiv
    1st Marine Air Wing, 94, 220
    1st Marine Division, 53, 59, 62-64, 71, 79, 94, 150, 185, 188
    III Marine Amphibious Force, 50, 53, 67, 71, 80, 95, 146
    3rd Marine Division, xxxi, 50-51, 62-63, 68, 176, 189, 224
    4th Regiment, 50
    5th Marine Division, 185, 220
    7th Marine Division, 60, 63
    9th Marine Amphibious Brigade, 71, 220
    26th Marine Regiment, 82, 220-223
    Battalion/Battalion Landing Team (BLT)
      1/3, 47, 173-190

1/4, 267-268
1/5, 71, 77
1/9, 94, 97, 181-182, 265
1/26, 82, 90-94
2/1, 53
2/3, xxxv, 64
2/4, 190
2/7, 49, 63
2/9, 267-268
2/11, 53
2/26, 221-223
3/3, 51, 63
3/4, xxvi
3/5, 79-81
3/7, 49, 53
3/9, 47, 182
3/26, 94, 221-222
3/36, 94
Firebases
  Con Thien, 180-182
  Gio Linh, 180
Marine Air Group 11 (MAG-11), 12 (MAG-12), 69
Medium Helicopter Squadron
  HMM-161, 50
  HMM-163, 49, 53, 57, 186, 188
  HMM-164, 182, 220, 222
  HMM-261, 57, 62, 65
  HMM-263, 173-179
  HMM-265, 220
  HMM-361, 189
  HMM-362, 65, 76, 94, 97, 181-188, 220, 222
  HMM-363, 80-81, 92-94
  HMM-364, 76-80
Regimental Landing Team 26, 220

Navy
  Amphibious Squadron
    Three, xxvii, 71, 189
    Five, 67, 178
    Nine, 174, 178
  Coastal Squadron One, 232-233
  Destroyer Squadron 23, 258, 260
  Explosive Ordnance Disposal Mobile Unit, Pacific (EODMUPAC), xviii, xxxix-xl, 202-203, 278
  Harbor (Harbour) Clearance/Defence Unit, Vung Tau, 217, 278
  Harbor (Harbour) Clearance Unit One, 235
  Helicopter Attack (Light) Squadron Three (HAL-3), 194, 232, 240

Index   363

Helicopter Combat Support Squadron One, 169
Helicopter Squadron HM-12, 249
Inshore Fire Support Division 93, 22, 157
Inshore Undersea Warfare Group One, xxxvii, 207, 302
Landing Ship Flotilla One, 129, 145,
Landing Ship Squadron (LandShipRon)
   One, 75, 139, 145, 150-151
   Two (former ResLandShipRon Two), 129, 134-141, 151
   Three, 129, 139, 141, 145-148, 151, 241-243
   Nine, 129, 143-145
Light Attack Squadron Four (VAL-4), 75, 202, 232, 240
Military Assistance and Advisory Group (MAAG) Navy Section, 43-44
Military Assistance Command Vietnam (MACV), 44, 49, 57, 64, 95, 106, 207, 219, 240, 278
Military Sea Transportation Service (MSTS), 135-136
Military Sealift Command, 143, 149, 259, 268, 271
Mine Flotilla One, 248
Mine Squadron 11 Detachment Alfa, 163, 165
Mobile Riverine Force (Task Force 117)/River Assault Flotilla One
   River Assault Squadron Nine (Task Group 117.1), 104-105, 116, 226
     River Assault Division 91, 104-105, 195
     River Assault Division 92, 105, 127
   River Assault Squadron Eleven (Task Group 117.2), 12, 105, 226
     River Assault Division 111, 2-3, 9, 12, 105, 127
     River Assault Division 112, 105, 109, 114, 125
   River Assault Squadron Thirteen, 106
   River Assault Squadron Fifteen, 106
   River Support Squadron Seven, 106, 108, 226
Mobile Riverine Group
   Alfa (Squadrons 9 and 11), 2, 106
   Bravo (Squadrons 13 and 15), 106
Naval Beach Group/Naval Beach Jumper, 144
Naval Forces Vietnam (NavFor),
   30th Naval Construction Regiment, 153
   Naval Supply Activity/Detachment
     Chu Lai, 136
     Danang, 148
     Dong Tam, 10
     My Tho, 167
     Saigon, 148, 193, 196
     Vinh Long, 192
Naval Inshore Operations Training Center, Mare Island, 235
Naval Ship Repair Facility,
   Yokosuka, 11
   Subic Bay, 237
Naval Explosive Ordnance Disposal Technology Division, Indian Head,

Maryland, 218
River Flotilla One, 226
River Patrol Force (Task Force 116)
  Division 55 Danang, 193
  River Division 51, 156, 193
    River Section 512, 156, 162, 169
  River Division 52, 193
  River Division 53, 165, 193
    Sections 531, 194, 313
    Section 532, 534, 194
  River Division 54, 193
    River Section 541, 156
  River Division 574, 226
  River Division 593, 232
  River Interdiction Division (RID) 42, 232
SEAL Team One, 74, 163
Strike Assault Boat Squadron Twenty, 233-235
UDT (Underwater Demolition Team)
  11, 67, 74-90
  12, xxxv, 59-60, 81, 91
Utter, Leon N., 49
Van Slyke Jr., James C., 243-245
Van Thoi, Nguyen, 126
Vanos, Jan, xxxv
Vanos, James George (Jesse Ventura), xxxv
Veile, Robert, 270
Veth, Kenneth L., 44, 105, 198

Vietnam/Vietnamese
 South
  An Loc, 247
  An Long, 235
  Annam Mountains, 91
  Ashau Valley, 171-173
  Ban Long Secret Zone, 124-125
  Bassac River, 136, 143, 160, 169, 194, 237
  Batangan Peninsula, 219-223
  Ben Goi, 54-55
  Ben Hai River, 176
  Ben Tre, 122, 194, 235-236
  Bien Hoa Province, 114, 124
  Binh Thuy, 136-137, 193, 305
  Binh Tuy Province, 82-83
  Bo De River, 146, 203-206
  Cai River, Cau River, 78
  Cam Ranh/Cam Ranh Bay, xxxvii, 23, 67, 210, 302
  Cam Son Secret Zone, 124-126

Can Tho, 136-137, 153, 160, 169, 193-194, 305
Cap Mui Lay, 176-177
Chu Lai, 31, 50-70, 135-137, 147, 150, 161-169, 220-221, 241-242
Co Chien River, 97-101, 193-195
Con Qui Island, 126
Con Son Island, 259-260
Cua Viet/Cua Viet River, xxxvii, 5, 91-92, 109, 146-148, 182-190, 239-241, 283-284
Danang, xxxv-xliii, 22, 38, 45-49, 60, 69, 71, 77, 80-81, 135-148, 153, 157, 174, 183, 193, 210, 241-248, 281-285
Dai Loc, 187
Dinh Tuong Province, 112, 117-127
Dong Ha, 81, 92, 181, 281-283
Dong Tam, 10, 110-127, 136-137, 193-196, 235-236, 305
Dong Tau, 125
Dong Tranh River, 155
Dua River, 170
Duc Pho, 242
Gia Dinh Province, 121
Go Cong Creek/Province, 117-118
Go Dau Ha, 111
Hai Lang Forest, 188
Ham Luong River, 97-98, 161, 170, 195, 236
Hieu Giang River, 91
Hoi An, 175, 183, 224
Hue, 5, 172-192, 239, 247, 306
Kien Hoa Province, 97-98, 124, 166, 194
Kien Phong Province, 125-127
Ky Phu Village, 63
La Rue Sans Joie (The Street without Joy), 178
Lai An, 92
Lang Ke Ga, 58-59
Long An Province, 116-124
Long Khanh Province, 83
Long Tau River, 113, 156, 161-170
May Tao Secret Zone, 83
Mekong River, 10, 38, 125-127, 166, 195, 231-238, 313
Military
  Air Force (RVNAF)
    Tan Son Nhut Air Base, 44, 256, 260
  Army (ARVN)
    1st Battalion, 5th Regiment, 60
    2nd Battalion, 115
    2nd Division, 223
    7th Division, 124
  Marine Corps (VNMC)

1st Battalion, 232
  4th Battalion, 97-98, 232
  5th Battalion, 125, 128, 232
  Brigade Force Bravo, 97
 Navy (VNN)
  Lien Doc Nguoi Nhia (LDNN frogmen), 74
  Nam Can Naval Base, 201
  Rach Soi Naval Base, xxiii
  River Assault Groups (RAG), 75, 104, 153, 155, 192
   RAG 21/33, 232
   RAG 22, 158
  Riverine Assault Interdiction Division
   RAID 70, RAID 71, RAID 73, RAID 74, RAID 75, 232
   RAID 72, 205, 232
Mo Cay, 194
Moc Hoa, 166
My Tho/My Tho River, xxxvii, 2, 9-10, 111-112, 125, 161-170, 193, 196, 236, 305, 313
Nam Thon River, 166-167
Nga Ba River, 170
Ngo Hiep Island, 165-167
Nha Be, 113-116, 137, 153-170, 193, 226
Nha Trang, xxxvii, 55, 67, 135, 227, 302
Nui Dat, 83-87
Phan Thiet, 59, 67
Phu Quoc Island, 17
Phu Thu Village, 58-59
Phu Vinh, 194
Phuoc Ha Valley/Phuoc Tuy Province, 4, 60, 83
Plain of Reeds, 125, 165-166
Pleiku, 247
Quang Nam, 173, 183, 187
Quang Ngai, 54, 67-71, 173, 220-221
Quang Tin, 70, 174-175, 183
Quang Tri, 80, 92, 173-189, 247, 281
Que Son, 60, 174, 185
Qui Nhon, xxxvii, 49, 54-58, 67, 78, 135-137, 172, 210, 302
Rai River, 87
Rung Sat Special Zone (RSSZ), xxxiii, xxxix, 71-75, 103-114, 153-165, 210
Sa Dec, 125-126, 193-195, 305
Saigon, xxxvii-xxxix, xlv-xlvi, 5, 38-59, 72-74, 82, 113-124, 136-137, 148, 153, 162-170, 191-196, 210, 227, 241-285
Soi Rap River, 113-125, 155-156, 170
Tam Quan, 54-56
Thach Ham River, Thach Hau, River, 91
Thach Tru, 68

Thanh Phong Secret Zone, 97
Thua Thien Province, 76, 173, 182, 185
Tra Cu, 111
Tuy Hoa, 137
Tuyho, 222
Vam Co River, 115-121, 155, 308
Vam Sat River, 75, 156
Van Tuong Peninsula, 50
Vinh Long, 146, 167, 192-195, 305
Vung Mu Peninsula, 32, 54-55
Vung Ro, 210
Vung Tau, xviii, xxxvi-xliii, 2, 82-87, 99-105, 112, 121-125, 135-140, 148, 161-165, 196, 203-219, 242-246, 255, 278-281, 300-302

North
  Vietnamese Army (NVA)
    5th Regiment, 6th Regiment, 188
    18th Regiment, 95th Regiment, 67
    71st Battalion, 175
    72nd (Local Forces) Battalion, 175, 183
    90th Regiment, 182
    721st Anti-aircraft Company, 87
    806th Battalion, 180
    Bo Doi Dac Cong ("soldiers in special forces") sappers, 4
      126th NVA Naval Sapper Regiment, 5, 210
      429th Sapper Group, 5
      Group 10 Viet Cong, 210
  Cam Pha, 250
  Haiphong, 5, 27, 40, 42, 208, 247-252
  Hanoi, 5, 37-40, 199, 247, 252
  Hon Gai, 250
  Hon Lai, 252
  Tet Offensive, 5, 191-199, 305
  Thanh Hoa Province, 5
  Viet Cong (National Liberation Front)
    1st Regiment, 50-51, 60
      40th Battalion, 60th Battalion, 51
    2nd Regiment, 67
    5th Division, 83, 87
    38th Main Force Regiment, 221
    48th Local Force Battalion, P-31st Local Force Company, 221
    65th Special Operations Group (National Liberation Front), 211
    261st Battalion, 514th Provincial Battalion, 119
    263rd Battalion, 119, 124
    274th Regiment, D445 Local Force Battalion, 83
    275th Regiment, 83, 87
    306th Battalion, 308th Battalion, 195

324th B. Division, 92
502nd Battalion, 127
514th Main Force Battalion, 124
C-95th Sapper Company, 221, 223
V25 Local Force Battalion, 183, 187
Vietnam Revolutionary League (Vinh Minh), 39
Vinh Linh City, 5

Walt, Lewis, 50
Ward, Norvell G., 44, 153
Waterman, Jack E., 69
Weeks, Robert Eugene, 92
Wells, Wade C., 102-105, 120, 127
Weschler, Thomas R., 56-59
Westervelt, John D., 97-98
Westmoreland, William C., 44, 49, 57-58, 65-67, 73-80, 154, 164, 176, 276
Wheeler, Earle, 225
Whitmire, Donald B., 254-259
Wickwise, Peter A., 173
Williams, Harlan Dale, 98
Williams, James Elliott, 166-168, 313-314
Williams, John, E., 220
Wilson, Barry W., xlii, 203-204
Wilson, Daniel M., 189
Wilson, Robert R., 222
Winstead, Edwin G., 55
Witham Jr., Boyd B., 154
Wojcik, Bogdan K., xxxviii, 244, 281
Wortman, Harry D., 97
Wulzen, Donald W., 46-58
Zipse, Robert L., 140
Zumwalt Jr., Elmo R., 200-202, 225-226, 233, 240

About the Author

Commander David D. Bruhn, U.S. Navy (Retired) served twenty-two years on active duty and two in the Naval Reserve, as both an enlisted man and as an officer, between 1977 and 2001.

Following completion of basic training, he served as a sonar technician aboard USS *Miller* (FF-1091) and USS *Leftwich* (DD-984). He was commissioned in 1983 following graduation from California State University at Chico. His initial assignment was to USS *Excel* (MSO-439), serving as supply officer, damage control assistant, and chief engineer. He then served in USS *Thach* (FFG-43) as chief engineer and Destroyer Squadron Thirteen as material officer.

After graduation from the Naval Postgraduate School, Commander Bruhn was assigned to Secretary of the Navy and Chief of Naval Operation staffs as a budget analyst and resources planner before attending the Naval War College in 1996, following which he commanded the mine countermeasures ships USS *Gladiator* (MCM-11) and USS *Dextrous* (MCM-13) in the Persian Gulf.

Commander Bruhn's final assignment was executive assistant to a senior (SES 4) government service executive at the Ballistic Missile Defense Organization in Washington, D.C.

Following military service, he was a high school teacher and track coach for ten years, and is now a USA Track & Field official. He lives in northern California with his wife Nancy and has two grown sons, David and Michael.

Heritage Books by Cdr. David D. Bruhn, USN (Retired)

Battle Stars for the "Cactus Navy":
America's Fishing Vessels and Yachts in World War II

Enemy Waters:
Royal Navy, Royal Canadian Navy, Royal Norwegian Navy,
U.S. Navy, and Other Allied Mine Forces Battling the
Germans and Italians in World War II
Cdr. David D. Bruhn, USN (Retired) and Lt. Cdr. Rob Hoole, RN (Retired)

Eyes of the Fleet:
The U.S. Navy's Seaplane Tenders and Patrol Aircraft in World War II

Gators Offshore and Upriver:
The U.S. Navy's Amphibious Ships and Underwater Demolition Teams,
and Royal Australian Navy Clearance Divers in Vietnam

Home Waters:
Royal Navy, Royal Canadian Navy, and U.S. Navy
Mine Forces Battling U-Boats in World War I
Cdr. David D. Bruhn, USN (Retired) and Lt. Cdr. Rob Hoole, RN (Retired)

Ingram's Fourth Fleet:
U.S. and Royal Navy Operations Against German Runners,
Raiders, and Submarines in the South Atlantic in World War II

MacArthur and Halsey's "Pacific Island Hoppers":
The Forgotten Fleet of World War II

Nightraiders:
U.S. Navy, Royal Navy, Royal Australian Navy, and
Royal Netherlands Navy Mine Forces Battling the
Japanese in the Pacific in World War II
Cdr. David D. Bruhn, USN (Retired) and Lt. Cdr. Rob Hoole, RN (Retired)

On the Gunline:
U.S. Navy and Royal Australian Navy Warships off Vietnam, 1965–1973
Cdr. David D. Bruhn, USN (Retired) and
STGCS Richard S. Mathews, USN (Retired)

We Are Sinking, Send Help!:
The U.S. Navy's Tugs and Salvage Ships in the African,
European, and Mediterranean Theaters in World War II

Wooden Ships and Iron Men:
The U.S. Navy's Ocean Minesweepers, 1953–1994

Wooden Ships and Iron Men:
The U.S. Navy's Coastal and Motor Minesweepers, 1941–1953

Wooden Ships and Iron Men:
The U.S. Navy's Coastal and Inshore Minesweepers,
and the Minecraft that Served in Vietnam, 1953–1976

www.ingramcontent.com/pod-product-compliance
Lightning Source LLC
Chambersburg PA
CBHW071436300426
44114CB00013B/1465